Poems

A New Anthology of
Leaving Certificate Poetry
(Higher Level 2012)
Cian Hogan

Editor: Kristin Jensen

Design: Karen Hoey

Layout: Oisín Burke

Cover Design: Karen Hoey

ISBN 978-1-84741-584-4

Produced in Ireland by Folens Publishers, Hibernian Industrial Estate, Greenhills Road, Tallaght, Dublin 24.

Cover image
Desc: The night of Jealousy 1893 dedicated to 2nd wife Frida Uhl
Artist: STRINDBERG, Johan August : 1849-1912 : Swedish
Credit: [The Art Archive / Strindberg Museum Stockholm / Alfredo Dagli Orti]
Ref: AA345696

Contents

Higher Level Poets and Poems

Poems prescribed at both Higher and Ordinary Levels are marked (**HL + OL**) in the table of contents.

Eavan Boland (1944–)   **1**

Robert Frost (1874–1963)   **28**

Sylvia Plath (1932–63)   176

Adrienne Rich (1929–)   201

The Unseen Poem

Acknowledgements

I am deeply grateful to Tara Lyons, Jim Lusby, Tom Brady, Denis Craven, Linda Golden and John Scally for their input and encouragement during the writing of this book. I also have to acknowledge the insight and honest opinions of my present Leaving Certificate class. I would like to thank Paul McCormack for his generous help with the essay-writing section of the book. For their courtesy and patience, I wish to thank Kristin Jensen, Oisín Burke and all the staff at Folens who contributed to this anthology. Finally, I would like to thank Tom O'Flaherty and Victor Flynn of Rochestown College.

Cian Hogan, 2010

Dedication

For Mr Alphoncy

Using This Anthology

This anthology includes all of the prescribed poets for the 2012 Higher Level English Leaving Certificate Examination. The prescribed poems for Ordinary Level are also included. Following close consultation with teachers and students, this book has been designed to facilitate mixed-level teaching.

Each prescribed poet is introduced with a short note on the poet. Each prescribed poem is then followed by a detailed glossary and three short questions referring to the poem just studied. The three short questions and exam-style unseen poem questions mirror the types of question that appear on the unseen poetry section of the examination. The intention is that students will become familiar with the modes of thinking and answering that are demanded by the unseen poem, while at the same time stimulating discussion of the poem they have just read. For ease of use, each glossary contains the page number on which the critical commentary for that poem can be found. All technical words that are included in the glossary of literary terms are highlighted in bold italics.

Every chapter in this anthology is designed to assist students in developing essay-writing techniques. Having studied a poet, students are encouraged to attain an overview of the work of that poet. Additionally, each chapter contains longer questions and, where applicable, past Leaving Certificate questions and marking schemes. These questions provide scope for real development of expression. Before starting to write, students need to move away from the tendency that we all have to only say what the poem is about. Remember that you will be given very few marks for simply paraphrasing the poem. The marking scheme will reward you for your knowledge of the content of the work and for features of the poet's style that strike you as important. Demonstrating this knowledge is not easy and will take many attempts to perfect, so be patient and reassure yourself that you are making progress every time you write.

For students who wish to make use of secondary criticism, the book contains a short biography of each of the prescribed poets, along with a detailed analysis of each poem on the course. These critical analyses are organised under three separate headings that reflect examination requirements: content, stylistic features and essay writing. Where the poet speaks directly about his or her work, a separate handwriting font has been used.

The approach to the unseen poem is given detailed consideration in this book. It is hoped that the experience garnered from answering the three short questions following each prescribed poem will prepare students for this section of the exam. In addition to unseen poems, the poems for study at Ordinary Level are also included in the book. They are presented in such a manner as to allow Higher Level students to make use of the texts as well.

Finally, the selection of poems in this anthology is challenging, varied and exciting. Thankfully, the new Leaving Certificate syllabus rewards you for your ability to express how these poems make you feel. You should never forget this as you prepare for the examination.

Higher Level Poets and Poems

Eavan Boland (1944–)

Eavan Boland's poetry offers us a unique perspective on the world in which we live. Historically, women in Irish literature have been either silenced or idealised. Her poems seek to change this. The result is a thoroughly modern and feminine voice that forces us to question our relationship with the past and to reassess our preconceived notions about poetry itself. Very often, she transports poetry from its more traditional settings to a modern urban landscape that most of us are familiar with. Her poems oppose violence in all its guises and speak out for the weak and the marginalised. While much of her work addresses matters of public concern, she has also written deeply personal and honest poems that reveal intimate details about her daily life and relationships. If you would like to read more about Boland's life, you will find a short biography on p. 266.

The War Horse

This dry night, nothing unusual
About the clip, clop, casual

Iron of his shoes as he stamps death
Like a mint on the innocent coinage of earth.

I lift the window, watch the ambling feather   5
Of hock and fetlock, loosed from its daily tether

In the tinker camp on the Enniskerry Road,
Pass, his breath hissing, his snuffling head

Down. He is gone. No great harm is done.
Only a leaf of our laurel hedge is torn –   10

Of distant interest like a maimed limb,
Only a rose which now will never climb

The stone of our house, expendable, a mere
Line of defence against him, a volunteer

You might say, only a crocus, its bulbous head   15
Blown from growth, one of the screamless dead.

But we, we are safe, our unformed fear
Of fierce commitment gone; why should we care

If a rose, a hedge, a crocus are uprooted
Like corpses, remote, crushed, mutilated?   20

He stumbles on like a rumour of war, huge
Threatening. Neighbours use the subterfuge

Of curtains. He stumbles down our short street
Thankfully passing us. I pause, wait,

Then to breathe relief lean on the sill   25
And for a second only my blood is still

With atavism. That rose he smashed frays
Ribboned across our hedge, recalling days

Of burned countryside, illicit braid:
A cause ruined before, a world betrayed.   30

Glossary

See the critical commentary on p. 268.

2 *clip, clop, casual* – the poet uses **consonance** and **onomatopoeia** in order to give the line a carefree feel. Perhaps she is saying something about our attitude to violence.

7 *the tinker camp* – tinker, derived from the old English word *tinkere* and the Irish *na tincéri*, is a reference to the Irish Travellers. This in itself is a clever **allusion** to the violence of Cromwell. Some believe that the origins of the Travellers lie in the ruthless clearances of Cromwell.

7 *Enniskerry Road* – a road in Dublin and Wicklow.

22 *subterfuge* – a ruse, ploy or trick. Here, the poet uses the trick of hiding behind the curtains. In this manner, she manages to shield herself from the reality of the violence around her.

27 *atavism* – the tendency to resemble your remote ancestors. This obscure noun is important when it comes to understanding this poem. The poem deals with cycles of violence and our tendency to repeat the mistakes of our ancestors.

29 *illicit* – unlawful or illegitimate.

29 *braid* – a plait or tress; this word is often associated with the tassels of a military uniform.

Questions

Go to   p. 27   for more questions on Eavan Boland.

1. Comment on the poet's choice of title. In what ways is the title important to our understanding of the poem?
2. What do you think the horse represents or symbolises in the poem?
3. How well does the poet convey the fragility of the domestic setting in the face of violence?

Exam-style Unseen Poem Questions

1. Choose three images from the poem that you find particularly powerful and explain why.
2. Write a response to 'The War Horse', highlighting aspects of it that you liked and/ or disliked.
3. Briefly describe the mood or feeling you get from reading this poem and illustrate your answer from the text.

Child of our Time

(for Aengus)

Yesterday I knew no lullaby
But you have taught me overnight to order
This song, which takes from your final cry
Its tune, from your unreasoned end its reason;
Its rhythm from the discord of your murder   5
Its motive from the fact you cannot listen.

We who should have known how to instruct
With rhymes for your waking, rhythms for your sleep,
Names for the animals you took to bed,
Tales to distract, legends to protect   10
Later an idiom for you to keep
And living, learn, must learn from you dead,

To make our broken images, rebuild
Themselves around your limbs, your broken
Image, find for your sake whose life our idle   15
Talk has cost, a new language. Child
Of our time, our times have robbed your cradle.
Sleep in a world your final sleep has woken.

17 May 1974

Glossary

See the critical commentary on p. 271.

The title and date of this poem refer to the death of a child in the Dublin and Monaghan bombings on 17 May 1974. The bombings killed 33 people – the largest number of casualties in any incident in the Troubles in Ireland. Three car bombs exploded within a few minutes of each other in the centre of Dublin. They were followed shortly after by a fourth car bomb in Monaghan.

3 *This song, which takes from your final cry | Its tune* – notice how the poem refers more than once to language and music. It is valid to read the poem as a commentary on the failure of language to cope with extreme violence.

4 *unreasoned end its reason* – the poem tries to create order out of the mindless violence that has resulted in the murder of an innocent child.

11 *keep | And living, learn, must learn from you dead* – the word order, or **syntax**, of the poem breaks down in several places. In this way, Boland allows the language of her poem to mirror the chaos created by the bomb. In the same fashion, the rhyming scheme of this poem is erratic and broken.

18 *Sleep in a world your final sleep has woken* – the full stop at the end of the final line provides us with a powerful reminder of the finality of the child's death.

Questions

Go to p. 27 for more questions on Eavan Boland.

1. Comment on the poet's use of language in the poem. In what ways does the language add to the elegiac mood of the poem?

2. What does the poet mean when she says that the dead child has 'taught' her to 'order | This song'?

3. It has been said of 'Child of our Time' that it is a political poem. Would you agree with this assessment of the poem?

Exam-style Unseen Poem Questions

1. Write a response to 'Child of our Time', highlighting the impact it has made on you.

2. Choose one image from the poem that you found particularly striking and briefly explain why.

3. Does this poem make you feel hopeful or unhopeful? Briefly explain why.

The Famine Road

'Idle as trout in light Colonel Jones
these Irish, give them no coins at all; their bones
need toil, their characters no less.' Trevelyan's
seal blooded the deal table. The Relief
Committee deliberated: 'Might it be safe,   5
Colonel, to give them roads, roads to force
from nowhere, going nowhere of course?'

   one out of every ten and then
   another third of those again
   women – in a case like yours.   10

Sick, directionless they worked fork, stick
were iron years away; after all could
they not blood their knuckles on rock, suck
April hailstones for water and for food?
Why for that, cunning as housewives, each eyed –   15
as if at a corner butcher – the other's buttock.

   anything may have caused it, spores,
   a childhood accident; one sees
   day after day these mysteries.

Dusk: they will work tomorrow without him.   20
They know it and walk clear. He has become
a typhoid pariah, his blood tainted, although
he shares it with some there. No more than snow
attends its own flakes where they settle
and melt, will they pray by his death rattle.   25

   You never will, never you know
   but take it well woman, grow
   your garden, keep house, good-bye.

'It has gone better than we expected, Lord
Trevelyan, sedition, idleness, cured   30
in one; from parish to parish, field to field;
the wretches work till they are quite worn,
then fester by their work; we march the corn
to the ships in peace. This Tuesday I saw bones
out of my carriage window. Your servant Jones.'   35

    Barren, never to know the load
    of his child in you, what is your body
    now if not a famine road?

Glossary

See the critical commentary on p. 273.

'*The Famine Road*' – during the Irish Famine, the government dictated that aid could not be given without demanding something in return. As a result, a series of public work programmes was initiated. In return for aid, the starving population was required to work on pointless construction projects.

3 *Trevelyan* – Sir Charles Edward Trevelyan (1807–86) served as secretary for Ireland during the Famine years. Prof. Joe Lee estimates that 10 per cent of the population died during Trevelyan's stewardship.

8 *one out of every ten* – the narrative changes here. We are now in a consultant's rooms. Notice how the detached tone of the consultant mirrors the coldness of Trevelyan and his subordinate.

17 *anything may have caused it, spores* – we return to the second narrative. Notice again the detachment of the doctor. The mention of spores recalls the fungal spores that caused the Famine.

22 *typhoid* – a disease of the blood transmitted by lice.

22 *pariah* – a social outcast.

30 *sedition* – the act of plotting against the state; subversive behaviour.

Questions

Go to p. 27 for more questions on Eavan Boland.

1. Choose two phrases from the poem – one from the narrative dealing with the Famine and one from the narrative dealing with the woman visiting the doctor – and show how they mirror one another.

2. To what extent does Boland manage to bring history to life in this poem?

3. Compare and contrast the tones of voice of the doctor and the Relief Committee in the poem.

Exam-style Unseen Poem Questions

1. Write a short personal response to this poem.

2. Does this poem give a realistic vision of suffering and oppression? Support your answer by close reference to the poem.

3. In your opinion, what is the central message of this poem?

The Shadow Doll

*(This was sent to the bride-to-be in Victorian times, by her
dressmaker. It consisted of a porcelain doll, under a dome of glass,
modelling the proposed wedding dress.)*

They stitched blooms from the ivory tulle
to hem the oyster gleam of the veil.
They made hoops for the crinoline.

Now, in summary and neatly sewn –
a porcelain bride in an airless glamour –   5
the shadow doll survives its occasion.

Under glass, under wraps, it stays
even now, after all, discreet about
visits, fevers, quickenings and lusts

and just how, when she looked at   10
the shell-tone spray of seed pearls,
the bisque features, she could see herself

inside it all, holding less than real
stephanotis, rose petals, never feeling
satin rise and fall with the vows   15

I kept repeating on the night before –
astray among the cards and wedding gifts –
the coffee pots and the clocks and

the battered tan case full of cotton
lace and tissue-paper, pressing down, then   20
pressing down again. And then, locks.

Glossary

See the critical commentary on p. 278.
The author's note at the beginning of the poem is very helpful. Notice how the doll can be viewed as a *metaphor* for marriage. In the past, women had very few choices open to them and were often viewed as decorative creatures rather than fully rational agents.

1   *tulle* – named after the French town from which it comes, this is a delicate, thin silk fabric.

8   *discreet about | visits, fevers, quickenings and lusts* – Boland imagines the doll having witnessed the intimate details of this family's life. She takes the doll's silence as discretion.

9   *quickenings* – a word sometimes used to describe the stage in pregnancy, usually towards the end of the second trimester, when the mother becomes aware of her child's movements.

12 *bisque* – a type of unglazed, white porcelain.

12 *she could see herself | inside it all* – here, Boland tries to capture the bride's feelings on the night of her wedding all those years ago. The glass dome that encases the shadow doll can be viewed as being symbolic of the oppression that the institution of marriage represented for women.

14 *stephanotis* – a type of flower cultivated for its scent. These were often used in garlands or wreaths.

16 *I kept repeating on the night before* – the poem changes direction here. Now we return to the present and Boland's voice intrudes. The use of the personal pronoun 'I' arouses the reader's interest.

21 *And then, locks* – the final line is short. The final verb is *onomatopoeic* and thus captures perfectly the sound of the case shutting. It also rounds off the poem nicely.

Questions

Go to p. 27 for more questions on Eavan Boland.

1. How well do you think Boland describes the differences between the past and the present in this poem?

2. 'This poem is typical of Boland's poetic style.' Discuss this view, supporting your answer by appropriate quotation or reference.

3. Suggest an alternative tile for this poem. Support your answer by close reference to the poem.

Exam-style Unseen Poem Questions

1. Write a personal response to this poem. Your answer should make close reference to the text.

2. Briefly describe the mood or feeling you get from reading this poem and illustrate your answer from the text.

3. Choose a line or two that you find particularly appealing and explain why.

White Hawthorn in the West of Ireland

I drove West
in the season between seasons.
I left behind suburban gardens.
Lawnmowers. Small talk.

Under low skies, past splashes of coltsfoot,   5
I assumed
the hard shyness of Atlantic light
and the superstitious aura of hawthorn.

All I wanted then was to fill my arms with
sharp flowers,   10
to seem, from a distance, to be part of
that ivory, downhill rush. But I knew,

I had always known
the custom was
not to touch hawthorn.   15
Not to bring it indoors for the sake of

the luck
such constraint would forfeit –
a child might die, perhaps, or an unexplained
fever speckle heifers. So I left it   20

stirring on those hills
with a fluency
only water has. And, like water, able
to re-define land. And free to seem to be –

for anglers,   25
and for travellers astray in
the unmarked lights of a May dusk –
the only language spoken in those parts.

Glossary

See the critical commentary on p. 281.

1   *I drove West* – the opening line is very important; it indicates movement and a sense of journey. More importantly, the West is where indigenous Irish culture still flourishes.

2   *the season between seasons* – given the strong associations that hawthorn has with the ancient May festival of Bealtaine, the season referred to here is late spring or early summer. Bealtaine comes from the Irish *Bealtaine*, meaning 'Bel-fire'. Named after the Celtic God of Light – *Bel, Beli* or *Balor* – Bealtaine is the traditional first day of summer and celebrations used to begin at sundown of the preceding day. Druids would kindle great bale fires on the tops of the nearest beacon hill. Believing that these fires had healing properties, people would jump through the flames to purify themselves and ensure protection. People would also drive their cattle between two such bonfires before taking them to their summer pastures.

5   *coltsfoot* – a plant with a shaggy stalk and large leaves.

7   *Atlantic light* – the light of the Atlantic seaboard is unique and is, perhaps, one of the defining qualities of Ireland.

14 *the custom was | not to touch hawthorn* – it is considered very bad luck to pick hawthorn. This is especially true of the branches of a solitary white hawthorn.

20 *heifers* – young cows. Given the importance of the cow to the rural economy, it is not surprising that many superstitions should have grown up around them.

28 *the only language spoken in those parts* – the final line of the poem suggests that superstitions and traditions can be viewed as a language in their own right. This language connects us to our ancestors and speaks of an undocumented past.

Questions

Go to p. 27 for more questions on Eavan Boland.

1. Comment on Boland's use of language in this poem. You may wish to mention the manner in which the poem's language is both abstract and concrete.

2. How important is the title to our overall understanding of the poem?

3. What themes or issues are raised in this poem? Support your answer by close reference to the poem.

Exam-style Unseen Poem Questions

1. 'I found this poem very moving.' Respond to this statement, referring closely to the language used by Boland in the poem.

2. Write down one phrase from the poem that shows how the poet feels about the hawthorn.

3. Do you think the poem gives a surprising insight into Irish traditions and folklore? In your answer, you might consider:
    *   The pattern of the speaker's thinking.
    *   The words and images in the poem.

Outside History

There are outsiders, always. These stars –
these iron inklings of an Irish January,
whose light happened

thousands of years before
our pain did: they are, they have always been   5
outside history.

They keep their distance. Under them remains
a place where you found
you were human, and

a landscape in which you know you are mortal.   10
And a time to choose between them.
I have chosen:

out of myth into history I move to be
part of that ordeal
whose darkness is   15

only now reaching me from those fields,
those rivers, those roads clotted as
firmaments with the dead.

How slowly they die
as we kneel beside them, whisper in their ear.   20
And we are too late. We are always too late.

Glossary

See the critical commentary on p. 282.
The title, 'Outside History', hints at the main concern of the poem. Much of Boland's poetry focuses on those who are forgotten and voiceless.

1   *These stars* – the stars here emphasise the brevity of human life. The time it takes a star to form is vast in comparison to time as understood by human beings. The stars in this poem are remote. They suggest the distance between the present and the past and they also remind us of the impossibility of changing the past.

2   *iron inklings* – the adjective 'iron' is intended to convey the coldness of the stars. This is very apt given their distance.

3   *whose light happened | thousands of years before | our pain did* – it can take the light from some stars thousands of years to reach earth. In this sense, the light emitted from the star comes from a time that has long since passed.

18   *firmaments* – the heavens or skies.

Questions

Go to   p. 27   for more questions on Eavan Boland.

1. What do you think is the theme of this poem? Refer closely to the poem in your answer.

2. Comment on the following statement about 'Outside History': 'The poem deals with those who have been forgotten by history.'

3. In your opinion, what is the mood of this poem?

Exam-style Unseen Poem Questions

1. Did you like this poem? Briefly state your reasons for liking or not liking this poem.

2. Write down one phrase from the poem that shows how the poet feels about 'outsiders'. Say why you have chosen this phrase.

3. Does this poem make you feel hopeful or unhopeful? Briefly explain why.

The Black Lace Fan my Mother Gave me

It was the first gift he ever gave her,
buying it for five francs in the Galeries
in pre-war Paris. It was stifling.
A starless drought made the nights stormy.

They stayed in the city for the summer.   5
They met in cafés. She was always early.
He was late. That evening he was later.
They wrapped the fan. He looked at his watch.

She looked down the Boulevard des Capucines.
She ordered more coffee. She stood up.   10
The streets were emptying. The heat was killing.
She thought the distance smelled of rain and lightning.

These are wild roses, appliqued on silk by hand,
darkly picked, stitched boldly, quickly.
The rest is tortoiseshell and has the reticent,   15
clear patience of its element. It is

a worn-out, underwater bullion and it keeps,
even now, an inference of its violation.
The lace is overcast as if the weather
it opened for and offset had entered it.   20

The past is an empty café terrace.
An airless dusk before thunder. A man running.
And no way now to know what happened then –
none at all – unless, of course, you improvise:

The blackbird on this first sultry morning,   25
in summer, finding buds, worms, fruit,
feels the heat. Suddenly she puts out her wing –
the whole, full, flirtatious span of it.

Glossary

See the critical commentary on p. 284.

2   *Galeries* – most likely a reference to the Galeries Lafayette, an upmarket store in Paris.

3   *pre-war Paris* and *stormy* (line 4) – these references must be read as a deliberate **allusion** to the lightning war, or blitzkrieg, of the German army. Notice how the poem makes great use of the **caesura**, or internal break within a line. These breaks in the line give the poem a jerky or grainy quality, similar to an old black and white film. For more on this, see the critical commentary on p. 284.

9   *Boulevard des Capucines* – an area of Paris made famous in a well-known painting by Claude Monet.

12   *the distance smelled of rain and lightning* – an allusion to the impending war.

15   *reticent* – unforthcoming, restrained, uncommunicative. The fan, being made of 'tortoiseshell', contains something of the tortoise it was made from.

22   *A man running* – notice the strange use of the present continuous. This allows us to access the narrative more easily.

24   *of course, you improvise* – because Boland has not lived this event herself, she is forced to improvise.

25   *The blackbird on this first sultry morning* – suddenly, the poem returns to the present. This is characteristic of Boland's poetry. The past, pre-war Paris and the story of her mother and father's courtship blend with the here and now.

Questions

Go to   p. 27   for more questions on Eavan Boland.

1.   In your view, how well does Boland describe the fan? Refer to the poem in your answer.

2.   Comment on Boland's treatment of time in this poem.

3.   In your opinion, what does the fan symbolise for the poet? Support your answer by close reference to the poem.

Exam-style Unseen Poem Questions

1.   Write a response to the above poem, highlighting the impact it makes on you.

2.   Briefly describe the mood or feeling you get from reading this poem and illustrate your answer from the text.

3.   Choose a line or two that you find particularly appealing and explain why.

This Moment

A neighbourhood.
At dusk.

Things are getting ready
to happen
out of sight.   5

Stars and moths.
And rinds slanting around fruit.

But not yet.

One tree is black.
One window is yellow as butter.   10

A woman leans down to catch a child
who has run into her arms
this moment.

Stars rise.
Moths flutter.   15
Apples sweeten in the dark.

Glossary

See the critical commentary on p. 289.
The title of the poem is very informative. This poem is literally about a moment in time.

1 *A neighbourhood* – once again, Boland turns her gaze towards suburbia.

7 *rinds slanting around fruit* – Boland takes the moment and slows it down so that usually imperceptible events become visible.

10 *yellow as butter* – there is something very homely about this **simile**.

11 *A woman leans down to catch a child* – this **image** is a beautiful representation of how wonderful the ordinary can be.

16 *Apples sweeten in the dark* – the poem ends with a depiction of an event that normally remains hidden.

Questions

Go to p. 27 for more questions on Eavan Boland.

1. This poem is almost cinematic in its presentation of its scene. In your opinion, how does Boland manage to achieve this effect?

2. Choose an alternative title for this poem. Support your choice by referring closely to the poem in your answer.

3. How does the poem's imagery contribute to the atmosphere in 'This Moment'?

Exam-style Unseen Poem Questions

1. Choose one or two images from the poem that you found appealing. In the case of each image, say why you have chosen it.

2. Do you like the scene that the poet describes in this poem? Give reasons for your answer, supporting them by reference to the text.

3. Briefly describe the mood or feeling you get from reading this poem and illustrate your answer from the text.

The Pomegranate

The only legend I have ever loved is
the story of a daughter lost in hell.
And found and rescued there.
Love and blackmail are the gist of it.
Ceres and Persephone the names.   5
And the best thing about the legend is
I can enter it anywhere. And have.
As a child in exile in
a city of fogs and strange consonants,
I read it first and at first I was   10
an exiled child in the crackling dusk of
the underworld, the stars blighted. Later
I walked out in a summer twilight
searching for my daughter at bed-time.
When she came running I was ready   15
to make any bargain to keep her.
I carried her back past whitebeams
and wasps and honey-scented buddleias.
But I was Ceres then and I knew
winter was in store for every leaf   20
on every tree on that road.
Was inescapable for each one we passed.
And for me.
        It is winter
and the stars are hidden.   25
I climb the stairs and stand where I can see
my child asleep beside her teen magazines,
her can of Coke, her plate of uncut fruit.
The pomegranate! How did I forget it?
She could have come home and been safe   30
and ended the story and all
our heart-broken searching but she reached
out a hand and plucked a pomegranate.

She put out her hand and pulled down

the French sound for apple and   35

the noise of stone and the proof

that even in the place of death,

at the heart of legend, in the midst

of rocks full of unshed tears

ready to be diamonds by the time   40

the story was told, a child can be

hungry. I could warn her. There is still a chance.

The rain is cold. The road is flint-coloured.

The suburb has cars and cable television.

The veiled stars are above ground.   45

It is another world. But what else

can a mother give her daughter but such

beautiful rifts in time?

If I defer the grief I will diminish the gift.

The legend will be hers as well as mine.   50

She will enter it. As I have.

She will wake up. She will hold

the papery flushed skin in her hand.

And to her lips. I will say nothing.

Glossary

See the critical commentary on p. 290.
The title of the poem, 'The Pomegranate', is very important, as it frames the poem. A pomegranate is a type of fruit. In Greek **mythology**, the pomegranate grows at the entrance to Hades, the underworld.

2 *hell* – this reference to hell is not meant to indicate Judaeo-Christian notions of hell. Rather, it is a direct **allusion** to Hades, the Greek underworld.

5 *Ceres and Persephone* – for the ancient Greeks, Ceres was the Goddess of the Earth. As a result of her seduction by Zeus, she had a daughter, Persephone, by him. Persephone was reputed to be one of the most beautiful of Zeus' many daughters. Consequently, her uncle Hades fell in love with her. One day while Persephone was picking flowers, the ground opened and Hades dragged her against her will into the underworld.

Ceres decided to abandon her duties as Goddess of the Earth until her daughter was returned to her. Ceres' self-imposed exile made the earth sterile. Zeus, as leader of the gods, ordered his brother Hades to return Persephone. However, that was no longer possible. During her stay in the underworld, Persephone had eaten a pomegranate seed, which linked her forever to the underworld. Finally, a compromise was reached by which Persephone spent half the year with her mother and the other half in the underworld.

9 *a city of fogs* – this is a reference to London. Once renowned for its fogs, London was home to Boland in the 1950s. Her father, F.H. Boland, was a diplomat who was posted to London during this period.

11 *crackling dusk* – look out for references to dusk, twilight and darkness in the poem. These references lend the poem a dark aspect. This is itself reminiscent of Hades.

19 *I knew | winter was in store for every leaf* – this is a vivid reminder that the effects of the passing of time are the inescapable lot of humankind.

24 *It is winter* – notice how the tense shifts from past to present. This mirrors the shift from myth to personal experience.

27 *my child asleep beside her teen magazines, | her can of Coke* – this is another example of Boland using the ordinary, even banal, setting of suburban life in order to create poetry.

49 *If I defer the grief I will diminish the gift* – this is an important line in the poem. Here, the poet states that it is possible to offset or delay the pain of growing up. However, to do so would lessen or diminish the freedom of the child.

52 *She will hold | the papery flushed skin in her hand* – this is a reference to the act of biting into the pomegranate. However, in the context of her daughter's growing up, this can also be read as an allusion to sexual awakening.

Questions

Go to p. 27 for more questions on Eavan Boland.

1. In your view, how well does Boland manage to link the story of Ceres and Persephone to her own life?

2. Comment on the manner in which Boland explores her relationship with her daughter in the poem.

3. In your opinion, what is the theme of this poem?

Exam-style Unseen Poem Questions

1. Do you think the poem gives an insight into the mother–daughter relationship? In your answer, you might consider:
   - The pattern of the speaker's thinking.
   - The words and images in the poem.

2. Write a response to 'The Pomegranate', highlighting aspects of it that you liked and/or disliked.

3. Choose a phrase or line from the poem that impressed you. Explain your choice.

Love

Dark falls on this mid-western town
where we once lived when myths collided.
Dusk has hidden the bridges in the river
which slides and deepens
to become the water   5
the hero crossed on his way to hell.

Not far from here is our old apartment.
We had a kitchen and an Amish table.
We had a view. And we discovered there
love had the feather and muscle of wings   10
and had come to live with us,
a brother of fire and air.

We had two infant children one of whom
was touched by death in this town
and spared: and when the hero   15
was hailed by his comrades in hell
their mouths opened and their voices failed and
there is no knowing what they would have asked
about a life they had shared and lost.

I am your wife.   20
It was years ago.
Our child was healed. We love each other still.
Across our day-to-day and ordinary distances
we speak plainly. We hear each other clearly.

And yet I want to return to you   25
on the bridge of the Iowa river as you were,
with snow on the shoulders of your coat
and a car passing with its headlights on:

I see you as a hero in a text –
the image blazing and the edges gilded –   30
and I long to cry out the epic question
my dear companion:

Will we ever live so intensely again?
Will love come to us again and be
so formidable at rest it offered us ascension   35
even to look at him?

But the words are shadows and you cannot hear me.
You walk away and I cannot follow.

Glossary

See the critical commentary on p. 294.
The title of the poem is powerful and captivating.

1   *mid-western town* – Boland was a member
    of the International Writing Program at the
    University of Iowa. During this time, she lived
    in the midwest of the United States.

5   *the water | the hero crossed* – this is a complex
    allusion to Homer's *Odyssey*. Odysseus,
    the hero of Homer's poem, travels to the
    underworld in an attempt to hasten his voyage
    home. Deeply in love with his wife, Penelope,
    the Greek hero mirrors many of the sentiments
    of this poem.

6   *hell* – this is a reference to Hades, the Greek
    underworld. Notice how the poem opens in
    darkness.

10 *love had the feather and muscle of wings* – like a
    bird's wing, love is simultaneously fragile and
    strong.

12 *brother of fire and air* – Boland views love
    as being elemental. Together with earth and
    water, fire and air make up the four elements.

17 *their mouths opened and their voices failed* –
    according to mythology, dead souls are unable
    to speak unless they drink from a special
    potion.

38 *You walk away and I cannot follow* – she can't
    follow him because the intense love they once
    experienced is now part of their past. It is
    unlikely to be lived again.

Questions

Go to   p. 27   for more questions on Eavan Boland.

1. Do you think the central theme of this poem is love or the passing of time?
    Support your answer by referring closely to the poem.

2. How does the myth used by Boland mirror the poem's theme?

3. What does the poet mean when she says, 'words are shadows [...] | You walk away
    and I cannot follow'?

Exam-style Unseen Poem Questions

1. Choose a line or two from 'Love' that you find particularly appealing and explain
    why.

2. Write down one phrase from the poem that shows how the speaker feels about
    her husband. Say why you have chosen this phrase.

3. Write a personal response to this poem. Your answer should make close reference
    to the text.

Eavan Boland: An Overview

Now that you have read a selection of Boland's poetry, you should take the time to look at the following general points. The purpose of these is not to tell you what to think, but rather to help you to form your own opinions. When you have read these points, you may wish to take the time to reread Boland's poetry. You should notice that the general points made here can be used to form the backbone of your paragraphs when it comes to writing on poetry. From now on, try to think about Boland's poems in terms of what they say and how they say it. Open your mind to any reasonable interpretation of the poems; remember, your opinions are as valid as anything printed. However, you must be prepared to ground these opinions in fact. If you find this process difficult, that is entirely normal. Remember that a poem is not meant to be studied and dissected in the manner that the Leaving Certificate requires of us. While we have to keep the exam in mind, you should not allow it to detract from your enjoyment of the poetry on the course.

1. Boland's poems on the course tend to create a sense of immediacy by drawing us into the narrative. Some techniques employed by her to great effect are:
   a. Use of the personal pronoun 'I'.
   b. The revelation of personal and intimate details about her own life.
   c. Use of concise language that is to the point.
2. You should also look at the manner in which Boland chooses to situate her poems in a suburban setting. Her poetry makes it clear that the modern housing estate is a place where the magic of poetry exists.
3. One of the more interesting aspects of Boland's poetry is its tendency to call into question the traditional divisions that exist between the order of suburbia and the wildness of the countryside.
4. Boland's poetry looks at history (both personal and public) in a unique fashion. The blending of past and present can result in an interesting experience for the reader. Notice how, on occasion, her narratives exist in the past and in the present. As a result, the barriers between past and present become worn down. In this sense, Boland's poetry achieves a feeling of timelessness.

5. Her poetry deals with powerful emotions and human relationships in an honest and open fashion. Nowhere is this more apparent than in her treatment of the experience of being in love.

This list of general points is, of course, in no way exhaustive; there are quite literally thousands of perfectly valid observations to be made about Boland's poetry. Remember, your opinion is as valid as any of the points mentioned above.

Past Leaving Certificate Questions

Boland first appeared on the 2002 Leaving Certificate paper. On that paper, students were asked to do the following:

> **Write a personal response to the poetry of Eavan Boland. Support the points you make by reference to the poetry of Eavan Boland that you have studied.**

The correctors were told to allow for a wide range of approaches in the candidates' answers. They were also told to consider the following possibilities:

- Her life and its links with her work.
- The themes and issues she explores in the poems.
- The appeal of the poems and/or the impact of the poetry on the reader.
- Her style – vision, language, imagery.

In 2005, the following question was asked:

> **'The appeal of Eavan Boland's poetry.'**
> **Using the above title, write an essay outlining what you consider to be the appeal of Boland's poetry. Support your points by reference to the poetry of Eavan Boland on your course.**

Sample Questions

Before you try these questions, you may wish to consult the examination technique guidelines on p. 548.

1. 'The impact of Eavan Boland's poetry.'
   Write a speech to be delivered to your classmates on the impact Eavan Boland's poetry had on you. Your answer should focus both on themes and the use of imagery/language. Support your points with the aid of suitable reference to the poems on your course.

2. Write a letter to Eavan Boland in which you discuss the experience of reading her poetry.

3. Write an essay introducing the poetry of Eavan Boland.

4. 'Eavan Boland expresses her themes in an interesting and thought-provoking fashion.'
   You have been asked by your local radio station to give a talk on the poetry of Eavan Boland. Write out the text of the talk you would deliver in response to the above title. You should refer to both style and subject matter. Support the points you make by reference to the poetry on your course.

5. Write a personal response to the poems by Eavan Boland on your course. Support your points with reference to the poetry on your course.

6. 'Eavan Boland poses interesting questions delivered by means of a unique style.'
   Do you agree with this assessment of her poetry? Your answer should focus on both themes and stylistic features. Support your points with the aid of suitable reference to the poems you have studied.

7. Write an introduction to the poetry of Eavan Boland for new readers. Your introduction should cover the following:
   • The ideas that are most important to her.
   • How you responded to her use of language and imagery.
   Refer closely to the poems by Eavan Boland that you have studied.

8. 'What Evan Boland's poetry means to me.'
   Write an essay in response to the above title. Your essay should include a discussion of her themes and the way she expresses them. Support the points you make by reference to the poetry on your course.

9. Write an article for a school magazine introducing the poetry of Eavan Boland to Leaving Certificate students. Tell them what she wrote about and explain why you liked her writing, suggesting some poems that you think they would find interesting. Support your points by reference to the poetry of Eavan Boland that you have studied.

Robert Frost (1874–1963)

Robert Frost looms as a giant figure on the American literary landscape. By concentrating on the countryside, language and experiences of America, his poetry has done much to establish an American poetic identity. In fact, his wry, countrified, New England narrative voice has often been praised as the quintessential voice of American literature. His determination to weave poetry out of everyday experience distinguishes him from most other poets of his age. His poems are honest, open and autobiographical. It has often been said of Frost that he never really tired of retelling the story of his own life. He was also the undisputed master of poetic forms. Writing in a period dominated by free verse, in a time when poetry seemed to have given up on punctuation and capital letters, Frost insisted that poetry have a definite form, that it be dramatic and that it rely on voice tones to vary the effect of its rhythms. If you are reading the poetry of Robert Frost for the first time, one of the things that should strike you straight away is that his poems are deceptive. What at first appears to be a simple nature poem will often yield complex and interesting interpretations. If you would like to read more about Robert Frost's life, there is a short biography on p. 297.

The Tuft of Flowers

I went to turn the grass once after one
Who mowed it in the dew before the sun.

The dew was gone that made his blade so keen
Before I came to view the leveled scene.

I looked for him behind an isle of trees;   5
I listened for his whetstone on the breeze.

But he had gone his way, the grass all mown,
And I must be, as he had been—alone,

"As all must be," I said within my heart,
"Whether they work together or apart."   10

But as I said it, swift there passed me by
On noiseless wing a bewildered butterfly,

Seeking with memories grown dim o'er night
Some resting flower of yesterday's delight.

And once I marked his flight go round and round,   15
As where some flower lay withering on the ground.

And then he flew as far as eye could see,
And then on tremulous wing came back to me.

I thought of questions that have no reply,
And would have turned to toss the grass to dry;   20

But he turned first, and led my eye to look
At a tall tuft of flowers beside a brook,

eaping tongue of bloom the scythe had spared
le a reedy brook the scythe had bared.

The mower in the dew had loved them thus,   25
By leaving them to flourish, not for us,

Nor yet to draw one thought of ours to him,
But from sheer morning gladness at the brim.

The butterfly and I had lit upon,
Nevertheless, a message from the dawn,   30

That made me hear the wakening birds around,
And hear his long scythe whispering to the ground,

And feel a spirit kindred to my own;
So that henceforth I worked no more alone;

But glad with him, I worked as with his aid,   35
And weary, sought at noon with him the shade;

And dreaming, as it were, held brotherly speech
With one whose thought I had not hoped to reach.

"Men work together," I told him from the heart,
"Whether they work together or apart."   40

Glossary

See the critical commentary on p. 299.

1 *to turn the grass* – to toss grass so that it will dry.

2 *dew* – moisture that is deposited from the air in small drops on plants, especially at night.

3 *keen* – enthusiastic, sharp.

6 *whetstone* – a stone on which the gardener would sharpen the blade of his knife or his scythe.

12 *bewildered* – confused, dazed or disorientated.

13 *grown dim* – become faint or dark.

18 *tremulous* – quivering or trembling.

22 *brook* – a small stream.

23 *A leaping tongue of bloom* – perhaps the speaker is echoing the Bible here. In the Bible, a tongue of flames descended on the Apostles (Christ's followers). For the speaker (and, indeed, for the butterfly), the tuft of flowers offers a moment of insight and inspiration that brings him into closer harmony with the natural world.

24 *scythe* – a long, curved blade used for mowing long grass.

26 *to flourish* – to grow in abundance or to thrive.

29 *lit upon* – met or came upon.

33 *kindred* – very close or similar to.

33 *a spirit kindred to my own* – here, the speaker feels so close to the absent gardener that it is as if they are working in the field together.

Questions

Go to **p. 52** for more questions on Robert Frost.

1. In your opinion, what is the theme of this poem?

2. Trace the shifts of mood and tone in this poem. Support your answer by close reference to the poem.

3. What do you think the poet means when he says, '"Men work together […] | "Whether they work together or apart"'?

Exam-style Unseen Poem Questions

1. Choose three images from the poem that you found particularly striking. In the case of each image, say why you have chosen it.

2. What do you think the flowers represent or symbolise?

3. Write a short personal response to this poem. You may want to comment on the effect that the imagery and the central message of the poem had on you.

Mending Wall

Something there is that doesn't love a wall,
That sends the frozen-ground-swell under it
And spills the upper boulders in the sun,
And makes gaps even two can pass abreast.
The work of hunters is another thing: 5
I have come after them and made repair
Where they have left not one stone on a stone,
But they would have the rabbit out of hiding,
To please the yelping dogs. The gaps I mean,
No one has seen them made or heard them made,   10
But at spring mending-time we find them there.
I let my neighbor know beyond the hill;
And on a day we meet to walk the line
And set the wall between us once again.
We keep the wall between us as we go.   15
To each the boulders that have fallen to each.
And some are loaves and some so nearly balls
We have to use a spell to make them balance:
"Stay where you are until our backs are turned!"
We wear our fingers rough with handling them.   20
Oh, just another kind of outdoor game,
One on a side. It comes to little more:
There where it is we do not need the wall:
He is all pine and I am apple orchard.
My apple trees will never get across   25
And eat the cones under his pines, I tell him.
He only says, "Good fences make good neighbors."
Spring is the mischief in me, and I wonder
If I could put a notion in his head:
"*Why* do they make good neighbors? Isn't it   30
Where there are cows? But here there are no cows.
Before I built a wall I'd ask to know
What I was walling in or walling out,
And to whom I was like to give offense.
Something there is that doesn't love a wall,   35

That wants it down." I could say "Elves" to him,
But it's not elves exactly, and I'd rather
He said it for himself. I see him there,
Bringing a stone grasped firmly by the top
In each hand, like an old-stone savage armed.   40
He moves in darkness as it seems to me,
Not of woods only and the shade of trees.
He will not go behind his father's saying,
And he likes having thought of it so well
He says again, "Good fences make good neighbors."   45

See the critical commentary on p. 302.

4 *abreast* – alongside one another.

5 *The work of hunters is another thing* – here, the speaker is referring back to 'that doesn't love a wall'.

9 *yelping* – barking.

24 *He is all pine and I am apple orchard* – the speaker is describing the two types of woodland on either side of the wall.

28 *Spring is the mischief in me* – springtime brings out the poet's mischievous side. The speaker would like to put a 'notion' in his neighbour's 'head' but refrains from doing so. The things that he would like to say remain unsaid. As a result, the poem then becomes a **monologue**, or a conversation that the speaker has with himself.

36 *Elves* – small, supernatural creatures of human form that supposedly inhabit woodlands. In folklore, elves are often associated with mischief-making.

40 *an old-stone savage* – a primitive man. Perhaps the speaker is making a comment on his neighbour's primitive views.

41 *He moves in darkness* – the speaker suggests that his neighbour has failed to develop any sense of personal philosophy.

43 *He will not go behind his father's saying* – again, this is another reference to his neighbour's failure to become enlightened. He remains trapped in an archaic way of thinking and fails to challenge the views held by his father.

Questions

Go to p. 52 for more questions on Robert Frost.

1. Do you think that this poem is about more than simply mending a wall? Give reasons for your answer.

2. What do you think the speaker means when he says: 'He is all pine and I am apple orchard'?

3. How well does the poem demonstrate that walls can unite as well as divide? Support your answer by close reference to the poem.

Exam-style Unseen Poem Questions

1. Write a response to 'Mending Wall', highlighting aspects of it that you liked and/ or disliked.

2. Choose a line or two that you find particularly appealing and explain why.

3. What impression of the speaker do you get from this poem? Support your answer by referring closely to the poem.

After Apple-Picking

My long two-pointed ladder's sticking through a tree
Toward heaven still,
And there's a barrel that I didn't fill
Beside it, and there may be two or three
Apples I didn't pick upon some bough.   5
But I am done with apple-picking now.
Essence of winter sleep is on the night,
The scent of apples: I am drowsing off.
I cannot rub the strangeness from my sight
I got from looking through a pane of glass   10
I skimmed this morning from the drinking trough
And held against the world of hoary grass.
It melted, and I let it fall and break.
But I was well
Upon my way to sleep before it fell,   15
And I could tell
What form my dreaming was about to take.
Magnified apples appear and disappear,
Stem end and blossom end,
And every fleck of russet showing clear.   20
My instep arch not only keeps the ache,
It keeps the pressure of a ladder-round.
I feel the ladder sway as the boughs bend.
And I keep hearing from the cellar bin
The rumbling sound   25
Of load on load of apples coming in.
For I have had too much
Of apple-picking: I am overtired
Of the great harvest I myself desired.
There were ten thousand thousand fruit to touch,   30
Cherish in hand, lift down, and not let fall.
For all
That struck the earth,
No matter if not bruised or spiked with stubble,
Went surely to the cider-apple heap   35

As of no worth.

One can see what will trouble

This sleep of mine, whatever sleep it is.

Were he not gone,

The woodchuck could say whether it's like his   40

Long sleep, as I describe its coming on,

Or just some human sleep.

Glossary

See the critical commentary on p. 306.
The title, 'After Apple-Picking', is very important.
The poem takes place after a hard day's work
harvesting apples. Frost describes the drowsy state
of being that comes over the exhausted apple-
picker.

7   *Essence of winter sleep* – the scent of winter
    sleep. The smell of the apples reminds
    the speaker of the coming of winter and
    hibernation. In the past, apples used to be kept
    in a darkened room in order to preserve them.
    These apple stores were known for their sweet
    smell.

10   *glass* – ice.
11   *drinking trough* – a container from which
     animals drink water.
12   *hoary* – snow-white.
20   *russet* – auburn or reddish coloured.
22   *ladder-round* – the rung on the ladder on
     which he has been standing.
40   *woodchuck* – an indigenous North American
     squirrel-like animal, sometimes called a
     groundhog.
41   *Long sleep* – hibernation.

Questions

Go to   p. 52   for more questions on Robert Frost.

1. 'This poem is about more than just picking apples.' Comment on this statement.
   Refer closely to the poem in your answer.

2. How well does Frost appeal to the senses in this poem?

3. Someone has said that 'a dreamlike quality pervades "After Apple-Picking".'
   Do you agree with this assessment of the poem? Support your answer by close
   reference to the poem.

Exam-style Unseen Poem Questions

1. Did you like this poem? Briefly state your reasons for liking or not liking 'After
   Apple-Picking'.

2. Choose a phrase or line from the poem that impressed you. Explain your choice.

3. Briefly describe the mood or feeling you get from reading this poem and illustrate
   your answer from the text.

The Road Not Taken

Two roads diverged in a yellow wood,
And sorry I could not travel both
And be one traveler, long I stood
And looked down one as far as I could
To where it bent in the undergrowth;   5

Then took the other, as just as fair,
And having perhaps the better claim,
Because it was grassy and wanted wear;
Though as for that, the passing there
Had worn them really about the same,   10

And both that morning equally lay
In leaves no step had trodden black.
Oh, I kept the first for another day!
Yet knowing how way leads on to way,
I doubted if I should ever come back.   15

I shall be telling this with a sigh
Somewhere ages and ages hence:
Two roads diverged in a wood, and I—
I took the one less traveled by,
And that has made all the difference.   20

See the critical commentary on p. 310.

In this poem, Frost forces us to interpret the choice that he faces on a symbolic level. The fact that the poet intends for us to react in this manner is obvious from the degree of importance he attaches to this choice in the last stanza.

1 *diverged* – separated, went in different directions. This, of course, adds a certain degree of urgency to the poet's choice.

1 *yellow wood* – the time of the year is autumn. This time of year has often been associated with the approach of old age.

5 *the undergrowth* – the vegetation growing at the base of the trees.

8 *wanted wear* – the path had not been walked on recently.

12 *trodden* – walked on.

16 *I shall be telling this with a sigh* – by using the future tense here, the poet is implying that the journey has not yet ended.

17 *ages hence* – in a long time to come.

Questions

Go to p. 52 for more questions on Robert Frost.

1. Describe the speaker's attitude to the choice he faces. Refer closely to the poem in your answer.

2. Suggest an alternative title for this poem. Support your answer by reference to or quotation from the poem.

3. In your opinion, what do the two roads represent or symbolise in this poem?

Exam-style Unseen Poem Questions

1. Write a response to 'The Road Not Taken', highlighting the impact it makes on you.

2. Choose a phrase or line from the poem that impressed you. Explain your choice.

3. Do you think the poem gives an interesting insight into the choices we all face in life? In your answer, you might consider:
   • The pattern of the speaker's thinking.
   • The words and images in the poem.

Birches

When I see birches bend to left and right
Across the lines of straighter darker trees,
I like to think some boy's been swinging them.
But swinging doesn't bend them down to stay
As ice storms do. Often you must have seen them   5
Loaded with ice a sunny winter morning
After a rain. They click upon themselves
As the breeze rises, and turn many-colored
As the stir cracks and crazes their enamel.
Soon the sun's warmth makes them shed crystal shells   10
Shattering and avalanching on the snow crust—
Such heaps of broken glass to sweep away
You'd think the inner dome of heaven had fallen.
They are dragged to the withered bracken by the load,
And they seem not to break; though once they are bowed   15
So low for long, they never right themselves:
You may see their trunks arching in the woods
Years afterwards, trailing their leaves on the ground
Like girls on hands and knees that throw their hair
Before them over their heads to dry in the sun.   20
But I was going to say when Truth broke in
With all her matter of fact about the ice storm,
I should prefer to have some boy bend them
As he went out and in to fetch the cows—
Some boy too far from town to learn baseball,   25
Whose only play was what he found himself, -
Summer or winter, and could play alone.
One by one he subdued his father's trees
By riding them down over and over again
Until he took the stiffness out of them,   30
And not one but hung limp, not one was left
For him to conquer. He learned all there was
To learn about not launching out too soon
And so not carrying the tree away

Clear to the ground. He always kept his poise   35
To the top branches, climbing carefully
With the same pains you use to fill a cup
Up to the brim, and even above the brim.
Then he flung outward, feet first, with a swish,
Kicking his way down through the air to the ground.   40
So was I once myself a swinger of birches.
And so I dream of going back to be.
It's when I'm weary of considerations,
And life is too much like a pathless wood
Where your face burns and tickles with the cobwebs   45
Broken across it, and one eye is weeping
From a twig's having lashed across it open.
I'd like to get away from earth awhile
And then come back to it and begin over.
May no fate willfully misunderstand me   50
And half grant what I wish and snatch me away
Not to return. Earth's the right place for love:
I don't know where it's likely to go better.
I'd like to go by climbing a birch tree,
And climb black branches up a snow-white trunk   55
Toward heaven, till the tree could bear no more,
But dipped its top and set me down again.
That would be good both going and coming back.
One could do worse than be a swinger of birches.

Glossary

See the critical commentary on p. 313.
The title, 'Birches', refers to a deciduous forest tree that has a smooth white bark.

5 *Often you must have seen them* – the use of the personal pronoun 'you' draws the reader into the poem. This single instance of the pronoun transforms the poem from a private consideration of the trees into a **monologue** aimed at the listener.

7 *They click upon themselves* – here, the poet is describing the noise that the trees make when they knock against one another.

9 *crazes* – cracks or shatters.

9 *enamel* – glossy surface.

10 *crystal shells* – the poet here is describing the melting ice on the trees.

11 *avalanching* – pouring down.

14 *bracken* – ferns.

31 *limp* – wilted or flaccid.

39 *swish* – whoosh or rustle.

44 *life is too much like a pathless wood* – here, the speaker describes the difficult nature of finding one's way in life.

50 *willfully* – purposefully.

Questions

Go to p. 52 for more questions on Robert Frost.

1. Comment on Frost's use of language in this poem. You may wish to mention the manner in which the poem's language is both abstract and concrete.

2. How does the poet support his claim that 'One could do worse than be a swinger of birches'?

3. To what extent do the rhythm and metre of 'Birches' add to the mood and atmosphere in the poem?

Exam-style Unseen Poem Questions

1. Do you like the scene that the poet describes in this poem? Give reasons for your answer, supporting them by reference to the text.

2. Choose a line or two that you find particularly appealing and explain why.

3. Describe the impact this poem makes on you as a reader.

"Out, Out—"

The buzz saw snarled and rattled in the yard
And made dust and dropped stove-length sticks of wood,
Sweet-scented stuff when the breeze drew across it.
And from there those that lifted eyes could count
Five mountain ranges one behind the other   5
Under the sunset far into Vermont.
And the saw snarled and rattled, snarled and rattled,
As it ran light, or had to bear a load.
And nothing happened: day was all but done.
Call it a day, I wish they might have said   10
To please the boy by giving him the half hour
That a boy counts so much when saved from work.
His sister stood beside them in her apron
To tell them "Supper." At the word, the saw,
As if to prove saws knew what supper meant,   15
Leaped out at the boy's hand, or seemed to leap—
He must have given the hand. However it was,
Neither refused the meeting. But the hand!
The boy's first outcry was a rueful laugh,
As he swung toward them holding up the hand,   20
Half in appeal, but half as if to keep
The life from spilling. Then the boy saw all—
Since he was old enough to know, big boy
Doing a man's work, though a child at heart—
He saw all spoiled. "Don't let him cut my hand off—   25
The doctor, when he comes. Don't let him, sister!"
So. But the hand was gone already.
The doctor put him in the dark of ether.
He lay and puffed his lips out with his breath.
And then—the watcher at his pulse took fright.   30
No one believed. They listened at his heart.
Little—less—nothing!—and that ended it.
No more to build on there. And they, since they
Were not the one dead, turned to their affairs.

Glossary

See the critical commentary on p. 317.
The title is an ***allusion*** to Shakespeare's *Macbeth*. See p. 317 of the critical commentaries to read the speech.

1   *snarled* – growled. 'Snarled' can also mean to be knotted or tangled. This helps us envision the blade of the saw more accurately.

6   *Vermont* – a state in the United States of America.

7   *And the saw snarled and rattled, snarled and rattled* – notice how the ***onomatopoeic*** effect precisely captures the sound of the saw.

12   *when saved from work* – there is a dreadful irony contained in these lines. A half-hour of free time would have saved the young boy's life.

19   *rueful* – regretful, remorseful.

23   *big boy | Doing a man's work, though a child at heart* – here, the poet highlights some of his own ambiguous feelings about life and death.

28   *the dark of ether* – ether is an anaesthetic. The mention of the word 'dark' also anticipates the boy's death.

Questions

Go to   p. 52   for more questions on Robert Frost.

1.   Comment on the poet's use of language in this poem. You may wish to mention the manner in which the sound of the saw is recreated and the manner in which the accident is foreshadowed.

2.   How effectively does the poet evoke the sense of shock and terror felt by the boy?

3.   In your opinion, what is the theme of this poem?

Exam-style Unseen Poem Questions

1.   'I found this poem very moving.' Respond to this statement, referring closely to the language used by Frost in the poem.

2.   Choose one image from the poem that you found particularly striking. Give reasons for your choice.

3.   Write a short personal response to this poem.

Spring Pools

These pools that, though in forests, still reflect
The total sky almost without defect,
And like the flowers beside them, chill and shiver,
Will like the flowers beside them soon be gone,
And yet not out by any brook or river,   5
But up by roots to bring dark foliage on.

The trees that have it in their pent-up buds
To darken nature and be summer woods—
Let them think twice before they use their powers
To blot out and drink up and sweep away   10
These flowery waters and these watery flowers
From snow that melted only yesterday.

Glossary

See the critical commentary on p. 319.
In 1928, Frost made a nostalgic return to England. In the same year, he also published the collection *West-Running Brook*, from which this poem is taken.

1 *reflect* – this word is very important to our reading of this poem. 'Spring Pools' is a poem that asks us to think and reflect. Of course, the pools also reflect the light.

2 *defect* – a flaw or imperfection.

5 *brook* – a small river.

6 *foliage* – undergrowth, green plants.

Questions

Go to p. 52 for more questions on Robert Frost.

1. In your opinion, what is the central message of this poem? In your answer, you may wish to outline the argument of the poem.

2. To what extent do the sound patterns in 'Spring Pools' contribute to the poem's atmosphere?

3. How well does Frost manage to capture the sense that the world is in a constant state of change? Support your answer by close reference to the poem.

Exam-style Unseen Poem Questions

1. Describe the impact this poem makes on you as a reader.

2. Do you think the poem gives an interesting insight into the natural world? In your answer, you might consider:
   • The pattern of the speaker's thinking.
   • The words and images in the poem.

3. Choose a line or two that you find particularly appealing and explain why.

Acquainted with the Night

I have been one acquainted with the night.
I have walked out in rain—and back in rain.
I have outwalked the furthest city light.

I have looked down the saddest city lane.
I have passed by the watchman on his beat   5
And dropped my eyes, unwilling to explain.

I have stood still and stopped the sound of feet
When far away an interrupted cry
Came over houses from another street,

But not to call me back or say good-by;   10
And further still at an unearthly height
One luminary clock against the sky

Proclaimed the time was neither wrong nor right.
I have been one acquainted with the night.

Glossary

See the critical commentary on p. 321.   1   *Acquainted with* – familiar with.

Questions

Go to   p. 52   for more questions on Robert Frost.

1. What do you think the poet means when he says that he has been 'acquainted with the night'?
2. In your own words, describe the scene in this poem.
3. In your opinion, what is the theme of this poem?

Exam-style Unseen Poem Questions

1. Write a short response to 'Acquainted with the Night' in which you outline your reasons for liking or not liking this poem.
2. Choose one or two phrases from the poem that you found particularly appealing and say why.
3. Does this poem make you feel hopeful or unhopeful? Briefly explain why.

Design

I found a dimpled spider, fat and white,
On a white heal-all, holding up a moth
Like a white piece of rigid satin cloth—
Assorted characters of death and blight
Mixed ready to begin the morning right,   5
Like the ingredients of a witches' broth—
A snow-drop spider, a flower like a froth,
And dead wings carried like a paper kite.

What had that flower to do with being white,
The wayside blue and innocent heal-all?   10
What brought the kindred spider to that height,
Then steered the white moth thither in the night?
What but design of darkness to appall?—
If design govern in a thing so small.

Glossary

See the critical commentary on p. 323.
The title, 'Design', alludes to the belief that the natural design of the world is proof that God exists.

1 *dimpled* – indented. The spider obviously has a small hollow on its body.

2 *heal-all* – a type of plant that was often used to produce medicines.

4 *blight* – a disease caused by fungus. However, the word can also mean anything that has an extremely negative effect.

6 *witches' broth* – these broths were said to be made from disgusting ingredients.

13 *appall* – literally to make pale, to shock or disgust.

Questions

Go to p. 52 for more questions on Robert Frost.

1. How important is the title to our understanding of the poem?

2. Comment on the poet's use of the colour white in this poem.

3. It what ways does the poem's form contribute to our understanding of the poem? In your answer, you may wish to comment on the fact that the poem is a sonnet and that there is a clear division in thought between the octet and the sestet.

Exam-style Unseen Poem Questions

1. Write a response to 'Design', highlighting aspects of it that you liked and/or disliked.

2. Do you think the poem gives a surprising insight into nature? In your answer, you might consider:
   - The pattern of the speaker's thinking.
   - The words and images in the poem.

3. Does this poem make you feel hopeful or unhopeful? Briefly explain why.

Provide, Provide

The witch that came (the withered hag)
To wash the steps with pail and rag
Was once the beauty Abishag,

The picture pride of Hollywood.
Too many fall from great and good   5
For you to doubt the likelihood.

Die early and avoid the fate.
Or if predestined to die late,
Make up your mind to die in state.

Make the whole stock exchange your own!   10
If need be occupy a throne,
Where nobody can call *you* crone.

Some have relied on what they knew,
Others on being simply true.
What worked for them might work for you.   15

No memory of having starred
Atones for later disregard
Or keeps the end from being hard.

Better to go down dignified
With boughten friendship at your side   20
Than none at all. Provide, provide!

Glossary

See the critical commentary on p. 325.

2 *pail* – bucket.

3 *Abishag* – she was a beautiful virgin who was brought to King David for the purpose of rejuvenating his ageing body and mind (1 Kings 1: 3–4). During this time, she became his closest friend.

4 *Hollywood* – this town has long been a symbol of superficiality. It is a place where people are valued and judged by the image they present.

12 *crone* – a witch or hag.

17 *Atones* – makes amends for.

20 *boughten* – bought or purchased.

21 *Provide, provide!* – the repetition, together with the use of the exclamation mark at the end of the poem, emphasises the degree to which Frost is being cynical.

Questions

Go to p. 52 for more questions on Robert Frost.

1. Comment on the tone of the speaker's voice in this poem. Make sure you refer to or quote from the poem in your answer.

2. Did you agree or disagree with the speaker's advice in this poem? Give reasons for your answer.

3. In your opinion, what is the theme of this poem? Support your answer by close reference to the poem.

Exam-style Unseen Poem Questions

1. Write a response to 'Provide, Provide', highlighting the impact it makes on you.

2. Do you think the poem gives an interesting insight into ageing?

3. Choose a line or two that you find particularly appealing and explain why.

Robert Frost: An Overview

Now that you have read a selection of Frost's poetry, you should take the time to look at the following general points. The purpose of these is not to tell you what to think, but rather to help you form your own opinions. When you have read these points, you may wish to take the time to reread Frost's poetry. You should notice that the general points made here can be used to form the backbone of your paragraphs when it comes to writing on poetry. From now on, try to think about Frost's poems not only in terms of what they say, but also in terms of how they say it. Open your mind to any reasonable interpretation of the poems; remember, your opinions are as valid as anything printed. However, you must be prepared to ground these opinions in fact. If you find this process difficult, that is entirely normal. Remember that a poem is not meant to be studied and dissected in the manner that the Leaving Certificate requires of us. While we have to keep the exam in mind, you should try not to allow it to detract from your enjoyment of the poetry on the course.

1. Frost was fascinated with the sound, and what he termed the 'noise', of words. In order to make these 'noises' more powerful, he placed them in tension with traditional rhythms and rhymes. What he succeeded in creating was, in effect, a poetry that fused everyday speech with formal poetic techniques.
2. Leaves, trees, grass, woods, spring pools: all of these feature repeatedly in Frost's poetry and the notion of the cycle of nature is a theme to which he returns again and again. However, you need to be careful when reading Frost. Much of the seeming simplicity of his poetry masks a far greater level of complexity.
3. Nearly all of Frost's poems on the course are open to *metaphorical* readings.
4. Frost had a difficult life. While his poems tend to appear uplifting, especially on a first reading, it is possible to see an awareness of life's darker aspects in his work.
5. The selection of poems by Frost on the course includes some beautiful poems that, in the words of the poet himself, provide 'a momentary stay against the confusion' of life.

This list of general points is, of course, in no way exhaustive; there are quite literally thousands of perfectly valid observations to be made about the poetry of Robert Frost and your opinion is as valid as any of the points mentioned here. Try to consult these points frequently, as they will help you when it comes to writing essays.

Past Leaving Certificate Questions

A question on Robert Frost appeared on the 2003 Leaving Certificate. Students were asked the following:

> **'We enjoy poetry for its ideas and for its language.'**
> **Using the above statement as your title, write an essay on the poetry of Robert Frost. Support your points by reference to the poetry by Robert Frost on your course.**

This question is asking you to perform two specific tasks. In your essay, you need to explore the ideas in Robert Frost's poetry and also the manner in which the language he uses complements these ideas. Correctors that year were told to 'expect candidates to deal with both elements of the question – ideas and language – but not necessarily separately'. In other words, in order to obtain full marks, you had to deal with both parts of the question.

Correctors were also told to look out for the following possible points:

- The poet's views on life/experience.
- The habitual concerns in the poems.
- The elegant plainness of his expression.
- Typical patterns of imagery.
- The variety of register in the texts.

Sample Questions

Before you try these questions, you may wish to consult the examination technique guidelines on p. 548.

1. 'Introducing Robert Frost.'
   Write out the text of a short presentation you would make to your friends or class group under the above title. Support your point of view by reference to or quotation from the poetry of Robert Frost that you have studied.

2. 'Often we love a poet because of the feelings his/her poems arouse in us.' Write about the feelings Robert Frost's poetry inspires in you and the aspects of the poems (their content and/or style) that help to create those feelings. Support your points by reference to the poetry by Frost that you have studied.

3. Write an essay in which you outline your reasons for liking or disliking the poetry of Robert Frost. Support your points by reference to the poetry of Frost that you have studied.

4. What impact did the poetry of Robert Frost make on you as a reader? In shaping your answer, you might consider some of the following:
    a. Your overall sense of the personality or outlook of the poet.
    b. The poet's use of language and imagery.
    c. Your favourite poem or poems.

5. Write a personal response to the poems by Frost on your course. Support your points with reference to the poetry on your course.

6. 'The impact of Robert Frost's poetry.'
    Write a speech to be delivered to your classmates on the impact that Robert Frost's poetry had on you. Your answer should focus on both the themes and the use of imagery/language. Support your answer with the aid of suitable reference to the poems on your course.

7. 'Robert Frost draws inspiration from ordinary events. In particular, he is inspired by the natural world.'
    Write an introduction to the poetry of Robert Frost based on the above statement. Your introduction should address his themes and the impact of his poetry on you as a reader. Support your points with reference to the poems you have studied.

8. Write an introduction to the poetry of Robert Frost for new readers. Your introduction should cover the following:
    •   The ideas that were most important to him.
    •   How you responded to his use of language and imagery.
    Refer closely to the poems by Robert Frost that you have studied.

9. 'What Robert Frost's poetry means to me.'
    Write an essay in response to the above title. Your essay should include a discussion of his themes and the way he expresses them. Support the points you make by reference to the poetry on your course.

10. 'Robert Frost – a deceptive poet.'
    Write an overview of Frost's poetry using the above title. Your overview should examine the way in which Robert Frost's poetry can at first appear straightforward, but on closer examination is thought provoking and complex. Support your points by reference to the poems you have studied.

Seamus Heaney (1939–)

Seamus Heaney was born in 1939 in the townland of Mossbawn, County Derry, in Northern Ireland. By the mid-1960s, his poetry was appearing regularly in literary magazines. Since then he has achieved what can only be described as a meteoric rise to fame. In 1995 he won the Nobel Prize for Literature and is now widely regarded as one of the leading poets of his generation and the greatest Irish poet since Yeats. The poems on your course by Seamus Heaney are representative of his body of work as a whole. They are by turns mythological and grounded in everyday reality, erotic and innocent, rural and cosmopolitan. Heaney's poetry is, to borrow from Harold Bloom, 'keyed and pitched unlike any other significant poet at work in the language anywhere'. In his Nobel Prize acceptance speech, Heaney praised the undisputed achievement of W.B. Yeats, whose work he felt 'does what the necessary poetry always does, which is to touch the base of our sympathetic nature while taking in at the same time the unsympathetic nature of the world'. This could easily be read as an assessment of Heaney's own poetry. If you would like to read more about Seamus Heaney's life, please see the short biography on p. 328.

The Forge

All I know is a door into the dark.
Outside, old axles and iron hoops rusting;
Inside, the hammered anvil's short-pitched ring,
The unpredictable fantail of sparks
Or hiss when a new shoe toughens in water.   5
The anvil must be somewhere in the centre,
Horned as a unicorn, at one end square,
Set there immoveable: an altar
Where he expends himself in shape and music.
Sometimes, leather-aproned, hairs in his nose,   10
He leans out on the jamb, recalls a clatter
Of hoofs where traffic is flashing in rows;
Then grunts and goes in, with a slam and flick
To beat real iron out, to work the bellows.

Glossary

See the critical commentary on p. 331.
Forge – a furnace used to heat metal to a very high temperature.

3 *anvil* – a strong piece of iron used by a blacksmith to beat metal into shape.

7 *unicorn* – a mythical animal usually described as being a white horse with a long white mane and a straight horn growing from its forehead. The mention of the unicorn hints at the magical process of creation that Heaney associates with the forge.

8 *immoveable* – fixed or permanent.

9 *expends* – uses up energy.

14 *bellows* – a piece of equipment that is expanded to draw air in and then contracted to push the air out.

Questions

Go to p. 85 for more questions on Seamus Heaney.

1. In your opinion, why is the young poet attracted to the blacksmith's forge?
2. From the description of the blacksmith that Heaney provides, what sort of person do you believe him to be?
3. Why does Heaney describe the blacksmith's anvil as being like an altar? Give reasons for your answer.

Exam-style Unseen Poem Questions

1. Write a brief personal response to this poem, highlighting aspects of it that you liked and/or disliked.
2. Do you think the poem provides an interesting perspective on the nature of artistic creation? In your answer, you might consider:
   - The words and images in the poem.
   - The pattern of the poet's thought.
3. Choose one or two phrases from the poem that you particularly enjoyed. Give reasons for your answer.

Bogland

for T.P. Flanagan

We have no prairies
To slice a big sun at evening –
Everywhere the eye concedes to
Encroaching horizon,

Is wooed into the cyclops' eye   5
Of a tarn. Our unfenced country
Is bog that keeps crusting
Between the sights of the sun.

They've taken the skeleton
Of the Great Irish Elk   10
Out of the peat, set it up,
An astounding crate full of air.

Butter sunk under
More than a hundred years
Was recovered salty and white.   15
The ground itself is kind, black butter

Melting and opening underfoot,
Missing its last definition
By millions of years.
They'll never dig coal here,   20

Only the waterlogged trunks
Of great firs, soft as pulp.
Our pioneers keep striking
Inwards and downwards,

Every layer they strip   25
Seems camped on before.
The bogholes might be Atlantic seepage.
The wet centre is bottomless.

Glossary

See the critical commentary on p. 333.

T.P. Flanagan – Terry Flanagan is a well-known Irish landscape watercolourist who was born in Enniskillen, County Fermanagh, in 1929.

1 *prairies* – the prairies are treeless grass-covered plains that stretch across the Midwestern and western United States and the provinces of Manitoba, Alberta and Saskatchewan in Canada. The prairies hold a special historical place in America for both the indigenous North American tribes, such as the Sioux, Cheyenne, Crow and Comanche, and the European settlers.

4 *Encroaching* – approaching, intruding or moving beyond its limits.

5 *cyclops* – in Greek mythology, the Cyclopes are a race of giants who had only one eye in the middle of their foreheads. Here, Heaney likens the setting of the sun to the one-eyed Cyclops.

10 *Irish Elk* – The Irish Elk, or *Megaloceros*, is a giant extinct deer, and the largest deer species that lived. Standing up to seven feet at the shoulder, with antlers spanning up to 12 feet, these animals once were found throughout Northern Europe.

13 *Butter* – owing to the acidity of the peat in the Irish bogs, butter has been found that has been edible even after hundreds of years.

23 *pioneers* – the name given to the white Europeans who settled the North American plains in the 19th century.

Questions

Go to   p. 85   for more questions on Seamus Heaney.

1. What parallels does the poet draw between the boglands of Ireland and the prairies of North America?

2. In the poem, Heaney looks beyond the surface of the bog. Describe how he does this in both a literal and a figurative sense.

3. In your opinion, what is the tone of this poem?

Exam-style Unseen Poem Questions

1. Write a personal response to this poem. In your answer, you may wish to consider the impact that the imagery has on you.

2. Choose one or two phrases from the poem that you found particularly interesting. Give reasons for your choice.

3. What do you think the poet means when he says that the 'wet centre [of the bog] is bottomless'? Give reasons for your answer.

The Tollund Man

Some day I will go to Aarhus
To see his peat-brown head,
The mild pods of his eyelids,
His pointed skin cap.

In the flat country nearby   5
Where they dug him out,
His last gruel of winter seeds
Caked in his stomach,

Naked except for
The cap, noose and girdle,   10
I will stand a long time.
Bridegroom to the goddess,

She tightened her torc on him
And opened her fen,
Those dark juices working   15
Him to a saint's kept body,

Trove of the turfcutters'
Honeycombed workings.
Now his stained face
Reposes at Aarhus.   20

II

I could risk blasphemy,
Consecrate the cauldron bog
Our holy ground and pray
Him to make germinate

The scattered, ambushed   25
Flesh of labourers,
Stockinged corpses
Laid out in the farmyards,

Tell-tale skin and teeth
Flecking the sleepers   30
Of four young brothers, trailed
For miles along the lines.

III

Something of his sad freedom
As he rode the tumbril
Should come to me, driving,   35
Saying the names

Tollund, Grauballe, Nebelgard,
Watching the pointing hands
Of country people,
Not knowing their tongue.   40

Out there in Jutland
In the old man-killing parishes
I will feel lost,
Unhappy and at home.

Glossary

See the critical commentary on p. 338.
The title refers to the Tollund Man, a corpse that is displayed at the National Museum of Denmark. According to the museum, the Tollund Man is an 'unusually well-preserved body of an adult male who was approximately 30 to 40 years old when he died. It is probably the most well-preserved body from pre-historic times in the world. Only the side of the body which had been turned upwards in the excavation of the peat bog showed signs of decomposition. On his right side, which had been turned downwards in the grave, the skin was well-preserved whereas the body itself had shrunk, thus making folds in the skin. Different measurements showed that he measured 161 centimetres when he was discovered, but it is very likely that he shrank a little during his stay in the bog.'

1 *Aarhus* – the capital of Jutland in Denmark.
7 *gruel* – a thin cereal made by boiling oatmeal in water.
10 *girdle* – a ring of material used as a belt.
12 *the goddess* – a reference to Nerthus, an ancient Germanic goddess who was associated with fertility and renewal.
13 *torc* – a metal necklace frequently made from gold or bronze.
14 *fen* – an inland area of low-lying marshy or boggy ground.
17 *Trove* – a collection of valuable items.
21 *blasphemy* – acting in a manner that disrespects God or sacred things.
24 *germinate* – to grow from a seed or spore.
31 *four young brothers* – a reference to the massacre of four brothers at the hands of Protestant paramilitaries. In a barbaric act of inhumanity, the bodies of the dead men were desecrated by dragging them along railway tracks.
34 *tumbril* – a farm cart. The tumbril, or tumbrel, is often associated with the French Revolution, where condemned prisoners were carried to their deaths by such a cart.
37 *Tollund, Grauballe, Nebelgard* – these are all places in Jutland associated with the discovery of bog people.

Questions

Go to **p. 85** for more questions on Seamus Heaney.

1. Describe the tone of the opening stanza of the poem. How does the tone contribute to the feeling that this poem resembles a prayer?

2. What links does Heaney make in the course of the poem between the fate of the Tollund Man and the situation in Northern Ireland?

3. Why does the poet say at the end of the poem that he 'will feel lost, | Unhappy and at home' in Aarhus?

Exam-style Unseen Poem Questions

1. How did this poem make you feel? In your answer, you may wish to consider the impact that the imagery had on you as a reader.

2. Imagine that you have been asked to choose a poem for a forthcoming edition of poetry entitled *Cycles of History*. You choose this poem. Give reasons for that choice.

3. Choose two phrases from the poem that you feel are particularly striking. Give reasons for your choice.

Mossbawn: Two Poems in Dedication

for Mary Heaney

I Sunlight

There was a sunlit absence.
The helmeted pump in the yard
heated its iron,
water honeyed

in the slung bucket   5
and the sun stood
like a griddle cooling
against the wall

of each long afternoon.
So, her hands scuffled   10
over the bakeboard,
the reddening stove

sent its plaque of heat
against her where she stood
in a floury apron   15
by the window.

Now she dusts the board
with a goose's wing,
now sits, broad-lapped,
with whitened nails   20

and measling shins:
here is a space
again, the scone rising
to the tick of two clocks.

And here is love   25
like a tinsmith's scoop
sunk past its gleam
in the meal-bin.

Glossary

See the critical commentary on p. 342.

Mary Heaney – the poem is dedicated to Mary Heaney, the poet's aunt who lived with him on the Heaney family farm.

2 *helmeted pump* – a type of water pump that used to be common in rural Ireland.

7 *griddle* – a flat metal plate heated and used for cooking food.

11 *bakeboard* – a board used for baking bread.

18 *goose's wing* – in the past, the wing of a goose was often used as a duster.

21 *measling* – spotty.

27 *gleam* – shine.

28 *meal* – any cereal crop that has been ground to a powder.

Questions

Go to p. 85 for more questions on Seamus Heaney.

1. This poem has been compared by more than one critic to a painting. In your opinion, how well does Heaney manage to paint a picture of Mossbawn?

2. From your reading of the poem, what sort of person do you think Mary Heaney was?

3. How well does Heaney confer a sense of timelessness to Mossbawn?

Exam-style Unseen Poem Questions

1. Write a brief personal response to this poem.

2. Choose two images from the poem that you liked or disliked. Give reasons for your choice.

3. Imagine that you have been asked to recommend a poem for a forthcoming collection of poetry entitled *Memories of Childhood*. You decide to choose this poem. Give reasons for that choice.

A Constable Calls

His bicycle stood at the window-sill,
The rubber cowl of a mud-splasher
Skirting the front mudguard,
Its fat black handlegrips

Heating in sunlight, the 'spud'   5
Of the dynamo gleaming and cocked back,
The pedal treads hanging relieved
Of the boot of the law.

His cap was upside down
On the floor, next his chair.   10
The line of its pressure ran like a bevel
In his slightly sweating hair.

He had unstrapped
The heavy ledger, and my father
Was making tillage returns   15
In acres, roods, and perches.

Arithmetic and fear.
I sat staring at the polished holster
With its buttoned flap, the braid cord
Looped into the revolver butt.   20

'Any other root crops?
Mangolds? Marrowstems? Anything like that?'
'No.' But was there not a line
Of turnips where the seed ran out

In the potato field? I assumed   25
Small guilts and sat
Imagining the black hole in the barracks.
He stood up, shifted the baton-case

Farther round on his belt,
Closed the domesday book,   30
Fitted his cap back with two hands,
And looked at me as he said goodbye.

A shadow bobbed in the window.
He was snapping the carrier spring
Over the ledger. His boot pushed off   35
And the bicycle ticked, ticked, ticked.

Glossary

See the critical commentary on p. 346.
The constable in the title of the poem is a member of the Royal Ulster Constabulary (RUC). The RUC was formed in 1922 following the partition of Ireland, replacing the Royal Irish Constabulary. Unlike other police forces in the United Kingdom, the RUC was armed and tasked with dealing with paramilitary activities. When the political situation in Northern Ireland worsened, the RUC began to lose the trust and respect of the Catholic minority. Following the beginnings of the peace process, repeated claims of brutality and even accusations of collusion in the murder of prominent Catholics and Republicans made the RUC's position as a police force untenable.

11 *bevel* – a slanting edge on the surface of something.

15 *tillage* – land that has been tilled or prepared for growing crops.

16 *roods* – an imperial unit of area equal to 0.1 hectare.

16 *perches* – an imperial unit of measurement equal to 5.03 metres.

17 *Arithmetic* – the area of mathematics that deals with addition, subtraction, multiplication and division.

19 *braid* – something that is made of three or more interwoven strands of cord.

22 *Mangolds* – a large variety of beet that is grown as food for livestock.

22 *Marrowstems* – a part of a plant in the cucumber family.

27 *black hole* – this evokes images of the Black Hole of Calcutta, which was a prison in India. Given the shared colonial history of Ireland and India, it is interesting that Heaney should **allude** to this prison.

30 *domesday book* – in 1085, William the Conqueror demanded that a record of all the land in England, its value and its ownership be made. This record became knows as the Domesday Book because it was said that it would be used on the Day of Judgement to ascertain the material belongings of everyone in England. In August 2006, a complete online version of Domesday Book was made available for the first time by the National Archives in the United Kingdom.

Questions

Go to p. 85 for more questions on Seamus Heaney.

1. To what extent can the constable's bicycle be regarded as a metaphor for the repression that he represents?

2. From your reading of the poem, what evidence is there that the constable is not welcome in the Heaney household?

3. Comment on the ending of the poem. How well does Heaney manage to capture a sense of threat and impending violence?

Exam-style Unseen Poem Questions

1. Write a response to this poem, highlighting the impact it made on you.

2. Briefly describe the mood or feeling you get from reading this poem. Illustrate your answer from the text.

3. To what extent does this poem illustrate Heaney's ability to describe a scene?

The Skunk

Up, black, striped and damasked like the chasuble
At a funeral Mass, the skunk's tail
Paraded the skunk. Night after night
I expected her like a visitor.

The refrigerator whinnied into silence.   5
My desk light softened beyond the verandah.
Small oranges loomed in the orange tree.
I began to tense as a voyeur.

After eleven years I was composing
Love-letters again, broaching the word 'wife'   10
Like a stored cask, as if its slender vowel
Had mutated into the night earth and air

Of California. The beautiful, useless
Tang of eucalyptus spelt your absence.
The aftermath of a mouthful of wine   15
Was like inhaling you off a cold pillow.

And there she was, the intent and glamorous,
Ordinary, mysterious skunk,
Mythologized, demythologized,
Snuffing the boards five feet beyond me.   20

It all came back to me last night, stirred
By the sootfall of your things at bedtime,
Your head-down, tail-up hunt in a bottom drawer
For the black plunge-line nightdress.

Glossary

See the critical commentary on p. 350.

1 *damasked* – a reversible cotton, linen or silk fabric with a pattern woven into it. Much like damask, the skunk's tail is reversible.

1 *chasuble* – a loose outer garment worn by a Christian priest when celebrating Mass or Communion.

5 *whinnied* – neighed or made the sound of a horse.

6 *verandah* – a roofed porch that extends along the outside wall of a building.

8 *voyeur* – a person who finds watching others pleasurable. Voyeurs take special pleasure in remaining unseen while watching other people's bodies or the sexual acts in which they participate.

12 *mutated* – changed or transformed.

14 *eucalyptus* – an evergreen tree with particularly aromatic leaves.

22 *sootfall* – this **neologism** connotes the soft sound his wife's clothes make as they fall to the ground.

Questions

Go to p. 85 for more questions on Seamus Heaney.

1. How does Heaney set the scene in the first two stanzas? Give reasons for your answer.

2. Why does the poet say that he began to feel as 'tense as a voyeur'?

3. In your opinion, is 'The Skunk' a good love poem? Support your answer by close reference to the poem.

Exam-style Unseen Poem Questions

1. Write a brief personal response to this poem. In your response, outline how the poem made you feel.

2. Choose two phrases from the poem that you particularly enjoyed. Give reasons for your answer.

3. In your opinion, what is the tone of this poem? Support your answer by reference to or quotation from the text.

The Harvest Bow

As you plaited the harvest bow
You implicated the mellowed silence in you
In wheat that does not rust
But brightens as it tightens twist by twist
Into a knowable corona,   5
A throwaway love-knot of straw.

Hands that aged round ashplants and cane sticks
And lapped the spurs on a lifetime of gamecocks
Harked to their gift and worked with fine intent
Until your fingers moved somnambulant: 10
I tell and finger it like braille,
Gleaning the unsaid off the palpable,

And if I spy into its golden loops
I see us walk between the railway slopes
Into an evening of long grass and midges,   15
Blue smoke straight up, old beds and ploughs in hedges,
An auction notice on an outhouse wall –
You with a harvest bow in your lapel,

Me with the fishing rod, already homesick
For the big lift of these evenings, as your stick   20
Whacking the tips off weeds and bushes
Beats out of time, and beats, but flushes
Nothing: that original townland
Still tongue-tied in the straw tied by your hand.

The end of art is peace   25
Could be the motto of this frail device
That I have pinned up on our deal dresser –
Like a drawn snare
Slipped lately by the spirit of the corn
Yet burnished by its passage, and still warm.   30

Glossary

See the critical commentary on p. 353.

1 *harvest bow* – a bow that was traditionally made from straw and worn to celebrate the harvest.

2 *implicated* – in this context, the word means interweaved or knitted.

2 *mellowed* – comfortingly soft or easygoing.

5 *corona* – a ring of light that is visible around a luminous body. The word is often associated with the moon. Perhaps Heaney has the harvest moon in mind.

8 *spurs* – a sharp spike on the legs of some male birds such as pheasants.

8 *gamecocks* – male wild animals or fish that have been killed for sport.

9 *Harked* – listened.

10 *somnambulant* – sleepwalking.

11 *braille* – a system of writing consisting of patterns of raised dots that is used by people who are visually impaired.

12 *Gleaning* – gathering.

12 *palpable* – something that can be felt physically.

15 *midges* – small flies.

25 *The end of art is peace* – Heaney is **alluding** to the English poet Coventry Patmore, who claimed that the purpose of art was to create peace.

Questions

Go to   p. 85   for more questions on Seamus Heaney.

1. What picture of Heaney's father emerges from this poem? Refer to the poem in your answer.

2. In your opinion, what does the harvest bow symbolise in this poem? Support your answer by close reference to the text.

3. What does Heaney mean when he says, '*The end of art is peace*'?

Exam-style Unseen Poem Questions

1. Do you think this poem gives an interesting insight to the relationship between Heaney and his father? In your answer, you might consider:
   • The words and images in the poem.
   • The tone of the poem.

2. Briefly describe the mood or feeling you get from reading this poem. Illustrate your answer from the text.

3. Write a response to this poem, highlighting the impact it makes on you.

The Underground

There we were in the vaulted tunnel running,
You in your going-away coat speeding ahead
And me, me then like a fleet god gaining
Upon you before you turned to a reed

Or some new white flower japped with crimson   5
As the coat flapped wild and button after button
Sprang off and fell in a trail
Between the Underground and the Albert Hall.

Honeymooning, mooning around, late for the Proms,
Our echoes die in that corridor and now   10
I come as Hansel came on the moonlit stones
Retracing the path back, lifting the buttons

To end up in a draughty lamplit station
After the trains have gone, the wet track
Bared and tensed as I am, all attention   15
For your step following and damned if I look back.

Glossary

See the critical commentary on p. 356.

The Underground – The London Underground transport system. The poem's title also hints at the underworld of Greek *mythology*, where the underworld is a kingdom that remains hidden in the earth. It is ruled over by Hades, a greedy god who is driven by the desire to increase his subjects. Although some Greek heroes managed to enter the underworld while living, escape, as in the case of Orpheus, proved altogether more difficult. In early Greek imagination, the underworld was a dreary place full of shadows and without hope. Having entered the underworld, the dead slowly faded away into oblivion.

1 *vaulted* – arched or domed.

3 *fleet god* – this is most likely an *allusion* to the Greek myth of Pan and Syrinx. In her attempts to escape from Pan, Syrinx was turned to a reed by her father.

5 *japped* – splashed.

5 *crimson* – a deep, rich red colour.

8 *Albert Hall* – the Royal Albert Hall is a music and entertainment venue in South Kensington, London.

9 *mooning* – wandering around in a dreamy state.

16 *damned if I look back* – an allusion to the Greek myth of Orpheus and Eurydice. Orpheus entered the underworld in order to rescue his lover, Eurydice.

Questions

Go to p. 85 for more questions on Seamus Heaney.

1. In your opinion, why did Heaney choose the title 'The Underground' for this poem? Support your answer by close reference to the text.

2. How well does Heaney create a sense of excitement in the first two stanzas?

3. What is the mood of the final stanza? Support your answer by reference to the text.

Exam-style Unseen Poem Questions

1. Write a personal response to this poem, highlighting the impact it made on you.

2. Choose two images from the poem that you found to be particularly effective. In the case of each image, say why you have chosen it.

3. In your opinion, is 'The Underground' a love poem? Give reasons for your answer.

Postscript

And some time make the time to drive out west
Into County Clare, along the Flaggy Shore,
In September or October, when the wind
And the light are working off each other
So that the ocean on one side is wild   5
With foam and glitter, and inland among stones
The surface of a slate-grey lake is lit
By the earthed lightning of a flock of swans,
Their feathers roughed and ruffling, white on white,
Their fully grown headstrong-looking heads   10
Tucked or cresting or busy underwater.
Useless to think you'll park and capture it
More thoroughly. You are neither here nor there,
A hurry through which known and strange things pass
As big soft buffetings come at the car sideways   15
And catch the heart off guard and blow it open.

Glossary

See the critical commentary on p. 359.
Postscript – a short message added onto the end
of a correspondence. Interestingly, it is possible to
read this poem as acting as a postscript to another
poem by Heaney from his 1996 collection, *The
Spirit Level*, entitled 'The Peninsula'.
2 *Flaggy Shore* – the flat slabs of limestone that
   form the Burren in County Clare run right up
   to the edge of the shore. This part of the shore
   is known locally as the Flaggy Shore.

11 *cresting* – in this instance, the ridge of the
    swans' heads.
15 *buffetings* – the shaking of a wing caused by
    strong winds.

Questions

Go to   p. 85   for more questions on Seamus Heaney.

1. In your opinion, why did Heaney choose this title for this poem? Support your
   answer by relevant quotation from the text.
2. How well does Heaney describe the landscape of County Clare in this poem?
   Illustrate your answer by reference to the poem.
3. What does Heaney mean in the final line of the poem?

Exam-style Unseen Poem Questions

1. Write a personal response to 'Postscript' in which you highlight the effect the
   poem had on you.
2. Choose a line or two from the poem that you like or disliked. Give reasons for
   your choice.
3. In your opinion, would this poem be suitable for inclusion in an Irish tourist
   brochure? Support your answer by reference to the text.

A Call

'Hold on,' she said, 'I'll just run out and get him.
The weather here's so good, he took the chance
To do a bit of weeding.'
                              So I saw him
Down on his hands and knees beside the leek rig,
Touching, inspecting, separating one   5
Stalk from the other, gently pulling up
Everything not tapered, frail and leafless,
Pleased to feel each little weed-root break,
But rueful also…
                              Then found myself listening to
The amplified grave ticking of hall clocks   10
Where the phone lay unattended in a calm
Of mirror glass and sunstruck pendulums…

And found myself then thinking: if it were nowadays,
This is how Death would summon Everyman.

Next thing he spoke and I nearly said I loved him.   15

Glossary

See the critical commentary on p. 362.

12 *pendulums* – the rod that controls the movement of certain types of clock.

14 *Everyman* – the name of one of the best-known morality plays of the Middle Ages. Most literary historians now feel that this play was a translation from a Dutch play composed towards the end of the 15th century. In the play, God sends Death to summon Everyman, who represents all mankind. The play centres on an account of Everyman's journey to this final judgement. The author of *Everyman*, who remains unknown, attempts to show us not only how every man should face death, but how every man should live his life.

Questions

Go to   p. 85   for more questions on Seamus Heaney.

1. From your reading of this poem, what impression do you get of Heaney's father?

2. In your opinion, why does the poet place such emphasis on the 'grave ticking of hall clocks'?

3. What do you think the poet means in the following lines?

   > And found myself then thinking: if it were nowadays,
   >
   > This is how Death would summon Everyman.

Exam-style Unseen Poem Questions

1. How did this poem make you feel? In your answer, refer to the images and the language of the poem.

2. What do you think is the mood of this poem? Illustrate your answer by close reference to the text.

3. Comment on the final line of 'A Call'. Do you find this to be a satisfactory ending to this poem? Give reasons for your answer.

Tate's Avenue

Not the brown and fawn car rug, that first one
Spread on sand by the sea but breathing land-breaths,
Its vestal folds unfolded, its comfort zone
Edged with a fringe of sepia-coloured wool tails.

Not the one scraggy with crusts and eggshells   5
And olive stones and cheese and salami rinds
Laid out by the torrents of the Guadalquivir
Where we got drunk before the corrida.

Instead, again, it's locked-park Sunday Belfast,
A walled back yard, the dust-bins high and silent   10
As a page is turned, a finger twirls warm hair
And nothing gives on the rug or the ground beneath it.

I lay at my length and felt the lumpy earth,
Keen-sensed more than ever through discomfort,
But never shifted off the plaid square once.   15
When we moved I had your measure and you had mine.

Glossary

See the critical commentary on p. 365.

Tate's Avenue is a street in Belfast, County Antrim. Seamus Heaney's wife, Marie, used to share a flat on Tate's Avenue in the 1960s, when the couple was courting.

3 *vestal* – chaste or virginal. The word relates to the Roman Vesta, the virgin goddess of house, hearth and home.

4 *sepia* – a deep reddish-brown, originally made from the ink sacs of cuttlefish. The word is often used in relation to old-fashioned photography or drawing.

7 *torrents* – in this instance, a very fast-flowing river.

7 *Guadalquivir* – a major river measuring 657 km that flows through southern Spain.

8 *corrida* – bullfighting.

Questions

Go to p. 85 for more questions on Seamus Heaney.

1. In your opinion, what do each of the two rugs represent in the first two stanzas? Give reasons for your opinion and refer closely to the text.

2. Describe the contrast between Spain and Belfast that is established in the third and fourth stanzas.

3. Comment on the allusions present in the poem to the political situation in Belfast.

Exam-style Unseen Poem Questions

1. Write a personal response to this poem, outlining the way it made you feel. In your answer, comment on the impact of:
   - The imagery in the poem.
   - The language used by the poet.

2. What do you think is the mood of the final stanza? Give reasons for your answer.

3. Do you think this is a good love poem? Give reasons for your answer.

The Pitchfork

Of all implements, the pitchfork was the one
That came near to an imagined perfection:
When he tightened his raised hand and aimed with it,
It felt like a javelin, accurate and light.

So whether he played the warrior or the athlete   5
Or worked in earnest in the chaff and sweat,
He loved its grain of tapering, dark-flecked ash
Grown satiny from its own natural polish.

Riveted steel, turned timber, burnish, grain,
Smoothness, straightness, roundness, length and sheen.   10
Sweat-cured, sharpened, balanced, tested, fitted.
The springiness, the clip and dart of it.

And then when he thought of the probes that reached the farthest,
He would see the shaft of a pitchfork sailing past
Evenly, imperturbably through space,   15
Its prongs starlit and absolutely soundless –

But has learned at last to follow that simple lead
Past its own aim, out to an other side
Where perfection – or nearness to it – is imagined
Not in the aiming but the opening hand.   20

Glossary

See the critical commentary on p. 368.

1 *implements* – tools.

6 *chaff* – the outer part of grains and other grass seeds that are separated by threshing. In previous times, this threshing was done manually, though nowadays the chaff is removed by a combine harvester.

7 *tapering* – something that is narrower at one end.

11 *cured* – preserved. Normally leather or wood is cured by drying, but here the poet imagines that his father's sweat has cured the handle of the pitchfork.

14 *shaft* – handle.

15 *imperturbably* – unworried or bothered.

Questions

Go to p. 85 for more questions on Seamus Heaney.

1. In your opinion, how well does this poem demonstrate Heaney's powers of observation?

2. What do we learn about Heaney's father from this poem?

3. Comment on the significance of the final line of the poem. You may refer to the rest of the text in your answer.

Exam-style Unseen Poem Questions

1. Write a personal response to this poem. Support your answer by close reference to the text.

2. What do you think is the mood of the poem?

3. Choose a line or two from the poem that you felt was particularly interesting. Give reasons for your choice.

Lightenings viii

The annals say: when the monks of Clonmacnoise
Were all at prayers inside the oratory
A ship appeared above them in the air.

The anchor dragged along behind so deep
It hooked itself into the altar rails   5
And then, as the big hull rocked to a standstill,

A crewman shinned and grappled down the rope
And struggled to release it. But in vain.
'This man can't bear our life here and will drown,'

The abbot said, 'unless we help him.' So   10
They did, the freed ship sailed, and the man climbed back
Out of the marvellous as he had known it.

Glossary

See the critical commentary on p. 371.

1 *the annals* – a record of events arranged chronologically by year. Many medieval monasteries such as Clonmacnoise kept historical and social records of the events they witnessed.

2 *oratory* – a small, often private devotional room set aside for prayer. In many monasteries, the oratory is a secluded chapel within a larger church.

7 *shinned* – climbed down using hands and legs.

Questions

Go to p. 85 for more questions on Seamus Heaney.

1. The poem is built around a series of contrasts. Identify as many of these as possible.

2. To what extent does this poem blur the lines between what is real and what is imaginary?

3. Comment on the form and structure of the poem. To what extent do they mirror the poem's thematic concerns?

Exam-style Unseen Poem Questions

1. How did this poem make you feel? In your answer, refer to the language and the imagery of the poem.

2. Choose two phrases from the poem that you found particularly effective. Give reasons for your choice.

3. Imagine you have been asked to select a poem for a forthcoming edition of poetry entitled *A Magical Experience*. You choose this poem. Explain your choice.

Seamus Heaney: An Overview

Now that you have read a selection of Seamus Heaney's poetry, you should take the time to look at the following general points. The purpose of these is not to tell you what to think, but rather to help you to form your own opinions. When you have read these points, you may wish to take the time to reread Heaney's poetry. You should notice that the general points made here can be used to form the backbone of your paragraphs when it comes to writing on poetry. From now on, try to think about Heaney's poems in terms of what they say and how they say it. Open your mind to any reasonable interpretation of the poems; remember, your opinions are as valid as anything printed. However, you must be prepared to ground these opinions in fact. If you find this process difficult, that is entirely normal. Remember that a poem is not meant to be studied and dissected in the manner that the Leaving Certificate requires of us. While we have to keep the exam in mind, you should not allow it to detract from your enjoyment of the poetry on the course.

1. Heaney is a poet who is acutely aware of his identity. The traditions, the people and the places of his birthplace inform and direct his poetry. In particular, his exploration of identity highlights the importance of vanishing traditions. In many of his poems on the course, he attempts to link the artistic process to the agricultural cycle.
2. Nostalgia and the search for lost innocence, coupled with a need to reinterpret his past, are very much to the fore in Heaney's poetry. The past of his childhood is often seen as a place of comfort and security. However, the past is not empty or stale, as it offers the poet a reassuring sense of continuity with the present. Memories of anxiety and worry are also allowed to surface in Heaney's poems.
3. Heaney was living in Belfast when political and religious tensions erupted into civil strife and violence in the 1960s. As a Catholic, and a nationalist, he felt the need to comment on the horrors unfolding before him. Many of the poems on the course contain **allusions** to the political realities of Northern Ireland.
4. In Heaney's imagination, the boglands of Ireland and the sacrificial victims who were buried in the bogs of Denmark became **metaphors** for Ireland's own tragic situation. In his own words:

    > The unforgettable photographs of these victims blended in my mind with photographs of atrocities, past and present, in the long rites of Irish political and religious struggles.

Writing in *The New York Review of Books*, Tom Murphy has said that Heaney's bog poems trace 'modern terrorism back to its roots in the early Iron Age, and mysterious awe back to the bone house of language itself'. In Heaney's poetry, the bog is a *symbol* that unifies time, person and place; it contains, preserves and yields up terror as well as childlike awe and wonder.

5. Heaney's poetry displays an acute sensitivity to the subtleties of language. Many readers can instantly recognise a poem by Seamus Heaney simply from the pattern of the words. There is an undeniable depth and richness to the verbal patterning of Heaney's poetry. He delights in the sounds and histories of words, using language to create what he has termed 'the music of what happens'. His masterly control of sound and expressive use of *rhythm* is plain to see in the poems on the course. In his lecture *Feelings into Words*, which was published in 1974, Heaney outlines the joy he feels when hearing a good poem:

> You hear something in another writer's sounds that flows in through your ear and enters the echo-chamber of your head and delights your whole nervous system in such a way that your reaction will be 'Ah, I wish I had said that, in that particular way'. This other writer, in fact, has spoken something essential to you, something you recognise instinctively as a true sounding of aspects of yourself and your experience.

6. Heaney's poetry is rooted in the landscape of Ireland. It has been said of his poetry that it treats nature with a lover's intensity. Images of farm and village and the wider countryside dominate many of the poems on the course. Ultimately, Heaney's poetry takes direction from and seeks renewal in the rural experience.

7. The poetic exploration of the imagination is at the heart of many of the poems on the course by Heaney. In many ways, the poems on the course can be read as an attempt to mediate between the real world and that of artistic or imaginative experience. Very often in Heaney's poetry, an ordinary experience, place or person is transformed through the power of the imagination into something extraordinary. Consider such poems as 'The Forge', 'The Harvest Bow' or 'Lightenings viii'. These are as much about the power of the imagination to order, create and transform the world in which we live as anything else.

8. Love is an important theme in this selection of poems. The love of place and family are matched by the erotic love the poet feels for his wife.

9. Heaney's treatment of childhood is another important aspect of the poems that have been selected for study on the Leaving Certificate course. While Heaney looks on childhood in a largely nostalgic way that recreates its innocence and security, he is also sensitive to its fears and anxieties.

Past Leaving Certificate Questions

Seamus Heaney has only appeared once on the Leaving Certificate paper, in 2003. In that year, students were asked the following question.

> **Dear Seamus Heaney ...**
> **Write a letter to Seamus Heaney telling him how you responded to some of his poems on your course. Support the points you make by detailed reference to the poems you choose to write about.**

That year, correctors were told to reward responses that showed clear evidence of engagement with the poems and/or the poet. They were also told that while the question suggests a conversational approach, they should expect and allow for a wide variety of approaches in candidates' answering.

Candidates were free to challenge and 'confront' the poet. Meanwhile, correctors were also told to accept treatment of positive and negative aspects of Heaney's poetry.

Some of the possible points correctors were told to look out for included:

- Powerful use of everyday language.
- Vividly detailed imagery.
- The poet's focus on memory, especially memories of childhood.
- The personal character of the writing.
- The political and social perspectives of the poems.
- The striking love poetry.

Sample Questions

Before you try these questions, you may wish to consult the examination technique guidelines on p. 548.

1. What impact did the poetry of Seamus Heaney make on you as a reader? Your answer should deal with the following:

- Your overall sense of the personality of the poet.
- The poet's use of language/imagery.

2. 'Seamus Heaney explores relationships in an interesting way.'
   Do you agree with this assessment of his poetry? Write a response, supporting your points with the aid of suitable reference to the poems you have studied.

3. 'I found Seamus Heaney's poetry both honest and thought provoking.'
   Referring to more than one poem by Heaney that you have read, comment on this statement.

4. Write an introduction to the poetry of Seamus Heaney for new readers of his poetry. Your introduction should cover the following:
   - The ideas that are most important to him.
   - How you responded to his use of language and imagery.
   Refer to the poems by Seamus Heaney that you have covered.

5. 'Seamus Heaney expresses his themes in a clear and precise fashion.'
   You have been asked by your local radio station to give a talk on the poetry of Seamus Heaney. Write out the text of the talk you would deliver in response to the above title. You should refer to both style and subject matter. Support the points you make by reference to the poetry on your course.

6. 'Seamus Heaney explores people and places in his own distinctive style.'
   Write your response to this statement, supporting your points with the aid of suitable reference to the poems you have studied.

7. Write a personal response to the poetry of Seamus Heaney that you have studied. Support the points you make with the aid of suitable reference to the poems you have studied.

8. 'For works of lyrical beauty and ethical depth, which exalt everyday miracles and the living past.'
   In light of the above assessment of Seamus Heaney's poetry by the Swedish Academy, write an essay outlining your reasons for liking/not liking the poems you have studied.

9. Write about the feelings that Seamus Heaney's poetry create in you and the aspects of his poetry (content/or style) that help to create those feelings. Support your points by reference to the poetry by Seamus Heaney that you have read.

10. 'Seamus Heaney: A poet for our time.'
    Using this title, write an essay outlining what you consider to be the appeal of Seamus Heaney's poetry to a modern audience. Support your points by reference to the poetry of Seamus Heaney on your course.

Patrick Kavanagh (1904–67)

The poetry by Patrick Kavanagh in this anthology appeals to the reader through its fresh, concrete imagery and the colloquial force of its language. In many respects, Kavanagh achieved the near impossible task of giving an authentic voice to rural Ireland while at the same time appealing to a much wider audience. His poetry rejects the romanticised notions of Ireland espoused by so many of his predecessors in favour of an uncompromisingly realistic representation of a way of life that he knew intimately. The poems on the Leaving Certificate draw widely on Kavanagh's understanding of the natural world. They range from autobiographical poems such as 'A Christmas Childhood' and 'Inniskeen Road: July Evening' to his epic masterpiece, 'The Great Hunger'. His brush with death and rebirth as a poet led him to look on nature and the world around him in a completely new light. Finally, it is difficult to ignore the haunting musicality of Kavanagh's work. In particular, poems such as 'On Raglan Road' have not only entertained generations of readers, but have quite literally become part of our shared cultural heritage. If you would like to read more about the life of Patrick Kavanagh, please see the short biography on p. 374.

Inniskeen Road: July Evening

The bicycles go by in twos and threes –
There's a dance in Billy Brennan's barn tonight,
And there's the half-talk code of mysteries
And the wink-and-elbow language of delight.
Half-past eight and there is not a spot   5
Upon a mile of road, no shadow thrown
That might turn out a man or woman, not
A footfall tapping secrecies of stone.

I have what every poet hates in spite
Of all the solemn talk of contemplation.   10
Oh, Alexander Selkirk knew the plight
Of being king and government and nation.
A road, a mile of kingdom, I am king
Of banks and stones and every blooming thing.

Glossary

See the critical commentary on p. 377.

The title, 'Inniskeen Road', refers to Inniskeen, which is an area close to the Louth border set in the heart of the poet's birthplace, County Monaghan.

8   *footfall* – the sound of someone's footsteps.

10 *solemn* – sombre or serious.

10 *contemplation* – thought, meditation, consideration.

11 *Alexander Selkirk* – a British sailor (1676–1721) who was the inspiration for Daniel Defoe's *Robinson Crusoe*. Selkirk shared something in common with Kavanagh in that he too was the son of a shoemaker and tanner. Following an argument over the seaworthiness of his vessel, he put ashore on one of the Juan Fernández Islands about 600 miles off the coast of Chile. For four years Selkirk battled to survive, living on wild goats and berries. He was rescued on 2 February 1709. Kavanagh's poem is to some extent inspired by another poem, 'The Solitude of Alexander Selkirk' (1782) by William Cowper, which was also inspired by Selkirk's adventure:

> *I am monarch of all I survey,*
> *My right there is none to dispute;*
> *From the centre all round to the sea,*
> *I am lord of the fowl and the brute.*

Questions

Go to p. 113 for more questions on Patrick Kavanagh.

1. How well does Kavanagh capture the atmosphere of that July evening in Inniskeen?

2. Comment on the comparison that the poet makes between himself and Alexander Selkirk.

3. How important is the last line to our understanding of the poem?

Exam-style Unseen Poem Questions

1. Choose two images from the poem that you felt were particularly effective. In the case of each image, say why you chose it.

2. Write a personal response to this poem. Your answer should make close reference to the text.

3. Briefly describe the mood or feeling you get from reading this poem and illustrate your answer from the text.

Shancoduff

My black hills have never seen the sun rising,
Eternally they look north towards Armagh.
Lot's wife would not be salt if she had been
Incurious as my black hills that are happy
When dawn whitens Glassdrummond chapel.   5

My hills hoard the bright shillings of March
While the sun searches in every pocket.
They are my Alps and I have climbed the Matterhorn
With a sheaf of hay for three perishing calves
In the field under the Big Forth of Rocksavage.   10

The sleety winds fondle the rushy beards of Shancoduff
While the cattle-drovers sheltering in the Featherna Bush
Look up and say: 'Who owns them hungry hills
That the water-hen and snipe must have forsaken?
A poet? Then by heavens he must be poor'   15
I hear and is my heart not badly shaken?

Glossary

See the critical commentary on p. 381.
Shancoduff is an anglicised spelling of the Irish Shanco Dubh. The title refers to a small north-facing farm in County Monaghan that Kavanagh inherited.

2 *Armagh* – known as the 'cathedral city', Armagh is the ecclesiastical capital of Ireland.

3 *Lot's wife* – the story of Lot and his family is told in the Book of Genesis, chapters 11–14 and 19. In the Bible, the cities of Sodom and Gomorrah were destroyed by God because they were corrupt, vice-ridden places. However, God chose to spare Lot's family, warning them not to look back at the city. Lot's wife's curiosity got the better of her and she looked back. As a result, she was turned to a pillar of salt: 'Then the Lord rained upon Sodom and upon Gomorrah brimstone and fire from the Lord out of heaven; And he overthrew those cities, and all the plain, and all the inhabitants of the cities, and that which grew upon the ground. But his wife looked back from behind him, and she became a pillar of salt.' (Genesis 19:23)

6 *shillings* – a former British and then Irish coin and subunit of currency, in use until 1971, that was equivalent to one-twentieth of one old pound. Here Kavanagh is probably referring to the silver colour of frost.

8 *Matterhorn* – the Matterhorn is one of the highest peaks in the Alps. The mountain peak forms a sharp, isolated rock pyramid with steep, narrow ridges jutting from surrounding glaciers.

9 *sheaf of hay* – a bundle of hay.

10 *Forth* – here Kavanagh attempts to mimic the local pronunciation of the word 'fort'.

11 *sleety* – here Kavanagh turns the noun 'sleety' into an adjective. It is a technical feature of Kavanagh's poetry that he employs such **neologisms**. In the same line, he transforms the noun 'rush' into the adjective 'rushy'.

14 *snipe* – a small bird with a long, straight bill that is usually found in boggy areas.

Questions

Go to p. 113 for more questions on Patrick Kavanagh.

1. How would you describe the speaker's relationship with Shancoduff?
2. Comment on the tone of the poem.
3. In the closing lines of the poem, Kavanagh asks, 'is my heart not badly shaken?' In your opinion, what does the poet mean by this?

Exam-style Unseen Poem Questions

1. Write a personal response to 'Shancoduff', highlighting the impact it makes on you.
2. Briefly describe the mood or feeling you get from reading this poem and illustrate your answer from the text.
3. Choose a phrase or line from the poem that impressed you. Explain your choice.

from The Great Hunger: Section I

I

Clay is the word and clay is the flesh
Where the potato-gatherers like mechanized scare-crows move
Along the side-fall of the hill – Maguire and his men.
If we watch them an hour is there anything we can prove
Of life as it is broken-backed over the Book   5
Of Death? Here crows gabble over worms and frogs
And the gulls like old newspapers are blown clear of the hedges,
    luckily.
Is there some light of imagination in these wet clods?
Or why do we stand here shivering?   10
                Which of these men
Loved the light and the queen
Too long virgin? Yesterday was summer. Who was it promised
    marriage to himself
Before apples were hung from the ceilings for Hallowe'en?   15
We will wait and watch the tragedy to the last curtain,
Till the last soul passively like a bag of wet clay
Rolls down the side of the hill, diverted by the angles
Where the plough missed or a spade stands, straitening the way.

A dog lying on a torn jacket under a heeled-up cart,   20
A horse nosing along the poised headland, trailing
A rusty plough. Three heads hanging between wide-apart
Legs. October playing a symphony on a slack wire paling.
Maguire watches the drills flattened out
And the flints that lit a candle for him on a June altar   25
Flameless. The drills slipped by and the days slipped by
And he trembled his head away and ran free from the world's
    halter,
And thought himself wiser than any man in the townland
When he laughed over pints of porter   30
Of how he came free from every net spread

In the gaps of experience. He shook a knowing head
And pretended to his soul
That children are tedious in hurrying fields of April
Where men are spanging across wide furrows,   35
Lost in the passion that never needs a wife –
The pricks that pricked were the pointed pins of harrows.
Children scream so loud that the crows could bring
The seed of an acre away with crow-rude jeers.
Patrick Maguire, he called his dog and he flung a stone in the   40
    air
And hallooed the birds away that were the birds of the years.
Turn over the weedy clods and tease out the tangled skeins.
What is he looking for there?
He thinks it is a potato, but we know better   45
Than his mud-gloved fingers probe in this insensitive hair.

'Move forward the basket and balance it steady
In this hollow. Pull down the shafts of that cart, Joe,
And straddle the horse,' Maguire calls.
'The wind's over Brannagan's, now that means rain.   50
Graip up some withered stalks and see that no potato falls
Over the tail-board going down the ruckety pass –
And *that's* a job we'll have to do in December,
Gravel it and build a kerb on the bog-side. Is that Cassidy's ass
Out in my clover? Curse o' God –   55
Where is that dog?
Never where he's wanted.' Maguire grunts and spits
Through a clay-wattled moustache and stares about him from the
    height.
His dream changes again like the cloud-swung wind   60
And he is not so sure now if his mother was right
When she praised the man who made a field his bride.

Watch him, watch him, that man on a hill whose spirit
Is a wet sack flapping about the knees of time.
He lives that his little fields may stay fertile when his own body   65
Is spread in the bottom of a ditch under two coulters crossed in
    Christ's Name.

He was suspicious in his youth as a rat near strange bread
When girls laughed; when they screamed he knew that meant
The cry of fillies in season. He could not walk   70
The easy road to his destiny. He dreamt
The innocence of young brambles to hooked treachery.
O the grip, O the grip of irregular fields! No man escapes.
It could not be that back of the hills love was free
And ditches straight.   75
No monster hand lifted up children and put down apes
As here.
                          'O God if I had been wiser!'
That was his sigh like the brown breeze in the thistles.
He looks towards his house and haggard. 'O God if I had been   80
    wiser!'
But now a crumpled leaf from the whitethorn bushes
Darts like a frightened robin, and the fence
Shows the green of after-grass through a little window,
And he knows that his own heart is calling his mother a liar.   85
God's truth is life – even the grotesque shapes of its foulest fire.

The horse lifts its head and cranes
Through the whins and stones
To lip late passion in the crawling clover.
In the gap there's a bush weighted with boulders like morality,   90
The fools of life bleed if they climb over.

The wind leans from Brady's, and the coltsfoot leaves are holed
    with rust,
Rain fills the cart-tracks and the sole-plate grooves;
A yellow sun reflects in Donaghmoyne   95
The poignant light in puddles shaped by hooves.
Come with me, Imagination, into this iron house
And we will watch from the doorway the years run back,
And we will know what a peasant's left hand wrote on the page.
Be easy, October. No cackle hen, horse neigh, tree sough, duck   100
    quack.

Glossary

See the critical commentary on p. 384.

This is an extract from 'The Great Hunger', which is a very long poem in 14 sections. The poem tells the story of the peasant small farmer, Patrick Maguire, who leads a life of spiritual, social and sexual impoverishment. The poem is the most controversial of Kavanagh's published works and sparked a wave of outrage due to its overt attack on the sexual and religious oppression of the Catholic Church. In his later life, Kavanagh denounced 'The Great Hunger' as being 'stillborn' because it had at its heart a social statement. He believed that the poet should stand apart from the people and should not be a social commentator.

The title is a clear **allusion** to the Great Irish Famine, or the Great Hunger (*An Gorta Mór*). In this case, Kavanagh is referring to Maguire's spiritual impoverishment.

1   *Clay is the word* – the opening line of the poem alludes to the Bible. In particular, it echoes the opening of St John's Gospel, the book of Genesis and the Catholic prayer, the Angelus: 'In the beginning was the Word, and the Word was with God, and the Word was God' (John 1:1); 'In the beginning when God created the heavens and the earth' (Genesis 1:1).

5–6 *Book | Of Death* – this may be a reference to the essay of the same title by Isaac D'Israeli (1766–1848). It may also be another allusion to the Bible. Revelations 20:12 mentions the Book of Life, which is a register of all those souls who will gain eternal life. Kavanagh might well be contrasting the hope of eternal life with the hopelessness of Maguire's situation.

12–13 *the queen | Too long virgin* – in the Catholic faith, the queen and the virgin are synonyms for Mary, mother of God.

20 *heeled-up cart* – a cart that is not attached to a horse.

21 *posied* – flowery.

28 *halter* – a bridle or rein that is used to guide, train or tie up an animal. Halters are most commonly used on horses but are sometimes used on cattle, dogs, goats and other animals.

35 *spanging* – walking in long strides.

37 *harrows* – in farming, a harrow is an implement for cultivating the surface of the soil in such a manner as to loosen the soil.

51 *Graip* – a type of dung fork. Here Kavanagh uses the word as a verb.

52 *ruckety* – jagged or bumpy.

58 *clay-wattled moustache* – a moustache that has been caked with mud.

66 *coulters* – blades or wheels attached to the beam of a plough that make vertical cuts in the soil in advance of the ploughshare.

70 *fillies* – young female ponies or horses.

80 *haggard* – an area in a farm where hay is stored.

92 *coltsfoot* – a plant that is often used in medicines.

94 *sole-plate* – the area to which a horseshoe is attached.

95 *Donaghmoyne* – the parish of Donaghmoyne in County Monaghan.

100 *sough* – a soft murmuring or rustling sound, as of the wind or a gentle surf.

Questions

Go to p. 113 for more questions on Patrick Kavanagh.

1. 'The Great Hunger' is perhaps Kavanagh's most critically acclaimed poem. In your opinion, what elements of this extract of the poem contribute to this reputation?
2. Comment on the poem's title. How does it contribute to your understanding of the poem?
3. From your reading of the poem, write a brief character sketch of Maguire. Support your answer by close reference to the poem.

Exam-style Unseen Poem Questions

1. Choose a phrase or two from the poem that you found particularly appealing. Give reasons for your choice.
2. Describe the impact that this poem makes on you as a reader.
3. Discuss the ways in which this poem captures the emptiness of Maguire's existence. Support your answer by close reference to the poem.

Advent

We have tested and tasted too much, lover—
Through a chink too wide there comes in no wonder.
But here in the Advent-darkened room
Where the dry black bread and the sugarless tea
Of penance will charm back the luxury   5
Of a child's soul, we'll return to Doom
the knowledge we stole but could not use.

And the newness that was in every stale thing
When we looked at it as children: the spirit-shocking
Wonder in a black slanting Ulster hill   10
Or the prophetic astonishment in the tedious talking
Of an old fool will awake for us and bring
You and me to the yard gate to watch the whins
And the bog-holes, cart-tracks, old stables where Time begins.

O after Christmas we'll have no need to go searching   15
For the difference that sets an old phrase burning—
We'll hear it in the whispered argument of a churning
Or in the streets where the village boys are lurching.
And we'll hear it among decent men too
Who barrow dung in gardens under trees,   20
Wherever life pours ordinary plenty.
Won't we be rich, my love and I, and please
God we shall not ask for reason's payment,
The why of heart-breaking strangeness in dreeping hedges
Nor analyse God's breath in common statement.   25
We have thrown into the dust-bin the clay-minted wages
Of pleasure, knowledge and the conscious hour—
And Christ comes with a January flower.

Glossary

See the critical commentary on p. 391.
The title, 'Advent', refers to the four-week period leading up to Christmas, beginning on the fourth Sunday before Christmas Day. The four Sundays of Advent are often traditionally celebrated with four candles, with one to be lit each Sunday. Each candle has a specific meaning associated with different aspects of Christ's birth. The first one almost always symbolises hope and is sometimes associated with prophecy. The others are organised around characters or themes as a means to unfold the story of Christ's birth and direct attention to the celebrations and worship in the season, such as Peace, Love and Joy. The third (and sometimes fourth) is generally symbolic of Joy at the imminence of the coming of Christ. A fifth white or gold candle – called a 'Christ Candle' – is often lit in a church on Christmas Eve and/or Christmas Day to signify Christ's birth. During Advent, many Roman Catholics abstain from luxury items. The Roman Catholic Church believes that all people are obliged by God to perform some penance for their sins, and that these acts of penance are both personal and corporate. The Catholic Church requires Catholics to perform some specific acts of penance, which includes fasting and abstaining at times each year, including Advent. This poem centres on the spiritual renewal that such acts can yield.

1 *We* – many critics believe the 'We' in the first line is in fact referring to Kavanagh's soul.

5 *penance* – self-punishment or an act of religious devotion performed to show sorrow for having committed a sin.

6 *we'll return to Doom* – we will reject that knowledge that results in death.

11 *prophetic* – here the word is used as an adjective. The noun 'prophetic' refers to the act of predicting or foreshadowing something that does eventually happen.

11 *tedious* – boring owing to being long, monotonous or repetitive.

14 *stables* – a reference to the place of Christ's birth.

14 *Time begins* – this is a reference to the Western calendar, which uses the birth of Christ as its starting point for the modern era.

17 *churning* – the slow turning of cream in a special barrel so as to produce butter.

24 *dreeping* – this is another example of Kavanagh's use of **neologisms**. This word has been coined by Kavanagh in order to capture the slow, sad sound of water dripping from hedges.

Questions

Go to p. 113 for more questions on Patrick Kavanagh.

1. Do you think the central message of this poem is still relevant today?

2. What do you think the poet means when he says, 'please I God we shall not ask for reason's payment'?

3. Trace the poet's use of religious imagery throughout the poem. How important is an understanding of this imagery to your appreciation of the poem?

Exam-style Unseen Poem Questions

1. Write a personal response to 'Advent'. Your answer should make close reference to the text.

2. Do you think the poem gives a surprising insight into Advent? In your answer, you might consider:
   • The pattern of the poet's thinking.
   • The words and images in the poem.

3. Choose a line or two that you find particularly appealing and explain why.

A Christmas Childhood

I

One side of the potato-pits was white with frost—
How wonderful that was, how wonderful!
And when we put our ears to the paling-post
The music that came out was magical.

The light between the ricks of hay and straw   5
Was a hole in Heaven's gable. An apple tree
With its December-glinting fruit we saw—
O you, Eve, were the world that tempted me

To eat the knowledge that grew in clay
And death the germ within it! Now and then   10
I can remember something of the gay
Garden that was childhood's. Again

The tracks of cattle to a drinking-place,
A green stone lying sideways in a ditch
Or any common sight the transfigured face   15
Of a beauty that the world did not touch.

II

My father played the melodeon
Outside at our gate;
There were stars in the morning east
And they danced to his music.   20

Across the wild bogs his melodeon called
To Lennons and Callans.
As I pulled on my trousers in a hurry
I knew some strange thing had happened.

Outside in the cow-house my mother   25
Made the music of milking;
The light of her stable-lamp was a star
And the frost of Bethlehem made it twinkle.

A water-hen screeched in the bog,
Mass-going feet   30
Crunched the wafer-ice on the pot-holes,
Somebody wistfully twisted the bellows wheel.

My child poet picked out the letters
On the grey stone,
In silver the wonder of a Christmas townland,   35
The winking glitter of a frosty dawn.

Cassiopeia was over
Cassidy's hanging hill,
I looked and three whin bushes rode across
The horizon—the Three Wise Kings.   40

An old man passing said:
'Can't he make it talk'—
The melodeon. I hid in the doorway
And tightened the belt of my box-pleated coat.

I nicked six nicks on the door-post   45
With my penknife's big blade—
There was a little one for cutting tobacco.
And I was six Christmases of age.

My father played the melodeon,
My mother milked the cows,   50
And I had a prayer like a white rose pinned
On the Virgin Mary's blouse.

Glossary

See the critical commentary on p. 395.
This is one of a series of Christmas poems that Kavanagh wrote while living and working in Dublin.

1 *potato-pits* – storage area for potatoes.

3 *paling-post* – a fence formed by a line of pointed wooden stakes placed in the ground.

5 *ricks* – a large amount of hay or straw normally stacked into a rectangular shape and covered at the top to protect it from rain.

6 *gable* – normally the triangular top portion of a side wall on a building with a pitched roof that fills the space beneath where the roof slopes meet. However, here Kavanagh imagines that the stacks of hay are a window in heaven's gable.

11 *gay* – having or showing a carefree spirit or being full of light-heartedness and merriment.

15 *transfigured* – changed. To transfigure means to change the appearance of someone or something, usually so as to reveal great beauty, spirituality or magnificence. The word also has specific religious connotations. The Transfiguration of Christ is recorded in the first three Gospels (Matthew 17:1–9; Mark 9:2–9; Luke 9:28–36): 'And the Word was made flesh, and dwelt among us.'

17 *melodeon* – a small reed organ that uses suction bellows to draw air through the reeds in order to produce music. This small accordion is favoured by German and Irish folk musicians.

32 *wistfully* – deep in sad reflection or thinking deeply about something that has been lost.

32 *bellows wheel* – a mechanical device that compresses air in order to help with lighting a fire.

37 *Cassiopeia* – a constellation shaped like the letter W in the sky of the northern hemisphere. In Greek **mythology**, the Egyptian queen Cassiopeia was chained to her throne and placed in the sky to circle the Northern Star.

39 *whin* – gorse bush or furze bush.

40 *Three Wise Kings* – in Christian tradition, the Magi, also known as the Three Wise Men or the Three Kings, are Median Zoroastrian priests who came from the east to Jerusalem to worship Jesus Christ. According to Matthew, they navigated by following a star which came to be known as the Star of Bethlehem.

44 *box-pleated coat* – a coat with a double fold of material.

52 *the Virgin Mary* – the mother of Christ.

Questions

Go to p. 113 for more questions on Patrick Kavanagh.

1. In your opinion, how well does 'A Christmas Childhood' combine ordinary, everyday imagery with extraordinary observations?

2. Comment on the religious imagery used by Kavanagh in the poem.

3. How well does Kavanagh manage to create a sense of childlike wonder in this poem?

Exam-style Unseen Poem Questions

1. Do you like the world that the poet describes in 'A Christmas Childhood'? Give reasons for your answer, supporting them by reference to the text.

2. Write a response to 'A Christmas Childhood', highlighting the impact it makes on you.

3. What impression of Kavanagh's childhood do you get from reading this poem?

Epic

I have lived in important places, times
When great events were decided, who owned
That half a rood of rock, a no-man's land
Surrounded by our pitchfork-armed claims.
I heard the Duffys shouting 'Damn your soul'   5
And old McCabe stripped to the waist, seen
Step the plot defying blue cast-steel—
'Here is the march along these iron stones'
That was the year of the Munich bother. Which
Was most important? I inclined   10
To lose my faith in Ballyrush and Gortin
Till Homer's ghost came whispering to my mind
He said: I made the Iliad from such
A local row. Gods make their own importance.

Glossary

See the critical commentary on p. 398.
Regarding the title, in poetry, an **epic** is a lengthy narrative poem in elevated language celebrating the adventures and achievements of a legendary or traditional hero, such as Homer's *Iliad*. In this poem, Kavanagh successfully writes about a very local dispute in the context of global conflict.

7   *blue cast-steel* – here Kavanagh is referring to pitchforks, which were often the preferred weapon of farmers in disputes over land.

8   *march* – an area along the border between two countries, especially an outlying area that is subject to territorial disputes and hostile incursions by one or other of the opposing countries.

9   *Munich bother* – this is a reference to the Munich Crisis, which was an agreement regarding the Sudetenland Crisis among the major powers of Europe after a conference held in Munich, Germany in September 1938. The Sudetenland was of immense strategic importance to Czechoslovakia, as most of its border defences were situated there. The purpose of the conference was to discuss the future of Czechoslovakia in the face of territorial demands made by German dictator Adolf Hitler. In the end, Sudetenland was divided between Nazi Germany, Poland and Hungary.

11   *Ballyrush and Gortin* – small townlands in County Monaghan.

12   *Homer* – the name given to the author of the early Greek epic poems the *Iliad* and the *Odyssey*, composed from the 8th to 7th century BC. Homer's works begin the Western canon and are universally praised for their poetic genius. By convention, the compositions are also often taken to initiate the period of classical antiquity.

13   *Iliad* – no other texts in the Western imagination occupy as central a position in our understanding of what defines Western culture as the two epic poems of Homer, the *Iliad* and the *Odyssey*. They both concern the great defining moment of Greek culture, the Trojan War. This war, however, fired the imaginations of the Greeks and became the defining cultural moment in their history. Since the Greeks regarded the Trojan War as the defining moment in the establishment of Greek national character, they were obsessed about the events of that great war and told them repeatedly with great variety; as the Greek idea of cultural identity changed, so did their stories about the Trojan War.

Questions

Go to   p. 113   for more questions on Patrick Kavanagh.

1. How important is the title to your understanding of this poem?
2. To what extent does the language used by Kavanagh undermine the poem's title?
3. 'Gods make their own importance.' What do you think Kavanagh means when he says this?

Exam-style Unseen Poem Questions

1. Choose a phrase or line from the poem that impressed you. Explain your choice.
2. Write a response to 'Epic', highlighting aspects of it that you liked and/or disliked.
3. Briefly describe the mood or feeling you get from reading this poem and illustrate your answer from the text.

Canal Bank Walk

Leafy-with-love banks and the green waters of the canal
Pouring redemption for me, that I do
The will of God, wallow in the habitual, the banal,
Grow with nature again as before I grew.
The bright stick trapped, the breeze adding a third   5
Party to the couple kissing on an old seat,
And a bird gathering materials for the nest for the Word,
Eloquently new and abandoned to its delirious beat.
O unworn world enrapture me, encapture me in a web
Of fabulous grass and eternal voices by a beech,   10
Feed the gaping need of my senses, give me ad lib
To pray unselfconsciously with overflowing speech,
For this soul needs to be honoured with a new dress woven
From green and blue things and arguments that cannot be proven.

Glossary

See the critical commentary on p. 400.
In 1955, Kavanagh was a patient in the Rialto Hospital in Dublin, suffering from lung cancer. He had one lung removed and, surviving this drastic operation, he walked out into a warm summer and sat down on the banks of the Grand Canal between Baggot and Leeson Street bridges in Dublin. It was then, according to his *Self-Portrait*, that he became a poet. During this extraordinary period of poetic output, the bitterness of Kavanagh's early poetry was replaced by praise of the commonplace and the discovery of wonder in the ordinary.

1   *Leafy-with-love banks* – this is yet another example of Kavanagh's tendency to employ **neologisms**.

2   *redemption* – in Christianity, the deliverance from the sins of humanity by the death of Jesus Christ on the Cross.

3   *habitual* – done regularly and frequently or continuing in some practice as a result of an ingrained tendency.

3   *banal* – ordinary, boringly commonplace and lacking in originality.

7   *Word* – the use of capitalisation recalls the gospel of St John: 'In the beginning was the Word, and the Word was with God, and the Word was God.'

11   *gaping* – wide open and deep.

11   *ad lib* – without any advance preparation. The term is the shortened form, derived from the Latin *ad libitum*, meaning 'at one's pleasure'. Usually, ad lib is the adjective or adverb; here ad lib is the verb or noun form.

Questions

Go to p. 113 for more questions on Patrick Kavanagh.

1. Why do you think the poet is compelled to exalt the 'banal'?

2. In this poem, the poet expresses a heartfelt wish 'To pray unselfconsciously with overflowing speech'. To what extent has this wish been granted?

3. Suggest an alternative title for this poem. Give reasons for your choice of title.

Exam-style Unseen Poem Questions

1. Briefly describe the mood or feeling you get from reading this poem and illustrate your answer from the text.

2. Write a response to 'Canal Bank Walk', highlighting aspects of it that you liked and/or disliked.

3. Choose a phrase or line from the poem that impressed you. Explain your choice.

Lines Written on a Seat on the Grand Canal, Dublin

'Erected to the Memory of Mrs Dermod O'Brien'

O commemorate me where there is water,
Canal water preferably, so stilly
Greeny at the heart of summer. Brother
Commemorate me thus beautifully
Where by a lock Niagarously roars   5
The falls for those who sit in the tremendous silence
Of mid-July. No one will speak in prose
Who finds his way to these Parnassian islands.
A swan goes by head low with many apologies,
Fantastic light looks through the eyes of bridges –   10
And look! a barge comes bringing from Athy
And other far-flung towns mythologies.
O commemorate me with no hero-courageous
Tomb – just a canal-bank seat for the passer-by.

Glossary

See the critical commentary on p. 404.
The subtitle is a reference to the seat that was erected in the memory of Mrs Dermod O'Brien. Kavanagh was attracted to the idea of being commemorated in such a manner.

3   *Brother* – it is unclear whether or not Kavanagh is referring to his brother Peter Kavanagh or in the broader sense to his fellow man.

5   *lock* – a short section of a canal or river with gates at each end and a mechanism for letting water in and out.

5   *Niagarously* – this is yet another example of Kavanagh's use of *neologism*. Niagara Falls is a set of enormous waterfalls located on the Niagara River, straddling the international border separating the Canadian province of Ontario and the US state of New York. Here, Kavanagh turns the word into an adverb in order to convey something of the power that the canal lock holds over his imagination.

8   *Parnassian* – Mount Parnassus is a mountain of barren limestone in central Greece that towers above the ancient oracle at Delphi, north of the Gulf of Corinth, and offers scenic views of the surrounding olive groves and countryside. The name Parnassus in literature typically refers to its distinction as the home of poetry, literature and learning. In this poem, Kavanagh **alludes** to the waters of Castalia, a spring on Mount Parnassus, near Delphi. It is said to have been created when the winged-horse Pegasus struck the ground with his hoof and was frequented by the Muses and Apollo and has thus come to be known as a fount of poetic inspiration.

12   *mythologies* – a group or body of myths that belong to a particular people or culture and tell about their ancestors, heroes, gods and other supernatural beings and history.

Questions

Go to ⟨ p. 113 ⟩ for more questions on Patrick Kavanagh.

1. Compare and contrast this poem to another poem by Kavanagh that you have studied.

2. In the opening line, Kavanagh beseeches his brother to 'commemorate [him] where there is water'. How does he justify this imperative in the course of the poem?

3. In your opinion, what is the theme of this poem?

Exam-style Unseen Poem Questions

1. Choose two lines from the poem that you found particularly appealing. Give reasons for your choice.

2. Write a personal response to this poem. Your answer should make close reference to the text.

3. Discuss the ways in which this poem captures the emotions felt by the poet.

The Hospital

A year ago I fell in love with the functional ward
Of a chest hospital: square cubicles in a row,
Plain concrete, wash basins – an art lover's woe,
Not counting how the fellow in the next bed snored.
But nothing whatever is by love debarred,   5
The common and banal her heat can know.
The corridor led to a stairway and below
Was the inexhaustible adventure of a gravelled yard.

This is what love does to things: the Rialto Bridge,
The main gate that was bent by a heavy lorry,   10
The seat at the back of a shed that was a suntrap.
Naming these things is the love-act and its pledge;
For we must record love's mystery without claptrap,
Snatch out of time the passionate transitory.

Glossary

See the critical commentary on p. 407.
The title, 'The Hospital', refers to Rialto Chest Hospital in Dublin, which until its closure was part of the Municipal Tuberculosis Service.

1 *functional* – practical.
3 *an art lover's woe* – the hospital lacks any artistic or aesthetic value.
5 *debarred* – excluded from entering or taking part in something.
6 *banal* – boringly ordinary and lacking in originality; commonplace.

12 *pledge* – something delivered as security for the keeping of a promise or the payment of a debt or as a guarantee of good faith.
13 *claptrap* – pompous or important-sounding nonsense.
14 *transitory* – fleeting, not permanent or lasting, existing only for a short time.

Questions

Go to p. 113 for more questions on Patrick Kavanagh.

1. The imagery in this poem is not the normal stuff of poetry. How successful is Kavanagh in transforming everyday objects into sources of poetic inspiration?
2. In your opinion, what is the theme of this poem?
3. 'We must record love's mystery without claptrap'. What do you think Kavanagh means by this?

Exam-style Unseen Poem Questions

1. Briefly describe the mood or feeling you get from reading this poem and illustrate your answer from the text.
2. Write a response to 'The Hospital', highlighting the impact it makes on you.
3. Choose a phrase or line from the poem that impressed you. Explain your choice.

On Raglan Road

On Raglan Road on an autumn day I met her first and knew
That her dark hair would weave a snare that I might one day rue;
I saw the danger, yet I walked along the enchanted way,
And I said, let grief be a fallen leaf at the dawning of the day.

On Grafton Street in November we tripped lightly along the ledge   5
Of the deep ravine where can be seen the worth of passion's pledge,
The Queen of Hearts still making tarts and I not making hay –
O I loved too much and by such, by such, is happiness thrown away.

I gave her gifts of the mind, I gave her the secret sign that's known
To the artists who have known the true gods of sound and stone   10
And word and tint. I did not stint for I gave her poems to say
With her own name there and her own dark hair like clouds over fields of May.

On a quiet street where old ghosts meet I see her walking now
Away from me so hurriedly my reason must allow
That I had wooed not as I should a creature made of clay –   15
When the angel woos the clay he'd lose his wings at the dawn of day.

Glossary

See the critical commentary on p. 409.
'On Raglan Road' was written by Patrick Kavanagh in 1946. The poem was originally published as 'Dark Haired Miriam Ran Away' and was inspired by his unrequited love for Hilda Moriarty. The poem has been recorded in song by many artists, including Luke Kelly, Van Morrison, Sinéad O'Connor and Mary Black. There is also an RTÉ recording of Kavanagh singing the poem. Writer Benedict Kiely remembers the day, in the office of *The Standard* journal, that Patrick Kavanagh first showed him the words of 'On Raglan Road'. It is clear from Kiely's account that the poet had always intended the poem to be sung to the air of 'The Dawning of the Day'. In his youth, Kavanagh was a member of the Inniskeen pipers' band and 'The Dawning of the Day' was one of three tunes that the young poet mastered.

1   *Raglan Road* – Raglan Road runs between Pembroke Road and Clyde Road in Ballsbridge, Dublin. Kavanagh lived in this area from 1946 to 1959.

2   *snare* – a trap, usually for small animals, that operates like a noose. In a general sense, the word describes a situation that is both alluring and dangerous.

2   *rue* – to feel regret or sorrow, usually for something in the past.

5   *Grafton Street* – one of the main shopping streets in Dublin.

6   *ravine* – a deep, narrow valley or gorge, normally formed by running water.

6   *pledge* – something delivered as security for the keeping of a promise or the payment of a debt or as a guarantee of good faith.

11   *tint* – a shade or colour, especially a pale one.

11   *stint* – to be ungenerous in offering or providing something, to hold back.

14   *reason* – mind.

Questions

Go to   p. 113   for more questions on Patrick Kavanagh.

1. 'On Raglan Road' is best known as a song. Identify the musical elements of the poem.

2. In your opinion, what is the dominant mood in this poem?

3. Suggest an alternative title for this poem. Give reasons for your suggestion.

Exam-style Unseen Poem Questions

1. Write a response to 'On Raglan Road', highlighting the impact it makes on you.

2. Briefly describe the mood or feeling you get from reading this poem and illustrate your answer from the text.

3. Do you think the poem gives a surprising insight into the experience of being in love? In your answer, you might consider:
   - The pattern of the poet's thinking.
   - The words and images in the poem.

Patrick Kavanagh: An Overview

Now that you have read a selection of Kavanagh's poetry, you should take the time to look at the following general points. The purpose of these is not to tell you what to think, but rather to help you to form your own opinions. When you have read these points, you may wish to take the time to reread Kavanagh's poetry. You should notice that the general points made here can be used to form the backbone of your paragraphs when it comes to writing on poetry. From now on, try to think about Kavanagh's poems not only in terms of what they say, but also in terms of how they say it. Open your mind to any reasonable interpretation of the poems; remember, your opinions are as valid as anything printed. However, you must be prepared to ground these opinions in fact. If you find this process difficult, that is entirely normal. Remember that a poem is not meant to be studied and dissected in the manner that the Leaving Certificate requires of us. While we have to keep the exam in mind, you should try not to allow it to detract from your enjoyment of the poetry on the course.

1. Kavanagh, perhaps more than any other contemporary poet, captured rural Ireland in a realistic and at times uncompromising fashion.
2. Kavanagh looks on nature with an almost lover's intensity. From his early poems rooted in the Monaghan of his birth to the uplifting and memorable 'canal poems' of his later life, the poet is inspired by the natural world.
3. Kavanagh can be deeply spiritual at times. His views on God and religion can be both conventional and idiosyncratic.
4. It is difficult to ignore Kavanagh's technical mastery. In particular, his control of **rhythm** and **metre** can lead to hauntingly beautiful musical effects.
5. The descriptive power of Kavanagh's poetry is evidenced in the Leaving Certificate selection. His **imagery** and intense depictions, in particular of remembered events from his childhood, allow the reader to share fully in the experience.
6. Unlike many of the other poets on the course, Kavanagh is entirely approachable. His poetry appeals to the heart more than the mind.

This list of general points is, of course, in no way exhaustive; there are quite literally thousands of perfectly valid observations to be made about the poetry of Kavanagh. Finally, as you reread his poems in this anthology, try to do so with an open mind. Remember, your opinion is as valid as any of the points mentioned above. Try to consult these points frequently, as they will help you when it comes to writing essays.

Past Leaving Certificate Questions

In 2004, students were asked to answer the following question on Kavanagh:

> **Imagine you were asked to select one or more of Patrick Kavanagh's poems from your course for inclusion in a short anthology entitled *The Essential Kavanagh*. Give reasons for your choice, quoting from or referring to the poem or poems you have chosen.**

In that year, the correctors were told to look out for the following possible points:

- The early poems provide an insight into rural Irish life.
- The poems celebrate the ordinary, familiar world.
- The poems reveal an ironic affection for the local milieu.
- The mood/atmosphere of the poems.
- The presence of distinctive patterns of language and imagery.

Sample Questions

Before you try these questions, you may wish to consult the examination technique guidelines on p. 548.

1. Imagine you were asked to select one or more of Kavanagh's poems from your course for inclusion in a short anthology entitled *Kavanagh: An Irish Poet*. Give reasons for your choice, quoting from or referring to the poem or poems you have chosen.

2. What impact did the poetry of Kavanagh make on you as a reader? Your answer should deal with the following:
   - Your overall sense of the personality of the poet.
   - The poet's use of language/imagery.

   Refer to the poems by Patrick Kavanagh that you have studied.

3. Write about the feelings that Kavanagh's poetry creates in you and the aspects of his poetry (content and/or style) that help to create those feelings. Support your points by reference to the poetry by Patrick Kavanagh that you have read.

4. Write a personal response to the poetry by Kavanagh that you have studied.

5. 'There are many reasons why the poetry of Patrick Kavanagh appeals to his readers.' In response to this statement, write an essay on the poetry of Kavanagh. Your essay should focus clearly on the reasons why the poetry is appealing and you should refer to the poetry on your course.

6. 'Speaking of Patrick Kavanagh…' Write out the text of a public talk you might give on the poetry of Patrick Kavanagh. Your talk should make reference to the poetry on your course.

7. Write a personal response to the poems by Patrick Kavanagh on your course. Support your points with reference to the poetry on your course.

8. Write an introduction to the poetry of Patrick Kavanagh for new readers. Your introduction should cover the following:
   - The ideas that were most important to him.
   - How you responded to his use of language and imagery.

9. Write an article for a school magazine introducing the poetry of Patrick Kavanagh to Leaving Certificate students. Tell them what he wrote about and explain why you liked his writing, suggesting some poems that you think they would find interesting. Support your points by reference to the poetry of Kavanagh that you have studied.

10. 'Patrick Kavanagh draws profound conclusions from the most ordinary of things.'

    Do you agree with this assessment of his poetry? Your answer should focus on both themes and stylistic features. Support your points with the aid of suitable reference to the poems you have studied.

Thomas Kinsella (1928–)

Thomas Kinsella ranks among the most distinguished of modern Irish poets. While he may not be as well known outside literary circles as some of his contemporaries, his work over the past 50 years has enriched the poetic landscape. Born in Dublin in 1928, he attended University College Dublin and entered the Irish civil service but quickly abandoned his job in the Department of Finance in order to pursue a career as a poet. Although he has lived on and off in the United States for over 50 years, his work is for the most part rooted in the people and places of his native Dublin. Yet despite the essentially local nature of his poetry, Kinsella is now perceived as being at the vanguard of modern literature. The poems on the course by Thomas Kinsella are entirely representative of his work as a whole in that they combine intense explorations of self with social commentary and satire. His poetry dramatises these explorations through the use of myth, historical narrative and elegy. Many of the poems by Kinsella contained in this anthology examine the origins of the creative process. Although Kinsella can be perplexing at times, close attention to his poetry compensates the reader for any difficulty encountered. The poems on the course by Kinsella illuminate the depth of the poet's insight and the scope of his artistic vision. In the words of poet himself, they ask us to share in his search for meaning and to follow him 'back to the dark | and the depth that I came from'. If you would like to read more about Thomas Kinsella, please consult the biography on p. 413.

Thinking of Mr D.

A man still light of foot, but ageing, took
An hour to drink his glass, his quiet tongue
Danced to such cheerful slander.

He sipped and swallowed with a scathing smile,
Tapping a polished toe.   5
His sober nod withheld assent.

When he died I saw him twice.
Once as he used retire
On one last murmured stabbing little tale
From the right company, tucking in his scarf.   10

And once down by the river, under wharf-
Lamps that plunged him in and out of light,
A priest-like figure turning, wolfish-slim,
Quickly aside from pain, in a bodily plight,
To note the oiled reflections chime and swim.   15

Glossary

See the critical commentary on p. 415.

3 *slander* – offending someone or saying something false or malicious that damages someone's reputation.

4 *scathing* – severely critical and/or scornful.

6 *assent* – an expression of agreement or acceptance.

9 *murmured* – said quietly or in an indistinct manner.

11 *wharf* – a structure used as a landing place for boats and ships.

14 *plight* – a difficult or dangerous situation.

15 *chime* – ringing.

Questions

Go to p. 148 for more questions on Thomas Kinsella.

1. What picture of Mr D. emerges from this poem?
2. Do you think the poet liked Mr D.? Give reasons for your answer.
3. What is the mood of this poem? Support your answer by reference to the text.

Exam-style Unseen Poem Questions

1. Choose two phrases from the poem that impressed you. Explain your choice.
2. Write a personal response to this poem. In your answer, you should make close reference to the text.
3. Discuss the ways in which the poet creates atmosphere in this poem.

Dick King

In your ghost, Dick King, in your phantom vowels I read
That death roves our memories igniting
Love. Kind plague, low voice in a stubbled throat,
You haunt with the taint of age and of vanished good,
Fouling my thought with losses.   5

Clearly now I remember rain on the cobbles,
Ripples in the iron trough, and the horses' dipped
Faces under the Fountain in James's Street,
When I sheltered my nine years against your buttons
And your own dread years were to come: 10

And your voice, in a pause of softness, named the dead,
Hushed as though the city had died by fire,
Bemused, discovering ... discovering
A gate to enter temperate ghosthood by;
And I squeezed your fingers till you found again   15
My hand hidden in yours.

                    I squeeze your fingers:

            Dick King was an upright man.
            Sixty years he trod
            The dull stations underfoot.   20
            Fifteen he lies with God.

            By the salt seaboard he grew up
            But left its rock and rain
            To bring a dying language east
            And dwell in Basin Lane.   25

            By the Southern Railway he increased:
            His second soul was born
            In the clangour of the iron sheds,
            The hush of the late horn.

An invalid he took to wife. 30
She prayed her life away;
Her whisper filled the whitewashed yard
Until her dying day.

And season in, season out,
He made his wintry bed. 35
He took the path to the turnstile
Morning and night till he was dead.

He clasped his hands in a Union ward
To hear St James's bell.
I searched his eyes though I was young, 40
The last to wish him well.

Glossary

See the critical commentary on p. 418.
In the preface to this poem, which appeared in Kinsella's 2006 collection *A Dublin Documentary*, Kinsella had the following to say:

An elderly neighbour lived in one of the cottages with his delicate and very pious wife. Born in the West of Ireland, a native speaker of Irish, he had come to Dublin and found work in the Great Southern Railway. He seemed to be always there: a friend of the family, a protector of my unformed feelings. I would visit him and his wife — leaving the shop and crossing the yard [...] I wrote two poems for him, in memory of his importance during those early years. Neither of the poems achieved completeness, but their parts came together.

1   *phantom* – a ghost or apparition.
4   *taint* – an imperfection or something that spoils the quality of something.
5   *Fouling* – clogging or obstructing.
13 *Bemused* – confused, puzzled, engrossed or mystified.
14 *temperate* – soft, mild or restrained in behaviour or attitude.
19 *trod* – walked.
24 *dying language* – Irish.
25 *Basin Lane* – an area in Dublin 8.
26 *Southern Railway* – possibly a reference to the Great Southern Railway.
28 *clangour* – peal or ringing.

Questions

Go to   p. 148   for more questions on Thomas Kinsella.

1. Outline the poet's memories of Dick King as they appear in the poem.
2. From your reading of the poem, what sort of person do you think Dick King was?
3. This poem contains many references to sound. Why do you think so many of Kinsella's memories of Dick King are associated with sounds?

Exam-style Unseen Poem Questions

1. Write a personal response to this poem. Your answer should make close reference to the text.
2. Choose a phrase from the poem that you liked and explain your choice.
3. Do you think the poem gives an interesting insight into the poet's childhood? In your answer, you might consider:
   - The poet's relationship with Dick King.
   - The words and images in the poem.

Mirror in February

The day dawns with scent of must and rain,
Of opened soil, dark trees, dry bedroom air.
Under the fading lamp, half dressed – my brain
Idling on some compulsive fantasy –
I towel my shaven jaw and stop, and stare,   5
Riveted by a dark exhausted eye,
A dry downturning mouth.

It seems again that it is time to learn,
In this untiring, crumbling place of growth
To which, for the time being, I return.   10
Now plainly in the mirror of my soul
I read that I have looked my last on youth
And little more; for they are not made whole
That reach the age of Christ.

Below my window the awakening trees,   15
Hacked clean for better bearing, stand defaced
Suffering their brute necessities,
And how should the flesh not quail that span for span
Is mutilated more? In slow distaste
I fold my towel with what grace I can,   20
Not young and not renewable, but man.

Glossary

See the critical commentary on p. 422.

1 *must* – the condition of being musty or mouldy. The word adds to the overall atmosphere of staleness that dominates the first stanza.

4 *compulsive* – exerting a powerful or unstoppable attraction.

14 *the age of Christ* – Christ is thought to have been 33 years old when he died.

16 *Hacked clean for better bearing* – it is important to understand this **paradox**. In order for the trees to bear fruit, they must be pruned, or hacked.

17 *brute* – cruel or savage.

18 *quail* – to tremble with fear.

20 *grace* – dignity.

Questions

Go to p. 148 for more questions on Thomas Kinsella.

1. Why do you think Kinsella chose the title 'Mirror in February' for this poem?
2. Explain the following phrase:

   It seems again that it is time to learn,

   In this untiring, crumbling place of growth

3. How important is the final line of the poem to your understanding of 'Mirror in February'?

Exam-style Unseen Poem Questions

1. Write a short personal response to this poem.
2. Choose a line or phrase from the poem that you found particularly appealing and say why.
3. Briefly describe the mood or feeling you get from reading this poem and illustrate your answer from the text.

Chrysalides

Our last free summer we mooned about at odd hours
Pedalling slowly through country towns, stopping to eat
Chocolate and fruit, tracing our vagaries on the map.

At night we watched in the barn, to the lurch of melodeon music,
The crunching boots of countrymen – huge and weightless   5
As their shadows – twirling and leaping over the yellow concrete.

Sleeping too little or too much, we awoke at noon
And were received with womanly mockery into the kitchen,
Like calves poking our faces in with enormous hunger.

Daily we strapped our saddlebags and went to experience   10
A tolerance we shall never know again, confusing
For the last time, for example, the licit and the familiar.

Our instincts blurred with change; a strange wakefulness
Sapped our energies and dulled our slow-beating hearts
To the extremes of feeling – insensitive alike   15

To the unique succession of our youthful midnights,
When by a window ablaze softly with the virgin moon
Dry scones and jugs of milk awaited us in the dark,

Or to lasting horror: a wedding flight of ants
Spawning to its death, a mute perspiration   20
Glistening like drops of copper, agonised, in our path.

Glossary

See the critical commentary on p. 425.
The title, 'Chrysalides', refers to the gold-coloured
pupa of a butterfly.

1   *mooned* – wandered aimlessly.
3   *vagaries* – an unpredictable or erratic change,
    action or idea.
4   *melodeon* – a small reed organ that uses
    bellows to draw air through its reeds.

14 *Sapped* – drained.
17 *virgin moon* – new moon.
20 *Spawning* – germinating or giving rise to.
20 *mute* – silent.
21 *Glistening* – shining brightly.

Questions

Go to p. 148 for more questions on Thomas Kinsella.

1. Why do you think the poet chose this title for this poem? Give reasons for your answer by referring to the poem.

2. Trace the poet's use of nature imagery in the poem. In what ways does it add to the poem?

3. What does the poet mean when he says, 'Our instincts blurred with change'? Support your answer by close reference to the poem.

Exam-style Unseen Poem Questions

1. Write a short personal response to 'Chrysalides' in which you outline how the poem made you feel.

2. Imagine you have been asked to suggest a poem for a forthcoming book of poetry entitled *Memories of Youth*. You choose this poem. Give reasons why.

3. Briefly describe the mood or feeling you get from reading this poem and illustrate your answer from the text.

from Glenmacnass VI: Littlebody

Up on the high road, as far as the sheepfold
into the wind, and back. The sides of the black bog channels
dug down in the water. The white cottonheads
on the old cuttings nodding everywhere.
Around one more bend, toward the car shining in the distance. 5

From a stony slope half way, behind a rock prow
with the stones on top for an old mark,
the music of pipes, distant and clear.

*

I was climbing up, making no noise
and getting close, when the music stopped,   10
leaving a pagan shape in the air.

There was a hard inhale,
a base growl,
and it started again, in a guttural dance.

I looked around the edge   15
– and it was Littlebody. Hugging his bag
under his left arm, with his eyes closed.

I slipped. Our eyes met.
He started scuttling up the slope with his gear
and his hump, elbows out and neck back.   20

But I shouted:
                'Stop, Littlebody!
I found you fair and I want my due.'

He stopped and dropped his pipes,
and spread his arms out, waiting for the next move.   25
I heard myself reciting:

'Demon dwarf
with the German jaw,
surrender your purse
with the ghostly gold.'   30

He took out a fat purse,
put it down on a stone
and recited in reply, in a voice too big for his body:

'You found me fair,
and I grant your wishes.   35
But we'll meet again,
when I dance in your ashes.'

He settled himself down once more
and bent over the bag,
                    looking off to one side.   40

'I thought I was safe up here.
You have to give the music a while to itself sometimes,
up out of the huckstering

– jumping around in your green top hat
and showing your skills   45
with your eye on your income.'

He ran his fingers up and down the stops,
then gave the bag a last squeeze.
His face went solemn,

his fingertips fondled all the right places,   50
and he started a slow air
                    out across the valley.

*

I left him to himself.

And left the purse where it was.

I have all I need for the while I have left   55

without taking unnecessary risks.

And made my way down to the main road

with my mind on our next meeting.

Glossary

See the critical commentary on p. 428.

1   *sheepfold* – an enclosure or shelter for sheep.
3   *cottonheads* – presumably the flower heads of bog cotton.
6   *prow* – the forward part of something.
11 *pagan* – someone who does not acknowledge the God of the Bible, the Torah or the Koran. This is often used as an offensive term.
13 *base* – low.
14 *guttural* – a harsh, grating sound from the back of the throat made while speaking.
43 *huckstering* – selling or peddling goods, often in an aggressive or underhanded manner.
49 *solemn* – being, having or showing sincerity or gravity.

Questions

Go to **p. 148** for more questions on Thomas Kinsella.

1. What elements of the poem suggest that Littlebody may be a figment of the poet's imagination?

2. In your opinion, what does Littlebody represent in this poem? Give reasons for your answer.

3. Why do you think the speaker refuses to take Littlebody's gold at the poem's end?

Exam-style Unseen Poem Questions

1. Discuss the ways Kinsella creates a surreal atmosphere in this poem.

2. Write a response to this poem, highlighting aspects of it that you liked and/or disliked.

3. Do you think this poem gives a surprising insight into the poetic process? In your answer, you might consider unusual words and images in the poem.

Tear

I was sent in to see her.
A fringe of jet drops
chattered at my ear
as I went in through the hangings.

I was swallowed in chambery dusk.   5
My heart shrank
at the smell of disused
organs and sour kidney.

The black aprons I used to
bury my face in   10
were folded at the foot of the bed
in the last watery light from the window

(Go in and say goodbye to her)
and I was carried off
to unfathomable depths.   15
I turned to look at her.

She stared at the ceiling
and puffed her cheek, distracted,
propped high in the bed
resting for the next attack.   20

The covers were gathered close
up to her mouth,
that the lines of ill-temper still
marked. Her grey hair

was loosened out like a young woman's   25
all over the pillow,
mixed with the shadows
criss-crossing her forehead

and at her mouth and eyes,
like a web of strands tying down her head   30
and tangling down toward the shadow
eating away the floor at my feet.

I couldn't stir at first, nor wished to,
for fear she might turn and tempt me
(my own father's mother)   35
with open mouth

– with some fierce wheedling whisper –
to hide myself one last time
against her, and bury my
self in her drying mud.   40

Was I to kiss her? As soon
kiss the damp that crept
in the flowered walls
of this pit.

Yet I had to kiss.   45
I knelt by the bulk of the death bed
and sank my face in the chill
and smell of her black aprons.

Snuff and musk, the folds against my eyelids,
carried me into a derelict place   50
smelling of ash: unseen walls and roofs
rustled like breathing.

I found myself disturbing
dead ashes for any trace
of warmth, when far off   55
in the vaults a single drop

splashed. And I found
what I was looking for

– not heat nor fire,
not any comfort,   60

but her voice, soft, talking to someone
about my father: 'God help him, he cried
big tears over there by the machine
for the poor little thing.' Bright

drops on the wooden lid   65
for my infant sister.
My own wail of child-animal grief
was soon done, with any early guess

at sad dullness and tedious pain
and lives bitter with hard bondage.   70
How I tasted it now –
her heart beating in my mouth!

She drew an uncertain breath
and pushed at the clothes
and shuddered tiredly.   75
I broke free

and left the room
promising myself
when she was really dead
I would really kiss.   80

My grandfather half looked up
from the fireplace as I came out,
and shrugged and turned back
with a deaf stare to the heat.

I fidgeted beside him for a minute   85
and went out to the shop.
It was still bright there
and I felt better able to breathe.

Old age can digest
anything: the commotion   90
at Heaven's gate – the struggle
in store for you all your life.

How long and hard it is
before you get to Heaven,
unless like little Agnes   95
you vanish with early tears.

Glossary

See the critical commentary on p. 431.

15   *unfathomable* – something that is too deep to be measured.

37   *wheedling* – to try and persuade somebody to do something using flattery, guile or other indirect means.

49   *musk* – a pungent smell.

50   *derelict* – something that is in poor condition owing to neglect.

69   *tedious* – boring, monotonous or repetitive.

70   *bondage* – the condition of being restrained by something that limits one's freedom, either physically or figuratively.

75   *shuddered* – trembled uncontrollably.

95   *little Agnes* – Kinsella's little sister, who died as a child.

Questions

Go to   p. 148   for more questions on Thomas Kinsella.

1. From your reading of this poem, how close do you think Kinsella was to his grandmother?

2. Why do you think Kinsella chose the title 'Tear' for this poem?

3. What devices does Kinsella use to create atmosphere in this poem?

Exam-style Unseen Poem Questions

1. Write a short personal response to this poem.

2. Briefly describe the mood or feeling that you get from reading this poem and illustrate your answer from the text.

3. Choose two phrases from this poem that you found particularly interesting and/ or moving.

Hen Woman

The noon heat in the yard
smelled of stillness and coming thunder.
A hen scratched and picked at the shore.
It stopped, its body crouched and puffed out.
The brooding silence seemed to say 'Hush…'   5

The cottage door opened,
a black hole
in a whitewashed wall so bright
the eyes narrowed.
Inside, a clock murmured 'Gong…'   10

(I had felt all this before.)

She hurried out in her slippers
muttering, her face dark with anger,
and gathered the hen up jerking
languidly. Her hand fumbled.   15
Too late. Too late.

It fixed me with its pebble eyes
(seeing what mad blur).
A white egg showed in the sphincter;
mouth and beak opened together;   20
and time stood still.

Nothing moved: bird or woman,
fumbled or fumbling – locked there
(as I must have been) gaping.

                    *

There was a tiny movement at my feet,   25
tiny and mechanical; I looked down.

A beetle like a bronze leaf
was inching across the cement,
clasping with small tarsi
a ball of dung bigger than its body.   30

The serrated brow pressed the ground humbly,
lifted in a short stare, bowed again;
the dung-ball advanced minutely,
losing a few fragments,
specks of staleness and freshness.   35

*

A mutter of thunder far off
– time not quite stopped.
I saw the egg had moved a fraction:
a tender blank brain
under torsion, a clean new world.   40

As I watched, the mystery completed.
The black zero of the orifice
closed to a point
and the white zero of the egg hung free,
flecked with greenish brown oils.   45

It fell and turned over slowly.
Dreamlike, fussed by her splayed fingers,
it floated outward, moon-white,
leaving no trace in the air,
and began its drop to the shore.   50

*

I feed upon it still, as you see;
there is no end to that which, not understood,
may yet be hoarded in the imagination,

in the yolk of one's being, so to speak,
there to undergo its (quite animal) growth,   55

dividing blindly, twitching, packed with will,
searching in its own tissue
for the structure in which it may wake.
Something that had – clenched in its cave –
not been now as was: an egg of being.   60

Through what seemed a whole year it fell
– as it still falls, for me, solid and light,
the red gold beating in its silvery womb,
alive as the yolk and white of my eye.
As it will continue to fall, probably, until I die,   65
through the vast indifferent spaces
with which I am empty.

                              *

It smashed against the grating
and slipped down quickly out of sight.
It was over in a comical flash.   70
The soft mucous shell clung a little longer,
then drained down.

She stood staring, in blank anger.
Then her eyes came to life, and she laughed
and let the bird flap away.   75

                        'It's all the one.
There's plenty more where that came from!'

Glossary

See the critical commentary on p. 437.

5 *brooding* – ominous or containing some silent threat or danger.

10 *murmured* – a low sound coming from some distance away.

15 *languidly* – lacking vigour or moving slowly.

19 *sphincter* – a ring of muscle that surrounds a passageway in the body and narrows or closes the opening by contracting.

29 *tarsi* – the distal part of the leg of an arthropod, usually divided into segments.

31 *serrated* – edged with notches or with projections looking very much like the teeth of a saw.

40 *torsion* – the distortion caused by twisting something or moving something into a twisted shape.

42 *orifice* – an opening, especially into a cavity or passage in the body.

71 *mucous* – resembling, containing or covered with mucus.

Questions

Go to p. 148 for more questions on Thomas Kinsella.

1. How well do you think Kinsella builds tension in this poem? Give reasons for your answer.

2. From your reading of the poem, what sort of relationship do you think Thomas Kinsella had with his grandmother?

3. How does Kinsella manage to create a vivid impression of the events of that day?

Exam-style Unseen Poem Questions

1. In your opinion, why does Kinsella have such vivid memories of this seemingly unimportant event?

2. Write a personal response to this poem. Your answer should make close reference to the text.

3. Do you think the poem gives an interesting insight into the poet's childhood?

His Father's Hands

I drank firmly
and set the glass down between us firmly.
You were saying.

My father
Was saying.   5

His finger prodded and prodded,
marring his point. Emphas-
emphasemphasis.

I have watched
his father's hands before him   10

      cupped, and tightening the black Plug
between knife and thumb,
carving off little curlicues
to rub them in the dark of his palms,

or cutting into new leather at his bench,   15
levering a groove open with his thumb,
insinuating wet sprigs for the hammer.

He kept the sprigs in mouthfuls
and brought them out in silvery
units between his lips.   20

I took a pinch out of their hole
and knocked them one by one into the wood,
bright points among hundreds gone black,
other children's – cousins and others, grown up.

      Or his bow hand scarcely moving,   25
scraping in the dark corner near the fire,
his plump fingers shifting on the strings.

To his deaf, inclined head
he hugged the fiddle's body
whispering with the tune   30
with breaking heart
whene'er I hear
in privacy, across a blocked void,

the wind that shakes the barley.
The wind ...   35
round her grave ...

on my breast in blood she died ...
But blood for blood without remorse
I've ta'en ...

Beyond that.   40

                              *

Your family, Thomas, met with and helped
many of the Croppies in hiding from the Yeos
or on their way home after the defeat
in south Wexford. They sheltered the Laceys
who were later hanged on the Bridge in Ballinglen 45
between Tinahely and Anacorra.

From hearsay, as far as I can tell
the Men Folk were either Stone Cutters
or masons or probably both.
                        In the 18   50
and late 1700s even the farmers
had some other trade to make a living.

They lived in Farnese among a Colony
of North of Ireland or Scotch settlers left there
in some of the dispersions or migrations   55

which occurred in this Area of Wicklow and Wexford
and Carlow. And some years before that time
the Family came from somewhere around Tullow.

Beyond that.

*

Littered uplands. Dense grass. Rocks everywhere,   60
wet underneath, retaining memory of the long cold.
First, a prow of land
chosen, and wedged with tracks;
then boulders chosen
and sloped together, stabilized in menace.   65

I do not like this place.
I do not think the people who lived here
were ever happy. It feels evil.
Terrible things happened.
I feel afraid here when I am on my own.   70

*

Dispersals or migrations.
Through what evolutions or accidents
toward that peace and patience
by the fireside, that blocked gentleness ...

That serene pause, with the slashing knife,   75
in kindly mockery,
as I busy myself with my little nails
at the rude block, his bench.

The blood advancing
– gorging vessel after vessel –   80
and altering in them
one by one.

Behold, that gentleness already
modulated twice, in others:
to earnestness and iteration;   85
to an offhandedness, repressing various impulses.

*

Extraordinary … The big block – I found it
years afterward in a corner of the yard
in sunlight after rain
and stood it up, wet and black: 90
it turned under my hands, an axis
of light flashing down its length,
and the wood's soft flesh broke open,
countless little nails
squirming and dropping out of it.   95

Glossary

See the critical commentary on p. 443.

11 *Plug* – plug tobacco. A hard form of tobacco that is cut or shaved so as to be smoked by pipe.

13 *curlicues* – an ornamental twist that is often used in calligraphy or design.

17 *insinuating* – hinting at or implying something.

42 *Croppies* – the derogatory nickname given to the Irish Rrebels who took part in the 1798 rebellion.

42 *Yeos* – members of the military.

49 *masons* – someone who works with stone.

62 *prow* – the front part.

84 *modulated* – changed.

Questions

Go to p. 148 for more questions on Thomas Kinsella.

1. Give a brief account of the Kinsella family history as it is described in this poem.

2. From your reading of this poem, how influential do you think Kinsella's father was in the poet's growth as a writer?

3. Comment on the final stanza of the poem. What significance do you think this stanza holds to our overall understanding of 'His Father's Hands'?

Exam-style Unseen Poem Questions

1. Imagine you have been asked to select a poem for a forthcoming edition of poetry entitled *Family*. You decide to select this poem. Give reasons for your choice.

2. Write a response to this poem, highlighting aspects of it that you liked and/or disliked.

3. Do you think this poem gives an interesting insight into the importance of family history? In your answer, you might consider:
   • The manner in which the Kinsella family history unfolds.
   • The words and images in the poem.

from Settings: Model School, Inchicore

Miss Carney handed us out blank paper and marla,
old plasticine with the colours
all rolled together into brown.

You started with a ball of it
and rolled it into a snake curling   5
around your hand, and kept rolling it
in one place until it wore down into two
with a stain on the paper.

We always tittered at each other
when we said the adding-up table in Irish   10
and came to her name.

*

In the second school we had Mr Browne.
He had white teeth in his brown man's face.

He stood in front of the black board
and chalked a white dot.   15

'We are going to start
decimals.'

I am going to know
everything.

*

One day he said: 20
'Out into the sun!'
We settled his chair under a tree
and sat ourselves down delighted
in two rows in the greeny gold shade.

A fat bee floated around   25
shining amongst us
and the flickering sun
warmed our folded coats
and he said: 'History …!'

*

When the Autumn came   30
and the big chestnut leaves
fell all over the playground
we piled them in heaps
between the wall and the tree trunks
and the boys ran races   35
jumping over the heaps
and tumbled into them shouting.

*

I sat by myself in the shed
and watched the draught
blowing the papers   40
around the wheels of the bicycles.

Will God judge
     our most secret thoughts and actions?
God will judge
     our most secret thoughts and actions   45
and every idle word that man shall speak
he shall render an account of it
on the Day of Judgment.

*

The taste
of ink off   50
the nib shrank your
mouth.

Glossary

See the critical commentary on p. 449.
The title refers to Kinsella's primary school in Inchicore, Dublin 8.
  1 *marla* – the Irish word for plasticine modelling clay.
51 *nib* – the tip of a fountain pen.

Questions

Go to p. 148 for more questions on Thomas Kinsella.

1. From your reading of this poem, do you think that Thomas Kinsella enjoyed his time in school? Explain your answer.
2. Imagine you have been asked to select a poem for a forthcoming edition of poetry entitled *School Days*. You choose this poem. Give reasons for your answer.
3. Can you identify with Kinsella's memories of his time in school?

Exam-style Unseen Poem Questions

1. Choose a line or two from this poem that you find particularly appealing and say why.
2. What do you think is the theme of this poem? Give reasons for your answer.
3. Write a personal response to the poem 'Model School, Inchicore'.

from The Familiar: VII

I was downstairs at first light,
looking out through the frost on the window
at the hill opposite and the sheets of frost
scattered down among the rocks.

The cat back in the kitchen.   5
Folded on herself. Torn and watchful.

*

A chilled grapefruit
– thin-skinned, with that little gloss.
I took a mouthful, looking up along the edge of the wood

at the two hooded crows high in the cold   10
talking to each other,
flying up toward the tundra, beyond the waterfall.

*

I sliced the tomatoes in thin discs
in damp sequence into their dish;
scalded the kettle; made the tea,   15

and rang the little brazen bell.
And saved the toast.
                          Arranged the pieces

in slight disorder around the basket.
Fixed our places, one with the fruit   20
and one with the plate of sharp cheese.

*

And stood in my dressing gown
with arms extended
over the sweetness of the sacrifice.

Her shade showed in the door.   25
Her voice responded:
'You are very good. You always made it nice.'

Glossary

See the critical commentary on p. 452.

10 *hooded crows* – a large grey and black crow.

12 *tundra* – the level or nearly level plain with very little vegetation and no trees between the ice cap and the timber line of North America, Europe and Asia that remains permanently frozen.

15 *scalded* – made hot by running boiling water over it.

25 *shade* – the term given in ancient Greek literature to describe the ghosts of the dead.

Questions

Go to   p. 148   for more questions on Thomas Kinsella.

1. Imagine you have been asked to select a poem for a forthcoming edition of poetry entitled *Everyday Events*. You choose this poem. Give reasons for your answer.
2. Comment on the mood of this poem.
3. How did this poem make you feel? Explain your answer.

Exam-style Unseen Poem Questions

1. Choose two images from the poem that you found particularly striking. Give reasons for your choice.
2. From your reading of the poem, what impression do you get of Kinsella's relationship with his wife?
3. Comment on the following statements, supporting your answers by reference to the poem.
   • The poem makes effective allusions to classical mythology.
   • The poem uses ordinary language to celebrate the beauty of everyday, familiar events.

from Belief and Unbelief: Echo

He cleared the thorns
from the broken gate,
and held her hand
through the heart of the wood
to the holy well.   5

They revealed their names
and told their tales
as they said that they would
on that distant day
when their love began.   10

And hand in hand
they turned to leave.
When she stopped and whispered
a final secret
down to the water.   15

See the critical commentary on p. 455.

Questions

Go to   p. 148   for more questions on Thomas Kinsella.

1. Comment on the mood of the poem.
2. How does the language of the poem contribute to that mood?
3. How does this poem make you feel? Support your answer by close reference to the poem.

Exam-style Unseen Poem Questions

1. Write a short personal response to this poem.
2. Suggest a different title for this poem. Give reasons for your suggestion.
3. Choose two phrases from the poem that you particularly liked or disliked. Support your answer by close reference to the text.

Thomas Kinsella: An Overview

Now that you have read a selection of Thomas Kinsella's poetry, you should take the time to look at the following general points. The purpose of these is not to tell you what to think, but rather to help you form your own opinions. When you have read these points, you may wish to take the time to reread Kinsella's poetry. You should notice that the general points made here can be used to form the backbone of your paragraphs when it comes to writing on poetry. From now on, try to think about Kinsella's poems in terms of what they say and how they say it. Open your mind to any reasonable interpretation of the poems; remember, your opinions are as valid as anything printed. However, you must be prepared to ground these opinions in fact. If you find this process difficult, that is entirely normal. Remember that a poem is not meant to be studied and dissected in the manner that the Leaving Certificate requires of us. While we have to keep the exam in mind, you should not allow it to detract from your enjoyment of the poetry on the course.

1. Thomas Kinsella's poetry is rooted in the Dublin of his birthplace. The people and places associated with his childhood are present in nearly every poem by Kinsella on the course. Frequently, the poet's recollections of his youth pave the way for deeper meditations on the passing of time and the inevitability of decay.
2. Kinsella's poetry concerns itself with the development of the imagination. In fact, it has been said of Kinsella that one of his most remarkable qualities is 'the owlish vigil the poet keeps over the workings of the imagination and the care with which he shapes its productions'.
3. Towards the latter half of his career, Kinsella became interested in the writings of Carl Jung. As a result, many of the poems on the course contain *allusions* to and examples of Jungian archetypes. According to Jung, these archetypes were representative of innate, universal dispositions from which the basic themes of human life emerge. In the poems on the course by Kinsella, the archetypal symbols that appear are those of the witch, the egg, the mother and the father. While these archetypes are obviously drawn from real life, in Kinsella's poetry they have an undeniable *symbolic* function. Very often they serve to shed light on the development of the poet's psyche.

4. Many of the poems by Kinsella on the course deal with primal aspects of the human experience. Nowhere is this more obvious than in his treatment of death. Speaking about his poetry, Kinsella has said:

> Some of the poems which I like most of mine are the cold–blooded lamentations for individuals whom I've known and liked and who have died.

5. Linked to but separate from Kinsella's treatment of the theme of death is his examination of the passing of time. Speaking about this aspect of his poetry, Kinsella has said:

> I have a distinct feeling, for instance, that one of the main impulses to poetry or, for that matter, to any art, is an attempt more or less to stem the passing of time; it's the process of arresting the erosion of feelings and relationships and objects which is being fought by the artist, not particularly because one relationship or one object has all his love at the moment, but simply that he is there to combat the erosion.

Many of the poems on the course examine the passing of time. In particular, poems such as 'Mirror in February' and 'His Father's Hands' highlight the spiritual and physical effects of time on the human soul.

6. Kinsella's language is a curious mixture of straightforward, even **colloquial** English and complex allusions to **myth** and history. In this respect, his poetry can at times be deceptive. What appears as a straightforward poem can, on closer inspection, prove to be very thought provoking and multi-layered.

Sample Questions

Before you try these questions, you may wish to consult the examination technique guidelines on p. 548.

1. What impact did the poetry of Thomas Kinsella make on you as a reader? Your answer should deal with the following:
   - Your overall sense of the personality of the poet
   - The poet's use of language/imagery.

2. 'Thomas Kinsella draws on the people and places of his native Dublin to produce a rich and interesting body of poetry.'
   Do you agree with this assessment of his poetry? Write a response, supporting your points with the aid of suitable reference to the poems you have studied.

3. 'I found Thomas Kinsella's poetry both complex and thought provoking.'
   Referring to more than one poem by Kinsella that you have read, comment on this statement.

4. Write an introduction to the poetry of Thomas Kinsella for new readers of his poetry. Your introduction should cover the following:
   • The ideas that are most important to him.
   • How you responded to his use of language and imagery.
   Refer to the poems by Kinsella that you have covered.

5. 'Thomas Kinsella draws on the power of memory to engage and fascinate his readers.'
   You have been asked by your local radio station to give a talk on the poetry of Thomas Kinsella. Write out the text of the talk you would deliver in response to the above title. You should refer to both style and subject matter. Support the points you make by reference to the poetry on your course.

6. 'Thomas Kinsella explores people and places in his own distinctive style.'
   Write your response to this statement, supporting your points with the aid of suitable reference to the poems you have studied.

7. Write a personal response to the poetry of Thomas Kinsella that you have studied. Support the points that you make with the aid of suitable reference to the poems you have studied.

8. 'Kinsella uses his poetry as a medium to express universal human experiences.'
   In light of the above assessment of Kinsella's poetry, write an essay outlining your reasons for liking or not liking the poems you have studied.

9. Write about the feelings that Thomas Kinsella's poetry creates in you and the aspects of his poetry (content/or style) that help to create those feelings. Support your points by reference to the poetry by Kinsella you have read.

10. 'Kinsella: A Dublin poet who speaks to us all.'
   Using this title, write an essay outlining what you consider to be the appeal of Thomas Kinsella's poetry to a modern audience. Support your points by reference to the poetry of Kinsella on your course.

Philip Larkin (1922–85)

The poetry of Philip Larkin in this anthology is thoroughly modern. It combines a homely, sophisticated language with detailed and accurate descriptions that are narrated for the most part by an entirely personal voice. His poetry manages to capture the moment in an uncompromisingly realistic fashion that can sometimes appear pessimistic. Larkin's verse can be sneering and contemptuous of society at large, yet, at the same time, he can be hilariously funny and self-deprecating. For all its bleak realism, Larkin's poetry is open and warm. He bemoans the certainty of death, yet affirms the possibility of continuity and renewal glimpsed in nature. You should approach Larkin's poetry with an open mind. If read without prejudice, it will force you to reassess many of your most deeply held beliefs. If you would like to read more about Philip Larkin's life, there is a short biography on p. 457.

Wedding-Wind

The wind blew all my wedding-day,
And my wedding-night was the night of the high wind;
And a stable door was banging, again and again,
That he must go and shut it, leaving me
Stupid in candlelight, hearing rain,   5
Seeing my face in the twisted candlestick,
Yet seeing nothing. When he came back
He said the horses were restless, and I was sad
That any man or beast that night should lack
The happiness I had.   10

            Now in the day
All's ravelled under the sun by the wind's blowing.
He has gone to look at the floods, and I
Carry a chipped pail to the chicken-run,
Set it down, and stare. All is the wind   15
Hunting through clouds and forests, thrashing
My apron and the hanging cloths on the line.
Can it be borne, this bodying-forth by wind
Of joy my actions turn on, like a thread
Carrying beads? Shall I be let to sleep   20
Now this perpetual morning shares my bed?
Can even death dry up
These new delighted lakes, conclude
Our kneeling as cattle by all-generous waters?

Glossary

See the critical commentary on p. 459.
The critic Martin Bruce feels that this poem is typical of Larkin's restraint in his use of figurative language. Here, the young bride employs two sets of metaphors – one natural or rural, the other religious – to express her combined joy and fear. She compares her blissful love to 'kneeling as cattle by all-generous waters' and 'a thread I Carrying beads', while wondering if the wind of death will dry up the waters or snap the thread.

12 *ravelled* – curiously, this word can mean to entangle or to disentangle. It also means to search. Here, it is probably intended to signify the clarity of day.

14 *pail* – a bucket.

16 *thrashing* – beating against.

18 *bodying-forth* – embodying. Here, the speaker questions whether the wind is capable of expressing accurately the joy she feels.

21 *perpetual* – continuous.

Questions

Go to p. 174 for more questions on Philip Larkin.

1. How do the images in the opening lines contribute to the overall mood of the poem?

2. In your opinion, why does the speaker describe the morning as being 'perpetual' at the end of the poem?

3. Imagining that you are the husband of the woman in this poem, write a response to 'Wedding-Wind'.

Exam-style Unseen Poem Questions

1. Write a response to 'Wedding-Wind', highlighting aspects of it that you liked and/ or disliked.

2. Write a short personal response to this poem. You may want to comment on the effect that the imagery used in the poem had on you.

3. Write down one phrase from the poem that shows how the speaker feels about her marriage. Say why you have chosen this phrase.

At Grass

The eye can hardly pick them out
From the cold shade they shelter in,
Till wind distresses tail and mane;
Then one crops grass, and moves about
—The other seeming to look on—   5
And stands anonymous again.

Yet fifteen years ago, perhaps
Two dozen distances sufficed
To fable them: faint afternoons
Of Cups and Stakes and Handicaps,   10
Whereby their names were artificed
To inlay faded, classic Junes—

Silks at the start: against the sky
Numbers and parasols: outside,
Squadrons of empty cars, and heat,   15
And littered grass: then the long cry
Hanging unhushed till it subside
To stop-press columns on the street.

Do memories plague their ears like flies?
They shake their heads. Dusk brims the shadows.   20
Summer by summer all stole away,
The starting-gates, the crowds and cries—
All but the unmolesting meadows.
Almanacked, their names live; they

Have slipped their names, and stand at ease,   25
Or gallop for what must be joy,
And not a fieldglass sees them home,
Or curious stop-watch prophesies:
Only the groom, and the groom's boy,
With bridles in the evening come.   30

Glossary

See the critical commentary on p. 462.

3 *mane* – the long hair on the back of the neck of a horse.

4 *crops* – cuts. In this case, the poet is referring to the horses eating the grass.

6 *anonymous* – unknown or nameless.

8 *sufficed* – were enough.

9 *To fable* – this is an unusual usage of the word. Here, 'fable' is used as the verb 'to make famous'.

10 *Cups and Stakes and Handicaps* – these are all horse-racing terms.

11 *artificed* – worked or designed.

12 *inlay* – a strip of fabric.

13 *Silks* – the shirts that jockeys wear on race day.

14 *parasols* – a light umbrella used to give shade from the sun or a decorative umbrella.

19 *plague* – pester.

23 *unmolesting meadows* – meadows that do no harm.

24 *Almanacked* – listed in an almanac or reference book.

27 *fieldglass* – binoculars.

28 *prophesies* – predictions.

29 *the groom* – the person charged with taking care of the horse.

30 *bridles* – the devices on horses' heads by which they are controlled.

Questions

Go to p. 174 for more questions on Philip Larkin.

1. How well does the poet evoke the world that the horses knew in their prime? Support your answer by relevant quotation from or reference to the poem.

2. To what extent can the horses' retirement be seen as a metaphor for the ageing process?

3. *Regret, nostalgia, acceptance*: which of these words best describes the tone of this poem? Justify your choice by reference to the poem.

Exam-style Unseen Poem Questions

1. 'I enjoyed (or did not enjoy) "At Grass".' Write a paragraph that responds to this statement. Refer closely to the poem.

2. Does this poem make you feel hopeful or unhopeful? Briefly explain why.

3. Choose a line or two that you find particularly appealing and explain why.

Church Going

Once I am sure there's nothing going on
I step inside, letting the door thud shut.
Another church: matting, seats, and stone,
And little books; sprawlings of flowers, cut
For Sunday, brownish now; some brass and stuff   5
Up at the holy end; the small neat organ;
And a tense, musty, unignorable silence,
Brewed God knows how long. Hatless, I take off
My cycle-clips in awkward reverence,

Move forward, run my hand around the font.   10
From where I stand, the roof looks almost new—
Cleaned, or restored? Someone would know: I don't.
Mounting the lectern, I peruse a few
Hectoring large-scale verses, and pronounce
'Here endeth' much more loudly than I'd meant.   15
The echoes snigger briefly. Back at the door
I sign the book, donate an Irish sixpence,
Reflect the place was not worth stopping for.

Yet stop I did: in fact I often do,
And always end much at a loss like this,   20
Wondering what to look for; wondering, too,
When churches fall completely out of use
What we shall turn them into, if we shall keep
A few cathedrals chronically on show,
Their parchment, plate and pyx in locked cases,   25
And let the rest rent-free to rain and sheep.
Shall we avoid them as unlucky places?

Or, after dark, will dubious women come
To make their children touch a particular stone;
Pick simples for a cancer; or on some   30
Advised night see walking a dead one?

Power of some sort or other will go on
In games, in riddles, seemingly at random;
But superstition, like belief, must die,
And what remains when disbelief has gone?   35
Grass, weedy pavement, brambles, buttress, sky,

A shape less recognisable each week,
A purpose more obscure. I wonder who
Will be the last, the very last, to seek
This place for what it was; one of the crew   40
That tap and jot and know what rood-lofts were?
Some ruin-bibber, randy for antique,
Or Christmas-addict, counting on a whiff
Of gown-and-bands and organ-pipes and myrrh?
Or will he be my representative,   45

Bored, uninformed, knowing the ghostly silt
Dispersed, yet tending to this cross of ground
Through suburb scrub because it held unspilt
So long and equably what since is found
Only in separation—marriage, and birth,   50
And death, and thoughts of these—for which was built
This special shell? For, though I've no idea
What this accoutred frowsty barn is worth,
It pleases me to stand in silence here;

A serious house on serious earth it is,   55
In whose blent air all our compulsions meet,
Are recognised, and robed as destinies.
And that much never can be obsolete,
Since someone will forever be surprising
A hunger in himself to be more serious,   60
And gravitating with it to this ground,
Which, he once heard, was proper to grow wise in,
If only that so many dead lie round.

Glossary

See the critical commentary on p. 464.

4 *sprawlings* – ragged bunches of flowers.

10 *font* – vessel for baptising.

13 *lectern* – a stand from which the scripture is read.

14 *Hectoring* – badgering or attempting to interrupt another person while he/she talks.

24 *chronically* – constantly.

25 *parchment* – writing paper.

25 *pyx* – a container in which wafers for the Eucharist are kept. In the Catholic religion, the Eucharist is bread and wine that has been consecrated and is consumed in remembrance of Jesus' death.

28 *dubious* – uncertain or doubtful.

30 *simples* – herbal cures.

38 *obscure* – unclear.

41 *rood-lofts* – galleries built above a rood screen. The rood screen was a common feature in late medieval churches. Its function was to separate the clergy from the laity, i.e. those in the congregation who weren't members of the clergy.

42 *ruin-bibber* – a bibber is someone who likes to drink. Here, the poet probably means someone who likes to sift through ruins.

42 *randy* – this word is usually associated with someone who displays frank, uninhibited sexuality. However, it can also be used to mean ill-mannered. Here, the poet probably intends the word to mean someone lusting after antiques.

44 *gown-and-bands* – ceremonial dress.

44 *myrrh* – an expensive, aromatic oil. Myrrh was one of the gifts taken to the baby Jesus by the Three Wise Men.

47 *Dispersed* – spread out.

53 *accoutred* – dressed or equipped.

53 *frowsty* – stuffy.

56 *compulsions* – irresistible impulses.

61 *gravitating* – moving towards.

Questions

Go to p. 174 for more questions on Philip Larkin.

1. Comment on the title of the poem. Do you think that the poet intended the title to be ambiguous?

2. Trace the mood of the poem as it changes and develops in the course of the poem.

3. In your opinion, is this poem optimistic or pessimistic? Justify your answer by close reference to the poem.

Exam-style Unseen Poem Questions

1. Write a personal response to this poem. Your answer should make close reference to the text.

2. Do you think the poem gives an interesting insight into religion? In your answer, you might consider:
   • The pattern of the poet's thinking.
   • The words and images in the poem.

3. Choose a line or two that you find particularly appealing and explain why.

An Arundel Tomb

Side by side, their faces blurred,
The earl and countess lie in stone,
Their proper habits vaguely shown
As jointed armour, stiffened pleat,
And that faint hint of the absurd—   5
The little dogs under their feet.

Such plainness of the pre-baroque
Hardly involves the eye, until
It meets his left-hand gauntlet, still
Clasped empty in the other; and   10
One sees, with a sharp tender shock,
His hand withdrawn, holding her hand.

They would not think to lie so long.
Such faithfulness in effigy
Was just a detail friends would see: 15
A sculptor's sweet commissioned grace
Thrown off in helping to prolong
The Latin names around the base.

They would not guess how early in
Their supine stationary voyage   20
The air would change to soundless damage,
Turn the old tenantry away;
How soon succeeding eyes begin
To look, not read. Rigidly they

Persisted, linked, through lengths and breadths   25
Of time. Snow fell, undated. Light
Each summer thronged the glass. A bright
Litter of birdcalls strewed the same
Bone-riddled ground. And up the paths
The endless altered people came,   30

Washing at their identity.
Now, helpless in the hollow of
An unarmorial age, a trough
Of smoke in slow suspended skeins
Above their scrap of history,   35
Only an attitude remains:

Time has transfigured them into
Untruth. The stone fidelity
They hardly meant has come to be
Their final blazon, and to prove   40
Our almost-instinct almost true:
What will survive of us is love.

Glossary

See the critical commentary on p. 468.

The title, 'An Arundel Tomb', refers to a tomb in Chichester Cathedral in England. Arundel is a town in West Sussex.

2 *lie in stone* – this refers to the carving on the tombstone. The word 'stone' is the first in a series of words that hint at a lack of movement.

4 *stiffened pleat* – hard fold. The words 'jointed' and 'pleat' suggest connection and relationship.

7 *pre-baroque* – the baroque style was characterised by a high degree of ornamentation. The statue is in keeping with the plain, unadorned style of the 'pre-baroque' era.

9 *gauntlet* – glove.

14 *effigy* – a sculpture of a person.

20 *supine* – inclined or lying on your back.

22 *tenantry* – those who live as tenants.

33 *unarmorial* – not containing armour or a crest of arms. The statue now exists in an age that has no interest in family crests of arms.

34 *skeins* – loosely tied coil or standard length of thread or yarn. Here, the speaker is probably referring to the coils of smoke as they rise.

Questions

Go to p. 174 for more questions on Philip Larkin.

1. How does Larkin manage to convey the passage of time in this poem?

2. What does the poet mean when he says that 'Time has transfigured them into | Untruth'?

3. Comment on the final line of the poem. How does it contribute to the overall mood of the poem?

Exam-style Unseen Poem Questions

1. Do you think the poem gives a surprising insight into the theme of love? In your answer, you might consider:
    *   The pattern of the speaker's thinking.
    *   The words and images in the poem.

2. Choose one or two phrases from the poem that you enjoyed and say why.

3. Write a response to 'An Arundel Tomb', highlighting aspects of it that you liked and/or disliked.

The Whitsun Weddings

That Whitsun, I was late getting away:
    Not till about
One-twenty on the sunlit Saturday
Did my three-quarters-empty train pull out,
All windows down, all cushions hot, all sense   5
Of being in a hurry gone. We ran
Behind the backs of houses, crossed a street
Of blinding windscreens, smelt the fish-dock; thence
The river's level drifting breadth began,
Where sky and Lincolnshire and water meet.   10

All afternoon, through the tall heat that slept
    For miles inland,
A slow and stopping curve southwards we kept.
Wide farms went by, short-shadowed cattle, and
Canals with floatings of industrial froth;   15
A hothouse flashed uniquely: hedges dipped
And rose: and now and then a smell of grass
Displaced the reek of buttoned carriage-cloth
Until the next town, new and nondescript,
Approached with acres of dismantled cars.   20

At first, I didn't notice what a noise
    The weddings made
Each station that we stopped at: sun destroys
The interest of what's happening in the shade,
And down the long cool platforms whoops and skirls   25
I took for porters larking with the mails,
And went on reading. Once we started, though,
We passed them, grinning and pomaded, girls
In parodies of fashion, heels and veils,
All poised irresolutely, watching us go,   30

As if out on the end of an event
    Waving goodbye
To something that survived it. Struck, I leant
More promptly out next time, more curiously,
And saw it all again in different terms: 35
The fathers with broad belts under their suits
And seamy foreheads; mothers loud and fat;
An uncle shouting smut; and then the perms,
The nylon gloves and jewellery-substitutes,
The lemons, mauves, and olive-ochres that   40

Marked off the girls unreally from the rest.
    Yes, from cafés
And banquet-halls up yards, and bunting-dressed
Coach-party annexes, the wedding-days
Were coming to an end. All down the line   45
Fresh couples climbed aboard: the rest stood round;
The last confetti and advice were thrown,
And, as we moved, each face seemed to define
Just what it saw departing: children frowned
At something dull; fathers had never known   50

Success so huge and wholly farcical;
    The women shared
The secret like a happy funeral;
While girls, gripping their handbags tighter, stared
At a religious wounding. Free at last,   55
And loaded with the sum of all they saw,
We hurried towards London, shuffling gouts of steam.
Now fields were building-plots, and poplars cast
Long shadows over major roads, and for
Some fifty minutes, that in time would seem   60

Just long enough to settle hats and say
 I nearly died,
A dozen marriages got under way.
They watched the landscape, sitting side by side
—An Odeon went past, a cooling tower,   65
and someone running up to bowl—and none
Thought of the others they would never meet
Or how their lives would all contain this hour.
I thought of London spread out in the sun,
Its postal districts packed like squares of wheat: 70

There we were aimed. And as we raced across
 Bright knots of rail
Past standing Pullmans, walls of blackened moss
Came close, and it was nearly done, this frail
Travelling coincidence; and what it held   75
Stood ready to be loosed with all the power
That being changed can give. We slowed again,
And as the tightened brakes took hold, there swelled
A sense of falling, like an arrow-shower
Sent out of sight, somewhere becoming rain.   80

Glossary

See the critical commentary on p. 471.
The title, 'The Whitsun Weddings', refers to Pentecost Sunday, which is the seventh Sunday after Easter. This was a time in the early Christian calendar when converts to the Church wore white robes in honour of their belief in the Holy Spirit. In this poem, there is the underlying notion that the wedding is the start of a new life, both for the married couple and for their respective families. To this day, Whitsun is a particularly popular time to celebrate a wedding.

19 *nondescript* – unremarkable or ordinary.

25 *skirls* – a shrill cry or sound.

28 *pomaded* – hair finished with pomade or another hair product.

30 *irresolutely* – waveringly or undecidedly.

40 *olive-ochres* – greenish-gold colours.

44 *annexes* – separate areas.

51 *farcical* – ridiculous.

55 *religious wounding* – here, the speaker is referring to the act of sexual intercourse. Once the couple has had sexual relations, the marriage is said to be consummated. When sexual intercourse takes place for the first time, the subsequent rupturing of the hymen can result in bleeding.

65 *Odeon* – a commonly used name for a cinema.

73 *Pullmans* – named after their inventor, George Pullman, these are luxury railway carriages or saloons.

Questions

Go to p. 174 for more questions on Philip Larkin.

1. Comment on the speaker's attitude to the wedding parties. In your answer, you may wish to mention the speaker's tone of voice.

2. How well does the speaker convey the atmosphere on the station platform and in the train?

3. What qualities have earned 'The Whitsun Weddings' the reputation as one of Larkin's best-loved poems? Refer closely to the poem in your answer.

Exam-style Unseen Poem Questions

1. Write a personal response to 'The Whitsun Weddings'.

2. Briefly describe the mood or feeling you get from reading this poem and illustrate your answer from the text.

3. Choose a phrase or line from the poem that impressed you. Explain your choice.

MCMXIV

Those long uneven lines
Standing as patiently
As if they were stretched outside
The Oval or Villa Park,
The crowns of hats, the sun   5
On moustached archaic faces
Grinning as if it were all
An August Bank Holiday lark;

And the shut shops, the bleached
Established names on the sunblinds,   10
The farthings and sovereigns,
And dark-clothed children at play
Called after kings and queens,
The tin advertisements
For cocoa and twist, and the pubs   15
Wide open all day;

And the countryside not caring:
The place-names all hazed over
With flowering grasses, and fields
Shadowing Domesday lines   20
Under wheat's restless silence;
The differently-dressed servants
With tiny rooms in huge houses,
The dust behind limousines;

Never such innocence,   25
Never before or since,
As changed itself to past
Without a word—the men
Leaving the gardens tidy,
The thousands of marriages   30
Lasting a little while longer:
Never such innocence again.

Glossary

See the critical commentary on p. 476.
The title, 'MCMXIV', is the year 1914 represented in roman numerals. The year 1914 saw the outbreak of World War One. Notice how the roman numerals lend the poem the appearance of a war monument.

4   *The Oval or Villa Park* – the Oval is the headquarters of English cricket and Villa Park is the home ground of the well-known English football team Aston Villa. Here, both these grounds act as **metaphors** for the class divisions in English society. The upper class traditionally supports cricket, while the lower and middle classes follow soccer.

6   *archaic* – old-fashioned.

11   *farthings and sovereigns* – types of coin used at this time.

13   *Called after kings and queens* – old-fashioned names, such as Albert and Victoria.

15   *cocoa* – a chocolate-flavoured drink.

15   *twist* – a twisted roll of tobacco.

20   *Domesday lines* – in 1086, William the Conqueror ordered that all the territorial divisions of England be recorded. The book in which these boundaries were recorded was known as the Domesday Book. Domesday is also the name given in the Bible to Judgement Day.

Questions

Go to   p. 174   for more questions on Philip Larkin.

1. How important are the title and the shape of 'MCMXIV' to the effect created in the poem?

2. What is the mood of this poem? Where in the language of the poem is this mood created?

3. How does the imagery of the poem convey a sense of threat and menace?

Exam-style Unseen Poem Questions

1. Write a response to 'MCMXIV', highlighting the impact it makes on you.

2. Briefly describe the mood or feeling you get from reading this poem and illustrate your answer from the text.

3. Choose a phrase or line from the poem that impressed you. Explain your choice.

Ambulances

Closed like confessionals, they thread
Loud noons of cities, giving back
None of the glances they absorb.
Light glossy grey, arms on a plaque,
They come to rest at any kerb: 5
All streets in time are visited.

Then children strewn on steps or road,
Or women coming from the shops
Past smells of different dinners, see
A wild white face that overtops   10
Red stretcher-blankets momently
As it is carried in and stowed,

And sense the solving emptiness
That lies just under all we do,
And for a second get it whole,   15
So permanent and blank and true.
The fastened doors recede. *Poor soul,*
They whisper at their own distress;

For borne away in deadened air
May go the sudden shut of loss   20
Round something nearly at an end,
And what cohered in it across
The years, the unique random blend
Of families and fashions, there

At last begin to loosen. Far   25
From the exchange of love to lie
Unreachable inside a room
The traffic parts to let go by
Brings closer what is left to come,
And dulls to distance all we are.   30

Glossary

See the critical commentary on p. 478.

1 *confessionals* – confession boxes. The act of confession is a sacred rite of the Catholic Church. During this sacrament, a Catholic is given the opportunity to repent his/her sins. This process normally takes place in a confession box.

2 *giving back | None of the glances they absorb* – the windows of the ambulance are blackened out.

13 *the solving emptiness* – here, the word 'solving' suggests a solution to some of life's central questions. However, when juxtaposed with the word 'emptiness', it loses some of its impact. In other words, the real questions go unanswered. The emptiness remains.

22 *cohered* – brought together.

Questions

Go to   p. 174   for more questions on Philip Larkin.

1. How does Larkin manage to capture the sound of the ambulance sirens?

2. In your opinion, what is the central message of this poem? Support your answer by close reference to the poem.

3. What does the poet mean when he says the following?

    And sense the solving emptiness

    That lies just under all we do

Exam-style Unseen Poem Questions

1. Does this poem make you feel hopeful or unhopeful? Briefly explain why.

2. Write a response to 'Ambulances', highlighting the impact it makes on you.

3. Do you think the poem gives a surprising insight into the theme of death? In your answer, you might consider:

    • The pattern of the speaker's thinking.

    • The words and images in the poem.

The Trees

The trees are coming into leaf
Like something almost being said;
The recent buds relax and spread,
Their greenness is a kind of grief.

Is it that they are born again   5
And we grow old? No, they die too.
Their yearly trick of looking new
Is written down in rings of grain.

Yet still the unresting castles thresh
In fullgrown thickness every May.   10
Last year is dead, they seem to say,
Begin afresh, afresh, afresh.

Glossary

See the critical commentary on p. 481.
9   *unresting castles* – here, the poet attempts to capture both the strength and movement of the trees.

Questions

Go to   p. 174   for more questions on Philip Larkin.

1. How would you describe the mood of the speaker in each of the three stanzas?
2. Someone has said of 'The Trees' that 'this poem provides us with a heartfelt celebration of the renewal to be glimpsed in the natural world'. Would you agree with this assessment of the poem?
3. Comment on the final couplet of the poem. To what extent do these lines emphasise the theme of 'The Trees'?

Exam-style Unseen Poem Questions

1. Write a response to 'The Trees', highlighting aspects of it that you liked and/or disliked.
2. Choose a line or two that you find particularly appealing and explain why.
3. Briefly describe the mood or feeling you get from reading this poem and illustrate your answer from the text.

The Explosion

On the day of the explosion
Shadows pointed towards the pithead:
In the sun the slagheap slept.

Down the lane came men in pitboots
Coughing oath-edged talk and pipe-smoke,   5
Shouldering off the freshened silence.

One chased after rabbits; lost them;
Came back with a nest of lark's eggs;
Showed them; lodged them in the grasses.

So they passed in beards and moleskins,   10
Fathers, brothers, nicknames, laughter,
Through the tall gates standing open.

At noon, there came a tremor; cows
Stopped chewing for a second; sun,
Scarfed as in a heat-haze, dimmed.   15

The dead go on before us, they
Are sitting in God's house in comfort,
We shall see them face to face—

Plain as lettering in the chapels
It was said, and for a second   20
Wives saw men of the explosion

Larger than in life they managed—
Gold as on a coin, or walking
Somehow from the sun towards them,

One showing the eggs unbroken.   25

Glossary

See the critical commentary on p. 483.
When reading 'The Explosion', one becomes aware that there is a perceptible shift in the poem from a realistic account of the disaster to a more surreal description of the survivors.

2 *pithead* – the top part of a mine including the shaft entrance and buildings.

3 *slagheap* – a man-made hill formed from the by-product of coal mining.

4 *pitboots* – heavy work boots worn by miners.

8 *lark's eggs* – the eggs of the skylark, a bird native to England and Ireland.

10 *moleskins* – a heavy-duty material worn by workmen, including miners.

15 *Scarfed* – wrapped up. The speaker could intend this to mean protected from the explosion.

Questions

Go to p. 174 for more questions on Philip Larkin.

1. What do you believe the theme of this poem is? Justify your answer by close reference to and quotation from the poem.

2. What impression do we get of the men in this poem? Where in the language of the poem is this impression created?

3. Comment on the final line of the poem. How important is this line to our understanding of 'The Explosion'?

Exam-style Unseen Poem Questions

1. Write a response to the above poem, highlighting the impact it makes on you.

2. Briefly describe the mood or feeling you get from reading this poem and illustrate your answer from the text.

3. Does this poem make you feel hopeful or unhopeful? Briefly explain why.

Cut Grass

Cut grass lies frail:
Brief is the breath
Mown stalks exhale.
Long, long the death

It dies in the white hours   5
Of young-leafed June
With chestnut flowers,
With hedges snowlike strewn,

White lilac bowed,
Lost lanes of Queen Anne's lace,   10
And that high-builded cloud
Moving at summer's pace.

Glossary

See the critical commentary on p. 486.

3 *exhale* – to breathe out.

10 *Queen Anne's lace* – a plant sometimes used in alternative medicine.

Questions

Go to p. 174 for more questions on Philip Larkin.

1. Comment on the form of the poem. Why do you think Larkin relies on short lines and a regular rhyming scheme in this poem? Support your answer by reference to or quotation from the poem.
2. What do you think the theme of this poem is?
3. Suggest an alternative title for this poem. Give reasons for your suggestion.

Exam-style Unseen Poem Questions

1. Write a response to 'Cut Grass', highlighting the impact it makes on you.
2. Choose a phrase or line from the poem that impressed you. Explain your choice.
3. Briefly describe the mood or feeling you get from reading this poem and illustrate your answer from the text.

Philip Larkin: An Overview

Now that you have read a selection of the poems by Philip Larkin on the course, you should take the time to look at the following general points. The purpose of this section is not to tell you what to think, but rather to help you to form your own opinions. When you have read these points, you may want to reread the poetry by Larkin on the course. You should notice that the general points made here could be used to form the backbone of your paragraphs when it comes to writing on Larkin's poetry. From now on, try to think about his poems not only in terms of what they say, but also in terms of how they say it. Open your mind to any reasonable interpretation of the poems; remember, your opinions are as valid as anything printed. However, you must be prepared to ground these opinions in fact. If you find this process difficult, that is entirely normal. Remember that a poem is not meant to be studied and dissected in the manner that the Leaving Certificate requires of us. While we have to keep the exam in mind, you should not allow it to detract from your enjoyment of the poetry on the course. Remember that Philip Larkin has long been recognised as one of the most important post-war English poets.

1. Larkin was deeply affected by his early family life. He viewed his parents' relationship as a reason to distrust the concept of lifelong commitment. Many of the poems on the course disparage the notion of enduring love.
2. Larkin's poetry tends to express a vision that is at once emotional and realistic. Poems such as 'Ambulances', 'An Arundel Tomb' and 'Church Going' are not afraid to confront difficult issues.
3. His poetry is often dominated by feelings of nostalgia for a way of life that has passed.
4. Typically, Larkin's poems tend to meditate on some ordinary object, place or event. While this meditation is normally provoked by everyday occurrences (the arrival of an ambulance, two racehorses in a field or an empty church), the conclusions reached are far from ordinary.
5. Larkin's poetry often draws on nature imagery to achieve its effect.
6. While the tone of his poems can be condescending or cynical, his poetry is also capable of exhibiting a warm tenderness.
7. The poems by Larkin on the Leaving Certificate course show that he is not afraid to tackle some of the more depressing realities of what it is to be alive. However, his poetry also affirms the possibility of continuity and a life after death.

Past Leaving Certificate Questions

The following question appeared on the Leaving Certificate paper of 2001.

> **Write an essay in which you outline your reasons for liking or disliking the poetry of Philip Larkin. Support your points by reference to the poetry of Philip Larkin that you have studied.**

The correctors were told to look out for the following points in any possible answer:

- The poet's unflinching honesty, his 'personality'.
- Modern, contemporary themes and ideas.
- His descriptive power – his use of interesting/powerful images.
- The disillusionment/pessimism of the work.
- His irony/his dry wit.
- His exploration of the dilemmas in the lives of ordinary people.

Sample Questions

Before you attempt these questions, you may want to consult the examination technique guidelines on p. 548.

1. 'Often we love a poet because of the feelings his or her poems create in us.'
   Write about the feelings that Philip Larkin's poetry creates in you and the aspects of the poems (their content and/or style) that help to create those feelings. Support your points by reference to the poetry by Larkin that you have studied.

2. Write a personal response to the poetry of Philip Larkin. Support the points you make by reference to or quotation from the poetry by Larkin you have studied.

3. 'The poetry of Philip Larkin appeals to the modern reader for many reasons.'
   Write an essay in which you outline the reasons why Philip Larkin's poetry has lasting appeal.

4. 'Larkin's poetry is realistic and uncompromising.'

   In light of this statement, write an overview of the poetry by Larkin that you have studied.

5. 'I found Larkin's poetry to be honest and interesting.'

   Referring to more than one poem by Larkin that you have studied, comment on this statement.

6. Imagine that you have been asked to edit a small selection of poetry by Philip Larkin. Say which poems you would include and why.

7. Comment on Larkin's use of language and imagery in his poetry. Support your answer by referring closely to or quoting from the poetry by Larkin on your course.

8. 'Philip Larkin's poetry provides us with thought-provoking explorations of universal themes.'

   Write an overview to the poetry by Philip Larkin that you have studied based on this statement.

9. 'Larkin is a deceptive poet. Often what appears as a straightforward commentary on a place or event can lead to much deeper discussion.'

   Referring to this statement, write a personal response to the poetry of Larkin that you have studied.

10. Imagine that you have been asked to compile a small collection of poetry by Philip Larkin entitled *Larkin: A Poet for All Mankind*. List the poems that you would choose and give reasons for their inclusion.

Sylvia Plath (1932–63)

Sylvia Plath grew up at a time of intense poetic ferment in the United States. It may surprise you to learn, however, that she wrote only two volumes of poetry before her suicide at the age of 31. During her short life, she craved fame but it was her posthumous collection, *Ariel*, which was published in 1965, that astonished the literary world. Despite its dark, brooding nature, this collection has become one of the best-selling volumes of poetry ever published.

Sylvia Plath is, quite simply, an iconic literary figure. From the myths that grew up around her following her suicide, she emerged larger than life. Her poems explore the depths of the human psyche and, as a result, can be confusing and difficult to understand. The mind is, after all, a confusing and difficult terrain to chart accurately. Yet notwithstanding its difficulty, her poetry is unforgettable. The harmony and musical quality of her language often give way to frighteningly dark statements about life and death. The unique and, at times, chillingly authentic voice that Plath fashioned from the tragedy of her life may not be one that you want to hear. Her poetry can be likened to dreams and nightmares. It is this ability to confront the darker sides of human consciousness that makes Plath's work so fascinating. If you would like to read more about Plath, please consult her biography on p. 487.

Black Rook in Rainy Weather

On the stiff twig up there
Hunches a wet black rook
Arranging and rearranging its feathers in the rain.
I do not expect a miracle
Or an accident   5

To set the sight on fire
In my eye, nor seek
Any more in the desultory weather some design,
But let spotted leaves fall as they fall,
Without ceremony, or portent.   10

Although, I admit, I desire,
Occasionally, some backtalk
From the mute sky, I can't honestly complain:
A certain minor light may still
Lean incandescent   15

Out of kitchen table or chair
As if a celestial burning took
Possession of the most obtuse objects now and then—
Thus hallowing an interval
Otherwise inconsequent   20

By bestowing largesse, honor,
One might say love. At any rate, I now walk
Wary (for it could happen
Even in this dull, ruinous landscape); skeptical,
Yet politic; ignorant   25

Of whatever angel may choose to flare
Suddenly at my elbow. I only know that a rook
Ordering its black feathers can so shine
As to seize my senses, haul
My eyelids up, and grant   30

A brief respite from fear
Of total neutrality. With luck,
Trekking stubborn through this season
Of fatigue, I shall
Patch together a content   35

Of sorts. Miracles occur,
If you care to call those spasmodic
Tricks of radiance miracles. The wait's begun again,
The long wait for the angel,
For that rare, random descent.   40

Glossary

See the critical commentary on p. 489.

8 *desultory* – aimless, random or disconnected.
10 *portent* – an omen or warning.
13 *mute* – silent.
15 *incandescent* – glowing or radiant.
17 *celestial* – heavenly.
18 *obtuse* – insensitive or thick.

19 *hallowing* – making holy.
20 *inconsequent* – illogical or disconnected.
21 *largesse* – generosity.
24 *ruinous* – disastrous or harmful.
31 *respite* – a break or interval.
37 *spasmodic* – intermittent or in fits and starts.
38 *radiance* – brightness.

Questions

Go to p. 199 for more questions on Sylvia Plath.

1. What do you think the rook symbolises in this poem?
2. Comment on the mood of the poem. Where in the language of the poem is this mood created?
3. What do you think the poet means when she says the rook grants her:

   A brief respite from fear
   Of total neutrality.

Exam-style Unseen Poem Questions

1. Write a short personal response to this poem. You may want to comment on the effect that the imagery and the central message of the poem had on you.
2. What impression of the speaker do you get from reading this poem? Support your view by reference to the poem.
3. Choose three images from the poem that you particularly liked or did not like. Give reasons for your choice.

The Times Are Tidy

Unlucky the hero born
In this province of the stuck record
Where the most watchful cooks go jobless
And the mayor's rôtisserie turns
Round of its own accord.   5

There's no career in the venture
Of riding against the lizard,
Himself withered these latter-days
To leaf-size from lack of action:
History's beaten the hazard.   10

The last crone got burnt up
More than eight decades back
With the love-hot herb, the talking cat,
But the children are better for it,
The cow milks cream an inch thick.   15

Glossary

See the critical commentary on p. 492.

2 *stuck record* – vinyl records preceded CDs and MP3 players as the most popular format for recorded music. Very often, the needle on a record player would become stuck. Here, the *image* of a stuck record is acting as a *metaphor* for things that remain stuck in their ways.

4 *rôtisserie* – a skewer that cooks meat.

11 *crone* – witch.

15 *The cow milks cream an inch thick* – it was believed that a cow's failure to produce creamy milk was the result of supernatural forces.

Questions

Go to 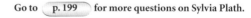 p. 199 for more questions on Sylvia Plath.

1. Referring closely to the poem, describe the speaker's attitude to the modern world.

2. Comment on the tone of this poem. Where in the language of the poem is the tone created?

3. What do you think the poet means when she says the following?

   There's no career in the venture

   Of riding against the lizard

Exam-style Unseen Poem Questions

1. Write a personal response to this poem. Your answer should make close reference to the text.

2. How effectively does the speaker contrast the past with the present in this poem? Support your answer by reference to or quotation from the poem.

3. Choose a phrase or line from the poem that impressed you. Explain your choice.

Morning Song

Love set you going like a fat gold watch.
The midwife slapped your footsoles, and your bald cry
Took its place among the elements.

Our voices echo, magnifying your arrival. New statue.
In a drafty museum, your nakedness   5
Shadows our safety. We stand round blankly as walls.

I'm no more your mother
Than the cloud that distills a mirror to reflect its own slow
Effacement at the wind's hand.

All night your moth-breath   10
Flickers among the flat pink roses. I wake to listen:
A far sea moves in my ear.

One cry, and I stumble from bed, cow-heavy and floral
In my Victorian nightgown.
Your mouth opens clean as a cat's. The window square   15

Whitens and swallows its dull stars. And now you try
Your handful of notes;
The clear vowels rise like balloons.

Glossary

2 *The midwife* – a person who is specialised in the delivery of babies.

3 *the elements* – in ancient times, the 'elements' were earth, air, fire and water.

7 *I'm no more your mother | Than the cloud that distills a mirror to reflect its own slow | Effacement* – here, Plath employs a complex **image** to describe the relationship between mother and child. The cloud produces the rain that forms puddles that, in turn, reflect the cloud.

8 *distills* – purifies.

9 *Effacement* – wiping or rubbing out.

13 *cow-heavy* – heavy with breast milk.

14 *Victorian* – a fashion typical of the period under Queen Victoria's reign (1837–1901). Here, Plath means that her nightdress is old-fashioned.

18 *vowels* – the letters a, e, i, o and u.

Questions

Go to p. 199 for more questions on Sylvia Plath.

1. Comment on the mood of the speaker at the end of this poem. Refer to the poem in your answer.

2. Suggest an alternative title for this poem. Give reasons for your suggestion.

3. What do you think the poet means when she says the following?

   I'm no more your mother

   Than the cloud that distills a mirror to reflect its own slow

   Effacement at the wind's hand.

Exam-style Unseen Poem Questions

1. Choose one phrase from this poem that you found particularly effective. Give reasons for your choice.

2. Write a short response to 'Morning Song' in which you outline your reasons for liking or not liking this poem. Refer closely to the poem in your answer.

3. Do you think the poem gives a surprising insight into the motherhood experience? In your answer, you might consider:
   - The precise and simple nature of the language.
   - The words and images in the poem.

(handwritten, top left) → Lands end

(handwritten, top right) → blank verse
Follows Rhythmic
pattern but not a
regular Rhyming
scheme

Finisterre

This was the land's end: the last fingers, knuckled and rheumatic,
Cramped on nothing. Black

(handwritten) Po 498

Admonitory cliffs, and the sea exploding
With no bottom, or anything on the other side of it,
Whitened by the faces of the drowned.   5
Now it is only gloomy, a dump of rocks—
Leftover soldiers from old, messy wars.
The sea cannons into their ear, but they don't budge.   *(handwritten)* – turbulent sea
Other rocks hide their grudges under the water.   *(handwritten)* – turbulent State of mind.

The cliffs are edged with trefoils, stars and bells   10
Such as fingers might embroider, close to death,
Almost too small for the mists to bother with.
The mists are part of the ancient paraphernalia—   *(handwritten)* Death
Souls, rolled in the doom-noise of the sea.
They bruise the rocks out of existence, then resurrect them.   15
They go up without hope, like sighs.   *(handwritten)* personification
I walk among them, and they stuff my mouth with cotton.   *(handwritten)* Cant talk about her Mental health
When they free me, I am beaded with tears.   *(handwritten)* (?)

Our Lady of the Shipwrecked is striding toward the horizon,
Her marble skirts blown back in two pink wings.   20
A marble sailor kneels at her foot distractedly, and at his foot
A peasant woman in black   *(handwritten)* Vasilating between two states of mind
Is praying to the monument of the sailor praying.
Our Lady of the Shipwrecked is three times life size,
Her lips sweet with divinity.   25
She does not hear what the sailor or the peasant is saying—
She is in love with the beautiful formlessness of the sea.

Gull-colored laces flap in the sea drafts   *(handwritten)* Stillance → Sea
Beside the postcard stalls.
The peasants anchor them with conches. One is told: 30
'These are the pretty trinkets the sea hides,

(handwritten) Retracts of Cliffs edge

beauty from times of anguish → Crucible

Ted Hughes?

Little shells made up into necklaces and toy ladies.

They do not come from the Bay of the Dead down there,

But from another place, tropical and blue,

We have never been to.

These are our crêpes. Eat them before they blow cold.'

Make the most of it 35

Glossary

plath Crucible - her hardship - Mental anguish

See the critical commentary on p. 496.
The title, 'Finisterre', refers to a *département* in the northernmost part of Brittany in France. The name 'Finisterre' means 'land's end'. Plath visited the area in 1961.

1 *rheumatic* – this is a reference to rheumatism. The hands and knuckles of people suffering from this condition often become disfigured. Plath is using the *image* of an arthritic hand to describe the Breton landscape. Notice, also, how the physical shape of the poem approximates the shape of a jagged coastline.

3 *Admonitory* – warning.

10 *trefoils* – any three-leafed plant, such as shamrock or clover. Trefoils often appear on coats of arms.

13 *paraphernalia* – equipment or bits and pieces.

19 *Our Lady of the Shipwrecked* – here, the poet refers to a statue of Our Lady (the mother of Jesus Christ) who prays for the dead souls of the shipwrecked sailors.

27 *formlessness* – without shape.

30 *conches* – large seashells.

31 *trinkets* – small, ornamental pieces of little value.

36 *crêpes* – this type of pancake is a speciality of Brittany.

Mettle - What you're made of

Questions

Go to p. 199 for more questions on Sylvia Plath.

1. Why do you think the poet chose the title 'Finisterre' for this poem? Give reasons for your answer.

2. What do you think the sea represents in this poem? Give reasons for your answer.

3. Comment on the manner in which the poet moves from the inner thoughts of the speaker to an objective view of the sea.

Exam-style Unseen Poem Questions

1. 'This is a disturbing poem.' Do you agree or disagree with this statement? Refer closely to the poem in your answer.

2. Describe the impact this poem makes on you as a reader.

3. Choose three images from this poem that you found particularly effective. Give reasons for your choice.

plaths mettle is tested as she goes through her crucible which is her life,

Mirror

I am silver and exact. I have no preconceptions.
Whatever I see I swallow immediately
Just as it is, unmisted by love or dislike.
I am not cruel, only truthful—
The eye of a little god, four-cornered.   5
Most of the time I meditate on the opposite wall.
It is pink, with speckles. I have looked at it so long
I think it is a part of my heart. But it flickers.
Faces and darkness separate us over and over.

Now I am a lake. A woman bends over me,   10
Searching my reaches for what she really is.
Then she turns to those liars, the candles or the moon.
I see her back, and reflect it faithfully.
She rewards me with tears and an agitation of hands.
I am important to her. She comes and goes.   15
Each morning it is her face that replaces the darkness.
In me she has drowned a young girl, and in me an old woman
Rises toward her day after day, like a terrible fish.

Glossary

See the critical commentary on p. 499.

1 *preconceptions* – fixed ideas.

3 *unmisted* – here, the poet uses this word to mean that the mirror's judgement is not clouded by love or any other emotions.

6 *meditate* – to ponder or contemplate.

11 *reaches* – range or extent of the mirror's surface.

14 *agitation of hands* – shaking of hands.

Questions

Go to p. 199 for more questions on Sylvia Plath.

1. How well does the language of the poem capture the mirror's essence? Refer to the poem in your answer.

2. What do you think the theme of this poem is? Support your answer by reference to or quotation from the poem.

3. Do you believe that the mirror is 'truthful'? Give reasons for your answer.

Exam-style Unseen Poem Questions

1. Choose a phrase or line from the poem that impressed you. Explain your choice.

2. Write a personal response to this poem. Your answer should make close reference to the text.

3. Discuss the ways in which this poem captures the darker side of the poet's personality.

Pheasant

You said you would kill it this morning.
Do not kill it. It startles me still,
The jut of that odd, dark head, pacing

Through the uncut grass on the elm's hill.
It is something to own a pheasant,   5
Or just to be visited at all.

I am not mystical: it isn't
As if I thought it had a spirit.
It is simply in its element.

That gives it a kingliness, a right.   10
The print of its big foot last winter,
The tail-track, on the snow in our court—

The wonder of it, in that pallor,
Through crosshatch of sparrow and starling.
Is it its rareness, then? It is rare.   15

But a dozen would be worth having,
A hundred, on that hill—green and red,
Crossing and recrossing: a fine thing!

It is such a good shape, so vivid.
It's a little cornucopia.   20
It unclaps, brown as a leaf, and loud,

Settles in the elm, and is easy.
It was sunning in the narcissi.
I trespass stupidly. Let be, let be.

Glossary

See the critical commentary on p. 501.

1 *You* – this is most likely a reference to her husband, the poet Ted Hughes.

3 *The jut* – the sticking out of, or the sharp movement. Here, the poet is attempting to capture the physical characteristics of the pheasant.

7 *mystical* – supernatural or spiritual.

12 *The tail-track* – a pheasant has a very long tail feather which brushes against the ground. In the snow, this tail would leave a trail.

13 *pallor* – whiteness or paleness.

14 *crosshatch* – shaded by intersecting lines.

14 *sparrow and starling* – small brown birds.

19 *vivid* – clear.

20 *cornucopia* – an abundance or profusion.

23 *narcissi* – brightly coloured spring flowers that resemble daffodils.

Questions

Go to p. 199 for more questions on Sylvia Plath.

1. In your opinion, how well does the speaker describe the pheasant? Support your answer by reference to or quotation from the poem.

2. Suggest an alternative title for this poem. Support your answer by close reference to the poem.

3. Comment on the final line of the poem. In your opinion, why does the poet decide to 'Let' the pheasant 'be'?

Exam-style Unseen Poem Questions

1. Write a response to 'Pheasant', highlighting the impact it makes on you.

2. Choose a phrase or line from the poem that impressed you. Explain your choice.

3. Write down one phrase from the poem that captures how the poet feels about the pheasant. Say why you have chosen this phrase.

Elm

For Ruth Fainlight

I know the bottom, she says. I know it with my great tap root:
It is what you fear.
I do not fear it: I have been there.

Is it the sea you hear in me,
Its dissatisfactions?   5
Or the voice of nothing, that was your madness?

Love is a shadow.
How you lie and cry after it
Listen: these are its hooves: it has gone off, like a horse.

All night I shall gallop thus, impetuously,   10
Till your head is a stone, your pillow a little turf,
Echoing, echoing.

Or shall I bring you the sound of poisons?
This is rain now, this big hush.
And this is the fruit of it: tin-white, like arsenic.   15

I have suffered the atrocity of sunsets.
Scorched to the root
My red filaments burn and stand, a hand of wires.

Now I break up in pieces that fly about like clubs.
A wind of such violence   20
Will tolerate no bystanding: I must shriek.

The moon, also, is merciless: she would drag me
Cruelly, being barren.
Her radiance scathes me. Or perhaps I have caught her.

I let her go. I let her go   25
Diminished and flat, as after radical surgery.
How your bad dreams possess and endow me.

I am inhabited by a cry.
Nightly it flaps out
Looking, with its hooks, for something to love.   30

I am terrified by this dark thing
That sleeps in me;
All day I feel its soft, feathery turnings, its malignity.

Clouds pass and disperse.
Are those the faces of love, those pale irretrievables?   35
Is it for such I agitate my heart?

I am incapable of more knowledge.
What is this, this face
So murderous in its strangle of branches?—

Its snaky acids kiss.   40
It petrifies the will. These are the isolate, slow faults
That kill, that kill, that kill.

Glossary

See the critical commentary on p. 503.

The title of the poem, 'Elm', refers to the majestic and stately deciduous tree. Ruth Fainlight is an American poet born in New York in 1931. The poem takes the form of a dialogue between the speaker and the elm tree. In the opening line, it is the elm that speaks first.

1 *tap root* – the principal root in the tree.

5 *dissatisfactions* – disappointments. Notice how the sound of the word approximates the sound of the rustling of leaves. This effect is known as **onomatopoeia**.

10 *impetuously* – impulsively, rashly.

15 *arsenic* – a powerful, white-coloured poison that kills almost instantly. The poet may be associating this **image** with snow.

16 *atrocity* – an extremely violent incident or massacre.

18 *filaments* – thin wires or fibres.

19 clubs – a thick stick used as a weapon. Here, the poet is likening the branches of the tree to clubs.

21 *shriek* – scream.

23 *being barren* – unable to conceive children.

24 *radiance* – brightness.

24 *scathes* – causes harm.

26 *flat, as after radical surgery* – in this disturbing **simile**, Plath compares the moon to a woman who has had her breasts removed.

27 *endow me* – bestow on me. Here, the speaker is asking the tree to bestow on her some of its qualities.

33 *malignity* – evil or illness.

34 *disperse* – scatter.

35 *irretrievables* – those things that cannot be returned to how they were.

36 *agitate* – worry or trouble.

40 *its snaky acids kiss* – its snake-like poisons. Note that some editions use the word 'hiss' instead of 'kiss' here.

41 *petrifies* – turns to stone or frozen with fear.

41 *isolate* – separate.

Questions

Go to p. 199 for more questions on Sylvia Plath.

1. 'This is a dark and disturbing poem.' Do you agree or disagree with this statement? Give reasons for your opinion.

2. Comment on the sound effects Plath employs in the poem.

3. It has been said of 'Elm' that it has 'the surreal quality of a nightmare'. Would you agree with this assessment of the poem? Support your answer by reference to the poem.

Exam-style Unseen Poem Questions

1. Do you think the poem gives an honest insight into the poet's state of mind? In your answer, you might consider:
   - The precise and simple nature of the language.
   - The words and images in the poem.

2. Comment on the way in which different voices emerge from the poem.

3. Write a personal response to this poem. Refer closely to the poem in your answer.

Poppies in July

Little poppies, little hell flames,
Do you do no harm?

You flicker. I cannot touch you.
I put my hands among the flames. Nothing burns.

And it exhausts me to watch you   5
Flickering like that, wrinkly and clear red, like the skin of a mouth.

A mouth just bloodied.
Little bloody skirts!

There are fumes that I cannot touch.
Where are your opiates, your nauseous capsules?   10

If I could bleed, or sleep!—
If my mouth could marry a hurt like that!

Or your liquors seep to me, in this glass capsule,
Dulling and stilling.

But colorless. Colorless.   15

Glossary

See the critical commentary on p. 507.
The title, 'Poppies in July', is significant. Opiates are extracted from the seeds of these small red flowers. Many opiate-based drugs, such as heroin, are obtained from poppies; as a result, the flower has often been associated with delirium.

1   *little hell flames* – given that the flowers are red, the speaker views them as being like flames.

9   *fumes* – this is a reference to the drugs that can be obtained from the poppies.

10   *opiates* – narcotics.

10   *nauseous* – sickening.

13   *liquors* – juices.

13   *glass capsule* – drugs are often contained in a glass vile.

15   *colorless* – this is most likely a reference to the general numbing of the senses that opiates can induce.

Questions

Go to   p. 199   for more questions on Sylvia Plath.

1.   Comment on the use of colour in 'Poppies in July'. Refer to the poem in your answer.

2.   Suggest an alternative title for this poem. Support your answer by close reference to the poem.

3.   What do you think the poppies symbolise in this poem? Give reasons for your answer by referring to the poem.

Exam-style Unseen Poem Questions

1.   Write a response to 'Poppies in July', highlighting aspects of it that you liked and/or disliked.

2.   How would you describe the poet's state of mind in this poem? Justify your answer by referring closely to the poem. In your answer, you might consider:
   •   The precise and simple nature of the language.
   •   The words and images in the poem.

3.   In your opinion, what is the mood of this poem?

The Arrival of the Bee Box

[handwritten annotation: Double meaning]

I ordered this, this clean wood box
Square as a chair and almost too heavy to lift. *[handwritten: Dark humour]*
I would say it was the coffin of a midget *[handwritten: Contrast]*
Or a square baby *[handwritten: tragic]*
Were there not such a din in it.   5

The box is locked, it is dangerous.
I have to live with it overnight
And I can't keep away from it.
There are no windows, so I can't see what is in there.
There is only a little grid, no exit.   10

I put my eye to the grid.
It is dark, dark,
With the swarmy feeling of African hands
Minute and shrunk for export,
Black on black, angrily clambering. *[handwritten: assonance]*   15

How can I let them out?
It is the noise that appalls me most of all,
The unintelligible syllables.
It is like a Roman mob,
Small, taken one by one, but my god, together!   20

I lay my ear to furious Latin.
I am not a Caesar.
I have simply ordered a box of maniacs.
They can be sent back.
They can die, I need feed them nothing, I am the owner.   25

I wonder how hungry they are.
I wonder if they would forget me
If I just undid the locks and stood back and turned into a tree.
There is the laburnum, its blond colonnades,
And the petticoats of the cherry.   30

[handwritten annotation: → assonance = Repetition of vowel sounds in middle of words]

They might ignore me immediately
In my moon suit and funeral veil.
I am no source of honey
So why should they turn on me? _[handwritten annotation: * Rhyming couplet]_
Tomorrow I will be sweet God, I will set them free.   35

The box is only temporary. _[handwritten: ?]_

[handwritten annotation: end Rhyming / Internal Rhyme = within a line]

Glossary

See the critical commentary on p. 509.
5   *din* – loud noise or racket.
10 *grid* – a metal grille.
13 *African hands* – most likely, the poet is referring to African bees.
17 *appalls* – shocks or upsets.
18 *unintelligible* – incoherent or garbled.
18 *syllables* – the sounds that make up the parts of a word.
19 *mob* – a noisy, often violent, gathering of people.

22 *Caesar* – Julius Caesar, the famous Roman ruler who laid the foundations for the Roman Empire.
23 *maniacs* – crazy people.
29 *laburnum* – a type of tree with long yellow flowers.
29 *colonnades* – pillars.
30 *petticoats* – underskirts.
32 *moon suit* – the protective suit worn by bee-keepers resembles that worn by astronauts.

Questions

Go to p. 199 for more questions on Sylvia Plath.

1. Why do you think the poet chooses to use the personal pronoun 'I' so much in this poem? Give reasons for your answer.
2. This poem has been described as 'providing a disturbing and frightening insight into Plath's state of mind'. Would you agree with this assessment of the poem? Support your answer by reference to the poem.
3. What do you think the central theme of this poem is? In your answer, refer to the tone and mood of the poem. _[handwritten annotation: → monotonous – boring]_

Exam-style Unseen Poem Questions

1. Choose two phrases from the poem that describe how the speaker feels. Write each one down and say, in each case, why you have chosen it.
2. Write a personal response to 'The Arrival of the Bee Box'.
3. Briefly describe the mood or feeling you get from reading this poem and illustrate your answer from the text.

Child

Your clear eye is the one absolutely beautiful thing.
I want to fill it with color and ducks,
The zoo of the new

Whose names you meditate—
April snowdrop, Indian pipe,   5
Little

Stalk without wrinkle,
Pool in which images
Should be grand and classical

Not this troublous   10
Wringing of hands, this dark
Ceiling without a star.

Glossary

See the critical commentary on p. 511.

5 *Indian pipe* – a small flower native to North America.

6 *Little | Stalk* – little stem of the plant.

9 *classical* – beautiful or statuesque.

10 *troublous* – agitated or full of trouble.

Questions

Go to p. 199 for more questions on Sylvia Plath.

1. Describe the speaker's feelings towards the child in the opening stanzas.

2. In what ways is the adult speaker contrasted with the child in the poem?

3. 'This poem uses beautiful language to capture a sad reality.' Comment on this statement by referring closely to the poem.

Exam-style Unseen Poem Questions

1. How did this poem make you feel? Justify your answer by making close reference to the poem.

2. Do you think the poem gives a surprising insight into the experience of parenthood? In your answer, you might consider:
   - The precise and simple nature of the language.
   - The words and images in the poem.

3. Choose a line or two that you find particularly appealing and explain why.

An Overview

ve read a selection of Plath's poetry, you should take the time to owing general points. The purpose of these is not to tell you what rather to help you to form your own opinions. When you have read these ʹ s, you may wish to take the time to reread Plath's poetry. You should notice that the general points made here can be used to form the backbone of your paragraphs when it comes to writing on poetry. From now on, try to think about Plath's poems not only in terms of what they say, but also in terms of how they say it. Open your mind to any reasonable interpretation of the poems; remember, your opinions are as valid as anything printed. However, you must be prepared to ground these opinions in fact. If you find this process difficult, that is entirely normal. Remember that a poem is not meant to be studied and dissected in the manner that the Leaving Certificate requires of us. While we have to keep the exam in mind, you should not allow it to detract from your enjoyment of the poetry on the course.

1. Plath's poetry is dark and disturbing. She confronts the murky recesses of her psyche in a bold and thoroughly unique manner.
2. Despite the latent violence and powerful emotions contained in so many of Plath's poems, her style is at all times measured and controlled.
3. Nearly all of the poems by Plath on the course contain the personal pronoun 'I'. In this sense, her poems tend to be brutally honest explorations of her deepest fears and desires.
4. Plath had a difficult life that ended in the tragedy of her suicide. This tragic aspect to her personality is fully represented in her poems.
5. The selection of poems by Plath on the course contains some very unusual and unexpected images, metaphors and similes. Plath often examines the world in obsessive detail. The result is a body of poetry that is as articulate as it is intense.

This list of general points is, of course, in no way exhaustive; there are quite literally thousands of perfectly valid observations to be made about the poetry of Sylvia Plath. Finally, as you reread her poems in this anthology, try to do so with an open mind. Remember, your opinion is as valid as any of the points mentioned here. Try to consult these points frequently, as they will help you when it comes to writing essays.

Past Leaving Certificate Questions

In 2004, students were asked to answer the following question on Sylvia Plath.

> **'I like (or do not like) to read the poetry of Sylvia Plath.'**
> **Respond to this statement, referring to the poetry by Sylvia Plath on your course.**

In that year, the correctors were told to look out for the following possible points:

- Striking originality – a distinctive poetic voice.
- Language and imagery are unusual, startling.
- Poetry offers insights into her life.
- Intensity and energy of the verse.
- An interesting preoccupation with life's darker side.
- The density, complexity of the poems.

Sample Questions

Before you try this question, you may wish to consult the examination technique guidelines on p. 548.

1. 'Reading Sylvia Plath.'
   Write out the text of a short article you would write for a school magazine using the above title as a starting point. Support your point of view by reference to the poetry of Plath that you have studied.
2. If you were asked to give a public reading of a small selection of Sylvia Plath's poems, which ones would you choose to read? Give reasons for your choices, supporting them by reference to the poems on your course.
3. Write an essay in which you outline your reasons for liking or disliking the poetry of Sylvia Plath. Support your points by reference to her poetry.
4. Write a personal response to the poems by Sylvia Plath on your course. Support your points with reference to the poetry on your course.

5. Write a speech to be delivered to your classmates on the impact that Sylvia Plath's poetry had on you. Your answer should focus on both themes and the use of imagery/language. Support your answer with the aid of suitable reference to the poems on your course.

6. 'Sylvia Plath – a poet who looks at the world in an unusual way.'
   Write an introduction to the poetry of Sylvia Plath using the above title. Your introduction should address her themes and the impact of her poetry on you as a reader. Support your points with reference to the poems you have studied.

7. Write an introduction to the poetry of Sylvia Plath for new readers. Your introduction should cover the following:
   • The ideas that were most important to her.
   • How you responded to her use of language and imagery.
   Refer closely to the poems by Sylvia Plath that you have studied.

8. 'What Sylvia Plath's poetry means to me.'
   Write an essay in response to the above title. Your essay should include a discussion of her themes and the way she expresses them. Support the points you make by reference to the poetry on your course.

9. Imagine you have been asked to edit a small collection of poetry by Sylvia Plath. State what poems you would suggest for inclusion and give reasons for your choice.

10. It has been said of Plath's poetry that 'it is too dark and depressing and should not be included on the Leaving Certificate syllabus'. Write a personal essay on the poetry of Sylvia Plath in which you argue for or against the inclusion of her poetry on the Leaving Certificate syllabus.

Adrienne Rich (1929–)

Adrienne Rich is one of America's most distinguished poets. Over the past 40 years, she has published more than 16 volumes of poetry and four books of prose essays. Rich's poems aim at self-exploration and at establishing the limits of the self, but they also reject any suggestion that such insights should remain solitary and unshared. She is deeply committed to the struggle for women's rights and social justice and much of her poetry reflects this. Her work has challenged assumptions about women and Western society and she has given many women the vocabulary to talk about their experiences. Rich's work exemplifies the idea that personal experience is political, meaning that the manner in which we lead our lives has civic and political consequences that affect the wider world. If you would like to read more about Adrienne Rich, please consult the biography on p. 514.

Aunt Jennifer's Tigers

Aunt Jennifer's tigers prance across a screen,
Bright topaz denizens of a world of green.
They do not fear the men beneath the tree;
They pace in sleek chivalric certainty.

Aunt Jennifer's fingers fluttering through her wool   5
Find even the ivory needle hard to pull.
The massive weight of Uncle's wedding band
Sits heavily upon Aunt Jennifer's hand.

When Aunt is dead, her terrified hands will lie
Still ringed with ordeals she was mastered by.   10
The tigers in the panel that she made
Will go on prancing, proud and unafraid.

Glossary

See the critical commentary on p. 519.

1 *prance* – to flounce, frolic or strut.

2 *topaz* – a translucent, yellow or sometimes pale blue precious stone.

2 *denizens* – occupants or dwellers.

4 *chivalric* – acting honourably or in accordance with the code of chivalry, as practised by medieval knights.

5 *fluttering* – trembling or flickering.

6 *ivory* – a hard, creamy white substance from which elephants' tusks are made. It can also be used as an adjective to describe something that is creamy or off-white in colour. Notice how many of the words used in the poem are associated with adventure and hunting.

11 *panel* – a flat board on which embroidery is sometimes placed. In this case, the tigers that Aunt Jennifer has embroidered are placed on a decorative board.

Questions

Go to p. 226 for more questions on Adrienne Rich.

1. What aspects of Aunt Jenifer's personality are revealed in her embroidery?

2. In your opinion, why does the poet describe 'Uncle's wedding band' as being like a 'massive weight'?

3. Comment on the final stanza of the poem. Do you think the poem ends on a positive note? Give reasons for your answer.

Exam-style Unseen Poem Questions

1. Write a short personal response to this poem.

2. What do you feel the tigers in the poem represent?

3. Choose a line from the poem that you found appealing and say why.

The Uncle Speaks in the Drawing Room

I have seen the mob of late
Standing sullen in the square,
Gazing with a sullen stare
At window, balcony, and gate.
Some have talked in bitter tones,   5
Some have held and fingered stones.

These are follies that subside.
Let us consider, none the less,
Certain frailties of glass
Which, it cannot be denied,   10
Lead in times like these to fear
For crystal vase and chandelier.

Not that missiles will be cast;
None as yet dare lift an arm.
But the scene recalls a storm   15
When our grandsire stood aghast
To see his antique ruby bowl
Shivered in a thunder-roll.

Let us only bear in mind
How these treasures handed down   20
From a calmer age passed on
Are in the keeping of our kind.
We stand between the dead glass-blowers
And murmurings of missile-throwers.

Glossary

See the critical commentary on p. 521.

1 *mob* – an angry crowd. The uncle watches this mob from his balcony. Notice how class distinctions are indicated in a subtle manner.

2 *sullen* – dour or grim.

7 *follies* – foolish activities.

16 *grandsire* – normally a grandfather, but it can also mean any ancestor.

16 *aghast* – amazed or horrified.

17 *ruby* – dark red.

Questions

Go to p. 226 for more questions on Adrienne Rich.

1. From your reading of the poem, what sort of person do you imagine the uncle to be?

2. Suggest an alternative title for this poem. Give reasons for your choice of title by referring closely to the poem.

3. What do you think the theme of this poem is? Refer closely to the poem in your answer.

Exam-style Unseen Poem Questions

1. Write a short personal response to this poem in which you outline how the poem made you feel. Support your answer by close reference to the poem.

2. Briefly describe the mood or feeling you get from reading this poem and illustrate your answer from the text.

3. Choose a phrase or line from the poem that impressed you. Explain your choice.

Power

Living   in the earth-deposits   of our history

Today a backhoe divulged   out of a crumbling flank of earth
one bottle   amber   perfect   a hundred-year-old
cure for fever   or melancholy   a tonic
for living on this earth   in the winters of this climate   5

Today I was reading about Marie Curie:
she must have known she suffered   from radiation sickness
her body bombarded for years   by the element
she had purified
It seems she denied to the end   10
the source of the cataracts on her eyes
the cracked and suppurating skin   of her finger-ends
till she could no longer hold   a test-tube or a pencil

She died   a famous woman   denying
her wounds   15
denying
her wounds   came   from the same source as her power

Glossary

See the critical commentary on p. 523.

1 *earth-deposits* – an archaeological term referring to material left in the earth from a previous age.

2 *backhoe* – a mechanical digger.

2 *flank* – side or border.

3 *amber* – an orange-yellowish colour. In terms of archaeology, amber is the name applied to a yellowish fossil resin.

4 *melancholy* – sadness. In the past, melancholy was the general term used to describe depression.

4 *tonic* – a stimulant designed to improve health or vitality.

6 *Marie Curie* – along with her husband, the Polish-born Marie Curie discovered two new elements: radium and polonium. Her work with radioactive material eventually killed her.

7 *radiation sickness* – when living flesh is exposed to radioactive rays, it is damaged. The resultant disease is known as radiation sickness. This condition was poorly understood until the attacks on Hiroshima and Nagasaki.

8 *bombarded* – attacked or bombed.

8 *element* – a substance that can't be broken down into smaller or simpler parts.

9 *purified* – cleansed or filtered.

11 *cataracts* – an eye condition where the lens of the eye becomes clouded over, making it impossible to see.

12 *suppurating* – oozing puss.

Questions

Go to p. 226 for more questions on Adrienne Rich.

1. What do you think is the theme of this poem? Illustrate your answer by close reference to the poem.

2. In your opinion, what impact did the life and work of Marie Curie have on the poet? Support your answer by close reference to the text.

3. How does the poet justify her claim in the final stanza that Marie Curie's wounds came from the same source as her power?

Exam-style Unseen Poem Questions

1. Describe the impact that this poem makes on you as a reader.

2. Choose a line or phrase from the poem that impressed you. Give reasons for your choice.

3. Is this poem still relevant today? Give reasons for your answer.

Storm Warnings

The glass has been falling all the afternoon,
And knowing better than the instrument
What winds are walking overhead, what zone
Of gray unrest is moving across the land,
I leave the book upon a pillowed chair   5
And walk from window to closed window, watching
Boughs strain against the sky

And think again, as often when the air
Moves inward toward a silent core of waiting,
How with a single purpose time has traveled   10
By secret currents of the undiscerned
Into this polar realm. Weather abroad
And weather in the heart alike come on
Regardless of prediction.

Between foreseeing and averting change   15
Lies all the mastery of elements
Which clocks and weatherglasses cannot alter.
Time in the hand is not control of time,
Nor shattered fragments of an instrument
A proof against the wind; the wind will rise,   20
We can only close the shutters.

I draw the curtains as the sky goes black
And set a match to candles sheathed in glass
Against the keyhole draught, the insistent whine
Of weather through the unsealed aperture.   25
This is our sole defense against the season;
These are the things that we have learned to do
Who live in troubled regions.

Glossary

See the critical commentary on p. 525.

1 *The glass* – a barometer or an instrument that measures the atmospheric pressure and can predict weather patterns.
7 *Boughs* – branches.
11 *undiscerned* – not recognised.

15 *averting* – preventing or avoiding.
16 *elements* – the weather.
17 *weatherglasses* – a barometer or device for predicting the weather.
25 *aperture* – opening or hole.

Questions

Go to ⟨ p. 226 ⟩ for more questions on Adrienne Rich.

1. Suggest an alternative title for this poem. Give reasons for your suggestion.
2. How well does the poet create a sense of tension and foreboding in the poem? Support your answer by reference to the poem.
3. What do you think the poet means when she says, 'These are the things that we have learned to do | Who live in troubled regions'?

Exam-style Unseen Poem Questions

1. Choose a line or two from the poem that you found particularly appealing and say why you chose it.
2. What impact did this poem have on you? Refer closely to the poem in your answer.
3. Do you think the poem gives a surprising insight into depression or a troubled state of mind? In your answer, you might consider:
    *   The pattern of the speaker's thinking.
    *   The words and images in the poem.

Living in Sin

She had thought the studio would keep itself;
no dust upon the furniture of love.
Half heresy, to wish the taps less vocal,
the panes relieved of grime. A plate of pears,
a piano with a Persian shawl, a cat   5
stalking the picturesque amusing mouse
had risen at his urging.
Not that at five each separate stair would writhe
under the milkman's tramp; that morning light
so coldly would delineate the scraps   10
of last night's cheese and three sepulchral bottles;
that on the kitchen shelf among the saucers
a pair of beetle-eyes would fix her own—
envoy from some village in the moldings ...
Meanwhile, he, with a yawn,   15
sounded a dozen notes upon the keyboard,
declared it out of tune, shrugged at the mirror,
rubbed at his beard, went out for cigarettes;
while she, jeered by the minor demons,
pulled back the sheets and made the bed and found   20
a towel to dust the table-top,
and let the coffee-pot boil over on the stove.
By evening she was back in love again,
though not so wholly but throughout the night
she woke sometimes to feel the daylight coming   25
like a relentless milkman up the stairs.

Glossary

See the critical commentary on p. 528.
The title, 'Living in Sin', is a term that was commonly used in the past to describe a couple who lived together without being married.

1   *studio* – a small apartment.
3   *heresy* – a belief which goes against traditional religious teachings.
4   *grime* – a film of dirt.
5   *Persian* – an adjective describing the ancient Persian Empire. Persia (modern-day Iran) was noted for its exquisite fabrics, especially rugs and tapestries; its empire dominated Mesopotamia (composing parts of Iraq, Turkey and Syria) from 612 to 330 BC.

6   *picturesque* – charming or visually pleasing.
7   *urging* – demand.
8   *writhe* – squirm or wriggle.
9   *tramp* – heavy or noisy walk.
10   *delineate* – define or mark out.
11   *sepulchral* – gloomy or tomblike.
14   *moldings* – American spelling for 'mouldings', the engraved wood or plasterwork in a building.
19   *jeered* – taunted.
19   *demons* – evil spirits or devils.

Questions

Go to   p. 226   for more questions on Adrienne Rich.

1. Comment on the title of the poem. Do you think it is in any way unusual? Support your answer by close reference to the poem.

2. How does the poet convey this young woman's sense of disappointment? Support your answer by reference to the poem.

3. What impression do we get of the man in the poem? Support your answer by reference to the text.

Exam-style Unseen Poem Questions

1. Do you like the world of this couple that the poet describes in this poem? Give reasons for your answer, supporting them by reference to the text.

2. Write down one phrase from the poem that shows how the woman feels about her relationship.

3. How does this poem make you feel? Briefly explain why. Support your answer by referring to or quoting from the poem.

The Roofwalker

—for Denise Levertov

Over the half-finished houses
night comes. The builders
stand on the roof. It is
quiet after the hammers,
the pulleys hang slack.   5
Giants, the roofwalkers,
on a listing deck, the wave
of darkness about to break
on their heads. The sky
is a torn sail where figures   10
pass magnified, shadows
on a burning deck.

I feel like them up there:
exposed, larger than life,
and due to break my neck.   15

Was it worth while to lay—
with infinite exertion—
a roof I can't live under?
—All those blueprints,
closings of gaps,   20
measurings, calculations?
A life I didn't choose
chose me: even
my tools are the wrong ones
for what I have to do.   25
I'm naked, ignorant,
a naked man fleeing
across the roofs
who could with a shade of difference
be sitting in the lamplight   30

against the cream wallpaper

reading—not with indifference—

about a naked man

fleeing across the roofs.

Glossary

See the critical commentary on p. 531.
The dedicatee was Denise Levertov (1923–97), an Anglo-American poet born in Ilford, Essex, England. After working as a nurse during the Second World War, she emigrated to the United States and became a US citizen in 1955. Her poetry often reflects on difficult social issues, such as the horrors of the Vietnam War.

5   *pulleys* – a winch or small crane used to lift building materials.
5   *slack* – loose.
7   *listing* – swaying or tilting.
7   *the wave | of darkness about to break* – here, the poet likens the sensation of swaying on the roof to a ship's deck.
17 *infinite exertion* – endless physical effort.
19 *blueprints* – plans for a building on paper.

Questions

Go to **p. 226** for more questions on Adrienne Rich.

1. Why do you think the poet finds it so easy to identify with the roofwalker?

2. In your opinion, what is the theme of this poem? Support your answer by close reference to the poem.

3. In your opinion, what does Rich mean when she says:

    A life I didn't choose

    chose me: even

    my tools are the wrong ones

    for what I have to do.

    Support your answer by close reference to the text.

Exam-style Unseen Poem Questions

1. Choose a phrase from the poem that you found particularly enjoyable and say why you found it so.

2. Write a personal response to this poem. Support your answer by referring to or quoting from the poem.

3. Do you think the poem gives a surprising insight into the creative process? In your answer, you might consider:
    *   The pattern of the speaker's thinking.
    *   The words and images in the poem.

Our Whole Life

Our whole life a translation
the permissible fibs

and now a knot of lies
eating at itself to get undone

Words bitten thru words   5

meanings burnt-off like paint
under the blowtorch

All those dead letters
rendered into the oppressor's language

Trying to tell the doctor where it hurts   10
like the Algerian
who has walked from his village, burning

his whole body a cloud of pain
and there are no words for this

except himself   15

Glossary

See the critical commentary on p. 535.

1   *translation* – conversion, usually from one language to another.
2   *permissible* – allowable or tolerable.

2   *fibs* – lies.
7   *blowtorch* – an instrument used to remove paint by burning.
9   *oppressor* – a persecutor.

Questions

Go to   p. 226   for more questions on Adrienne Rich.

1. What do you think the poet means when she says that she feels life to be 'a translation'?
2. In your opinion, what is the theme of this poem? Refer closely to the poem in your answer.
3. How do you imagine the poet's partner might have felt after having read this poem?

Exam-style Unseen Poem Questions

1. Write a short response to 'Our Whole Life' in which you outline your reasons for liking or not liking this poem.
2. Choose a line or two from the poem that you found particularly impressive. Give reasons for your choice.
3. Does this poem make you feel optimistic or pessimistic? Briefly explain why.

Trying to Talk with a Man

Out in this desert we are testing bombs,

that's why we came here.

Sometimes I feel an underground river
forcing its way between deformed cliffs
an acute angle of understanding   5
moving itself like a locus of the sun
into this condemned scenery.

What we've had to give up to get here—
whole LP collections, films we starred in
playing in the neighborhoods, bakery windows   10
full of dry, chocolate-filled Jewish cookies,
the language of love-letters, of suicide notes,
afternoons on the riverbank
pretending to be childern

Coming out to this desert   15
we meant to change the face of
driving among dull green succulents
walking at noon in the ghost town
surrounded by a silence

that sounds like the silence of the place   20
except that it came with us
and is familiar
and everything we were saying until now
was an effort to blot it out—
coming out here we are up against it   25

Out here I feel more helpless
with you than without you

You mention the danger
and list the equipment
we talk of people caring for each other   30
in emergencies—laceration, thirst—
but you look at me like an emergency

Your dry heat feels like power
your eyes are stars of a different magnitude
they reflect lights that spell out: EXIT   35
when you get up and pace the floor

talking of the danger
as if it were not ourselves
as if we were testing anything else.

Glossary

See the critical commentary on p. 537.

1 *desert* – during the 1940s and 1950s, the American military carried out a series of controlled nuclear explosions in the Nevada desert.
5 *acute angle* – an angle of less than 90 degrees.
6 *locus of the sun* – position of the sun.
7 *condemned* – following the explosion of a nuclear device, the land is rendered poisonous.

9 *LP collections* – record collections. In this line, the poet lists some of the typical items to be divided up following a separation.
28 *the danger* – the explosion of a nuclear bomb is obviously very dangerous.
31 *laceration* – a serious cut.

Questions

Go to p. 226 for more questions on Adrienne Rich.

1. Comment on the location and setting of 'Trying to Talk with a Man'. Refer closely to the poem in your answer.
2. What does the poet mean when she says the following?

    Out here I feel more helpless

    with you than without you

3. What is the mood of this poem? In your answer, show where in the poem this mood is created.

Exam-style Unseen Poem Questions

1. Write a short personal response to this poem. Support your answer by referring closely to the poem.
2. Choose one or two lines from the poem that you found particularly appealing. Give reasons for your choice by referring closely to the poem.
3. Do you think the poem gives a surprising insight into the end of a relationship? In your answer, you might consider:
   • The pattern of the speaker's thinking.
   • The words and images in the poem.

Diving into the Wreck

First having read the book of myths,
and loaded the camera,
and checked the edge of the knife-blade,
I put on
the body-armor of black rubber   5
the absurd flippers
the grave and awkward mask.
I am having to do this
not like Cousteau with his
assiduous team   10
aboard the sun-flooded schooner
but here alone.

There is a ladder.
The ladder is always there
hanging innocently   15
close to the side of the schooner.
We know what it is for,
we who have used it.
Otherwise
it's a piece of maritime floss   20
some sundry equipment.

I go down.
Rung after rung and still
the oxygen immerses me
the blue light   25
the clear atoms
of our human air.
I go down.
My flippers cripple me,
I crawl like an insect down the ladder   30
and there is no one
to tell me when the ocean
will begin.

First the air is blue and then
it is bluer and then green and then   35
black I am blacking out and yet
my mask is powerful
it pumps my blood with power
the sea is another story
the sea is not a question of power   40
I have to learn alone
to turn my body without force
in the deep element.

And now: it is easy to forget
what I came for   45
among so many who have always
lived here
swaying their crenellated fans
between the reefs
and besides   50
you breathe differently down here.

I came to explore the wreck.
The words are purposes.
The words are maps.
I came to see the damage that was done   55
and the treasures that prevail.
I stroke the beam of my lamp
slowly along the flank
of something more permanent
than fish or weed   60

the thing I came for:
the wreck and not the story of the wreck
the thing itself and not the myth
the drowned face always staring
toward the sun   65
the evidence of damage

worn by salt and sway into this threadbare beauty
the ribs of the disaster
curving their assertion
among the tentative haunters.   70

This is the place.
And I am here, the mermaid whose dark hair
streams black, the merman in his armored body
We circle silently
about the wreck   75
we dive into the hold.
I am she: I am he

whose drowned face sleeps with open eyes
whose breasts still bear the stress
whose silver, copper, vermeil cargo lies   80
obscurely inside barrels
half-wedged and left to rot
we are the half-destroyed instruments
that once held to a course
the water-eaten log   85
the fouled compass

We are, I am, you are
by cowardice or courage
the one who find our way
back to this scene   90
carrying a knife, a camera
a book of myths
in which
our names do not appear.

Glossary

See the critical commentary on p. 540.

1 *myths* – traditional stories, usually involving supernatural or imaginary persons. These tales, which may or may not be true, are often based on religious or quasi-religious beliefs.

5 *body-armor* – the poet likens the wetsuit to body armour.

6 *flippers* – flat, rubber attachments shaped like webbed feet that help a diver to swim more easily.

9 *Cousteau* – Jacques-Yves Cousteau (1910–97) was a famous French underwater explorer and author who made many well-known television documentaries in the 1970s and 1980s. He also helped to invent the scuba-diving apparatus.

10 *assiduous* – diligent or tireless.

11 *schooner* – a sailing ship with two or more masts.

20 *maritime* – naval or describing any activity taking place at sea.

20 *floss* – thread.

21 *sundry* – miscellaneous or different.

48 *crenellated* – with repeated indentations. This unusual adjective is used to describe the battlements on a castle. Here, the speaker imagines the ridges on the creatures that live underwater as resembling the walls or battlements on a castle.

49 *reefs* – ridges of jagged rock or coral.

58 *flank* – side or edge.

64 *drowned face* – here, the speaker is referring to one of the female figureheads that are often found on the bows of old sailing ships.

67 *threadbare* – shabby or frayed.

70 *tentative* – cautious or hesitant.

72 *mermaid* – a **mythical** creature said to be half-woman and half-fish.

73 *merman* – a mythical creature said to be half-man and half-fish.

80 *vermeil* – silver gilt, or any other metal that is covered with a precious metal such as gold.

Questions

Go to p. 226 for more questions on Adrienne Rich.

1. How does the poet suggest that this dive into the wreck is going to involve risk?

2. In your opinion, what is the theme of this poem? Support your answer by close reference to the poem.

3. What do you think the speaker means when she refers to the following?

> a book of myths
>
> in which
>
> our names do not appear.

Exam-style Unseen Poem Questions

1. 'This is a dark and powerful poem.' Write a short response to 'Diving into the Wreck' based on this statement. Support your answer by close reference to the poem.

2. Choose three images from the poem that you found particularly effective. In the case of each image, say why you have chosen it.

3. Do you think the speaker is exploring anything other than the wreck in this poem? Support your answer by close reference to the poem.

From a Survivor

The pact that we made was the ordinary pact
of men & women in those days

I don't know who we thought we were
that our personalities
could resist the failures of the race   5

Lucky or unlucky, we didn't know
the race had failures of that order
and that we were going to share them

Like everybody else, we thought of ourselves as special

Your body is as vivid to me   10
as it ever was: even more

since my feeling for it is clearer:
I know what it could and could not do

it is no longer
the body of a god   15
or anything with power over my life

Next year it would have been 20 years
and you are wastefully dead
who might have made the leap
we talked, too late, of making   20

which I live now
not as a leap
but a succession of brief, amazing movements

each one making possible the next

Glossary

The title, 'From a Survivor', is an emotionally charged one. The term 'survivor' is often used to describe those Jews that survived the Nazi concentration camps. Here, Rich uses the word to describe her feelings some 20 years after the end of her marriage.

1 *pact* – agreement or deal.

2 *in those days* – here, the poet is referring to the attitudes of men and women to marriage in the past.

5 *the failures of the race* – the general personality failings that all people are prone to.

10 *vivid* – clear.

12 *since my feeling for it is clearer* – now that she no longer feels a physical attraction for her lover, the speaker feels that she can see his body more clearly.

17 *would have been 20 years* – the following year would have been their twentieth wedding anniversary. The couple married in 1953 and this poem was written in 1972.

18 *wastefully dead* – this is a reference to Rich's husband, Alfred H. Conrad, who committed suicide in 1970.

Questions

Go to **p. 226** for more questions on Adrienne Rich.

1. In your view, how well does the poem capture the poet's feelings concerning her failed marriage? Illustrate your answer by reference to the language of the poem.

2. Comment on the relevance of the title to the poem's underlying themes.

3. What does the poet mean when she describes her life as being:

    but a succession of brief, amazing movements

    each one making possible the next

    Support your answer by close reference to the poem.

Exam-style Unseen Poem Questions

1. Choose one or two lines from the poem that you found particularly appealing and say why you found them so.

2. Write a response to the above poem, highlighting the impact it makes on you.

3. Does this poem make you feel hopeful or unhopeful? Briefly explain why.

Adrienne Rich: An Overview

Now that you have read a selection of Rich's poetry, you should take the time to look at the following general points. The purpose of these is not to tell you what to think, but rather to help you to form your own opinions. When you have read these points, you may wish to take the time to reread Rich's poetry. You should notice that the general points made here can be used to form the backbone of your paragraphs when it comes to writing on poetry. From now on, try to think about Rich's poems not only in terms of what they say, but also in terms of how they say it. Open your mind to any reasonable interpretation of the poems; remember, your opinions are as valid as anything printed. However, you must be prepared to ground these opinions in fact. If you find this process difficult, that is entirely normal. Remember that a poem is not meant to be studied and dissected in the manner that the Leaving Certificate requires of us. While we have to keep the exam in mind, you should try not to allow it to detract from your enjoyment of the poetry on the course.

1. Adrienne Rich, perhaps more than any other contemporary poet, crystallised in her work and life the consciousness of modern women. In this respect, her poems are overtly feminist in their outlook.
2. Her poems are confessional in that they often draw from her own life experience. While many poets tend to do this, Rich is unique among the poets in this anthology in that she uses these experiences to make political statements.
3. Her poems contain complex images and carefully worked-out rhythms that challenge the reader.
4. Rich tends to draw from everyday events and experiences in order to make complex ideas more accessible.

This list of general points is, of course, in no way exhaustive; there are quite literally thousands of perfectly valid observations to be made about the poetry of Adrienne Rich. Finally, as you reread her poems in this anthology, try to do so with an open mind. Remember, your opinion is as valid as any of the points mentioned above. Try to consult these points frequently, as they will help you when it comes to writing essays.

Past Leaving Certificate Questions

In 2008, students were asked to answer the following question on Rich.

> **'The desire to be heard – that is the impulse behind writing poems, for me.' (Adrienne Rich) Does the poetry of Adrienne Rich speak to you? Write your personal response, referring to the poems of Adrienne Rich that do/do not speak to you.**

That year, correctors were told to reward responses that showed clear evidence of personal engagement/involvement with the poetry of Adrienne Rich. Furthermore, correctors were told to bear in mind that students could draw material from the following points:

- Transcends stereotypical feminism.
- Challenges patriarchal society.
- Her poetry is/is not confessional.
- Imprints powerful images.
- Explores power politics.

Sample Questions

Before you try these questions, you may wish to consult the examination technique guidelines on p. 548.

1. Write an article for a school magazine introducing the poetry of Adrienne Rich to Leaving Certificate students. Tell them what she wrote about and explain what you liked in her writing, suggesting some poems you think they would enjoy reading. Support your points by reference to the poetry by Adrienne Rich that you have studied.

2. What impact did the poetry of Adrienne Rich make on you as a reader? Your answer should deal with the following and should refer to the poems by Adrienne Rich that you have studied:
   - Your overall sense of the poet's personality.
   - The poet's use of language/imagery.

3. 'The appeal of Adrienne Rich's poetry.'

   Using this title, write an essay outlining what you consider to be the appeal o
   Rich's poetry. Support your points by reference to the poetry of Adrienne Rich
   on your course.

4. Write about the feelings that Adrienne Rich's poetry creates in you and the
   aspects of her poetry (content and/or style) that help to create those feelings.
   Support your points by reference to the poetry by Adrienne Rich that you have
   read.

5. Imagine you were asked to select one or more of Adrienne Rich's poems from
   your course for inclusion in a short anthology entitled *The Essential Rich*. Give
   reasons for your choice, quoting from or referring to the poem or poems you
   have chosen.

6. 'Adrienne Rich expresses her themes in an interesting and precise fashion.'
   You have been asked by your local radio station to give a talk on the poetry of
   Adrienne Rich. Write out the text of the talk you would deliver in response to
   the above title. You should refer to both style and subject matter. Support the
   points you make by reference to the poetry on your course.

7. 'Adrienne Rich poses interesting questions delivered by means of a unique style.'
   Do you agree with this assessment of her poetry? Your answer should focus on
   both themes and stylistic features. Support your points with the aid of suitable
   reference to the poems you have studied.

8. 'I think my work comes out of both an intense desire for connection and what
   it means to feel isolated.' In light of Rich's own assessment of her poetry, write
   an essay outlining your reasons for liking or not liking her poetry. Support your
   points with the aid of suitable reference to the poems you have studied.

9. 'I like (or do not like) to read the poetry of Adrienne Rich.'
   Respond to this statement, referring to the poetry by Adrienne Rich on your
   course.

10. 'Adrienne Rich explores tensions and conflicts in an inventive way.'
    Do you agree with this assessment of her poetry? Write a response, supporting
    your points with the aid of suitable reference to the poems you have studied.

ən Poem

,en Poem: An Introduction

Very i. f us when listening to a song, watching a movie or reading a novel need to be told how to react. We engage with these art forms with a confidence that is often lacking in our approach to poetry. Most of us read a poem for the first time in school. As a result, we tend to wait to be told what the poem means. Of course, poetry is never meant to be read like this. When the poet Elizabeth Bishop lectured at Harvard in the 1970s, she rejected the idea that poems should be dissected and pored over by her students. In fact, Bishop insisted that her students learn poetry off by heart. She felt that by being able to recite poetry, students would come to appreciate better the sounds of poetry. Seamus Heaney, too, has advocated the rote learning of poems. Both of these poets believed that poetry could only be fully and properly experienced when listened to correctly.

Poetry embraces all of life in a condensed and concentrated form of language. This can pose problems for the reader, but it also makes poetry unique amongst art forms. A well-written poem appeals not only to our intelligence, but also to our senses, emotions and imagination. It is no wonder, then, that at times of great joy, sadness and uncertainty, people turn to poetry to express themselves. The poet achieves greater force per phrase and greater impact per poem by drawing more fully on a number of language devices. You will have encountered many such technical devices during your study of the poems on the syllabus. Among them are **metaphor, simile, image, symbol, allusion, onomatopoeia, rhythm** and **metre.**

Of course, the division in this book between seen and unseen poetry is a completely artificial one. Every poem, when we first encounter it, is an unseen poem. The three short questions and exam-style unseen poem questions that have followed each poem in this anthology should help you to come to terms with the type of unseen poetry question that appears on the exam paper. In this respect, you are already a well-read student of poetry, so when you approach the unseen poem, you should do so with confidence and without fear. For help with answering unseen poetry questions, please consult the examination technique section on p. 548.

With a little forethought and the considered application of some of the techniques that we have met in the prescribed poetry, you will do very well in this section of the exam. According to the Chief Examiner's report of 2001, most candidates responded well to the unseen poem question. They were, however, able to write about the content of the poem more effectively than they were able to express their own feelings as readers of the poem.

In future, try to consider the unseen poem under the following headings.

- **Title:** Give serious consideration to the title before reading the poem. The title or, indeed, the lack of a title can do much to alter the direction of a poem or the reader's response to it. Ask yourself how you feel about the title. Do this before and after you have read the poem. Has your attitude to the title been changed by the experience of reading the poem?
- **Form and shape:** Make a note of the form and the shape of the poem. For example, it is a *sonnet* or a *concrete poem*? How does the shape of the poem relate to its subject matter?
- **Mental paraphrase:** Translating the poem into a series of mental pictures or, indeed, your own words can yield very profitable results. While you are doing this, try to make a note of how you are feeling. Ask yourself why the poem makes you feel like this. Try to think about how the poet is producing these feelings in you.
- **Connotation:** The act of contemplating the poem for meaning beyond the literal one is the most important task a reader is required to perform. This alone can be enough to gain full marks in the personal response type of question. However, if you manage to unite this understanding of the deeper meaning of a poem with an exploration of how the poet achieves this, you will certainly impress the corrector.
- **Personal pronouns:** One of the most useful examinations of an unseen poem can be achieved through a consideration of the use of personal pronouns. The personal pronouns 'I' and 'we' can draw the reader in, creating a sense of immediacy between the reader and the poet.
- **Tone:** Pay close attention to the *tone* of the poem. In many respects, given the oral nature of poetry, the tone of a poem can reveal more than the actual words on the page.
- **Changes:** Note all changes in the poem's attitude or tone. Nearly every poem changes tone in some manner. To discover changes, look out for the following key words: *but, yet, however, although.* Changes in punctuation are also important (*dashes, full stops, colons, stanzas and/or line divisions*), as are changes in line or stanza length. The poet often relies on such changes to achieve his or her desired effect. Ask yourself how the poem develops. Are the *images* and

ideas developed chronologically, by cause and effect or by free association? Does the poem circle back to where it started or is the movement from one attitude to a different attitude (e.g. from despair to hope or openness to bitterness)? Remember, a poem never ends as it began. Never forget to question your own change in attitude during the course of the poem.

- **Imagery:** Look at the figurative language of the poem – *images*, *metaphors*, *similes*, *symbols*, etc. How do these images add to the meaning of the poem? Do they intensify the effect of the poem?

- **Syntax:** How many phrases are in the poem? Are the sentences simple or complicated? Where are the main verbs in the poem? Does the language pattern in the poem mirror that of normal speech?

- **Punctuation:** What kind of punctuation does the poet use? Does the punctuation always coincide with the end of a line? If so, this is called an end-stopped line. If there is no punctuation at the end of a line and the thought continues into the next line, this is called *enjambment*. Is there any punctuation in the middle of a line? Look out for *caesurae*, as these may indicate a change in the poem's direction. Ask yourself why the poet would want you to pause halfway through the line.

- **Theme:** At this stage, give consideration to the theme of the poem. In other words, determine what message the poet is trying to get across.

- **Devices:** Examine any and all poetic devices, focusing on how such devices contribute to the meaning and/or effect of the poem. (What is important is not that you can identify poetic devices, but that you can explain how these devices enhance the poem.) Note anything that is repeated, either individual words or complete phrases. Anything said more than once may be crucial to interpretation. Keep asking yourself how you feel about this. Examine the musical devices in the poem:

  - Rhyme scheme: Does the poem *rhyme*? Does the rhyme occur in a regular pattern or irregularly? Is the effect formal, satisfying, musical, funny, disconcerting?

  - *Rhythm* or *metre*: In most poems, there is a pattern of stressed and unstressed syllables in a word or words in a sentence. In poetry, the variation of stressed and unstressed syllables and words has a rhythmic effect. How does the rhythm of the poem impact on you as a reader?

  - Other sound effects include *alliteration, assonance, consonance* and repetition. How do these alter your response to the poem?

- **Mood:** It is important to ask yourself if the poem has created a change in *mood* for you.
- **Think again about the movement of the poem:** Rarely does a poem begin and end in the same place. Normally, the poet relates his or her experiences to us in a gradual manner. You should try to trace the changing feelings of the speaker from the beginning to the end, while paying particular attention to the poem's conclusion.

Of course, it is not possible to memorise this approach. However, if you follow this pattern every time you answer an unseen poem, it should become second nature to you.

The Unseen Poem: A Sample Answer

In 2005, the following unseen poem and questions appeared.

Back Yard

Shine on, O moon of summer.
Shine to the leaves of grass, catalpa and oak,
All silver under your rain tonight.

An Italian boy is sending songs to you tonight from an accordion.
A Polish boy is out with his best girl; they marry next month; tonight they
    are throwing you kisses.

An old man next door is dreaming over a sheen that sits in a cherry tree
    in his back yard.

The clocks say I must go—I stay here sitting on the back porch drinking
    white thoughts you rain down.

    Shine on, O moon,
Shake out more and more silver changes.

Carl Sandburg (1878–1967)

1. (a) Do you like the world that the poet describes in this poem? (10)

   (b) Choose a line or two that you find particularly appealing and explain why. (10)

OR

2. Write a personal response to the poem 'Back Yard'. (20)

Sample Answer 1(a)

I really enjoyed the world described by the poet in this poem. Firstly, it is one with which I am completely familiar. The mixture of cosmopolitan (reflected in the various nationalities) and nature (symbolised by the moon, grass and cherry tree) remind me so much of my native Galway. Although one suspects that this backyard is American, it could also be anywhere in the Ireland of 2005. On a different level, I genuinely enjoyed the atmosphere that the poem creates. The world of the poem is populated with people, yet the speaker has the space and time to contemplate the significance of the full moon. Furthermore, the reader is drawn into this world in a very clever fashion. The familiar sound of the accordion combines with the sight of the 'leaves of grass' and leads us to a point where we can almost taste the moonlight.

Sample Answer 1(b)

I have chosen the couplet that forms the second last stanza. I found these lines particularly appealing because they sum up the dreamy quality of this poem. The image of the poet sitting on the back porch is familiar and grounded in reality. Yet, at the same time, I found that this line evoked something of the imagery of a Hollywood movie. The personification of the clocks makes us aware of the urgencies of the outside world. The speaker's refusal to listen to their demands that he 'must go' increases our sense of a special place that is removed from day-to-day worries.

I particularly enjoyed the second line of this penultimate stanza. The confusion of the senses when the poet attempts to drink the moonlight is, in my opinion, the stuff of pure poetry. The beautifully slow pace created by the predominance of broad vowel sounds adds so much to these lines.

Sample Answer 2

I genuinely enjoyed reading this poem. In comparison to many of the poems I have studied this year, I felt 'Back Yard' to be an accessible, yet thought-provoking, poem. The energetic first line drew me in and from there on my attention was held in an unforced manner. At first, I expected this poem to be a conventional nature poem. However, as I read on, I quickly realised that this poem was not typical of that genre of poem. The setting of 'Back Yard' is, in fact, an urban one. Coming from a large city, this is something that really appealed to me. I enjoyed the cosmopolitan feel of the second stanza. The melting pot of what is presumably American culture is beautifully interlaced with the descriptions of the moonlight.

Another aspect of 'Back Yard' that appeals to me is the manner in which the poet manages to combine a uniquely personal experience with an overview of the neighbourhood in which he lives. The Polish boy and the romantic Italian are forced to share the stage with the old man. All three are seen to bathe in the beauty of the moonlight. This, somehow, makes the poem more inviting and open. Ultimately, however, this poem presents us with a personal moment of reflection: a moment that I enjoyed reading about.

Cosmopolitan = Including people from many different Countries

The Unseen Poem: A Selection of Suitable Poems 1

The following poems are prescribed for Ordinary Level for the Leaving Certificate 2012. The questions that follow each poem are intended to help you hone your unseen poetry skills. Please bear in mind that on the day of the examination, you will not be provided with a glossary.

Phenomenal Woman

Pretty women wonder where my secret lies.
I'm not cute or built to suit a fashion model's size
But when I start to tell them,
They think I'm telling lies.
I say,   5
It's in the reach of my arms,
The span of my hips,
The stride of my step,
The curl of my lips.
I'm a woman   10
Phenomenally.
Phenomenal woman,
That's me.

I walk into a room
Just as cool as you please,   15
And to a man,
The fellows stand or
Fall down on their knees.
Then they swarm around me,
A hive of honey bees.   20
I say,
It's the fire in my eyes,
And the flash of my teeth,
The swing in my waist,
And the joy in my feet.   25

I'm a woman
Phenomenally.
Phenomenal woman,
That's me.

Men themselves have wondered   30
What they see in me.
They try so much
But they can't touch
My inner mystery.
When I try to show them,   35
They say they still can't see.
I say,
It's in the arch of my back,
The sun of my smile,
The ride of my breasts,   40
The grace of my style.
I'm a woman
Phenomenally.
Phenomenal woman,
That's me.   45

Now you understand
Just why my head's not bowed.
I don't shout or jump about
Or have to talk real loud.
When you see me passing,   50
It ought to make you proud.
I say,
It's in the click of my heels,
The bend of my hair,
The palm of my hand   55
The need for my care.
'Cause I'm a woman
Phenomenally.
Phenomenal woman,
That's me.   60

Maya Angelou (1928–)

Glossary

Phenomenal – extraordinary, unique.

Questions

1. Describe the type of man that, in your opinion, would make a suitable partner for this woman. (10)
2. Do you think that the woman in this poem is happy? Give reasons for your answer. (10)

OR

3. How did this poem make you feel? (20)

Going Home to Mayo, Winter, 1949

Leaving behind us the alien, foreign city of Dublin,
My father drove through the night in an old Ford Anglia,
His five-year-old son in the seat beside him,
The rexine seat of red leatherette,
And a yellow moon peered in through the windscreen.   5
"Daddy, Daddy," I cried, "pass out the moon,"
But no matter how hard he drove he could not pass out the moon.
Each town we passed through was another milestone
And their names were magic passwords into eternity:
Kilcock, Kinnegad, Strokestown, Elphin,   10
Tarmonbarry, Tulsk, Ballaghaderreen, Ballavarry;
Now we were in Mayo and the next stop was Turlough,
The village of Turlough in the heartland of Mayo,
And my father's mother's house, all oil-lamps and women,
And my bedroom over the public bar below,   15
And in the morning cattle-cries and cock-crows:
Life's seemingly seamless garment gorgeously rent
By their screeches and bellowings. And in the evenings
I walked with my father in the high grass down by the river
Talking with him – an unheard-of thing in the city.   20

But home was not home and the moon could be no more outflanked
Than the daylight nightmare of Dublin City:
Back down along the canal we chugged into the city
And each lock-gate tolled our mutual doom;
And railings and palings and asphalt and traffic lights,   25
And blocks after blocks of so-called "new" tenements –
Thousands of crosses of loneliness planted
In the narrowing grave of the life of the father;
In the wide, wide cemetery of the boy's childhood.

Paul Durcan (1944–)

Glossary

2 *Ford Anglia* – a type of car made by Ford.
4 *rexine* – a brand of artificial leather.
4 *leatherette* – artificial leather.
17 *rent* – torn.
21 *outflanked* – moved around the side of.
23 *chugged* – here, the poet attempts to recreate the sound of the car.

24 *tolled* – a slow ringing, often associated with a funeral bell.
24 *mutual doom* – our shared destiny or misfortune.

Questions

1. Imagine you are the little boy in this poem. What would you write in your diary about your experience of going home to Mayo? (10)
2. Suggest an alternative title for this poem. Give reasons for your suggestion. (10)

OR

3. How did this poem make you feel? Give reasons for your answer. (20)

Daniel's Duck

for Frances

I held out the shot mallard, she took it from me,
looped its neck-string over a drawer of the dresser.
The children were looking on, half-caught.
Then the kitchen life — warm, lit, glowing —
moved forward, taking in the dead bird,   5
and its coldness, its wildness, were leaching away.

The children were sitting to their dinners.
Us too — drinking tea, hardly noticing
the child's quiet slide from his chair,
his small absorbed body before the duck's body,   10
the duck changing — feral, live —
arrowing up out of black sloblands
with the gleam of a river
falling away below.

Then the duck — dead again — hanging from the drawer-   15
  knob,
the green head, brown neck running into the breast,
the intricate silvery-greyness of the back;
the wings, their white bars and blue flashes,
the feet, their snakey, orange scaliness, small claws, piteous 20
  webbing,
the yellow beak, blooded,
the whole like a weighted sack —
all that downward-dragginess of death.

He hovered, took a step forward, a step back,   25
something appeared in his face, some knowledge
of a place where he stood, the world stilled,
the lit streaks of sunrise running off red
into the high bowl of morning.

She watched him, moving to touch, his hand out: 30
What is it, Daniel, do you like the duck?
He turned as though caught in the act,
saw the gentleness in her face and his body loosened.
I thought there was water on it —
he was finding the words, one by one,   35
holding them out, to see would they do us —
but there isn't.
He added this on, going small with relief
that his wing-drag of sounds was enough.

Kerry Hardie (1951–)

Glossary

1 *mallard* – a wild duck, the male of which has a deep green head with a white ring around its neck. The mallard is native to Ireland.
6 *leaching* – leaking.

11 *feral* – the word used to describe a wild animal.
12 *sloblands* – wetlands.

Questions

1. Comment on the final lines of this poem. What do you think the poet means here? (10)
2. Write a short personal response to this poem. (10)

OR

3. Choose two or three lines or phrases from this poem that you found particularly striking. Give reasons for your choice. (20)

When I Set Out for Lyonnesse

When I set out for Lyonnesse,
  A hundred miles away,
  The rime was on the spray,
And starlight lit my lonesomeness
When I set out for Lyonnesse   5
  A hundred miles away.

What would bechance at Lyonnesse
  While I should sojourn there
  No prophet durst declare,
Nor did the wisest wizard guess   10
What would bechance at Lyonnesse
  While I should sojourn there.

When I came back from Lyonnesse
  With magic in my eyes,
  All marked with mute surmise   15
My radiance rare and fathomless,
When I came back from Lyonnesse
  With magic in my eyes!

Thomas Hardy (1840–1928)

Glossary

The title refers to Lyonnesse, a mythical kingdom that was said to have sunk beneath the sea. In the English legend of Arthur and the Knights of the Round Table, Lyonnesse was the westernmost kingdom of Arthur's realm, extending beyond the end of Cornwall and joining the Isles of Scilly to the rest of Britain. Hardy's wife-to-be, Emma Gifford, hailed from Cornwall.

3 *rime* – a thin coating of frost.
3 *spray* – thin shoots or branches of a plant.
9 *durst* – archaic past tense of 'dare'.
11 *bechance* – happen.
12 *sojourn* – stay.
15 *mute* – silent.
15 *surmise* – guesswork.
16 *radiance* – joy and energy.
16 *fathomless* – too deep to be measured.

Questions

1. Write a response to 'When I Set Out for Lyonnesse', highlighting the impact it makes on you. (10)
2. Briefly describe the mood or feeling you get from reading this poem and illustrate your answer from the text. (10)

OR

3. Discuss the ways this poem captures the emotions felt by the poet. (20)

A Glimpse of Starlings

I expect him any minute now although
He's dead. I know he has been talking
All night to his own dead and now
In the first heart-breaking light of morning
He is struggling into his clothes,   5
Sipping a cup of tea, fingering a bit of bread,
Eating a small photograph with his eyes.
The questions bang and rattle in his head
Like doors and cannisters the night of a storm.
He doesn't know why his days finished like this   10
Daylight is as hard to swallow as food
Love is a crumb all of him hungers for.
I can hear the drag of his feet on the concrete path
The close explosion of his smoker's cough
The slow turn of the Yale key in the lock   15
The door opening to let him in
To what looks like release from what feels like pain
And over his shoulder a glimpse of starlings
Suddenly lifted over field, road and river
Like a fist of black dust pitched in the wind.   20

Brendan Kennelly (1936–)

Glossary

9 *cannisters* – a metal container with a lid, for storing tea, coffee or other dry goods.

15 *Yale key* – Yale is a manufacturer of locks commonly used in household doors.

20 *pitched* – thrown.

Questions

1. How did this poem make you feel? (10)
2. Choose two images from the poem that you found particularly effective. Give reasons for your choice. (10)

OR

3. Why, in your opinion, did Kennelly choose this title for his poem? (20)

What Were They Like?

1) Did the people of Viet Nam
   use lanterns of stone?
2) Did they hold ceremonies
   to reverence the opening of buds?
3) Were they inclined to quiet laughter?   5
4) Did they use bone and ivory,
   jade and silver, for ornament?
5) Had they an epic poem?
6) Did they distinguish between speech and singing?

1) Sir, their light hearts turned to stone.   10
   It is not remembered whether in gardens
   stone lanterns illumined pleasant ways.
2) Perhaps they gathered once to delight in blossom,
   but after the children were killed
   there were no more buds.   15
3) Sir, laughter is bitter to the burned mouth.
4) A dream ago, perhaps. Ornament is for joy.
   All the bones were charred.

5) It is not remembered. Remember,
   most were peasants; their life   20
   was in rice and bamboo.
   When peaceful clouds were reflected in the paddies
   and the water buffalo stepped surely along terraces,
   maybe fathers told their sons old tales.
   When bombs smashed those mirrors   25
   there was time only to scream.

6) There is an echo yet
   of their speech which was like a song.
   It is reported their singing resembled
   the flight of moths in moonlight.   30
   Who can say? It is silent now.

Denise Levertov (1923–97)

Glossary

The poem refers to the Vietnam War that was fought in Vietnam, Laos and Cambodia from 1959 to 30 April 1975. The war was fought between the communist North Vietnam, supported by its communist allies, and South Vietnam, supported by the United States and others. The war exacted a savage human cost. Nearly 4 million Vietnamese people on both sides of the conflict were killed, while just over 58,000 US soldiers died. The war had a major impact on US politics, culture and foreign relations, leading to mass demonstrations and widespread civil unrest throughout the 1960s and 1970s.

2 *lanterns* – a portable case with transparent sides that holds a light.

3 *ceremonies* – formal events that celebrate something, e.g. a wedding, an official opening or an anniversary.

4 *reverence* – feelings of deep respect or devotion.

5 *inclined* – moved or convinced to do something.

6 *ivory* – a hard, cream-colored substance that forms the tusks of animals such as an elephant.

8 *epic poem* – a long poem dealing with events of huge significance.

9 *distinguish* – tell the difference.

12 *illumined* – lit up.

22 *paddies* – fields covered in shallow water where rice is grown.

23 *terraces* – a flat, level strip of ground, bounded by a steep slope and constructed on a hillside so that the land can be cultivated.

Questions

1. Comment on the two voices in this poem. In your opinion, how effective is this technique? (10)

2. Choose two phrases from the poem that you found particularly interesting. Give reasons for your choice. (10)

OR

3. How did this poem make you feel? Refer closely to the poem in your answer. (20)

Meeting Point

Time was away and somewhere else,
There were two glasses and two chairs
And two people with the one pulse
(Somebody stopped the moving stairs):
Time was away and somewhere else.   5

And they were neither up nor down;
The stream's music did not stop
Flowing through heather, limpid brown,
Although they sat in a coffee shop
And they were neither up nor down.   10

The bell was silent in the air
Holding its inverted poise—
Between the clang and clang a flower,
A brazen calyx of no noise:
The bell was silent in the air.   15

The camels crossed the miles of sand
That stretched around the cups and plates;
The desert was their own, they planned
To portion out the stars and dates:
The camels crossed the miles of sand.   20

Time was away and somewhere else.
The waiter did not come, the clock
Forgot them and the radio waltz
Came out like water from a rock:
Time was away and somewhere else.   25

Her fingers flicked away the ash
That bloomed again in tropic trees:
Not caring if the markets crash

When they had forests such as these,
Her fingers flicked away the ash.   30

God or whatever means the Good
Be praised that time can stop like this,
That what the heart has understood
Can verify in the body's peace
God or whatever means the Good.   35

Time was away and she was here
And life no longer what it was,
The bell was silent in the air
And all the room one glow because
Time was away and she was here.   40

Louis MacNeice (1907–63)

Glossary

8 *heather* – a low-growing evergreen plant with spiky leaves and purple flowers that grows in clumps.

8 *limpid* – clear and transparent.

12 *inverted* – turned upside down, inside out or back to front.

12 *poise* – calm and self-assured.

14 *calyx* – a modified leaf that is usually green and is found around the outside of a flower. Another word for a calyx is a sepal.

23 *waltz* – a type of ballroom dance.

Questions

1. Choose a line or two that you find particularly appealing and explain why. (10)

2. Write a response to this poem, highlighting aspects of it that you liked and/or disliked. (10)

OR

3. Do you think this poem gives an interesting insight into the experience of being in love? Explain why or why not. (20)

Bearhugs

Whenever my sons call round we hug each other.
Bearhugs. Both bigger than me and stronger
They lift me off my feet, crushing the life out of me.

They smell of oil paint and aftershave, of beer
Sometimes and tobacco, and of women   5
Whose memory they seem reluctant to wash away.

They haven't lived with me for years,
Since they were tiny, and so each visit
Is an assessment, a reassurance of love unspoken.

I look for some resemblance to my family.   10
Seize on an expression, a lifted eyebrow,
A tilt of the head, but cannot see myself.

Though like each other, they are not like me.
But I can see in them something of my father.
Uncles, home on leave during the war.   15
At three or four, I loved those straightbacked men
Towering above me, smiling and confident.
The whole world before them. Or so it seemed.

I look at my boys, slouched in armchairs
They have outgrown. See Tom in army uniform   20
And Finn in air force blue. Time is up.

Bearhugs. They lift me off my feet
And fifty years fall away. One son
After another, crushing the life into me.

Roger McGough (1937–)

Glossary

2 *Bearhugs* – large embraces.

Questions

1. Suggest a different title for this poem. Support your suggestion by close reference to the poem. (10)
2. What do we learn about the poet Roger McGough from reading this poem? (10)

OR

3. 'One son | After another, crushing the life into me.' Do you think this is a good ending to the poem? Give reasons for your answer, supporting them by quotation from the poem. (20)

All Day Long

At school we see
Ink spilt on the floor.
Children get bored
Counting, conjucating verbs ….
All day long.   5

You never know
When some disappear
You never know
Where to find them.

Teachers are patient,   10
See with their eyes.
Children, not easily tamed,
See with their hearts,
And are made to sit in rows,
In blue and navy uniforms.   15

How can you know
When some disappear?
How can you know
Where to find them?

Principals, Deputy Principals,   20
Constantly counting the children,
Mornings and afternoons
Names and numbers put on files.

One never knows
When they go missing   25
One never knows
Where to find them.

Noel Monahan (1949–)

Glossary

4   *conjugating verbs* – declining a verb systematically in its different forms according to tense, mood, person and number.

Questions

1. Choose some words and phrases that you found enjoyable. Give reasons for your choice. (10)
2. From your reading of this poem, do you feel the writer understands what it is like to be in school? (10)

OR

3. 'This is an accessible yet thought-provoking poem.' Do you agree with this statement? Explain your answer. (20)

Anseo

When the Master was calling the roll
At the primary school in Collegelands,
You were meant to call back *Anseo*
And raise your hand
As your name occurred.   5
Anseo, meaning here, here and now,
All present and correct,
Was the first word of Irish I spoke.
The last name on the ledger
Belonged to Joseph Mary Plunkett Ward   10
And was followed, as often as not,
By silence, knowing looks,
A nod and a wink, the Master's droll
'And where's our little Ward-of-court?'

I remember the first time he came back   15
The Master had sent him out
Along the hedges
To weigh up for himself and cut
A stick with which he would be beaten.
After a while, nothing was spoken;   20
He would arrive as a matter of course
With an ash-plant, a salley-rod.
Or, finally, the hazel-wand
He had whittled down to a whip-lash,
Its twist of red and yellow lacquers   25
Sanded and polished,
And altogether so delicately wrought
That he had engraved his initials on it.

I last met Joseph Mary Plunkett Ward
In a pub just over the Irish border.   30
He was living in the open,
In a secret camp
On the other side of the mountain.

He was fighting for Ireland,

Making things happen.   35

And he told me, Joe Ward,

Of how he had risen through the ranks

To Quartermaster, Commandant:

How every morning at parade

His volunteers would call back *Anseo*   40

And raise their hands

As their names occurred.

Paul Muldoon (1951–)

Glossary

3   *Anseo* – the Irish for 'here'.
9   *ledger* – a large book used for recording data.
10 *Joseph Mary Plunkett Ward* – the boy was named after one of the seven signatories to the proclamation of the Irish Republic in 1916, who was imprisoned by the English army in the Richmond Barracks. Shortly before his execution in the courtyard of Kilmainham Jail, on the morning of 4 May 1916, he married his fiancée, Grace Gifford, in the jail's chapel. He died at the age of 28. Since the boy in the poem is named after this man, we presume that he is from a Republican background.

13 *droll* – funny or witty.
14 *Ward-of-court* – someone who has been placed under the protection of the state.
22–3 *ash-plant, a salley-rod [...] hazel-wand* – sticks made from tree branches.
25 *lacquers* – varnishes.
38 *Quartermaster* – a rank in the army, usually the person in charge of supplies.

Questions

1. Imagine you are Joe Ward. What would you write in your diary about your experience of going to school? (10)
2. From your reading of the poem, what sort of person do you feel the teacher to be? (10)

OR

3. How did this poem make you feel? (20)

Moonshine

To think
I must be alone:
To love
We must be together.

I think I love you   5
When I'm alone
More than I think of you
When we're together.

I cannot think
Without loving   10
Or love
Without thinking.

Alone I love
To think of us together:
Together I think   15
I'd love to be alone.

Richard Murphy (1927–)

Questions

1. Write a personal response to this poem. (10)
2. Choose a line or phrase from the poem that you found enjoyable. Give reasons for your choice. (10)

OR

3. Suggest an alternative title for this poem. Give a reason for your choice. (20)

The Sun

Have you ever seen
anything
in your life
more wonderful

than the way the sun,   5
every evening,
relaxed and easy,
floats toward the horizon

and into the clouds or the hills,
or the rumpled sea,   10
and is gone—
and how it slides again

out of the blackness,
every morning,
on the other side of the world,   15
like a red flower

streaming upward on its heavenly oils,
say, on a morning in early summer,
at its perfect imperial distance—
and have you ever felt for anything   20

such wild love—
do you think there is anywhere, in any language,
a word billowing enough
for the pleasure

that fills you,   25
as the sun
reaches out,
as it warms you

as you stand there,
empty-handed—   30
or have you too
turned from this world—

or have you too
gone crazy
for power,   35
for things?

Mary Oliver (1935–)

Glossary

10 *rumpled* – wrinkled or creased.   23 *billowing* – filling full of air.
19 *imperial* – very grand or majestic.

Questions

1. Write a personal response to 'The Sun'. (10)
2. Does this poem make you feel hopeful or unhopeful? Briefly explain why. (10)

                                    OR

3. Choose a line or two that you find particularly appealing and explain why. (20)

Ozymandias

I met a traveler from an antique land
Who said: Two vast and trunkless legs of stone
Stand in the desert ... Near them, on the sand,
Half sunk, a shattered visage lies, whose frown,
And wrinkled lip, and sneer of cold command,   5
Tell that its sculptor well those passions read
Which yet survive, stamped on these lifeless things,
The hand that mocked them, and the heart that fed:
And on the pedestal, these words appear:
"My name is Ozymandias, king of kings: 10

Look on my works, ye Mighty, and despair!"
Nothing beside remains. Round the decay
Of that colossal wreck, boundless and bare
The lone and level sands stretch far away.

Percy Bysshe Shelley (1792–1822)

Glossary

The title, 'Ozymandias', refers to Pharaoh Rameses
II of Egypt. Rameses II is widely held as providing
us with the most complete example of an imperial
ruler.

4   *visage* – a face.
13   *colossal* – huge.

Questions

1. What impression do you get of Ozymandias? (10)

2. What words or phrases from the poem best convey that impression to you? (10)

OR

3. Is this poem still worth reading in the twenty-first century? Give reasons for your answer. (20)

Jungian Cows

In Switzerland, the people call their cows
Venus, Eve, Salome, or Fraulein Alberta,
beautiful names
to yodel across the pastures at Bollingen.

If the woman is busy with child or book,   5
the farmer wears his wife's skirt
to milk the most sensitive cows.
When the electric milking-machine arrives,
the stalled cows rebel and sulk
for the woman's impatient skilful fingers   10
on their blowzy tough rosy udders,
will not give their milk;

so the man who works the machine

dons cotton skirt, all floral delicate flounces

to hide his denim overalls and big old muddy boots,   15

he fastens the soft folds carefully,

wraps his head in his sweetheart's sunday-best fringed scarf,

and walks smelling feminine and shy among the cows,

till the milk spurts, hot, slippery and steamy

into the churns,   20

Venus, Salome, Eve, and Fraulein Alberta,

lowing, half-asleep,

accepting the disguised man as an echo of the woman,

their breath smelling of green, of milk's sweet traditional climax.

Penelope Shuttle (1947–)

Glossary

The title refers to Carl Gustav Jung (1875–1961), the influential Swiss psychiatrist and theoretical psychologist. Jung believed that there was a lack of balance and harmony in the world. He also felt that Western man relied too heavily on science and had moved too far away from spirituality.

2 *Venus* – in Roman **mythology**, the goddess of love and beauty.

2 *Eve* – in the Bible, Eve was Adam's companion in the Garden of Eden and was the first woman.

2 *Salome* – in the Bible (Matthew 14:6–11 and Mark 6:21–28), Salome was the Herodias who demanded and received John the Baptist's head as reward for dancing before her stepfather.

2 *Fraulein* – German for Miss.

4 *yodel* – sing. Yodelling is a traditional alpine folk music.

4 *Bollingen* – a town in Germany.

14 *flounces* – frills.

22 *lowing* – the mooing sounds that cows make.

Questions

1. A friend asks you to tell him/her what this poem is about. Write what you would say. (10)

2. Suggest an alternative title for this poem. Explain your suggestion. (10)

OR

3. Someone has said of this poem that it is both 'amusing and thought provoking'. Would you agree with this assessment of the poem? (20)

Traveling through the Dark

Traveling through the dark I found a deer
dead on the edge of the Wilson River road.
It is usually best to roll them into the canyon:
that road is narrow; to swerve might make more dead.

By glow of the tail-light I stumbled back of the car   5
and stood by the heap, a doe, a recent killing;
she had stiffened already, almost cold.
I dragged her off; she was large in the belly.

My fingers touching her side brought me the reason—
her side was warm; her fawn lay there waiting,   10
alive, still, never to be born.
Beside that mountain road I hesitated.

The car aimed its lowered parking lights;
under the hood purred the steady engine.
I stood in the glare of the warm exhaust turning red;   15
around our group I could hear the wilderness listen.

I thought hard for us all—my only swerving—
then pushed her over the edge into the river.

William Stafford (1914–93)

Glossary

2 *Wilson River* – a river that flows through north-west Oregon in the United States.
3 *canyon* – a deep, often narrow valley with steep slopes.
6 *doe* – a mature female dear.
10 *fawn* – a young deer less than a year old.

Questions

1. Write a response to 'Traveling through the Dark', highlighting aspects of it that you liked and/or disliked. (10)
2. Choose a line or two that you find particularly appealing and explain why. (10)

OR

3. Briefly describe the mood or feeling you get from reading this poem and illustrate your answer from the text. (20)

A Summer Morning

Her young employers, having got in late
From seeing friends in town
And scraped the right front fender on the gate,
Will not, the cook expects, be coming down.

She makes a quiet breakfast for herself.   5
The coffee-pot is bright,
The jelly where it should be on the shelf.
She breaks an egg into the morning light,

Then, with the bread-knife lifted, stands and hears
The sweet efficient sounds   10
Of thrush and catbird, and the snip of shears
Where, in the terraced backward of the grounds,

A gardener works before the heat of day.
He straightens for a view
Of the big house ascending stony-gray   15
Out of his beds mosaic with the dew.

His young employers having got in late,
He and the cook alone
Receive the morning on their old estate,
Possessing what the owners can but own.   20

Richard Wilbur (1921–)

Glossary

3 *fender* – the corner part of a car that surrounds each wheel.

7 *jelly* – in this context, probably American English for jam.

15 *ascending* – rising.

16 *mosaic* – a picture of a design made with small pieces of coloured material.

Questions

1. Write a response to 'A Summer Morning', highlighting the impact it makes on you. (10)

2. Choose a line or two that you find particularly appealing and explain why. (10)

OR

3. What impression of the owners of the house do you get from reading this poem? (20)

The Unseen Poem: A Selection of Suitable Poems 2

On the day of the exam, you will generally be given a choice between two 10-mark questions and one 20-mark question. This layout is followed here. In an effort to replicate exam conditions, the poems in this section of the anthology are presented without glossaries.

Southern Cop

Let us forgive Ty Kendricks.
The place was Darktown. He was young.
His nerves were jittery. The day was hot.
The Negro ran out of the alley.
And so Ty shot.

Let us understand Ty Kendricks.
The Negro must have been dangerous,
Because he ran;
And there was a rookie with a chance
To prove himself a man.

Let us condone Ty Kendricks
If we cannot decorate.
When he found what the Negro was running for,
It was too late;
And all we can say for the Negro is
It was unfortunate.

Let us pity Ty Kendricks.
He has been through enough,
Standing there, his big gun smoking,
Rabbit-scared, alone,
Having to hear the wenches wail
And the dying Negro moan.

Sterling A. Brown (1901–89)

Questions

1. Do you think the speaker feels any pity for Ty Kendricks? Justify your answer by reference to the poem. (10)
2. Comment on the speaker's use of irony and understatement. (10)

OR

3. Write a personal response to the above poem, highlighting the impact it had on you. (20)

homage to my hips

these hips are big hips
they need space to
move around in.
they don't fit into little
petty places. these hips
are free hips.
they don't like to be held back.
these hips have never been enslaved,
they go where they want to go
they do what they want to do.
these hips are mighty hips.
these hips are magic hips.
i have known them
to put a spell on a man and
spin him like a top!

Lucille Clifton (1936–)

Questions

1. Did you enjoy this poem? Give reasons for enjoying or not enjoying this poem. (10)
2. What impact do the sounds of the poem have on your reading of 'homage to my hips'? Illustrate your answer by reference to the sound patterns in the poem. (10)

OR

3. The tone of voice in this poem could be described as playful. How does the poet create such a tone? (20)

Those Winter Sundays

Sundays too my father got up early
and put his clothes on in the blueblack cold,
then with cracked hands that ached
from labor in the weekday weather made
banked fires blaze. No one ever thanked him.

I'd wake and hear the cold splintering, breaking.
When the rooms were warm, he'd call,
and slowly I would rise and dress,
fearing the chronic angers of that house,

Speaking indifferently to him,
who had driven out the cold
and polished my good shoes as well.
What did I know, what did I know
of love's austere and lonely offices?

Robert Hayden (1913–80)

Questions

1. What evidence is there to suggest that the speaker's attitude to his father has changed? Give reasons for your answer. (10)
2. Do you think that the father cares for his family? Give reasons for your answer. (10)

OR

3. Choose two or three images from 'Those Winter Sundays' that you feel are important to the emotional concerns of the poem. (20)

The Embankment

The fantasia of a fallen gentleman on a cold, bitter night.

Once, in finesse of fiddles found I ecstasy,
In the flash of gold heels on the hard pavement.
Now see I
That warmth's the very stuff of poesy.
Oh, God, make small
The old star-eaten blanket of the sky,
That I may fold it round me and in comfort lie.

Thomas Ernest Hulme (1883–1917)

Questions

1. How did this poem make you feel? Give reasons for your answer. (10)
2. What does the poet mean when he says 'warmth's the very stuff of poesy'? (10)

OR

3. Choose one or two phrases from the poem that you found particularly striking. Support your answer by reference to the poem. (20)

Eily Kilbride

On the North side of Cork city
Where I sported and played
On the banks of my own lovely Lee
Having seen the goat break loose in Grand Parade

I met a child, Eily Kilbride
Who'd never heard of marmalade,
Whose experience of breakfast
Was coldly limited,

Whose entire school day
Was a bag of crisps,
Whose parents had no work to do,

Who went, once, into the countryside,
Saw a horse with a feeding bag over its head
And thought it was sniffing glue.

Brendan Kennelly (1936–)

Questions

1. The first verse includes a line from a popular and well-known song about Cork, 'On the banks of my own lovely Lee'. Why is that line included here? (10)
2. What part of Eily's experience would you see as the most upsetting? Explain your choice by describing the kind of picture it gives you and the feelings related to it. (10)

OR

3. How does the poet feel about Eily? Choose at least two from the following list of descriptive words which you think describe the way he is feeling: *sad, angry, gentle, happy, shocked, uncaring, frustrated*. Explain your choices. (20)

Eating Poetry

Ink runs from the corners of my mouth.
There is no happiness like mine.
I have been eating poetry.

The librarian does not believe what she sees.
Her eyes are sad
and she walks with her hands in her dress.

The poems are gone.
The light is dim.
The dogs are on the basement stairs and coming up.

Their eyeballs roll,
their blond legs burn like brush.
The poor librarian begins to stamp her feet and weep.

She does not understand.
When I get on my knees and lick her hand,
she screams.

I am a new man.
I snarl at her and bark.
I romp with joy in the bookish dark.

Mark Strand (1934–)

Questions

1. Why, in your opinion, does the librarian feel as she does? (10)
2. Write down one phrase from this poem that you found appealing. (10)

OR

3. Think about what has happened to the speaker in the poem. How does he convey the impact that reading the poem has had on him? (20)

Do Not Go Gentle into That Good Night

Do not go gentle into that good night,
Old age should burn and rave at close of day;
Rage, rage against the dying of the light.

Though wise men at their end know dark is right,
Because their words had forked no lightning they
Do not go gentle into that good night.

Good men, the last wave by, crying how bright
Their frail deeds might have danced in a green bay,
Rage, rage against the dying of the light.

Wild men who caught and sang the sun in flight,
And learn, too late, they grieved it on its way,
Do not go gentle into that good night.

Grave men, near death, who see with blinding sight
Blind eyes could blaze like meteors and be gay,
Rage, rage against the dying of the light.

And you, my father, there on the sad height,
Curse, bless, me now with your fierce tears, I pray.
Do not go gentle into that good night.
Rage, rage against the dying of the light.

Dylan Thomas (1914–53)

Questions

1. Comment on the poet's use of repetition in this poem. (10)
2. Write down one phrase from the poem that shows how the poet feels about death. Say why you have chosen this phrase. (10)

OR

3. Write a personal response to this poem, highlighting the impact it had on you. (20)

Biographies and Critical Commentaries

Eavan Boland (1944–)

A Short Biography

Eavan Boland was born in Dublin in 1944, daughter of Frederick Henry Boland, a career diplomat who served as Ireland's Permanent Representative to the United Nations, and Frances Kelly, an artist. She was educated in London, New York and Dublin. Aged only 22, Boland published her first book of poems, *New Territory*. The next year she started to lecture at Trinity. Shortly afterwards she was employed as a columnist for *The Irish Times*. In her columns, Boland began to argue that the great poets of the past had idealised our understanding of women – a woman was often used as a **symbol** for Ireland in Irish poetry. In this manner, Boland felt that women had become objects and symbols. Much of her poetic output attempts to combat these clichéd views of women. In *Object Lessons*, published in 1995, she tells us that she knew that 'the women of the Irish past were defeated'. What she objected to was 'that Irish poetry should defeat them twice'.

When she married Kevin Casey and moved to the suburbs in the Dublin foothills to raise their two daughters, Boland found herself part of what she calls a 'devalued class'. At times, she felt that the decision to move to the suburbs was akin to being in exile. Rather than accepting this exile, Boland's poetry strives to engage with the experience of being a mother in suburbia. Writing on this aspect of Boland's life, Diane Rogers has commented that:

> as she washed dishes at the kitchen sink, Boland also listened for the rhythmic grind of a neighbour's garden shears; as she watched her children in the yard, she followed the play of dappled sunlight on rowan trees. And once the girls were in bed at night, she could retreat to her desk to write, drilling deeply into the everyday cadences and planes that surrounded her for the sound and shape of her own poetic voice. 'I used to work out of notebooks, and I learned when I had young children that you can always do something,' she says. 'If you can't do a poem, you can do a line. And if you can't do a line, you can do an image – and that pathway that leads you along, in fragments, becomes astonishingly valuable.'

Thus, early on, Boland centred her poems on home and garden and included everyday, domestic language that had never before been heard in Irish poetry: a 'can of Coke', 'teen magazines', 'small talk' and 'cable television' can be found in the poems in this anthology. The collection *The War Horse* was published in 1975 and deals with outside threats to home and family. In 1986, she published *The Journey and Other Poems*, which provides us with a dramatic portrayal of the mission of the poet in society. The year 1990 saw the publication of *Outside History*. As the title suggests, this collection deals with those who have been forgotten by history. This collection was critically acclaimed and established Boland's presence in the world of contemporary poetry. Aside from teaching at Trinity, she has also taught at Bowdoin College in Maine, New England and has been a member of the International Writing Program at the University of Iowa. In this anthology, the poem 'Love' refers to this period of her life. She has also lectured at the University of Houston, the University of Utah and Washington University in St Louis and has been internationally recognised for many years.

In 1991, Boland was included in the *Field Day Anthology of Irish Poetry*. This publication was intended to be a complete compendium of Irish writing. However, she was one of only three women to be so honoured. In Boland's estimation, this was an unforgivable oversight. Much like she does in many of the poems in this anthology, Boland spoke out for those who had been excluded. In a series of public interviews, she launched scathing attacks on the establishment. American critic Jody Allen Randolph, who works on both sides of the Atlantic as a poetry reviewer for *The Irish Times* and the *Women's Review of Books*, went to Dublin in 1988 as a Mellon fellow in Irish Studies and has followed Boland's career closely since then. Talking about the *Field Day* aftermath in *Standard Magazine*, she says, 'God, but it was fun to watch.' Although many younger poets feared for their careers and stayed out of the fray, she says Boland 'almost single-handedly challenged what was a very oppressive male establishment, one that was still trying to set terms for what the permissible subjects of poetry were'.

However, Boland's career was progressing to such an extent that the establishment she once attacked could no longer ignore her. In 1997, she received the Irish Literature Award. Other awards include a Lannan Foundation Award in Poetry and an American/Ireland Fund Literary Award. When the new English curriculum came on stream in 2001, Eavan Boland took her place alongside other well-known Irish writers such as Seamus Heaney, Derek Mahon, Michael Longley and John Montague as one of the prescribed poets on the Leaving Certificate syllabus. She is currently Professor of English at Stanford University, California. She divides her time between Dublin and the United States and continues to write regularly for *The Irish Times*.

Critical Commentary: The War Horse

See the text of the poem on pp. 2–3.

1. Content

Like so much of Boland's poetry, 'The War Horse' originates in a specific incident and has a clear and identifiable setting. This is a poem steeped in historical reference. In a real sense, the horse becomes a poetic **symbol** for the violence that has characterised the past millennium of Irish history.

Like many of Boland's poems, the message of 'The War Horse' can be understood on several levels. Interestingly, the poem first confronts the issue of violence in an almost 'clip, clop, casual' fashion. The open rhyming **couplets** work to reinforce this carefree attitude. There is little to suggest from the rhyming scheme that this is a serious poem, dealing with serious issues. Boland is, in this sense, mirroring our own attitudes to violence.

To the young reader, it is difficult to imagine the attitude that Irish people had towards the violence in Northern Ireland in the 1970s. A general sense of apathy and disinterest predominated in the face of the daily toll of mayhem and destruction that came from the North. The temptation for many people was to change the channel on the television rather than confront the reality of the Troubles. While the violence in Northern Ireland may seem like history to you, this poem should still be readily accessible. The casual nature of our reaction to the destruction wrought by the horse mirrors the detachment and emotional fatigue of the television era. The parallel between the seemingly irrelevant news of the crocus's death and our lack of concern with the endless tally of statistics concerning Northern Ireland or, indeed, any other trouble spot should be comprehensible to most readers. As the horse arrives,

> [...] he stamps death
> Like a mint on the innocent coinage of earth.

However, all of this is 'Of distant interest like a maimed limb'. This shocking **simile** accurately conveys the modern attitude to violence. The only real casualty of the horse's incursion is a crocus. Boland views this dead flower as being 'expendable, a mere | [...] volunteer'. As in so many other wars, the first to perish are usually those who are most expendable. Yet, curiously, the poem tells us that none of this should matter. And why is this so? The reason is simple: 'we are safe'. The horse passes on while the speaker and her neighbours hide behind curtains. At this point, the poem takes on a different aspect.

The speaker's blood now becomes 'still | With atavism'. 'Atavism' is an unusual word. It can be defined as bearing a resemblance to one's ancestors. Earlier on in the poem, Boland mentioned that the horse came from the 'tinker camp on the Enniskerry Road'. The Travellers are a separate ethnic group who have, some claim, their origins in the violent clearances of Cromwell. This is the first hint that the poem may be commenting on ancestral violence. The horse's arrival forces Boland to recall a past characterised by 'burned countryside' and 'illicit braid'. However, the impact of the horse's arrival lies not in the physical destruction brought about, but rather in the realisation that the past can reach far into the here and now. The 'illicit braid' and 'burned countryside' of the final stanza stand as stark reminders of the power and relevance of history. John Goodby has this to say about the poem:

> the vocabulary ('rose', 'volunteer', 'war', 'maimed', 'blown', 'corpses', 'mutilated', 'ribboned') hints at the guilty conscience of Nationalists in the Republic over the 'betrayed cause' of national unity now manifest in Northern violence.

The war horse thus becomes symbolic of the cycles of violence that have dominated Ireland's history. It is a history created by a population that has been taught to hate and to embrace a cause that was 'ruined' and tainted long before they were born. Much like 'Child of our Time', 'The War Horse' may be viewed as an attempt to come to terms with the senseless and casual violence that has become so familiar to us all. The result is a poem that draws from the collective consciousness of Irish history to produce a fresh and unique view of race memory. The title, 'The War Horse', signals that the past, and particularly Ireland's past, will be recalled or evoked in this poem and in this sense the poem remains faithful to its title.

Interestingly, in an interview with Kathleen Fraser, published in *Parnassus: Poetry in Review*, Eavan Boland said that one of her more pressing artistic concerns was how the 'lyric would hold up in a time of violence: how a well-made poem, nurtured by British and Irish traditions, would sustain an assault on its subject matter and tone'. In light of this statement, the poem may be viewed as a poetic enquiry into, amongst other things, the impact of violence on our sensibilities.

As we have seen, the poem situates itself in a very recognisable suburban Irish setting, yet it is steeped in history. This is very important for both your understanding of the piece and your preparation for the examination.

The following are some points for you to consider when dealing with this poem in relation to other Boland poems you have studied.

a. As with 'The Black Lace Fan my Mother Gave me', 'The Famine Road', 'Outside History' and 'The Shadow Doll', history is brought into contact with the present in this poem. The incursion of the horse is a sharp reminder that history can leave destruction in its wake. It is history that uproots the present and all too often leaves 'corpses, remote, crushed, [and] mutilated'.

b. It is interesting to note that the intrusion of history sweeps aside the carefully ordered life of the Dublin suburb. This intrusion is accompanied by a challenge to our preconceived notions about identity, race, memory and violence.

c. In many ways, this is a poem built around tension and conflict. As we have seen, there is the obvious tension between past and present. However, there is an equally uneasy relationship between the suburban setting and the wild disorientation of the natural world. The war horse is untamed and free, paying no heed to the niceties of suburban living. The domesticated setting is made to cower and tremble as uninhibited nature is literally given free rein. The scant protection offered by the 'curtains' is a fitting symbol of the impotence of suburbia when confronted with the unrestrained power of the horse.

2. Stylistic Features

Technically, 'The War Horse' is a highly crafted poem. From the outset, the poem's rhyming scheme attempts to work in harmony with the themes we have just discussed. The sequence of open rhyming and half rhyming **couplets** is not allowed to settle down and must be read in a series of energetic gushes. This creates a carefree, open feel to the poem. In this manner, Boland tries to mirror the carefree attitude of most people to violence. It is a difficult poem to read slowly. The momentum of the horse's movement carries the reader along, until we too join in the sigh of relief at this horse's passing. Other techniques that Boland puts to good use include *onomatopoeia, assonance* and *alliteration*. Try to see if you can notice these. Their effect is to heighten our awareness of the horse's intrusion. Equally, the poem employs a series of muscular verbs in order to create a vibrant and powerful poetic pattern. The imagery of the poem is graphic and highly visual. Boland uses, amongst other things, an unusual series of *similes* and *metaphors* to great effect. Consider the impact of the torn leaf, which we learn is 'like a maimed limb'.

3. Essay Writing

When studying for the exam, consider the following.

a. 'The War Horse' manages to deconstruct the familiar divisions between past and present.
b. It causes us to reassess our relationship with violence and the past.
c. This is a layered poem that approaches its subject matter from more than one viewpoint.
d. At all times, there is a distinctly feminine voice to the poem.
e. The poetic process is given a new setting and suburbia is validated as a place of artistic worth.

Critical Commentary: Child of our Time

See the text of the poem on p. 4.

1. Content

All violence can be viewed as a direct result of an inability to communicate. The violence of the Dublin and Monaghan bombings in 1974 is no different. This poem can be read as a commentary on the failure of communication or as a searing condemnation of violence. At the heart of the poem is a powerful evocation of the loss, dismay and shock at the news of a child's murder. The poem was inspired by a newspaper photograph of the dead child (Aengus) being carried from the rubble in the arms of a fireman. However, this is also a poem that asks many questions of society. We are told that it is 'our time' that has 'robbed' this child of his 'cradle'.

This poem also examines the role that language has to play in the cycles of violence that have led to this child's murder. It is interesting to scrutinise the terminology of 'Child of our Time' in order to examine the degree to which violence and language have become linked within its narrative. The poem opens with an attempt to 'order' a lullaby. We are told that this 'lullaby' is inspired by the child's 'final cry'. However, the *rhythm* of this lullaby is uneven and discordant, or disharmonious. In this sense, it is a children's song that has failed. Boland causes the poem to fail as a lullaby in order to show how language itself has failed the child. No child would ever wish to be lulled to sleep by these lines of poetry. The poet uses the language of her poem to reinforce the notion that language itself is partially responsible for the death of the child. However, you should notice that the central *paradox* of this poem is that language may be our only hope. If violence is to end, people must talk.

Despite the criticism of 'idle talk' that lies at the heart of the poem, it is important to realise that this poem affirms Boland's belief that language is the only real defence against the barbarism of violence. Boland invites us to find 'a new language' so that we can end the violence that has resulted in this tragedy.

'Child of our Time' has, however, transcended the empty meaninglessness of violence to produce something beautiful. For a moment at least, the beauty of the poem, however poignant, eclipses the bitterness and hatred that have dogged Irish history. The shattered glass and the tragedy caused by this bomb are replaced, if only temporarily, by rhythm and meaning. There is nevertheless one final element of sadness to this poem: this child will never hear Boland's lullaby.

2. Stylistic Features

'Child of our Time' achieves much of its immediacy and impact through its language. The beautiful simplicity and restrained expression of the poem work to enhance its central message. A more conventional examination of the poem reveals a carefully worked-out grammar and *syntax*. The word order of the poem strives to mirror the seriousness of its subject matter. Boland does not allow the words to flow smoothly. This forces us to stop and consider the meaning of each word. The brutal meaninglessness of this killing is accurately reflected in Boland's choice of imagery. The *images* of 'broken [...] limbs', a lost childhood and an empty cradle work to reinforce the tragedy. The result is a finely tuned poem that delivers its message with poise and compassion. This tragic death is confronted because we 'must learn' from what has happened. A sense of haunting finality is created in the simplicity of 'you dead'. In a real sense, Boland is searching for an 'idiom' in order to explore this terrible event. This, perhaps, explains why the rhythm of the poem matches that of a lullaby. Curiously, however, this rhythm is never far from that of a *dirge*, or funeral march. The poet employs the personal pronoun 'we' and the possessive adjective 'our' to great effect. By making all of us share some of the responsibility for the child's death, Boland includes the reader in the process of mourning this murder. Notice how many times she employs language associated with the voice. It is as if she is attempting to give voice to the emotions engendered by the senseless death of a child.

3. Essay Writing

When you come to put your response to Boland's poetry into essay form, try to think of all her poetry rather than just one individual poem. The best paragraphs contain references to more than one poem and deal, instead, with one aspect of the poet's style or thematic concerns. If you want to use 'Child of our Time' in one or more of your paragraphs, consider the following.

a.   The poem deals with the poet's reaction to violence.
b.   It attempts to give a voice to the weak and vulnerable. In this manner, it is similar to some other poems by Boland on the course, such as 'The Famine Road' and 'Outside History'.
c.   The language of the poem is typical of the poetry of Eavan Boland. Its restrained simplicity and haunting realism work to enhance its central message.

Critical Commentary: The Famine Road

See the text of the poem on pp. 6–7.

1. Content

'The Famine Road' is a haunting poem. It is complex and can at first be difficult to read. You will have noticed two narratives in this poem. 'The Famine Road' opens with the voice of Trevelyan assuring his colonel that the Irish are lazy and in need of hard work. Interlaced with this narrative is the story of a woman visiting a gynaecologist. She is being told that she will not be able to conceive a child. As the poem progresses, Boland draws both narratives together to produce a memorable piece. In Boland's view, the tragedy of Irish history and the reality of being a woman are reflected in one another. This is what this poem attempts to convey through these two narratives. When asked about being Irish, Boland has stated:

> Apart from the fact that it connects me with a past, I find it a perspective on my womanhood as well. Womanhood and Irishness are metaphors for one another. There are resonances of humiliation, oppression and silence in both of them and I think you can understand one better by experiencing the other.

Thus, it is valid to read this poem as an attempt to join the experience of being a woman to the humiliation experienced during the Famine.

Let us first turn our attention to the narrative dealing with the Famine. The Great Famine is a horrific fault line in Irish history. After two successive years of blight on potato crops caused by mildew spores, many people chose to eat whatever seed they had rather than run the risk of planting a fresh crop of potatoes. Ironically and tragically, in 1847, there was little or no blight, but there was no crop either. The people had simply not planted enough to sustain themselves. 'Black 47', as it came to be known, saw the advent of fevers such as typhus, which rapidly spread through the weakened population. Workhouses were crammed with fever patients. Auxiliary workhouses were opened and fever sheds erected. Dr Daly reported from Newport in May 1847:

> Fever, dysentery and diarrhoea are greatly on the increase, beginning with vomiting, pains, headache very intense; coming to a crisis in about seven days, relapsing again once or twice, from which death occurred through mere debility or diarrhoea, caused and kept up by bad food, principally Indian meal, supplied to them in small quantities, and which they invariably swallow after only a few minutes boiling and sometimes cold and raw. The greatest mortality is among the labourers, men and women, on public roads, in cold, wet, boggy hills.

No other single event in the history of Ireland has so touched and shaped our identity. In *Outside History*, Eavan Boland explains how she first became aware of the Famine. She tells us that on a visit to Achill Island, she came into contact with an old woman who was:

the first person to talk to me about the famine. The first person, in fact, to speak to me with any force about the terrible parish of survival and death which the event had been in those regions. She kept repeating to me that they were great people, the people of the famine. Great people, I had never heard that before.

Having read the above, you should be able to understand the narrative in the poem that deals with the Famine. As we have said, the poem opens with Lord Trevelyan advising his subordinate on how to deal with the 'idle' and starving Irish population. The manner in which his seal bloodies the deal table is significant. Blood is a ***motif*** that runs through this poem. The attitude of these men is completely lacking in compassion and this is mirrored in their decision:

> [...] to give them roads, roads to force
> from nowhere, going nowhere of course [...]

Notice how the Irish themselves are denied any voice. Those in power decide the manner in which this population will die. The people have no say in this.

The poem now changes direction abruptly. The narrative in italics takes place in a doctor's rooms. We have moved through time to the present day. The cold, arrogant lack of compassion shown by the doctor mirrors the attitude of Jones, Trevelyan and the Relief Committee. Notice how the woman in question is also denied a voice. In the third stanza, we return to the 'Sick [and] directionless' Famine victims. The physical deprivation and suffering experienced by this starving population are accurately captured in the following lines:

> [...] after all could
> they not blood their knuckles on rock, suck
> April hailstones for water and for food?

The hunger and distress caused by being forced to work with inadequate tools in difficult conditions reduces them to the level of animals. They eye each other hungrily as their humanity is eroded.

The poem switches direction and once again we are in the doctor's surgery. The woman is informed that anything may have caused her defect. It may have even been '*spores*'. This links her plight to that of the Famine victims. The blight that affected the potatoes was carried by fungal spores. Despite the life-altering gravity of what the doctor is telling the woman, his ***tone*** remains detached. To him, it is an ordinary, everyday mystery, not to be questioned. She remains silent. In the fifth stanza, we return once again to the past. It is now dusk and the effects of the Famine are made more vivid. One of the work party has become a 'typhoid pariah'. As a result of the disease, his companions, even though some are relatives, shun him.

> Dusk: they will work tomorrow without him.
> They know it and walk clear […]

The image of the snow settling and melting is a powerful and poignant one. It captures in a simple and moving fashion the fragility of human life. Before we have time to consider fully the tragedy of this death, the narrative returns to the present. The tone of the doctor has changed slightly. Coldness and detachment now give way to an arrogant, patronising tone. The woman is told that she '*never will*' give birth. Instead of mothering a child, she is told to '*grow* | [her] *garden, keep house*'. The abrupt '*good-bye*' signals the point at which the doctor washes his hands of the woman. She remains silent.

In the seventh stanza, Colonel Jones makes his final, sickening report to his master, Trevelyan. Following the cruelty of the work programmes, he reports:

> […] sedition, idleness, cured
> in one; from parish to parish, field to field;
> the wretches work till they are quite worn,
> then fester by their work […]

There is an appalling lack of human compassion in these lines. This is followed by a shocking admission:

> […] we march the corn
> to the ships in peace […]

The Famine years saw a continuation of the export of cereal crops from Ireland. However shocking this may be, it is historically accurate. The starving Irish quite literally looked on while the food they needed to survive was exported. The poem ends with a return to the woman's narrative. She is still denied a direct voice. Then, in the final stanza, rhymed *aba* to round off the poem, we are told that she will never know the '*load* | *of [a] child in* [*her*]'. Her body is now barren. Like the Famine road itself, she lacks direction.

2. Stylistic Features

'The Famine Road' constitutes a poignant interlacing of voices. At first, Boland manages to make use of the private and public voices of the Relief Committee. We first meet the private voice of Trevelyan. It is a voice laced with contempt. The Irish are, in his view, 'Idle as trout in light' and should be given:

> [...] no coins at all; their bones
> need toil, their characters no less.' [...]

Notice how the Irish are objectified. They are, in Lord Trevelyan's eyes, 'these Irish'. The wheedling of the public works committee is matched by Trevelyan's coldness. The hypocrisy of the committee is such that it tries to sell the programmes as being 'safe'. The public decision of the committee to give them roads 'going nowhere of course' is sickening. The language of the committee continues to objectify the Irish. It is worth pointing out that, in this poem, the Irish are not permitted to speak; they, unlike the English, have no voice. The structure of 'The Famine Road' mirrors this fact. The two stanzas that outline the tortured and dehumanising experiences of the Irish people are framed by the two English stanzas. As a result, the Irish become little more than objects.

The narrative voice of the poem changes once again. The four *tercets* in italics concentrate on the condition of the woman unable to conceive. The italics show us that the woman's story is different. She is marginalised by her experience. In the first three tercets, the *tone* of the voice descends from professional impartiality to arrogance.

The final tercet attempts to acknowledge the individuality of the woman. While not allowing the woman to speak directly, the objective third person attempts to give voice to the woman's emotions:

> *Barren, never to know the load*
> *of his child in you, what is your body*
> *now if not a famine road?*

The result is a highly crafted poem that manages to convey its message through several voices.

3. Essay Writing

When it comes to essay writing, 'The Famine Road' is an interesting poem. If you are considering using this poem in your essays, you may want to include the poem in any paragraph that deals with the following.

a. Boland's tendency to move through time. In this manner, the poem links with 'The Black Lace Fan my Mother Gave me', 'The Pomegranate', 'Love' and 'Outside History'.
b. Boland's treatment of history.
c. The technical aspects of the poem: the interlacing of voices, the changes in tone and the powerful imagery.

Critical Commentary: The Shadow Doll

See the text of the poem on p. 9.

1. Content

Once again, we are taken on a journey through time. The lines between past and present are allowed to blur as Boland considers the shadow doll. According to the author's own explanatory note at the beginning of the poem:

> (*This was sent to the bride-to-be in Victorian times, by her dressmaker. It consisted of a porcelain doll, under a dome of glass, modelling the proposed wedding dress.*)

The poem opens with a description of the doll. It is stitched from delicate silk or 'ivory tulle'. The crinoline or petticoat is made of 'hoops'. In the second stanza, we learn that the doll is 'neatly sewn'. Thanks to the airless glass dome that contains the doll, it has survived long beyond the occasion it was intended for. It has survived to the present and is relatively untouched by the ravages of time. In the third stanza, Boland considers the lifespan of the doll. The words 'even now' highlight the return to the present and recall the same words used in her poem 'The Black Lace Fan my

Mother Gave me'. The wedding, the woman and her family are long since gone, but the doll remains. The lives it has witnessed, the 'fevers', the births and the 'lusts' have passed into history. Boland sees the doll as having been a discreet observer of these events.

In the fourth stanza, the poem changes direction ever so slightly. Boland presents us with the *image* of the woman staring at the shadow doll. Stanza five, in typical Boland fashion, transports us through the years to the night of that Victorian woman's wedding. The woman looking at the doll's glass case can see her reflection. Suddenly, the doll's case becomes a *metaphor* for marriage itself. The silence of the doll *symbolises* the silence of women and their inability to give voice to their feelings about marriage, sexuality and motherhood. The doll holding the flowers ('stephanotis') is encased and trapped, unable to feel the 'satin rise and fall with the vows'. The sixth stanza signals a further change in the narrative. The interjection of the poet's voice in the form of the personal pronoun 'I' grabs our attention. Here, Boland imagines herself as she was on the night of her own wedding:

> [...] among the cards and wedding gifts –
> the coffee pots and the clocks and
>
> the battered tan case full of cotton

As with so much of Boland's poetry in this anthology, the poem has managed to span the years. The use of the present tense underscores this process of transition from past to present. The speaker feels strangely lost or 'astray'. The emotion of her wedding night is captured beautifully in the poem's final action. As the poet leans on 'the battered tan case', it 'locks'. The sound that this action creates provides the poem with a tangible moment of closure. The final action is that of a woman who is directing the course of her own life.

2. Stylistic Features

On the whole, the language of the poem is straightforward and restrained. The poem is written in a series of seven *tercets*. The careful construction of the three-line stanzas mirrors the careful consideration of the shadow doll at the centre of the poem. The poem makes use of *rhyme* and *half-rhyme* as the stanzas flow into one another. Boland moves with ease from past to present and from detached observer to active agent. Some of the language in the poem is obscure. However, the choice of unusual words like 'tulle', 'crinoline' and 'stephanotis' is calculated. The doll described by Boland is a piece of history. The use of these words adds to the antiquated feel of the doll. One of the most effective linguistic devices employed by Boland is to be found in the final line. This short, terse line closes the poem off in a measured fashion. Given its length, the line is heavily punctuated. The use of the ***onomatopoeic*** verb 'locks' rounds the poem off perfectly.

3. Essay Writing

When framing your personal response to the poems by Boland on the course, you may wish to make reference to 'The Shadow Doll'. Remember that your paragraphs should centre on a particular point or issue rather than on a poem. While it may seem easier to write a paragraph on a particular poem, with practice you will come to see that a paragraph centred on one theme or issue is preferable. For more information on this, please consult the examination technique section of this book on p. 548. The following points may also prove useful.

a. This is yet another poem by Boland where the past and present come into contact with one another.
b. The poem examines its subject matter from the point of view of the outsider. In this instance, the Victorian woman is about to enter a marriage that in itself implies subjugation.
c. The manner in which this poem tells its story provides links to the other poems on the course. The simplicity of its language, the use of the personal pronoun 'I' and the honesty of the speaker are all hallmarks of Boland's poetry.

Critical Commentary: White Hawthorn in the West of Ireland

See the text of the poem on p. 11.

1. Content

The title, 'White Hawthorn in the West of Ireland', is essential to our understanding of this poem. White hawthorn has always had powerful superstitious associations for the Irish. In early summer, hawthorn blossoms into clumps of tiny white flowers; hawthorn also figures prominently in the ancient Bealtaine celebrations. This tree, especially if found growing alone, is considered to have magical properties. To ensure continuity of milking, it was considered a wise precaution to pour a few drops of milk on or near a solitary white hawthorn tree in a pasture field. However, it is also widely thought to be an unlucky tree. It was thought very unwise to cut or disturb this tree. To do so was to invite death into the household. The next time you are travelling through the Irish countryside, look out for pasture land containing solitary trees that have not been touched – these are probably hawthorn trees because these superstitions still persist.

The poem opens with the poet driving 'West' as she leaves the order of 'suburban gardens' and 'lawnmowers' behind her. As she moves further into the West of Ireland, she begins to assume something of its qualities, its 'hard shyness [...] and the superstitious aura of hawthorn'.

In the third stanza, the speaker notices the snowy cloud of hawthorn flowers. She longs to 'fill [her] arms with I sharp flowers, I [...] to be part of I that ivory, downhill rush'. However, she resists this urge. In the fourth stanza, she reminds us that she had always known that 'the custom was I not to touch hawthorn'. Such an act could tempt fate and result in a fever amongst livestock or, even worse, a 'child might die'.

The poem changes direction somewhat in the final two stanzas. The sight of the hawthorn, and the reminder of the tree's place in Irish tradition, connects the poet with an unspoken language. In essence, the poem can be read as a beautiful and unique commentary on being Irish. The 'small talk', the suburbs and the 'lawnmowers', which are all *symbolic* of modern Ireland, give way to the beauty of the West and its traditions. The hawthorn is a real link to our past and, suddenly, in the final two stanzas, Boland becomes part of that past. This experience is essentially indescribable. The landscape becomes strangely redefined for the poet as she partakes in 'the only language spoken in those parts'.

2. Stylistic Features

This poem is carefully measured and its structure reflects this fact. The opening line stands alone and is the only one in the first stanza not to be end stopped. This draws our attention to the importance of the journey about to be undertaken. The poem is written in *free verse* and this too is particularly suited to the idea of a journey about to be undertaken. When the poet encounters the white hawthorn in stanza three, a series of *run-on lines* or *enjambments* captures her excitement. These fluid, free-flowing lines also capture something of the hawthorn, as seen by the poet. It has, she tells us, a 'fluency I only water has'. In the final stanza, lines flow freely into one another until we reach the closing line. This rounds the poem off nicely.

3. Essay Writing

This poem shares many of the characteristic traits that we have seen in other Boland poems. The poem would be particularly suitable for any paragraph addressing the following subjects.

a. Boland's approach to the examination of history or, more specifically, her tendency to document unrecorded history.
b. Boland's interest in mythology.
c. Boland's inclination to trace the divisions between the order of suburbia and the freedom of the countryside. (You may wish to compare it to 'The War Horse'.)
d. Her use of language. (The techniques employed in the poem are very similar to those found in the other poems by Boland in this anthology.)

Critical Commentary: Outside History

See the text of the poem on p. 13.

1. Content

This poem opens with an inescapable fact. If you have read 'The Famine Road' or, indeed, if you just take a look at the world you live in, you will recognise that 'There are outsiders, always.' Much of Boland's poetry concerns itself with the plight of the outsider and the voiceless. From the child unable to speak about the outrage committed against it to the woman denied a voice by her doctor, her poems concern themselves with those on the margins. The stars of the first stanza stand apart from the history and pain of the Irish. Their light reaches us through the darkness of space. It is a light that has travelled through time. When you look at the light of a star, you are in fact gazing at a false image of a time that has long since passed. The remote distance of the stars that 'illuminate the sky' of 'an Irish January' throws the plight of the human population into sharp relief. Time, in human terms, seems so brief when compared to the life of a star. The **run-on line** pushes the first stanza into the second, where we learn that their 'light happened I thousands of years before I our pain did'. There is a beautiful, yet poignant, simplicity to these lines. Our loneliness and isolation in the darkness of space are made all the more distressing by the pain we inflict upon ourselves. The stars, however, continue to 'keep their distance', unmoved by our 'mortal' concerns.

In the fifth stanza, the poem changes significantly as Boland looks at history and, in particular, at our tendency to transform history into 'myth'. From here on, the poem can be read as a sharp criticism of the mythicisation of Irish history. Here, Boland tries to give voice to those who have actually lived the events of the past. Myth is seen as a deceiver that, much like the light of the stars, is nothing more than a fantasy or a chimera. **Mythology** is separate from Irish history, as lived by the people of the island. This is the central message of the poem. Myth and, above all, the attempt to dress the past in false clothes is a dangerous occupation that has yielded tragic results. In this respect, the poem uncovers the back roads and alleyways of history to reveal a past that is 'clotted as I firmaments with the dead.' There are as many people who have suffered and died as there are stars in heaven. This is a sobering thought. As Boland tries to speak to these shadows from the past, she realises that the span of years is too great:

And we are too late. We are always too late.

2. Stylistic Features

The language in this poem is straightforward and easily accessible. The punctuation and extensive use of the **run-on line**, or **enjambment**, allows the poem to flow freely. This fluidity mirrors the ebb and flow of time as examined in the poem. On a general level, Boland takes the language she employs to detail the stars in the first stanza and superimposes this on her descriptions of the human world. Both stars and people are viewed as a landscape to be described. The verb 'clotted', used to describe the roads and rivers crowded with the dead, could equally be applied to the stars. John Goodby has described Boland's style as 'deliberately unsophisticated and forceful … that is calculated to upset cherished stereotypes'. It is, he goes on to say, a style 'where vocabulary and *syntax* are simplified; rhythms are punchy; and *rhymes* obvious and frequent'. This is certainly true of 'Outside History'.

3. Essay Writing

As you think about organising your essay's paragraphs, consider some of the following possible ways to mention 'Outside History'.

a. This is a moving poem that delivers its message in a straightforward manner.
b. Once again, history is a central concern. You should now see that this is a major link when it comes to framing a written response to Boland's poetry. When considering history as a possible focus of your paragraph, remember the links between the 'The Black Lace Fan my Mother Gave me', 'The War Horse' and 'The Famine Road'.
c. Discuss the technical aspects of the poem: its tone, the restrained and powerful imagery and its aesthetic appeal.

Critical Commentary: The Black Lace Fan my Mother Gave me

See the text of the poem on p. 15.

1. Content

This is a complex, beautiful poem that deals with those classic themes of poetry – love, life and the passing of time. The poem opens in a very direct fashion. This black lace fan, we learn, was 'the first gift' Boland's father gave her mother. The fan becomes a symbol of her mother and father's courtship. As the poet has no way of knowing what happened during this stage in their relationship, she is forced to 'improvise'. The barriers between past and present become loosened, and the result is an emotionally charged poem. Through her study of the black lace fan,

Boland manages to reconstruct the courtship of her mother and father. By moving through the layers of the past, she throws fresh light on her understanding of their relationship.

This examination of the rituals that surround any love story leads to profound insights into the nature of existence, love and the passing of time. Boland brings us back to her parents' meetings in 'pre-war Paris'. We are told that the weather was 'stifling', 'the nights stormy' and that 'They met in cafés'. This is the stuff of a romance novel or a Hollywood love story. There is certainly something cinematic about these opening lines. Boland herself has stated that she wanted to create 'a jerky, grainy feel to the poem', much like the experience of watching an old black and white movie. This adds to the romance of the opening stanzas. However, in a very subtle manner, the poet manages to introduce a sense of urgency to the lovers' courtship. She informs us that:

> The heat was killing.
> She thought the distance smelled of rain and lightning.

This must be read as an **allusion** to the impending war and the blitzkrieg, or lightning warfare, of Nazi Germany. This reference to a historical event that had such an enormous impact on people's lives is a powerful reminder that nothing in this world lasts forever. Despite the careful, considered nature of Boland's treatment of the past, it is an improvisation and thus incomplete. So, before she completes this portrait of her parents' courtship, she returns to the present.

'The Black Lace Fan my Mother Gave me' is framed within a series of precise temporal references. We are made aware from the outset that this poem is dealing with a historical event. However, despite the obvious historical context of the opening stanzas, Boland chooses to introduce the continuous present tense. The effect of this is to blur the distinctions between history and the present. We are literally made to relive events. Her father is still 'buying' the fan, even though it is 'pre-war Paris'. This signals the beginning of the blending of the past and present and forms an essential characteristic of the poem. The sands of time shift again in stanza four as Boland gives closer consideration to the detail on the fan. We now return to the present. The 'wild roses' are a reminder of the romantic connotations associated with the gift. Yet for all the romance of its 'café terrace', the past cannot be relived.

We are told that the fan, like the 'tortoiseshell' from which it was made, has a 'reticent, | clear patience'. Here, the tone of the poem changes significantly and darkens. Even now, an 'inference' of the destruction or 'violation' that was necessary to create this fan can be detected. In the poet's eyes, the fan is transformed from an object symbolising love to one that reminds us that change is inevitable.

This is a beautiful poem. It takes us into the past to witness the romance and the emotion of a relationship in its early stages. In the process, we are made to confront some harsh realities concerning the passing of time. As the poem ends, Boland returns to the present and describes the blackbird in an act of courtship:

> [...] Suddenly she puts out her wing –
> the whole, full, flirtatious span of it.

2. Stylistic Features

It is rare to find a poet who is willing to explain the rationale behind the technical choices made in a poem. Given that Boland has provided us with a detailed account of how she crafted this poem in her book *Object Lessons*, it might be best to allow her to explain the techniques she has used:

This poem is about a black lace fan. The fan actually exists. As I write this, I know it is downstairs in a glass-fronted cupboard, all folded in, a bit crumpled and definitely faded. But in its first existence, as I imagine it here, it was fully spread out. The lace was crisp and scratchy. The tortoiseshell at the base of it had a yellow sheen. The tasselled cord looked silky and ungrimy.

This fan was the first gift my father gave my mother. They were in a heat wave in Paris in the thirties and, as she once told me, he went to the Galeries Lafayette, a big cluster of shops, and bought the fan just before he went on to keep his appointment with her.

Eventually my mother gave me the fan and told me its story. But the poem began in an image and not a story. The image was of an object, which was entirely silent. I could hold it and feel its mixture of smoothness and friction. But it would never be able to tell me whether my father rushed down the Boulevard des Capucines to be there on time. Did he rush? It would never be able to tell me what they said, or when the storm broke. What did they say? What did the storm look like?

Just asking these questions made me want to re-create the event: the storm, the man and the woman, the drama and poignancy of the first steps in a courtship. But first I had to make the fan vivid again: not the crumpled object I owned but the beautiful, surprising gift it had once been. To do that, I had to make some choices: practical technical choices. These can be hard to describe in hindsight, but here are two examples of those choices.

Firstly, I decided to make the opening stanza of the poem slip and slide a bit: to make the pronouns shimmer and disappear. To make the reader feel the ground of grammar shift and tip in a disconcerting way. So I used the word 'it' twice. The first 'it', of course, is the fan. It was the first gift he ever gave her. The second 'it' is evidently about the weather. It was stifling. But it looks back a little bit, like something disappearing in a car mirror, to the other it. And so the fan, the weather, the heat, the mystery are deliberately confused and merged by those pronouns.

In the second stanza I change the caesuras around. Perhaps the word is hardly used any more. And yet there hasn't been a replacement for it, so I will use it here. No one should be afraid of it. All a caesura means is where you break the line as you are writing it: after two beats, or three, or even one. Or not at all. Where you pause, or don't pause, in other words. The name may be rather artificial and off-putting. But the actual practice of breaking the line can yield very useful results for a poet and be instantly picked up as a slight, but important, shift in speed by the readers, even if they don't use that name for it. It's a little like the controls on a video; slowing down or speeding up the tape. Here I write four lines where I move the action along a little: to show they stayed in the city, were meeting in the cafes, were sometimes late for one another, and this time he was delayed by buying the fan. I use no caesura in the first or last line. Then in the following three lines I put the caesura or internal line-break after the second stress. That way I get a jerky, grainy feel to the stanza: a little like the frames of an old film. And that's what I wanted.

> They stayed in the city for the summer.
> They met in cafés. She was always early.
> He was late. That evening he was later.
> They wrapped the fan. He looked at his watch.

The fan, the story, the history of the object all had and have great meaning for me. But sometimes a poem's existence is decided in a split second. And that happened here. I had the fan; I knew the story. And still I hadn't the poem although I had thought about it. Then one late spring morning I was looking out my back window into the garden. A female blackbird was just in front of our apple tree, moving around, looking for worms. It was sunny and clear and the light was moving directly to that part of the grass. Suddenly, as I watched, she put out one brown wing: a wonderfully constructed fan-like movement, now open, now shut. There and then the existence of the poem was guaranteed. I had wanted to write about the fan, the past, the lost moment. I lacked the meaning. Now here, in this evocation in nature of the man-made object of courtship, I found the meaning I needed and the final image for the poem.

> The blackbird on this first sultry morning,
> in summer, finding buds, worms, fruit,
> feels the heat. Suddenly she puts out her wing –
> the whole, full, flirtatious span of it.

3. Essay Writing

'The Black Lace Fan my Mother Gave me' is an important poem and, as such, is certainly worth mentioning in any response to Boland's poetry. When writing about Boland's poetry, you should bear the following points in mind.

a. The poem deals with the passing of time. In *Object Lessons*, Boland has said that 'ordinary objects seemed to warn [her] that the body might share the world but could not own it'. In other words, the fan is a reminder of the passing of time. This links the poem to 'The Shadow Doll' and 'White Hawthorn in the West of Ireland'.

b. The poem moves through time and, in the process, past and present become blurred. This is, of course, true of other Boland poems on the course. Consider how this same process can be seen in 'The Shadow Doll', 'White Hawthorn in the West of Ireland', 'The Famine Road' and 'The War Horse'.

c. The poem is honest about the relationships in Boland's life. This can be used to form a link to 'Love' and 'The Pomegranate'.

Critical Commentary: This Moment

See the text of the poem on p. 17.

1. Content

There is something almost cinematic about this poem. Here, as elsewhere, Boland examines a condensed moment in time. The result is a simple, honest, yet deeply moving poem.

There is something so familiar about the scene that Boland presents to us. We are taken to a suburban neighbourhood. The time of year suggested by the early twilight, ripening fruit and fluttering moths is most likely autumn. Autumn brings with it a feeling of comfort and of natural abundance. Furthermore, and this again adds to the warmth of the poem, one can sense a feminine presence at work. The description of suburbia feels somehow safe and warm. This feeling of security finds its fullest expression in the unification of the mother and child. In *Object Lessons,* Boland asks the following question:

> Is there something about the repeated action — about lifting a child, clearing a dish, watching the season return to a tree and depart from a vista — which reveals a deeper meaning to existence and heals some of the worst abrasions of time?

Perhaps this is the best way to view 'This Moment' – as an attempt to heal 'those abrasions of time'. In any case, the poem does offer insights into the beauty that can exist in the ordinary. In his famous poem 'Canal Bank Walk', Patrick Kavanagh celebrated the everyday, the habitual, the 'banal'. This is what Boland attempts to do here. The ordinary is given new meaning and relevance and is celebrated with a lover's intensity. Here, Boland reinstates suburbia as a setting worthy of poetic expression.

2. Stylistic Features

This poem stands apart from the other poems by Boland on the course. Boland's poetry can be forceful and vigorous in its approach. Very often, the power of its message is matched by powerful language. Boland was determined to make her poems address the ordinary, everyday concerns that had never traditionally been the stuff of poetry.

This is precisely what she does here. The ordinary things in everyday life are celebrated. Reading this poem, we can easily recognise the picture she paints. It's dusk in autumn and 'Things are getting ready | to happen'. The uninhibited simplicity of the poem's language reflects the ordinariness of its *theme*. There is not one word in this poem that forces the reader to consult a dictionary. This is a very accessible poem.

3. Essay Writing

There are possible links betwen 'This Moment' and the other poems that you have studied. If you include 'This Moment' in a paragraph, consider some of these points.

a. The poem is readily accessible to most readers.
b. The language of the poem mirrors the simplicity of its message.
c. Once again, this is a poem by Boland that is situated in suburbia. Despite the unpoetic setting of 'This Moment', the poem provides the reader with wonderful poetry.
d. The imagery in the poem is almost cinematic. It is striking and memorable.

Critical Commentary: The Pomegranate

See the text of the poem on pp. 19–20.

1. Content

'The Pomegranate' draws on the Greek and Roman *myth* of Ceres and Persephone. Before engaging in any commentary on the poem, it is important first to understand the myth. Ceres is the Roman name for the Greek goddess Demeter. For the Greeks, Ceres was the Mother Goddess of the Earth. Seduced by Zeus, she had a daughter, Persephone, by him. Persephone grew up happily amongst the other daughters of Zeus but, as she was extremely beautiful, her uncle, god of the underworld, fell in love with her. One day while Persephone was picking flowers (it is said she was picking a narcissus), the ground opened and Hades appeared and dragged her down into the underworld. Persephone cried out as she vanished, but when Ceres arrived to where Persephone had been, there was no sign of her anywhere.

For nine days and nine nights, Ceres roamed the earth with a lighted torch in either hand, looking for her beloved daughter. Only on the tenth day did she meet Helios, the sun god. He was able to tell her what had really happened. In protest, Ceres decided to abandon her duties. This self-imposed exile from the divinities made the earth sterile, so Zeus ordered Hades to return Persephone. However, that was no longer possible. During her stay in Hades (this is sometimes the word used to describe the underworld), Persephone had eaten a pomegranate seed, which linked her forever to Hades. A compromise was reached by which Ceres would return to Mount Olympus, home of the gods of Greek mythology, and Persephone would divide the year, spending half of it with her mother and the other half in the underworld. When Persephone leaves the underworld to be with her mother, the earth blossoms, bringing spring and summer to the mortals as a sign of the joy of both deities. When the time comes for Persephone to leave her mother for the underworld, autumn and winter cover the earth as a sign of their grief. According to Greek mythology, the pomegranate is a fruit that tends to grow at the entrance to the underworld. In this poem, this fruit symbolises temptation and growth.

Boland uses the myth of Ceres and Persephone to highlight universal truths. In this case, insight is given into the relationship between mother and daughter. It is also worth bearing in mind that the poem suggests that the passing of time is inevitable. The poem not only spans the full extent of Boland's life, but it also traces the growth of her daughter through childhood and into early adulthood. It is worthwhile noting the process of change in the poem, as it provides useful links to Boland's other poems. Remember, when you come to write essays, these links should form the core of your paragraph structure.

'The Pomegranate' gives new life and relevance to ancient mythology. As the poem opens, we learn that Boland has always had a special relationship with the myth of Ceres and Persephone. It is a myth that she can 'enter […] anywhere'. As a child, she first encountered the myth while living in London, which was at the time a 'city of fogs and strange consonants'. One can imagine the young poet, already interested in the sound of language, drawn to a myth that deals with separation. The sombre fog and the 'crackling dusk' of the London cityscape mirror the gloomy landscape of Hades. This was Boland's first encounter with the myth. She was a child cut off from the world she had known in Ireland. In this sense, she was perfectly placed to empathise with Persephone, who was also 'a child in exile'.

'Later', Boland experienced the myth on a different level. A mother herself at this stage, she perceives the myth from the point of view of Ceres. Once again, 'twilight' and the darkness of Hades are recalled. However, on this occasion Boland is searching for her lost daughter. Such is her concern that she, like Ceres, is willing to 'make any bargain to keep her'. The evening reminds Boland of the changing nature of her relationship with her daughter. This, in turn, prompts the realisation that change is inevitable:

> winter was in store for every leaf
> on every tree on that road.

This is a remarkable shift in the poem's perspective. Before we are allowed to ponder the implications of this, the poem changes direction again. It is now 'winter | and the stars are hidden'. Notice how once again the physical environment mirrors the mythological landscape of Hades. As the speaker climbs the stairs, she is reminded of the myth. Her daughter's 'uncut fruit' leads her to recall the pomegranate. This forces the poet to recognise that her daughter has changed too. No longer the little girl who was once lost, she is now a teenager. At this point, Boland assesses the significance of this transformation. Here again, as elsewhere in the poem, she uses the myth to help her come to terms with the inevitability of her daughter's ageing. Her conclusion is that growth is unavoidable and that all growth involves pain of some sort. No matter how painful the transition from childhood to adulthood, each child must be given the space to make its way in the world.

This is an uncomfortable truth for any parent to accept. The parental desire to protect and shield the child from harm must yield to the child's need to be independent. The process of change that Boland alludes to is, most likely, linked to sexual awakening. The mention of the apple and its associations with temptation, together with the image of the daughter about to embrace 'the papery flushed skin', is evidence of this. The poem ends with a terse promise from Boland that she will 'say nothing'. Much like Ceres, Boland must let her daughter go, even though she knows that this process of separation will involve pain. Her daughter will have to experience this for herself. The temptations that life will offer cannot be mitigated by a mother's love:

> She will enter it. As I have.
> She will wake up. She will hold
> the papery flushed skin in her hand.
> And to her lips. I will say nothing.

2. Stylistic Features

The *mood, tone* and language of the poem display all the qualities of a good narrative. From the opening lines, we feel we are about to be told a story. Indeed, this is what happens: 'The Pomegranate' tells us the story of Boland's changing relationship with the myth of Ceres and Persephone. The *rhythm* is measured and thus matches the reflective nature of the poem. This poem is written in *blank verse*. This lack of rhyming scheme renders the feelings expressed in the poem more natural and honest. The use of the personal pronoun 'I' is arresting and draws the reader into the narative. The *allusions* to classical mythology give the poem an air of gravity. Once again, Boland's awareness of language becomes obvious to the reader. We learn that she first heard the myth in that 'city of fogs and strange consonants'. Finally, a myth is a unique and, in Boland's view, still valid expression of oftentimes hidden wisdom.

3. Essay Writing

Remember that the best way to frame your response to the poems by Boland on the course is to construct focused paragraphs that deal with one particular aspect of the poet's style or thematic concerns. For more complete help with essay-writing, please consult the examination technique section on p. 548 and bear the following points in mind.

a. This is a beautiful, complex poem.
b. It breathes new life into an ancient myth and, in this respect, it can be compared to the poem 'Love'.
c. This is another poem that unites past and present. In this sense, it links with 'The Famine Road', 'The Black Lace Fan my Mother Gave me' and 'The War Horse'.

Critical Commentary: Love

See the text of the poem on pp. 22–3.

1. Content

'Love' is a beautiful poem. Here again, Boland draws on **myth** in order to enrich her narrative. In this extract from an interview with *The New Yorker*, Boland talks about her experience writing this poem:

> When you write about marriage, you begin by writing about people and end by writing about time. That poem was about an incredibly intense moment of connection and endurance. Our second daughter had become sick. She was a year old and got meningitis and, for a short while, we really feared for her life. The meeting in the poem is about an encounter in that moment of fear and love. But it was a moment. And, when you think not of a moment together but of a life together, then you reflect differently.

'Love', then, is a deeply personal expression of a powerful emotion. Drawing on Homer's *Odyssey* and, in particular, book 11 of the poem, Boland uses the myth to throw light on the changing nature of her relationship with her husband. In book 11 of the *Odyssey*, Odysseus travels to the underworld in order to hasten his voyage home. Deeply in love with his wife, Penelope, the Greek hero braves the dangers of Hades so he can return to her sooner. In Homer's poem, Odysseus gives his view on marriage when he tells us that:

> nothing is greater or better than this, when man and wife dwell in a home in one accord, a great grief to their foes and a joy to their friends …

Boland's poem opens in North America and we are brought back to a specific moment in time. From this moment, Boland attempts to shed light on her relationship with her husband. We learn that when they lived in America, love 'had come to live with [them], I a brother of fire and air'. Love, then, is viewed by Boland as something elemental. The elements in the ancient Greek world were air, fire, water and earth. Three of these four elements are present in this poem. The speaker tells us that they had two children, one of whom 'was touched by death'. It is this event, this emotionally charged moment during her marriage, that Boland is drawn to explore. At this point in the poem, the speaker returns to Homer's *Odyssey*. When Odysseus journeyed to hell, he met many of his fallen comrades. However, the dead souls were unable to communicate with the living Odysseus. As we will see later, this is similar to Boland and her husband.

The poem then returns to the present. The event that prompted this poem 'was years ago', their child is now 'healed' and they 'love each other still'. Their relationship has, however, changed. While they now speak plainly and listen to each other, the poet still longs to return to that time in Iowa. The intense moment that gave rise to this poem still captivates the poet. In a series of charged lines, Boland sees her husband on that night in Iowa:

> with snow on the shoulders of [his] coat
> and a car passing with its headlights on:

In her eyes, he becomes 'a hero in a text – | the image blazing and the edges gilded'.

Her husband is crossing a bridge and moving away from her. There is something almost cinematic about the presentation of the scene. It is a cold, dark night and her husband has snow on his shoulders. However, it is what happens during this moment that is of interest to us. This recollection brings with it a heightened awareness of the nature of love itself. To further this process, Boland draws from the myth of Odysseus' journey into Hades. Like Odysseus, her husband embarks on a journey. While this journey is **metaphorical**, it is, much like the descent of the hero into hell, a labour of love. Odysseus braved hell in order to hasten his return to his wife. However, when he journeyed to the underworld, the Greek hero was unable to communicate with his former comrades. In the case of this poem, her husband's journey is connected to the sickness of one of their children. As she tries to communicate with her husband as he once was, Boland, like Odysseus in hell, is forced to realise that this is impossible. The past is but a 'shadow' and, for all its passion, can never be relived.

2. Stylistic Features

The language in 'Love' is restrained and simple. This simplicity mirrors the poem's theme. In the first stanza, the opening *run-on line,* or *enjambment,* mirrors the emotional rush the poet feels when she considers the intensity of the life she and her husband once shared. Halfway through the second stanza, the end-stopped lines give way to a series of lines without punctuation. This continues in the third stanza as the emotional intensity of the poem builds. The lack of punctuation makes the poem appear less contrived and more honest. However, some of the most intense lines in the poem are the shortest and the most contained. Boland opens stanza four with the deeply moving and stark admission – 'I am your wife.'

Here again, as with many other poems in this anthology, Boland moves between past and present. This movement through time is evident in Boland's choice of tense. The poem opens in the past imperfect tense ('we once lived'), changes to the present perfect tense ('has hidden') and then abruptly returns to the present indicative ('I am'). All of this adds to the poem's appeal. The sands of time are not allowed to settle fully and we are made to partake in the intensity of Boland's story.

3. Essay Writing

If you are thinking about using this poem in an essay on Boland's poetry, consider the following.

a. The poem deals with the passing of time and the inevitability of change in any relationship.
b. Much like 'The Pomegranate', 'Love' breathes new life into ancient mythology.
c. As with the other poems on the course by Boland, the language of this poem mirrors its subject matter. There is a restrained simplicity to the words she chooses.

Robert Frost (1874–1963)

A Short Biography

Robert Frost's reputation as one of the best-known American poets came very late in his life. He was 40 when, as he put it himself, his poetry 'caught on' with the American public. However, once he had established himself in the hearts and minds of his readership, he became one of the best-loved poets writing in the English language. Frost was born in San Francisco on 26 March 1874. His father, William, named him after Robert E. Lee, the famous Southern general in the American Civil War. Frost did not have an easy relationship with his father, who drank too much and was violent towards his wife and children.

Suffering from tuberculosis and continuing to drink heavily, Frost's father finally died in 1884. In his will, he stated that it was his wish to be buried in New England. Although William Frost had been an abusive father and husband, his wife and two children, Robert and Jeanie, respected his final wishes and headed east for the funeral. Lacking the funds to return to California, they settled in Salem, Massachusetts, where Mrs Frost was forced to resume her career as a schoolteacher in order to support her family. The move to New England had a profound effect on Robert. Previously, he had been a city boy with little interest in his studies, but he now became a keen student. Graduating from high school in 1891, he came top of his class alongside Elinor White, whom he married three years later.

Over the next 20 years, he enrolled for brief periods at Darthmoth and Harvard Colleges. He now had four children and brief spells as a teacher and a number of menial jobs failed to haul his growing family above the breadline. Frost became deeply depressed and even suicidal by what he saw as his tendency to mirror his own father's abusive and destructive behaviour. However, during this very difficult period in his life, he continued to write poetry. In 1894 he sold his first poem, 'My Butterfly', to the *New York Independent*. In 1900, his oldest son, Eliot, died of cholera, and in 1906, he himself came close to death after contracting pneumonia. Tragedy was to strike his family once again in 1907, when his second daughter, Elinor, died at just three days old. This grief and suffering, combined with his failure in business, forced Frost to take refuge more and more in his poetry.

In 1912, aged almost 40 and with only a few poems published, Frost sold his farm and used an allowance that he was receiving from his grandfather to go to England in order to devote his life to poetry. The family settled on a farm in Buckinghamshire and Frost continued to write. Ezra Pound, the expatriate American poet and one of the most influential figures in 20th-century literature, helped him to get published.

A Boy's Will appeared in 1913 and it was well received by critics. The collection was to be typical of Frost's style in that it was highly structured, yet incorporated the **colloquial** diction and rhythms of New England speech. The poem 'The Tuft of Flowers', which is on the Leaving Certificate course, first appeared in this anthology. These early poems displayed a clear inclination towards nature, seclusion and contemplation, towards the attractiveness of straightforward fact and towards a New England individuality that stresses the need for love and community.

Still living in England in 1914, Frost published *North of Boston*; this collection was made up mainly of **blank-verse monologues** and dramatic narratives. Two poems on the course, 'Mending Wall' and 'After Apple-Picking', appeared in this collection. His literary career had finally taken off and the success of his first two publications persuaded him that he was making enough of a name for himself to return home. However, the success he was to enjoy for the rest of his life came far too late to erase the bitter memories of his earlier years.

Returning to the US with his family in 1915, Frost bought a farm near Franconia, New Hampshire. He taught at Amherst College from 1916 to 1938 and, later, at Michigan University. In 1916, Frost was made a member of the National Institute of Arts and Letters. In the same year, his third collection of verse, *Mountain Interval*, appeared; it contained the poems 'The Road Not Taken' and 'Birches', which are also on the syllabus. Like so many of Frost's poems, these depict ordinary scenes that pave the way for far deeper explorations. Although perceived as a nature poet, he did not idealise nature. His work addressed not only its beauty, but also the desolation, bleakness and anxiety that anyone living close to the land has to endure.

In 1920, he moved to South Shaftsbury, Vermont. Four years later, in 1934, his daughter Marjorie died and in 1938 he lost his wife. During these troubled times he continued to suffer from depression and self-doubt. To a large extent, the speaker in many of Frost's poems is an alter ego: the kindly, calm person Frost would so dearly have loved to be but knew that he was not. However, even though the narrative voice in his poems may sound homespun and folksy, the poems themselves often tend to view the world as reflecting a design to 'frighten and appall'.

Frost recited two of his poems at the inauguration of President John F. Kennedy in 1961. In 1962, he travelled to the Soviet Union as a member of a goodwill group. In his later years, he received a remarkable number of literary and academic honours. At the time of his death on 29 January 1963, Frost was regarded as the elder statesman of American literature. His poetry continues to be read and, despite being out of tune with nearly every other major poet of his day, Frost has succeeded in realising his life's ambition: to write 'a few poems it will be hard to get rid of'.

Critical Commentary: The Tuft of Flowers

See the text of the poem on pp. 29–30.

1. Content

First published in the collection *A Boy's Will*, 'The Tuft of Flowers' revisits one of Frost's favourite subjects: the work associated with haymaking. In this poem, Frost moves from a belief that all men are individuals, leading separate lives, to a conviction that we all share a common bond of humanity. In the opening stanza, the poet tells us that he went down 'to turn the grass', so that it would dry. This grass had already been 'mowed [...] in the dew before the sun' by an unnamed person. In the second **heroic couplet**, the speaker makes it clear that some hours have passed since this person worked in the field. Nevertheless, the speaker looks and listens for signs of the worker:

> I looked for him behind an isle of trees;
> I listened for his whetstone on the breeze.

It soon becomes apparent that this man 'had gone his way' once his work was finished. The speaker is left completely on his own. In the fifth couplet, he contemplates the implications of his solitude and comes to the conclusion that ultimately all men are alone, 'Whether they work together or apart'. At that moment, a 'bewildered butterfly' stumbles into the poet's view. In the speaker's imagination, the butterfly is drawn to this place by the dim memory of the flower it visited the previous day. However, in the next couplet, we learn that that flower has been mowed and lies withering on the ground. Confused and lost, the creature flies 'round and round' until it almost vanishes from the poet's sight. The butterfly returns to the speaker's line of vision. This causes the poet to ponder over 'questions that have no reply'. Unable to come up with satisfactory answers to these unspecified questions, the speaker turns to 'toss the grass to dry'. Then, suddenly, in the eleventh and twelfth stanzas, the poet has a profound moment of **epiphany**, or revelation. As he turns to look in the direction of the brook, he has an almost religious, or spiritual, awakening. The sight of the flowers that have been unharmed by the worker who mowed the grass on the previous day moves the poet deeply. He now realises that 'The mower in the dew had loved them thus, | By leaving them to flourish, not for us'.

The speaker now feels that he is linked to the worker. The arrival of the butterfly and the sight of the unharmed flowers lead him to believe that he can see and hear the mower. You will remember that this is something he initially felt unable to do. The intensity of the speaker's feelings grows until he feels:

> [...] a spirit kindred to my own;
> So that henceforth I worked no more alone;

No longer alone, the poet now imagines himself working with the man. United by a common bond of fraternal love, he addresses his fellow worker directly:

> "Men work together," I told him from the heart,
> "Whether they work together or apart."

The poem's final heroic couplet reverses the speaker's previous belief that we are all alone and separate.

2. Stylistic Features

In 'The Tuft of Flowers', Frost uses a number of carefully worked-out *images* in order to convey his moment of epiphany. The poem opens with a depiction of the speaker's isolation. However, this sense of loneliness is not, as it first appears, simply a personal experience. It is *symbolic* of the loneliness of the human condition. As the speaker puts it, he is lonely, 'As all must be'. To begin with, the speaker feels confident that this is an undeniable truth that concerns all humankind, yet the arrival of a simple butterfly leads him to reassess this conviction. The butterfly heralds an awakening in the poet's consciousness. As the butterfly lands on the blossom, the poet is made aware of the mower's appreciation of the beauty of these same flowers. Many critics have pointed out the similarities between the work of the unnamed gardener and that of the poet. Both work in isolation and both professions appreciate a kind of beauty that many fail to see. In a letter that Frost wrote to his friend Sidney Cox, he had the following to say about flowers:

> I like flowers you know but I like 'em wild, and I am rather the exception than the rule in America. Far as I have walked in pursuit of flowers, I have never met another in the woods on the same quest. Americans

will dig for peas and beans and such like utilities but not if they know it for posies.

Thus, it is possible to read 'The Tuft of Flowers' as an extended **metaphor** for the creative process. In this poem, the speaker recognises in himself the appreciation of aesthetic beauty that led the mower to spare the flowers and, with this recognition, he senses a bond between his ideals and the other man's ideals, between his craft and the other man's craft. The flowers then become a symbol for artistic appreciation and the bonds of humanity that transcend ordinary, everyday experiences. Just as in the opening couplets Frost was willing to generalise his personal loneliness so that it became symbolic of the human condition, his delight now leads him to generalise his feelings of fraternal kinship for this unnamed man and his work. In the poem, the tuft of flowers serves as a catalyst that provokes in the poet feelings of common purpose with the entire human race.

However, this moment of spiritual recognition does not occur spontaneously; it is something that requires work. The act of cutting the grass becomes a metaphor for the spiritual journey that the poet must undertake. This is not an easy process, as it requires physical toil and labour. In this sense, it mirrors the process of spiritual awakening that the poet undergoes. This obligation to work, the resulting enjoyment of the fruits of our labour and even the difficultly and hardship that labour entails make the poet more aware of his own humanity. The image of the butterfly searching for a flower that 'lay withering on the ground' prevents the poem from becoming too sentimental. It provides us with a sharp reminder of the fact that all beauty is fleeting. There is a sense of understanding between the speaker and the mower because they both appreciate the beauty of these flowers.

In order to relate his feelings to us, Frost uses a number of particularly peaceful **images** and sound effects. The poem is set in a grassy field with a brook running through it. The soft sounds create an **onomatopoeic** effect of silent tranquillity. The speaker mentions the scythe 'whispering to the ground', he tells us that he can hear 'wakening birds around' and he listens for the 'whetstone on the breeze'. The regular rhyming scheme (*aa, bb*) offsets the poem's irregular **metre**. This, in part, gives the poem its insistent, old-fashioned and genteel sound. Some of the archaic-sounding words used by Frost add to this effect, such as 'o'er night' and 'henceforth'.

Most of the heroic couplets make use of **end rhyme** and each one contains a separate thought. This makes 'The Tuft of Flowers' easy to read and contributes to its peaceful and contemplative *tone*. One of the most striking stylistic features of the poem is the *paradox* that is used to highlight its central theme. The idea that 'Men work together […] Whether they work together or apart' is an unusual, if not contradictory, one. However, in order to grasp the meaning of the poem fully, it is necessary to embrace this notion. Finally, Frost employs a series of subtle *motifs* to highlight the idea that man is united to his fellow man. The poem suggests that we are all linked by our need to work, that we all share an instinctive appreciation of beauty and that men are driven by a need to respect living things. This is a beautiful poem that causes us to pause and consider the nature of the world in which we live.

3. Essay Writing

'The Tuft of Flowers' is a complex poem that is certainly worth mentioning in an essay. If you decide to include it, you might want to consider the following points.

a. The poem is typical of Frost's personal and *confessional* style.
b. 'The Tuft of Flowers' is highly structured. The poet's mastery of form leads to a restrained and contemplative tone of voice.
c. The final message of the poem is uplifting. Once again, this is typical of Frost. However, there are darker poems on the Leaving Certificate course and you may wish to contrast 'The Tuft of Flowers' with a dark poem like 'Design'.

Critical Commentary: Mending Wall

See the text of the poem on pp. 32–3.

1. Content

Writing about 'Mending Wall' in 1955, Frost said:

> It's about a spring occupation in my day. When I was farming seriously we had to set the wall up every year. You don't do that any more. You run a strand of barbed wire along it and let it go at that. We used to set the wall up. If you see a real wall set up you know it's owned by a

lawyer in New York — not a real farmer. This poem is about that spring occupation.

In this deceptively complex poem, the speaker opens with a bold statement:

> Something there is that doesn't love a wall,
> That sends the frozen-ground-swell under it
> And spills the upper boulders in the sun,
> And makes gaps even two can pass abreast.
> The work of hunters is another thing:

Here, the poet suggests that there are two types of people: those who like building walls and those who don't. The speaker says that he has arrived many times after the 'hunters' have damaged the wall. He has set himself the task of rebuilding the damaged sections of the wall. In line 11, he tells us that in springtime he has walked the line with this neighbour in order to help him to 'set the wall between [them] once again'. The speaker stays on his side of the wall and his neighbour keeps to his own side. Doggedly, they each replace the boulders that have landed on their side of the barrier. The work is tough and they 'wear [their] fingers rough with handling' these rocks. At one point in the work, it becomes clear that the wall is actually not necessary. His neighbour's land contains pine trees and Frost's field contains an apple orchard. The poet now engages in light-hearted criticism of his neighbour's need to maintain this wall. He would like to remind his neighbour that his:

> [...] apple trees will never get across
> And eat the cones under his pines, I tell him.

The only reply that this man can offer the speaker is that 'Good fences make good neighbors'. The speaker, in turn, would like to ask him: '*Why* do they make good neighbors?'

Seeing as there are 'no cows' to protect, the poet would like to know exactly what it is he is 'walling in or walling out'. Continuing in the same playful manner, the speaker would like to suggest that the land needs to be protected from 'elves'. Thinking of this, the poet sees his neighbour:

> Bringing a stone grasped firmly by the top
> In each hand, like an old-stone savage armed.

The *image* of the man struggling with the heavy stones leads the poet to believe that this man 'moves in darkness'. The darkness that he is referring to here is a *metaphorical* darkness of the mind. His refusal to look beyond his instinctive need for a wall is at the root of this darkness. The man simply 'will not go behind his father's saying […] He says again, "Good fences make good neighbors."'

2. Stylistic Features

While it may not seem like it on a first reading, 'Mending Wall' is complex and is open to multiple interpretations. The poem is built around the meeting of both neighbours as they repair a wall together. This is something that they have done on many occasions. The wall then becomes a *metaphor* for some of the traditional, grand themes of literature. It is possible to apply three separate metaphorical associations to the wall: firstly, the wall represents the human territorial need to segregate; secondly, the wall represents the dogged persistence of humankind in the face of enormous obstacles; and thirdly, the act of building the wall is a metaphor for the creative process itself.

If you choose to accept that the poem is criticising man's need to wall himself off from his fellow man, then the date of its composition is important. The poem was written in the 1950s, at the height of the Cold War. Perhaps one of the most obvious *symbols* of the divisions that threatened to plunge the world into World War Three was the Berlin Wall. In fact, when Frost visited the great enemy of the United States, the Soviet Union, he made a point of reading this poem. Bearing this in mind, it is possible to assume that Frost was passing comment on the foolhardy aggression of both superpowers as they scrambled for supremacy.

The second, more subtle reading of the poem addresses the idea that human beings continue to toil, regardless of the futility of their efforts. In order to understand this reading, it is necessary to look closely at some of the *images* employed by Frost in the poem. The poet draws on Greek *mythology* to express this complex notion. The image of both speaker and neighbour pushing the heavy boulders up the hill, safe in the knowledge that they will have to repeat the same task at a later time, recalls the myth of Sisyphus. According to this Greek legend, Sisyphus was doomed for all eternity to push a heavy boulder up a hill. Before he could reach the top and complete his task, Sisyphus' boulder would roll back down again. In a similar fashion, the poet and his neighbour commit themselves to the task of repairing the wall even though they know that it is futile.

As with so many of Frost's poems, 'Mending Wall' is open to further interpretation. The act of mending the wall can be likened to the artistic process itself. On a basic level, it is possible to see the similarities between the continual creation and destruction of the wall and the act of writing a work of literature. Every piece of art must first be created; however, once that act is completed, the ideas in the work of art challenge and even disrupt previously held beliefs. It is also possible to see that the acts of 'walk[ing] the line', building the wall and balancing each stone evoke the mysterious and arduous act of creating poetry. Interestingly, the process of building a wall is also directly applicable to Frost's poetic style. Frost was opposed to *free verse*. 'I had as soon write free verse,' he once declared, 'as play tennis without a net.' Richard Gray, writing about Frost's poetic style in *American Poetry of the Twentieth Century*, has pointed out that:

> For [Frost] traditional metres were a necessary discipline, something against which he could play off the urgencies of his own speaking voice, the chance movements of his emotions, the catch and tilt of his breath.

Frost preferred to use formal, traditional poetic forms. By maintaining and upholding the time-honoured customs of formal poetry, Frost, much like his neighbour, is traditional in his thinking.

This poem is written in unrhymed 10-syllable, or decasyllabic, lines. There are no stanza breaks, obvious **end rhymes** or rhyming patterns, but many of the end words share an **assonance** with the words that went before (e.g. 'wall', 'hill', 'balls', 'wall' and 'well'; 'sun', 'thing', 'stone', 'mean', 'line' and 'again'; and 'game', 'them' and 'him'). 'Mending Wall' also makes use of **internal rhymes** and **slanted rhymes** to create a relaxed, lilting quality. The **colloquial** style of the **monologue** allows the poet to enhance this relaxed tone of voice. The fact that the poem is written in unrhymed **iambic pentameter** also makes it seem more relaxed:

Something there **is** that **doesn't** **love** a **wall,**

This line contains five stressed *feet*; this is known as iambic pentameter. This is also the metre of normal, everyday speech. Other stylistic features employed by Frost in this poem include inversion, such as in the opening line. The poet also makes use of amplification to stress what he wants to say. The vocabulary is straightforward, relaxed and conversational. In fact, 'another' is the only word in the poem that exceeds two syllables.

3. Essay Writing

Once again, 'Mending Wall' is typical of Frost's poetic style. This makes it useful when it comes to writing essays. If you are thinking of using this poem in an essay, you may wish to include some of the following points:

a. The poem is open to metaphorical interpretation. This is typical of Frost's poetry.

b. This is yet another poem by Frost that centres on manual labour. This fact alone allows you to form links with such poems as 'After Apple-Picking' or 'The Tuft of Flowers'. Of course, rather than just simply state that all three poems centre on manual labour, you should explore the importance of work in the poetry of Frost.

c. As with so many of Frost's poems on the course, 'Mending Wall' is highly crafted. These traditional forms give the poem a stable platform that enables the poet to explore complex themes.

Critical Commentary: After Apple-Picking

See the text of the poem on pp. 35–6.

1. Content

'After Apple-Picking' opens with a description of a scene in which apples have just been harvested:

> My long two-pointed ladder's sticking through a tree
> Toward heaven still,
> And there's a barrel that I didn't fill
> Beside it, and there may be two or three
> Apples I didn't pick upon some bough.

The speaker is tired and his day's work is done. As he grows drowsy in the failing light of an autumn evening, he is reminded of the strangeness of an image that first greeted him earlier in the morning. This strange sight was caused by lifting a sheet of ice and looking through it. He held the ice in his hand until it melted and he was forced to let it fall. He then tells us that even though he is very tired now, he first felt dreamy and sleepy when he looked through this sheet of ice. Early that morning, with a full day's work ahead of him, the speaker could already tell what form his dreams would take. In his dreams:

> Magnified apples appear and disappear,
> Stem end and blossom end,
> And every fleck of russet showing clear.

Remaining in the present tense, the poet describes events that have already taken place. This can be confusing for the reader. He describes the sensation of the ladder swaying as the boughs of the tree move. He tells us that he can hear the apples rumble as they fall into the cellar bin. In line 28, he reminds the reader that he is overtired. He has 'had too much | Of apple-picking'.

The 'great harvest' is now stowed safely in the cellar. Some of the apples did not make the grade and they have been set aside for cider. Looking ahead to when his day's work is over, the speaker is sure that he will sleep. He goes on to say that in his overtired, restive sleep, he will dream of apple-picking. In a strange aside, he even wonders whether the 'woodchuck' experiences something similar during its long sleep or hibernation. The poem ends with the speaker anticipating this long and deserved sleep at the end of his day's work.

2. Stylistic Features

In an interview with *The Atlantic Monthly* in 1946, Robert Frost pointed out that:

> There are many other things I have found myself saying about poetry, but the chiefest of these is that it is the metaphor, saying one thing and meaning another, saying one thing in terms of another, that provides me with the greatest pleasure.

'After Apple-Picking' is obviously about harvesting apples. However, with its ladders pointing 'Toward heaven', with its sense of profound weariness and its thoughtful exploration of the harvest and the coming of winter, the reader is led to believe that the poem must harbour a different meaning. As the poet looks back on the scene of his day's labour in the orchard, he begins to confront truths about the human condition. It does not matter if you, as a reader, have never actually worked at apple-picking; 'After Apple-Picking' can still appeal directly to you. The poet's depiction of the scene is carefully grounded in actual experience. The issues that the poem raises (about life and death) are ones that everyone has to confront. In his dreamy, half-awake state, the poet's mind is more amenable to exploring the 'strangeness' that he perceives in the world.

The sequence of tenses in the poem is confusing and, as a result, we are forced to question what is dreamed and what is real about the day's events. Obviously, the speaker is exhausted following his labour in the orchard, but he also tells us that he was well on his way to sleep before he even began picking the apples. This gives us a clue about the poem's hidden *metaphorical* meaning. The fact that the poet has been entering a deep sleep since that morning is essential to our understanding of the poem. Sleep has long been used by writers as a metaphor for death. This lends a deeper significance to the long sleep 'coming on' at the end of the poem. The poet, in the autumn of his life, confronts the inevitability of the approaching winter.

Thus, it is possible to compare the acts of picking apples, of separating the good apples from the bad and of setting aside something to sustain one in the dark days of winter, to life itself. By looking through 'a pane of glass', the poet has entered into an altered state of consciousness. In this state of mind, the apples become 'Magnified' and his other senses are equally altered. Simply put, he begins to see things differently. In lines 28–9, the speaker tells us that he is 'overtired | Of the great harvest I myself desired'. He feels jaded. Yet this tiredness seems to be more than just a physical exhaustion. It would seem that he has 'desired' too much and this has taken its toll on him. The apple is a *symbol* of worldly knowledge in the Bible. The harvest, as we have said, can be read as a metaphor for life itself. However, the poet is purposely ambiguous about whether or not this harvest has been successful. Despite his best efforts, many of the apples have fallen by the wayside. Some are 'bruised' or 'spiked with stubble'. Obviously, these faults and imperfections 'trouble' the poet's 'sleep'.

There are other possible readings that we can apply to 'After Apple-Picking'. Many critics have pointed out that the act of picking the apples can be compared to the artistic process itself. If you have read the poem 'Mending Wall', you may have already considered this interpretation. The barrels of apples, in which good parts are separated from bad, can, of course, be likened to the act of writing a poem. In writing any poem, some lines are kept and some are set aside for use later.

As a poet, Frost set himself a number of stylistic goals. He always tried to capture with precision the sounds of New England speech. He also tried to create poems that would be easily understood because they were drawn from simple, natural phenomena and incorporated in standard verse forms. 'After Apple-Picking' is no different in this respect. The poem is carefully constructed. Firstly, it is built around a number of readily identifiable contrasts. Summer is opposed to winter, work is contrasted with rest, toil leads to reward and, of course, sleep is set alongside wakefulness. Together with the use of imagery associated with the sensation of movement, or **kinaesthetic** imagery, this careful construction gives the poem a tension that it would otherwise be lacking. It is written mostly in **iambic pentameter** and, despite the fact that it recounts events that happened earlier in the day, it remains in the present tense. Both of these effects combine to create a carefree tone.

In 'After Apple-Picking', Frost makes an assault on all of the senses. In the mind's eye of the poet, the apples become 'Magnified'. The dawn is presented to us in great *visual* detail. We can hear the *sounds* of the apples as they tumble into the barrels. When the poet makes an appeal to our sense of *smell*, we can sense the apples as they ripen in the cellar. Although not specifically mentioned, the *taste* of the apples is of course never far from the poem's narrative. The sense of *touch* is stimulated when the poet tells us that this fruit is something to 'Cherish in hand'.

3. Essay Writing

'After Apple-Picking' is perhaps the most difficult poem by Frost on the course. However, you should not let this fact deter you from using the poem in an essay on Frost. You may want to mention the following points.

a. The very fact that the poem is difficult might be worth mentioning in an essay that asks you to make a personal response to Frost. Sometimes, it can be a good idea when writing an essay to admit to finding a poem difficult. It goes without saying that you must always refer closely to the poem in saying why you found it difficult.

b. The poem uses complex imagery that appeals to all the senses.

c. This is yet another poem that has a much deeper meaning than the title suggests.

Critical Commentary: The Road Not Taken

See the text of the poem on p. 37.

1. Content

'The Road Not Taken', which Frost claimed was inspired by his friend Edward
Thomas, is perhaps one of the best-known poems in the English language. It opens
with a very straightforward statement:

> Two roads diverged in a yellow wood

It is autumn and the speaker, standing at a fork in the road, is faced with a choice. He
can take either road and there is nothing preventing him from doing so. He would
like to travel both roads but, of course, this is simply not possible. The speaker first
stares down one road to 'where it bent in the undergrowth'. Unwilling to commit
to this path, he decides to assess the other road. In the second *stanza*, he tells us
that this road is just as fair as the previous one. However, given that it is grassy, the
poet infers that it is less travelled than the other path. In the final line of the second
stanza, he admits that 'the passing there | Had [in truth] worn them really about the
same'. In the third stanza, it becomes clear that the poet has committed himself to
following one of the roads. He begins his journey in the morning:

> Yet knowing how way leads on to way,
> I doubted if I should ever come back.

The final stanza looks forward to a time 'ages hence' when he 'shall be telling [his
story] with a sigh'. His choice has been made and he has taken 'the [road] less
traveled by'. This life-altering choice 'has made all the difference'.

2. Stylistic Features

Many critics agree that 'The Road Not Taken' is typical of Frost's tendency to
write a poem that sounds noble, but is mischievous. In *Robert Frost: Selected Poems*
(London, 1973), Ian Hamilton says of this poem that:

the air of irretrievable error that hangs over the poem is a beguiling means of disguising its essential bleakness. To Frost, it doesn't seem to matter much which road he took, or didn't take. It is that indifference which should have been the real subject of the poem.

As previously mentioned, this poem was inspired by Frost's friend, the poet Edward Thomas. Thomas was forced to choose whether to enlist and fight in World War One or whether to follow Frost's advice and emigrate to America. He chose to fight in the trenches and was killed in action in 1917. Thomas's friendship and death had a great impact on Frost. Whatever the inspiration for 'The Road Not Taken' may have been, it is a complex and problematic poem. The poem is so perfectly written and its central *metaphor* is so appealing that many students simply fail to read the poem attentively. The title suggests that this poem is going to concern itself with the choice that the speaker failed to take. However, the opening of the poem presents us with a slightly different scenario. The poet actually focuses on the road that he *did* take. In the opening lines, the speaker finds himself in a readily identifiable and very human dilemma. We have all been faced with choices that are difficult to make. As the speaker considers both roads, *image, metaphor* and *symbol* blend into one another to produce a memorable representation of the notion of fate. Remember that Frost felt that the metaphor was an essential feature of poetry. In an essay entitled 'Education by Poetry', Frost pointed out:

> Poetry begins in trivial metaphors, pretty metaphors, grace metaphors, and goes on to the profoundest thinking that we have. Poetry provides the one permissible way of saying one thing and meaning another. People say, 'Why don't you say what you mean?' We never do that, do we, being all of us too much poets. We like to talk in parables and in hints and in indirections — whether from diffidence or from some other instinct.

The image of the crossroads has long been symbolic of fate and destiny. All human beings are, in one sense, free to choose. However, like the speaker, we can never really see the full implications of the choices that we make. When we examine the choice that confronts the poet, it becomes clear that there really is no great difference between the roads. Many readers like to interpret Frost's choice in this poem as being brave and groundbreaking. However, the speaker's own words dismiss this reading. He anticipates some future time when he will regret his choice or, at least, breathe a sigh when considering the action he has taken. Thus, even though one may read the poem as a brave affirmation of the merit of making original decisions in life, it can equally be read as a world-weary recognition of the fact that we must go on living with our choices.

The poem's form is quite unusual. The vocabulary is relaxed, even casual. Frost employs **colloquialisms** ('perhaps the better claim', 'really about the same', 'I doubted if I should ever come back') to reinforce this effect. However, despite the casual **tone** adopted by the speaker, the poem is actually quite formal in its construction. 'The Road Not Taken' is written in **tetrameter**, with four **feet** in each line:

> Two **roads** / di- **verged** / in a **yel-** / low **wood**
> *4 feet*

> And **sor-** / ry I **could** / not **trav-** / el **both**
> *4 feet*

> And **be** / **one** travel- / er **long** / I **stood**
> *4 feet*

> And **looked** / down **one** / as **far** / as I **could**
> *4 feet*

> To **where** / it **bent** / in the **un-** / der **growth**
> *4 feet*

The steady regularity of these four-beat lines creates a sense of peacefulness and thoughtfulness. While the lines all have the same number of feet, the **metre** is varied throughout. This wavering **rhythm** in the poem reflects the regretful condition of the speaker and his memory of his hesitancy. This creates a dramatic effect and makes the choice at the heart of the poem seem more important.

3. Essay Writing

'The Road Not Taken' is one of Frost's best-known and best-loved poems. This fact alone is worth mentioning in any essay that contains a reference to the poem. Other points you may want to mention include the following.

a. The poem is highly structured.
b. Once again, Frost presents us with a scene that is open to metaphorical interpretation.

c. The poem appeals to our senses of sight and hearing. The melancholic, regretful tone, coupled with the beauty of the language, makes 'The Road Not Taken' a memorable poem.

Critical Commentary: Birches

See the text of the poem on pp. 39–40.

1. Content

'Birches', another popular and beloved poem by Frost, was first published in the *Atlantic Monthly* in August 1915. In the poem, Frost presents us with a vivid, personal depiction of nature as he describes a boy playfully swinging on trees. As he often does in his poetry, Frost presents an ambiguous view of the natural world and uses that as a starting point for questioning larger issues. As he describes a hypothetical boy climbing up birches and then riding them down to the ground, the speaker raises questions about the nature of human existence. The poem opens with the adult voice of the narrator telling us that when he sees:

> [...] birches bend to left and right
> Across the lines of straighter darker trees,
> [He likes] to think some boy's been swinging them.

Initially, the poet believes that a boy has bent these trees. Obviously, the thought of the birches being bent down by someone swinging on them is drawn from personal memory. The speaker tells us that swinging on birches in the manner that he has described does not harm them. They bounce back into position. In the fourth line, he contradicts his initial assumption about how the trees have come to be bent. He points out that 'swinging doesn't bend them down to stay'.

There is a slight change in the poem's direction in the fifth line, when Frost assumes that these trees must have been bent by an ice storm. In the next four lines, the poet gives us a beautiful description of the frozen birches. However, this beautiful, frozen state is short lived. In line 9, the sun 'cracks and crazes their enamel' (i.e. the ice), which breaks and falls into the snow. The 'sun's warmth' makes the ice particles 'crystal shells'. In line 13, the poem's *tone* shifts again, when the poet is prompted to claim: 'You'd think the inner dome of heaven had fallen.'

The weight of snow and ice on the trees causes them to bend as far as the 'withered bracken'. However, once the trees have been bent this far, they never really return to the shape they once held. The poet tells us that:

> You may see their trunks arching in the woods
> Years afterwards, trailing their leaves on the ground

He feels that he would prefer if the trees had been bent by a young boy. He reminds us that this is what he was thinking before the 'Truth' about the snow and ice interrupted his thoughts. The speaker then describes the type of boy that he imagines bending the birches. The boy in question lives far from the city and its distractions, such as 'baseball'. He 'subdue[s] his father's trees', riding them until he takes the 'stiffness out of them', leaving him, in lines 31–3, absolutely victorious over the trees: 'not one was left | For him to conquer'.

In the section of the poem encompassing lines 41–2, Frost allows a note of nostalgia to creep in:

> So was I once myself a swinger of birches.
> And so I dream of going back to be.

This longing for the more innocent days of childhood is contrasted with the pain of adulthood, which is described as a 'pathless wood'. It is important to realise that in this section of the poem, Frost begins to contrast the imaginary world with the real world. The idea of the boy climbing the birch has been wholly imaginary. In line 48, he develops this idea of escaping into an imaginary world, telling us that he would 'like to get away from earth awhile'. However, in lines 52–3 he stresses that he does not want to leave the real world:

> […] Earth's the right place for love:
> I don't know where it's likely to go better.

In the concluding section of the poem, Frost unites all of these ideas in the *image* of the birch trees. Towards the end of the poem, the process of the imagination reaching beyond the limits of reality is compared to the act of climbing the birch tree. The swaying motion of the tree, which allows a person to reach its top only to return back to the ground, is in fact the way Frost would like his imagination to work. He would like his imagination to permit him only to reach 'heaven' and then to return him back to the real world. The poem's memorable concluding line tells us that: 'One could do worse than be a swinger of birches.'

2. Stylistic Features

Frost was very traditional in his thinking when it came to constructing his poems. 'Birches' is no different in this respect. The poem is written in **blank verse** in **iambic pentameter.**

> **When** I / **see** birch- / **es** bend / **to** left / **and** right
> *5 feet, or 5 stresses = iambic pentameter*
>
> A- gaint / **the** lines / **of** straight- / **er** dark- / **er** trees
> *5 feet, or 5 accents = iambic pentameter*
>
> I like / **to** think / **some boy's** / been **swing-** / ing them
> *5 feet, or 5 stresses = iambic pentameter*

This unrhymed, carefully metred type of poetry is perhaps the most commonly used in the English language. For example, it was the verse pattern used in most of Shakespeare's plays and many of Wordsworth's poems. Frost's obstinate use of traditional poetic forms not only reflects his personality, but also provides the poet with the necessary framework to deal with the complex themes in the poem.

A poem as richly textured as 'Birches' yields no shortage of interpretations. It invites the reader to look below the surface and build his or her own understanding. In 'Birches', as in many of Frost's poems, the limits forced on us by the real world are seen as a necessary part of being human. Frost believed that the borders of the world define a person and situate him or her in the real world. In many of Frost's poems, the thought of removing all of the barriers between oneself and the world at large is at best unwelcome and at worst frightening. It is for this reason that Frost pleads that 'no fate willfully misunderstand [him] | And half grant' what he hopes for and snatch him away. The removal of such barriers and limitations is a frightening thought for the poet, as it would leave him adrift. Throughout the poem, this idea of earthly limitation is explored. The imaginary young boy bends the tree, gravity pulls the speaker back to earth as he moves '*Toward* heaven' and in line 38, water is held within the confines of a cup. A similar conclusion is reached by the critic Floyd C. Watkins. In an essay published in *South Atlantic Quarterly*, Watkins explains that in 'Birches', Frost:

[…] contemplates a moment when the soul may be completely absorbed into a union with the divine. But he is earthbound, limited, afraid. No sooner does he wish to get away from earth than he thinks of 'fate' rather than God. And what might be a mystical experience turns into fear of death, a fear that he would be snatched away 'not to return'.

This poem also indirectly addresses the idea of conflict. The ice storm triumphs over the trees, bending them down so low that they almost appear to be bowing to the storm. Similarly, the young boy of Frost's imagination bends the trees, forcing them to accept his will. The critic James Ellis notes that the boy 'subdue[s]' his father's trees, implying a kind of conflict in which the boy must symbolically control his father in order to become his own person.

Finally, it is possible to read this poem as simply being a beautiful **pastoral** (a poem that deals with rural life). The typical pastoral presents the natural world as unspoiled and idyllic when compared to the hustle and bustle of city life. In some respects, 'Birches', as well as many other Frost poems, can be considered a pastoral in that it has a rustic setting and presents the boy's solitary life as uncomplicated.

3. Essay Writing

'Birches' is another well-known Frost poem that is worth including in almost any Leaving Certificate essay. Some of the following points might help you to organise your approach to the poem in an essay.

a. The poem presents us, yet again, with a detailed depiction of nature. This description of the natural world is then used to evoke a deeper meaning.
b. 'Birches' is highly structured. As with so many other poems by Frost on the course, the poet's evident mastery of form allows him to control his complex ideas.
c. The poem is a straightforward and personal account of the poet's feelings about the world as he perceives it.

Critical Commentary: "Out, Out—"

See the text of the poem on p. 42.

1. Content

'"Out, Out—"' deals with the tragic death of a young boy who dies as a result of cutting his hand using a saw. The poem opens with the sound of the saw as it 'snarled and rattled in the yard | And made dust and dropped stove-length sticks of wood'. The dust thrown up by the saw is sweet-smelling and, in the background, the sun is setting over the 'Five mountain ranges' of Vermont. The saw sets to its task with ease. The day's work '[is] all but done'. The narrator interrupts the narrative to beseech them to give the boy a break from his work. This is the first hint in the poem that something dreadful is about to happen. His sister then arrives to tell the boy that his supper is ready. As if to prove that it understood 'what supper meant', the saw 'seemed to leap' out at the boy's hand. The boy's hand is taken by the saw and his only reaction is to offer a 'rueful laugh'. However, owing to his age, the boy is fully aware of the seriousness of his situation. He is, after all, a 'big boy | Doing a man's work'.

The arrival of the doctor in line 28 brings with it the first hint that he may die. The doctor places the boy in the 'dark of ether'. Slowly, the boy's heartbeat becomes fainter and fainter until there is 'nothing' and the boy is dead. The others, 'since they | Were not the one dead', get on with the business of living their lives.

2. Stylistic Features

One of the most important features of '"Out, Out—"' is its title, which contains an **allusion** to one of the most famous soliloquies in all of English literature. It alludes to a passage in *Macbeth* in which Macbeth has just been told of his wife's death. The key moment in this speech is arrived at when Macbeth underscores the tragic brevity of human life.

> She should have died hereafter;
> There would have been a time for such a word.
> To-morrow, and to-morrow, and to-morrow,
> Creeps in this petty pace from day to day,

To the last syllable of recorded time;
And all our yesterdays have lighted fools
The way to dusty death. **Out, out,** brief candle!
Life's but a walking shadow, a poor player,
That struts and frets his hour upon the stage,
And then is heard no more. It is a tale
Told by an idiot, full of sound and fury,
Signifying nothing.

In this sense, the title captures perfectly the full meaning of this poem. By means of this allusion, Frost not only reinforces the emotions contained in the poem, but also helps to define its *theme*. The theme of '"Out, Out—"' is, of course, the uncertainty and unpredicability of life.

The opening of the poem attempts to capture the sound of the buzz saw. It rattles and snarls and is made to sound menacing. In order to draw us into the narrative, Frost appeals to all of the senses. We can feel the breeze as it draws across sticks of wood and the scent of the cut wood assails our sense of smell. Another effective feature of the poem is the manner in which the saw is *personified*. By giving the saw human attributes, Frost increases the emotional impact of the poem. The boy doesn't drop the saw, it 'leap[s] out at [his] hand'. This makes the saw seem aggressive and the boy, in turn, is made to seem an innocent victim of this aggression. In a similar fashion, Frost makes use of *metonymy* (the use of something closely related in place of the thing actually meant) when he describes the injured boy holding up his cut hand: 'as if to keep | The life from spilling'. Here, the poet literally means to keep the blood from spilling, but by substituting the word 'life' for blood, the poem gains in clarity, force and emotional intensity. This emotional intensity is mirrored in the poem's construction. '"Out, Out—"' is a narrative in *blank verse*, contained in a continuous structure. There are no stanzas and no physical breaks in the poem. By not structuring the poem in a formal manner, Frost does not attempt to confine the emotional response of the reader. Finally, while the poem provokes an emotional response in its readers, its *tone* is at all times impersonal. The narrator simply relates the truth of the boy's accident and death in a straightforward manner. It is left to us to respond emotionally to the event described.

3. Essay Writing

This shocking poem is different from the other, more gentle nature poems on the course. In this sense, you can use it to highlight Frost's ability to move beyond simple nature poetry. The following points might provide you with some ideas when using '"Out, Out—"' in an essay.

a. Once again, the poem is open to *metaphorical* readings. The shocking story of the boy's death acts as a metaphor for the unpredictability and brevity of life.
b. The poem's sound effects underscore its meaning. As you are by now well aware, this is typical of Frost's poetic style.
c. It is difficult to read this poem without being moved by the depiction of the boy's death. This is certainly a point worth making in a question that requires you to frame a personal response to Frost's poetry.

Critical Commentary: Spring Pools

See the text of the poem on p. 44.

1. Content

'Spring Pools' is a quiet, reflective poem that opens with a simple statement. We learn that even though the pools are subject to tree cover, they can still 'reflect | The total sky'. The narrator then goes on to point out that they will soon have disappeared. The pools will not vanish into a brook or river, but will be soaked up by the trees. The water from these pools will move up the roots of the trees and cause them to grow leaves, or 'dark foliage'.

In the second stanza, the poet admonishes these trees, asking them to think twice before they 'use their powers' to trap the water from the pools in their 'pent-up buds'. The poet recognises that the water from the pools will help the trees become 'summer woods'. Nevertheless, he does not want this transformation to be at the expense of the water and the 'watery flowers' that depend on the spring pools for their existence.

2. Stylistic Features

This beautiful *lyric* poem is perfectly formed. Written in two six-line stanzas, each composed of one sentence, the poem presents a striking scene, only to undermine it with the threat of mutability and extinction. To begin with, the poem observes a peaceful scene of natural continuity. However, it soon becomes apparent that this natural cycle has loss at its heart. The pools will not evaporate, they will not simply disappear; rather, they will be taken up 'by roots to bring dark foliage on'. Here, nature and its trees are 'dark'. The dark power of nature to destroy and create is something that the poet can acknowledge, but can't name. However, he does recognise that these powers of destruction result in a fleeting or ephemeral beauty. In simple terms, the poem can be read as a meditation on the natural process of destruction and renewal. All of nature is in a perpetual state of flux. Life implies death and this is an inescapable, if distasteful, truth about the natural world.

However, 'Spring Pools' is also open to other possible readings. Many commentators have pointed out that the pools can be interpreted as *metaphors* for the reflective consciousness. Other critics view the poem as a veiled commentary on the artistic process itself. If you choose to read the poem in this way, you should notice that the speaker is brought to realise his own limitations. If the pools are metaphors for poetic inspiration, then the creative juices evaporate in front of the poet's eyes.

As with so many of Frost's poems, this poem is formal in its construction. In order to support the concentrated level of contemplation at the heart of 'Spring Pools', Frost had to rely on graceful and poised lines. These stable, well-written lines prevent the reader from becoming distracted and maintain the peaceful and thoughtful *mood* that is so essential to the poem. Notice, too, the predominance of broad vowel sounds and 'l' sounds that capture the effect of water perfectly.

3. Essay Writing

If you are considering writing about 'Spring Pools' in an essay, you might want to consider the following points.

a. The poem is one of Frost's darker pieces. This allows you to contrast 'Spring Pools' with many of the other poems by Frost in this anthology.

b. Once again, Frost's mastery of sound and poetic form is apparent in this poem. For example, you may want to consider the manner in which the poet captures the sound of the pools.

c. The poem can be read as an extended metaphor for the creative process. This allows you to compare 'Spring Pools' with 'Mending Wall' and 'After Apple-Picking'.

Critical Commentary: Acquainted with the Night

See the text of the poem on p. 46.

1. Content

Unlike any of the other poems by Frost on the course, 'Acquainted with the Night' opens in the city. The poet tells us that he has known the city at night. He has walked in the rain further than the 'furthest city light'. In the second **tercet**, the speaker tells us that he has looked down the lonely, deserted city lanes. He has passed the 'watchman on his beat' and avoided making eye contact with him. In the third stanza, the speaker explains that he has been stopped in his tracks by the sound of a cry 'from another street'. However, the shout that he heard was not to call him back or 'say good-by'. Meanwhile, a giant clock forms the backdrop to this cityscape. The scale of the clock is not human. The speaker ends the poem by reminding us that he has been 'acquainted with the night'.

2. Stylistic Features

This is one of Frost's better-known poems. In the poem, the speaker uses the lonely cityscape as a **metaphor** for his inner despair. The strict form of the **lyric** testifies to Frost's mastery of poetic forms. Like a **sonnet**, the poem contains 14 lines, but its rhyming scheme, **terza rima**, is a formal arrangement that implies continual progression. It is interesting to note that Dante also used this form in his famous poem *The Inferno*, in which he makes an imaginative journey into hell.

Frost could be using the same form as a veiled and complicated *allusion* to Dante's poem. The night has always had strong associations with darkness and evil. Furthermore, the slow, measured *rhythm* of this sonnet form matches the slow pace of the poet as he walks through the city.

'Acquainted with the Night' is an intense expression of loneliness. Vast modern cities, in which millions of people live in close proximity to one another, can be extremely lonely places. In order to convey this loneliness, the poet employs repetition (both of lines and words) and produces a haunting, chant-like effect. In addition to this repetition, the poem is dominated by broad vowel sounds, which create a lonely, echoing sound. Frost coined a term to describe the unique sound pattern of his poems. He liked to identify what he called his poems' tune, which is separate from the *metre* and *rhythm*. While it is impossible to say exactly what he meant by this term, it is obvious that he was referring to the sound of the poems. Following a reading he gave of 'Acquainted with the Night', he proclaimed that the poem was 'all for the tune. Tune is everything.' On another occasion, he asked his readers to 'listen for the tune'. In any case, the sound effects used by Frost contribute to the ghostly, even surreal atmosphere that dominates the poem.

3. Essay Writing

It is worth considering 'Acquainted with the Night' for inclusion in an essay on Frost. The following points might help you to organise your thoughts if you choose to mention the poem.

a. The poem is set in a city. This fact alone means that you can contrast 'Acquainted with the Night' with nearly all of the other poems by Frost in this anthology.
b. The poem is dark in its outlook.
c. Yet again, the scene depicted can be read in a metaphorical light.

Critical Commentary: Design

See the text of the poem on p. 47.

1. Content

'Design' opens with a straightforward statement. The speaker tells us that he found a 'dimpled spider'. This 'fat and white' spider, situated on a flower, holds up a dead moth. This, along with the other 'Assorted characters of death and blight' trapped in the web, remind the speaker of a 'witches' broth'. In the second stanza, the poet suggests that the flower helped to camouflage the spider. '[B]eing white', it is the same colour as the spider and, for this reason, it is seen by the poet as aiding the spider to trap the moth. The *tone* towards the end of the poem is questioning. The poet acknowledges that there is a design to nature. However, this design has contributed to the death of the innocent moth. It 'steered [it] thither in the night' to its doom. The poet wonders what kind of design could produce such a dark and sinister plan:

> What but design of darkness to appall?—
> If design govern in a thing so small.

2. Stylistic Features

The starting point for the speaker's train of thought is what he sees as a remarkable coincidence: a white spider that has trapped a white moth by sitting on a white flower. This chance occurrence is even more unusual because the type of flower in question, a heal-all, is normally blue. In literature, the colour white has strong *symbolic* associations with purity and innocence. The language of the poem reinforces these symbolic associations through a number of subtle, carefully worked out *allusions*. The spider is described as being fat and white. This, of course, could also be a description of a white, newborn child. The dead moth is likened to a 'rigid satin cloth'. This could be an allusion to a bridal dress, itself a *symbol* of purity. In addition to all of these, heal-alls are normally used in medicine to cure and heal.

However, the poet quickly sweeps aside these positive associations in order to confront the speaker with the reality of the situation. By the end of the *octet*, the gruesome nature of the moth's death is made clear. While the scene that the poet has described contains elements of purity and innocence, it is also tainted by 'death' and 'blight'. The spider may resemble an innocent 'snow-drop' and the dead moth may look like a child's 'paper kite', but they are also the main ingredients in this awful and deadly 'witches' broth'.

If the octet presents the scene, then the **sestet** questions what the poet has just witnessed. This is important to bear in mind when reading the poem. 'Design' has to be one of the most unusual sonnets in the English language. The poet borrows an Italian sonnet form, only to alter it completely. 'Design' reverses the expected order of octave and sestet. Rather than posing a problem in the octave and answering it in the sestet, as an Italian sonnet traditionally does, 'Design' describes an event in the octet and then questions it in the sestet. This reversal of the traditional order suggests that the poet has no answer to the issues raised in the poem.

In the second half of the sonnet, the speaker wonders how the unusual set of circumstances that have contributed to the moth's death came to be. The speaker purposely avoids apportioning blame to the spider. It is, after all, 'kindred' to the flower. The **volta**, or change in the poem's direction, occurs in the closing **couplet**. Here, the poet offers us two possible conclusions that may be drawn from the circumstances that led to the moth's death. Firstly, the speaker suggests that the killing of the moth may have been the result of an evil force or presence at work in the universe. Cloaking itself in the white colour of virtue and purity, this evil presence destroys the innocent moth. The second explanation is perhaps even more troubling: in the closing line of the poem, the poet admits that there may be no purpose or order in the universe.

Most monotheistic religions (religions that believe that there is only one God) believe that God is all powerful and that His power extends even to the smallest creatures on earth. The speaker suggests that the 'design of darkness' could exist only if 'design govern in a thing so small'. This sentence is difficult to untangle. It seems to be suggesting that if there is no design governing such small creatures, then this might indicate that God does not exist. Thus, a poem that opened with a detailed consideration of a natural scene ends with an interesting explanation for the existence of evil in the world.

This is a dark, unsettling poem, in which Frost confronts the darker aspects of life. Remarkably, he chooses to frame this dark commentary on the nature of existence within an airy and light poetic form. The poem almost sounds like a child's song. Yet these nursery-rhyme **rhythms** and innocent-sounding stanzas expose the naïve fragility of humankind's ongoing struggle to make sense of the world.

3. Essay Writing

If you choose to include 'Design' in a response to any question on Frost that might appear, try to bear the following points in mind.

a. The poem is dark, which is in sharp contrast to many poems by Frost in this anthology.

b. It is highly structured. The innocent, childlike rhythms belie a far greater complexity of thought.

c. The poem forces us to question our own beliefs. This point is well worth making in any question that asks you to make a personal response to Frost.

Critical Commentary: Provide, Provide

See the text of the poem on p. 49.

1. Content

'Provide, Provide' opens with a direct statement of fact. The old witch that washes the steps was once the beautiful woman known as Abishag. In the Bible, this beautiful woman was presented as a gift to King David in order to make him young again.

In the second stanza, the poet bridges the span of years and moves from the reference to the biblical beauty Abishag to modern-day Hollywood starlets. These beautiful actresses, much like Abishag, will one day be cast aside in favour of younger, more attractive women.

In the third stanza, the speaker provides us with a way to avoid this grim reality:

> Die early and avoid the fate.
> Or if predestined to die late,
> Make up your mind to die in state.

In the fourth stanza, we are given some additional advice. In a sweeping series of imaginative *imperatives*, the poet advises us to make the 'whole stock exchange our own' and 'If need be occupy a throne'.

The fifth stanza changes tack slightly. Here, the speaker advises the reader that other people prepare for the future by 'simply being true'.

In the sixth stanza, the poet returns to the notion of the once beautiful woman who is now bent with age. In order to avoid this fate, he suggests that one is better off never having been famous. Out of the spotlight, the end of one's life is less harsh. In the final stanza, the speaker suggests that it would be better to buy friendship and thereby ensure a dignified end to your days.

2. Stylistic Features

'Provide, Provide', together with the poem 'Design', shows Frost confronting what he called the background of 'hugeness and confusion shading away [...] into black and utter chaos'. The poem, which first appeared in the collection *A Further Range*, is unlike any other poem by Frost on the Leaving Certificate course. It was, in fact, inspired by a charwomen's strike at Harvard University. According to the poet, 'Provide, Provide' was intended to be a *satirical* comment on President Roosevelt's welfare state. In fact, Frost liked to read the poem by adding the lines 'Or somebody else'll provide for you' at the end.

While the poem may be read as a political commentary on Roosevelt's attempts to introduce welfare for all, it is open to other readings. Firstly, the cynical *tone* of the speaker is simply not typical of Frost's poetry. Secondly, the poem does not contain the personal pronoun 'I'. This strongly suggests that Frost does not want to be identified with his speaker's pronouncements. The poem opens with a complex *allusion* to the biblical figure, Abishag. She was a beautiful virgin who was brought to King David for the purpose of rejuvenating his ageing body and mind. However, even this *symbol* of purity and innocence was reduced to the level of a hag and forced to wash the steps 'with pail and rag'. The main purpose of 'Provide, Provide' is to warn the reader to provide at any cost for the future. In order to reinforce this point, the speaker makes some strange demands on the reader. Speaking in the *imperative*, he demands that we become extremely wealthy or buy friendship. Failing this, the poem suggests that one is better off dead than facing old age on one's own.

As we have said previously, this poem is unlike any other poem by Frost on the course. It is dark, cynical and even mocking. This tone of voice is certainly not typical of Frost's overall style. However, the poem's strict control of form, which involves the speaker's ideas being put forward in a series of carefully structured *tercets*, is representative of Frost's style. Finally, given that so many of the poems by Frost on the syllabus are uplifting, the inclusion of this poem achieves a sense of balance on the course that might otherwise be lacking.

3. Essay Writing

This is the final poem by Frost in this anthology. If you are thinking of using it in an essay, you may want to include some of the following points.

a. The poem is the only one on the course that doesn't contain the personal pronoun 'I'. This may be an indication that the poet does not support the views expressed in the poem.
b. It is possible to contrast this poem with the more positive nature poems by Frost on the course.
c. Yet again, it is a carefully structured, well-balanced poem.

Seamus Heaney (1939–)

A Short Biography

Seamus Heaney was born on 13 April 1939, the first child of Patrick and Margaret Kathleen Heaney (née McCann). His father, who worked as a cattle dealer, was a taciturn man, and as a result Heaney had difficulty communicating with him. His mother took particular delight in the meanings and derivations of words and imparted something of her love of language to the young poet. Interestingly, Heaney has said that his own character embodied aspects of both his parents. According to the poet, the inner tension that he felt between the 'tongue tied' aspects of his father's character and the facets of his mother's character that he inherited was fundamental to the 'quarrel with himself' out of which his poetry was born.

The Heaney family lived on a 50-acre farm called Mossbawn in the townland of Taminarn in County Derry. There were nine in the family. Heaney attended the local primary school in Anahorish and was very happy. However, this family idyll was interrupted when at the age of 12 he won a scholarship to St Columb's boarding school in Derry. The regimented atmosphere of life in St Columb's contrasted sharply with the serene and carefree happiness he had known in Mossbawn. Heaney actively resented being sent to boarding school and would angrily throw any treats received from home over the school walls. Tragedy struck the family when his youngest brother, Christopher, was killed by a passing car. As a consequence, the family farm at Mossbawn was sold and the warm radiance of his childhood, so beautifully evoked in the poem 'Mossbawn: Two Poems in Dedication', effectively ended. The tragedy of this event is retold in one of his most memorable poems, 'Mid-Term Break'.

When he completed his secondary education, the young poet entered Queen's University in Belfast. While at Queen's he started to write, and between 1959 and 1961 – the same year he received a first-class honours degree – the university magazines *Q* and *Gorgon* published some of his first attempts at poetry. As a measure of his lack of confidence, Heaney wrote under the nom de plume of Incertus (Uncertain). His talent was noticed by his teachers, and the head of the English faculty at Queen's encouraged him to continue his studies at Oxford. However, Heaney's lack of belief in his own ability, or what he termed the lack of 'confidence, the nous and precedent', ruled out the move to England. Deciding that he needed to enter the workforce, he applied instead to prepare for a career in teaching. Once he graduated as a teacher from St Joseph's College in Belfast, he took up a job at St Thomas' Intermediate School, also in Belfast. However, he found classroom management trying and after only one year decided to give up teaching on the back of an offer of a lectureship at St Joseph's.

In 1965, he married Marie Devlin. Like Heaney, she was from a large family with artistic leanings. Her sister is the journalist Polly Devlin and her brother was the bassist in the rock group Horselips. He had met Marie in 1963 while studying to become a teacher, and from that point on she played a pivotal role in his development as a writer. They have three children together and she appears in many of the poems on the course, such as 'The Skunk', 'Tate's Avenue' and 'The Underground'. In 1966 many of his earliest poems appeared in his collection *Death of a Naturalist*. Speaking in April 2009 on the occasion of his seventieth birthday, Heaney described those early days of poetic inspiration:

> It all happened as if by magic. In my early twenties I walked through the ceo draoíchta of contemporary poetry — Irish, English, Scottish, Welsh and American poetry. During those first years of creative excitement when I discovered the company of other poets, young and old, north and south, it was as if the morning fog that had once hung over the fields of Patrick Kavanagh's Mucker, the fog where he met the god of awakened imagination, it was as if that fog had descended on my own home ground in Co. Derry. I rhymed to see myself, as the last lines of the last poem in that first book put it — 'to see myself,/To set the darkness echoing.'

Death of a Naturalist was followed by the 1969 collection *Door into the Dark*. Publication by a publishing house as prestigious as Faber & Faber was a remarkable achievement for a young poet and Heaney was fêted by critics and the wider public alike. To begin with, he was received as a 'bucolic poet'. This was not surprising given the extent to which his memories of life in rural Ireland dominated his early poems. However, much like his contemporaries Michael Longley, Derek Mahon and Paul Muldoon, Heaney was unable to ignore the awful direction his country was taking. Although he confronted the issues raised by the Troubles in a different manner to the other poets from the North, he was deeply affected by them. The tone and mood of many of his poems darkened in the 1970s as he struggled to come to terms with the internecine violence and bitterness that were ripping his society apart.

At the beginning of the 1970s, Heaney taught for a short spell at the University of California at Berkley. While there, he began to read some of the newer American poets such as William Carlos Williams, Robert Lowel and Robert Creeley. The open style of their verse had an impact on his own poetic style. The regular **metres**, **rhymes** and **half-rhymes** of Heaney's early poetry began to yield to the influence of these American writers. What emerged was a poetry defined by short unrhymed lines written in **free verse**. Such a willingness to change has always been a hallmark of Heaney's poetry. Writing in *The Irish Times*, Michael Hoffmann has said that the 'greatest thing about Heaney is his adventurous progress from book to book and poem to poem, his refusal to rest on his laurels'.

In 1972 he decided to move south to Glanmore in County Wicklow. For a period of three years he worked as a freelance writer before taking up the offer of a teaching job at Carysfort College of Education, where he stayed from 1975 to 1981. However, during this time he was also making regular visits to America and the contacts that he established there led to the offer of a guest professorship at Harvard University. Then, in 1985, he was made Boylston Professor of Rhetoric and Oratory at Harvard. His reputation continued to grow and from 1989 to 1994 he held the Oxford Professorship of Poetry. In 1995 he was awarded the Nobel Prize for Literature, which was followed by a Whitbread Prize for his collection *The Spirit Level*. In recent years he has continued to win prizes and has been the recipient of several honorary degrees. He was made a member of Aosdána; a Foreign Member of the American Academy of Arts and Letters; and a Commandeur de L'Ordre des Arts et Lettres by the French Ministry of Culture. It is difficult to underestimate the esteem and regard with which Seamus Heaney is held both at home and abroad. In 2007, his translation of *Beowulf* was adapted into a film and his most recent collection of poetry in 2006, *District and Circle*, was on bestseller lists in America and Europe.

Critical Commentary: The Forge

See the text of the poem on p. 55.

1. Content

This poem uses the relatively familiar image of the blacksmith to cast light on the poetic process. The *sonnet* opens with a memorable line of poetry that provided the title to Heaney's second published collection, *Door into the Dark*:

> All I know is a door into the dark.

Drawing on his childhood fascination and memories with the local forge, the poet paints a vivid picture of this place. We are told that outside, 'old axles and iron hoops' lie 'rusting'. Then, in the third line, attracted by the 'short-pitched ring' of the anvil, the poet's attention is drawn into the inside of the forge. One can imagine the young poet's eyes adjusting to the darkness of the forge, which is illuminated briefly by an 'unpredictable fantail of sparks'. Although the speaker does not see the anvil, he feels that it 'must be somewhere in the centre':

> Horned as a unicorn, at one end square,
> Set there immovable: an altar

The references to the 'unicorn' and the 'altar' convey the almost *mythical*, even sacred, light in which the young poet views the workings of the forge.

In the ninth line, the poet turns his attention to the smith. We learn that he 'expends himself in shape and music'. This is a rough, powerful man whose physical presence is palpable. A man from another era, he is 'leather-aproned', has 'hairs in his nose' and 'grunts' at the passing 'traffic'. The poem ends with a clear affirmation of the smithy's mastery of his art: he beats 'real iron out, to work the bellows'.

2. Stylistic Features

This poem is one of the most memorable examples of Heaney's meditative style. From a strictly formal point of view, 'The Forge' is a sonnet. However, the poem undermines the conventional sonnet form in that both the shape and the **rhyming** scheme of 'The Forge' depart from the typical sonnet.

In the poem, the forge becomes an **allegory** or **symbol** for the artistic process in general and the art of writing poetry in particular. The stylistic complexity of the poem can at first be seen in the opening line, where the **internal rhymes** and **half-rhymes** that exist between such words as 'know' and 'door' and 'door' and 'dark' create a memorable interplay that engages the reader's attention from the outset. The emphasis on sound continues throughout the rest of the poem. Notice how the 'short-pitched' description of the sound of the hammer striking the anvil evokes in its **consonance** the sound of metal on metal. This action leads to 'an unpredictable fantail of sparks'. Here, Heaney links sound to the unpredictable nature of the beauty that results from artistic creation. The vital energy that captivates the young poet is captured in the 'hiss' of the 'new shoe' as it 'toughens in water'.

At the heart of this process lies the anvil and the figure of the blacksmith. While Heaney goes out of his way to stress the sacred, unfathomable nature of what this man achieves, he is eager to emphasise his earthy ordinariness. What this man does is cloaked in darkness and thereby shrouded in mystery. For a brief moment in the sonnet, the associations between the smithy's work, the unicorn of classical mythology and even the sacramental altar lend him a priest-like aspect. It is as if he is a holy man transubstantiating the common and even banal occurrences of everyday life into some kind of rarefied artefact. However, Heaney quickly counters his instinctive urge to glorify the artisan by describing him in the most ordinary of ways. At the end of the poem, the speaker emphasises the secular rather than spiritual aspect of the blacksmith's work. Ultimately, the smith does not cast any illumination on life, but rather beats 'real iron out'. The 'real iron' is the end product, while the unknowable and ultimately indescribable creative inspiration remains deep in the darkness of the forge. The correspondence between the 'shape and music' that Heaney draws our attention to in the **sestet** highlights both the abstract and concrete nature of creation. The 'shape' of the artifice emphasises its concrete reality, while its 'music' is its abstract nature.

The forge and the smithy have longstanding associations with artistic endeavour in both classical and contemporary literature. In his famous poem 'Sailing to Byzantium', W.B. Yeats celebrates the ancient Byzantine goldsmiths, while Homer devotes a famous passage in the *Odyssey* to the story of Hephaestus, the blacksmith to the gods. In *A Portrait of the Artist as a Young Man*, James Joyce's Stephen Dedalus promised to 'forge in the smithy of [his] soul the uncreated conscience of [his] race'.

However, perhaps it is Shakespeare's 'quick forge and working-house of thought' in *Henry V* that Heaney has in mind in this poem.

Finally, it is interesting that the poem ends with a warning of sorts. Although the poet emphasises the power and mystery of the artificer's achievement, he also acknowledges the threats to his existence that lie beyond the forge. Outside, 'a clatter | Of hoofs' is now but a distant memory and the traffic that flashes by reminds us of a faster modern world that has little need for the skills of the blacksmith. Of course, it is not difficult to see that poetry faces similar threats to its existence from the modern world.

3. Essay Writing

If you are thinking of making reference to 'The Forge' in any response to Heaney's poetry that you may be asked to make, you may wish to keep the following points in mind.

a. Heaney makes use of the sonnet form in this poem. It may be possible to compare and contrast the form of this poem with the other poems on the course.
b. Heaney is interested in the artistic process. In this respect, you may be able to devote an entire paragraph to this aspect of Heaney's writing. It might be useful to compare this poem with 'The Harvest Bow'.
c. This is a complex and interesting poem that is rich in clever language devices and literary *allusion*.

Critical Commentary: Bogland

See the text of the poem on p. 57.

1. Content

In 1969, Heaney read *The Bog People*, a study of the discoveries made by the Danish archaeologist P.V. Glob, which had a profound influence on his work. A close examination of Heaney's earlier poetry demonstrates clearly the extent to which he was influenced by Glob's writing. However, even before Heaney first read *The Bog People*, he was using bog imagery as a *metaphor* for the elemental. 'Bogland' opens with a negative statement that seems designed to offer an alternative to our traditional image of the wide, sweeping prairies of North America:

> We have no prairies
> To slice a big sun at evening –

Instead of wide-open spaces, the countryside offers us a landscape where 'the eye concedes to I [the] Encroaching horizon'. In the second stanza, Heaney develops this idea further. The reflection of the sun setting over a mountain lake, or a 'tarn', is likened to 'cyclops' eye'. Where the American prairies contain vast stretches of unfenced country, the Irish alternative is 'bog that keeps crusting I Between the sights of the sun'.

The third stanza marks the beginning of a series of examples that demonstrate the natural, cultural, historical and social importance of bogland. The 'skeleton I Of the Great Irish Elk', which the poet describes as being 'An astounding crate full of air', has been found buried in the bog. The Great Irish Elk, or Giant Deer, was a species of *Megaloceros* and one of the largest deer that ever lived. While its range extended across Eurasia, it is in the boglands of Ireland that the greatest numbers of these creatures have been found.

In the fourth stanza, Heaney mentions the bog butter. In some cases, churns and wooden containers of butter dating back over three hundred years have been found in the bogs. The high level of acidity in bogs acts as a preservative that previous generations valued highly. In the speaker's opinion, the bog itself is:

> [...] kind, black butter

> Melting and opening underfoot,

Many students find this fifth stanza puzzling. When Heaney says that the bog is 'Missing its last definition I By millions of years', he is referring to the fact that the bog will eventually become coal. Over time, pressure will force the massive accumulation of dead plant life in the peat into bitumen, which will eventually be transformed into coal. However, for the time being, all that is to be found in these boglands is 'waterlogged trunks I Of great firs'.

In the final two lines of the penultimate stanza, Heaney **alludes** once again to North America. In the 1700s, the 'pioneers' were a groups of men and women who were the first Europeans to settle the American frontier. Whereas the American pioneers extended the frontier beyond the Appalachian Mountains and in later westward expansions beyond the Mississippi River, the Irish pioneers 'keep striking I Inwards and downwards'. The sense of expanding into virgin territory that was so much a part of the American experience seems absent here. Within the context of the Irish experience, 'Every layer [...] I Seems camped on before'. In the poet's imagination, the cultural depth that he associates with the bogholes is mirrored by a physical one that extends as far as the Atlantic Ocean and beyond. The **hyperbole** of the final line emphasises this depth further. The 'wet centre', we learn, 'is bottomless'.

2. Stylistic Features

This poem, which is one of a number of poems by Heaney that are inspired by the wetlands of Ireland and Northern Europe, concluded his 1969 collection, *Door into the Dark*. In his presentation speech on the occasion of Seamus Heaney's Nobel Prize in 1995, Östen Sjöstrand, a member of the Swedish Academy, said that Heaney 'has little time for the Emerald Isle of the tourist brochures. For him Ireland is first and foremost The Bogland.' Speaking about his own interest in boglands during a lecture called 'Feeling into Words,' given to the Royal Society of Literature in London on 17 October 1974, Heaney said:

> I began to get an idea of bog as the memory of the landscape, or as a landscape that remembered everything that happened in and to it. In fact, if you go round the National Museum in Dublin, you will realize that a great proportion of the most cherished material heritage of Ireland was found in a bog.

He also added that he:

> had been reading about the frontier and the west as an important myth in the American consciousness, so I set up — or rather, laid down — the bog as an answering Irish myth.

According to Neil Corcoran, this poem can be regarded as a kind of 'answering Irish poem to Theodore Roethke's American "In Praise of Prairie", in which "Horizons have no strangeness to the eye", and "distance is familiar as a friend. | The feud we kept with space comes to an end".'

Perhaps the most striking stylistic feature of the poem is the manner in which Heaney's mastery of form mirrors his descriptions of the bog. **Run-on lines**, **metre** and **rhythm** combine to produce memorable sound patterns that capture fully the sense of the bog. The run-on lines in particular help to create a sense of the interconnected layers of bog that connect the present with the past and store a wealth of culture and history:

> The ground itself is kind, black butter

> Melting and opening underfoot,
> Missing its last definition

According to Edna Longley, 'The poem alternates ampler development with sharp insertions. Thus the abrupt "They'll never dig coal here" interrupts **assonances** which imitate the wet softness of bog "Melting and opening underfoot". "Bogland" might be called not so much "a prospect of the mind" (to use Heaney's favourite Wordsworthian phrase for poet landscape) as a prospecting of the mind.'

For Heaney, the bog is a **mythological** landscape, a **symbol** of cultural identity and race memory. In this respect, he is heavily influenced by the writings of the Swiss psychoanalyst Carl Jung. This revolutionary and extremely influential thinker founded a type of psychoanalysis known as analytical psychology. Jung was virtually alone amongst 19th-century thinkers in believing that human beings had placed far too much emphasis on science and needed to return to the realms of the mythological and the spiritual in order to obtain a true understanding of what defines our humanity. In particular, Jung believed that beneath the personal unconscious lay the collective unconscious. According to Jung, this collective unconscious could be inherited as a race memory and passed on from generation to generation. In Heaney's imagination, the bog acts as a storehouse for our collective unconscious. Speaking directly about this poem, Heaney has said:

> The title of the poem refers to the bogs I knew while I was growing up and the stories I had heard about the things that could be preserved in the bog such as supplies of butter that were kept there, and about the

> things that were even more astonishing to a child, such as the skeleton
> of an Irish elk which our neighbours had dug out.

In the same address, he emphasised the lifelong hold that the bogland has held on his imagination:

> When I was a child and an adolescent I lived among peat-diggers and I
> also worked in the peat bog myself. I loved the structure the peat bank
> revealed after the spade had worked its way through the surface of
> the peat. I loved the mystery and silence of the place when the work
> was done at the end of the day and I would stand there alone while the
> larks became quiet and the lapwings started calling, while a snipe would
> suddenly take off and disappear...

In one respect, it is not surprising that Heaney should identify so strongly with the boglands of Ireland. In 1969, the date of the poem's publication, Derry's Bogside was at the centre of the civil rights marches in Northern Ireland. Furthermore, the English word 'bog' comes from the Irish for 'soft'. However, in English the word has often been a *synonym* for backwardness, shame and even filth. 'The bog' is slang for a toilet and 'a bogger' is often used as an insult in Hiberno-English. Yet Heaney dismisses such connotations for a view of the bog that is altogether more favourable.

3. Essay Writing

If you think you would like to make reference to 'Bogland' in any response to Heaney's poetry that you may be asked to make, you may wish to keep the following points in mind.

a. The poem is one of two poems by Heaney on the course that have the bog as their central *metaphor*. As such, you may wish to compare this poem to 'The Tollund Man'.

b. The language and *metre* of the poem attempt to capture the sense of the Irish bog.

c. Although Heaney is not an overtly political poet, it is possible to assign political significance to this and Heaney's other bog poem on the course. It might be possible to mention this in a paragraph on Heaney's attitude to violence.

Critical Commentary: The Tollund Man

See the text of the poem on pp. 59–60.

1. Content

Heaney was inspired to write this poem after he had read *The Bog People*, written by the Danish archaeologist P.V. Glob and published by Faber & Faber in 1969. Speaking of this poem, Heaney has said that he was drawn to the description of the violence and definite sense of place as outlined by Glob. The following is a brief extract from Glob's book:

> An early spring day – 8 May 1950. Evening was gathering over Tolland Fen in Bjaeldskov Dal. Momentarily, the sun burst in, bright and yet subdued, through a gate in blue thunderclouds in the west, bringing everything mysteriously to life. The evening stillness was only broken, now and again, by the grating love-call of the snipe. The dead man, too, deep down in the amber-brown peat, seemed to have come alive. He lay on his damp bed as though asleep, resting on his side, the head inclined a little forward, arms and legs bent. His face wore a gentle expression – the eyes tightly closed, the lips softly pursed, as in silent prayer. It was as though the dead man's soul had for a moment returned from another world, through the gate in the western sky.

Heaney's poem opens with a commitment by the speaker that someday he 'will go to Aarhus'. The purpose of this intended visit is to see the 'peat-brown head', the 'eyelids' and the 'pointed skin cap' of the Tollund Man. Then, in the next stanza, the poet imagines 'the flat country nearby | Where they dug him out'. In the final lines of the second stanza, the contents of the dead man's stomach are envisioned by the poet in almost forensic detail.

In the third stanza, the man's naked vulnerability is juxtaposed in a shocking fashion with the evidence of his execution:

> Naked except for
> The cap, noose and girdle,
> I will stand a long time.
> Bridegroom to the goddess,

The final line of the third stanza casts light on the reason for this man's death: he was offered up as a sacrifice, or as a 'Bridegroom to the goddess'. In keeping with the fact that this act of sacrifice was intended to form part of a fertility rite, the language in the fourth stanza becomes more sexual in nature. We learn that the earth goddess 'tightened her torc' and then opened the ground to envelop him, her juices (the acidity of the water in the bog) preserving his body until it becomes in the poet's imagination a 'saint's kept body'. Where this man once lay deep in the bog, 'his stained face' now 'Reposes at Aarhus'.

In the sixth stanza, the poet tells us that he 'could risk blasphemy' and 'Consecrate' the bog. Unusually, given the pagan nature of the ritual that led to the Tollund Man's death, the language used here is overtly Christian. The prayer that the speaker feels that he would like to intone concerns the germination or reanimation of the 'Stockinged corpses' of 'labourers' who died as a result of a Black and Tans atrocity in Northern Ireland during the 1920s.

In the next stanza, Heaney provides us with a series of disturbing glimpses into the level of the violence that was meted out to these brothers. We learn that their 'skin and teeth' flecked the sleepers of the railroad for 'miles along the lines'. Then, in an abrupt and jarring change that links the plight of these four young brothers to that of the Tollund Man, we are transported back in time to the day when he 'rode the tumbril' on his way to certain death. In an almost incantatory fashion, the poet then lists the names 'Tollund', 'Grauballe' and 'Nebelgard', all well-known sites where sacrificial victims have been found.

In the final stanza, the speaker tells us that he imagines he will feel a strange sense of affinity with the 'old man-killing parishes'. Such a sense of kinship that will cause him to 'feel lost, I Unhappy and at home' results, one can only imagine, from the shared history of violent sacrifice that exists between Northern Ireland and Jutland.

2. Stylistic Features

This is a complex poem that both rewards and demands our close attention. In the poem, the Tollund Man is emblematic of the victimisation and violence that have dominated recent history in Northern Ireland. Östen Sjöstrand, a member of the Swedish Academy who awarded Heaney the Nobel Prize in 1995, has said of 'The Tollund Man' that 'in his figure Heaney conjures forth, brutally and movingly, a culture that is both alien and familiar, a distinctive subject of ritual sacrifice, human voices silenced by the boggy landscape'. From the outset there are obvious parallels between the ritualistic violence that led to this man's brutal death and the awful violence that has been part of Ireland's history. The poem was inspired by the accounts of the ritualistic deaths that Heaney read in the late 1960s. According to the poet:

> the unforgettable photographs of these victims blended in [his] mind with photographs of atrocities, past and present, in the long rites of Irish political and religious struggles.

Archaeology and the act of digging have fascinated Heaney throughout his poetic career. In this poem, Heaney imaginatively digs down through the layers of the past in order to cast light on the present. The links that exist between the violence that led to the Tollund Man's death and Ireland's sad history are many. Firstly, this man was sacrificed to a female goddess as part of a fertility rite. The *mythology* surrounding the Irish Republican cause has always identified Ireland as a feminine presence. Secondly, the religious nature of his sacrifice is mirrored in the sectarian nature of the violence that has dogged Northern Ireland's recent past.

The religious imagery in the poem is particularly interesting. Through the religious symbolism, Heaney skilfully interweaves pagan ritual with Christianity in general and Catholicism in particular. The first instance of religious imagery in the poem is to be found in the poet's promise to undertake a pilgrimage to view the Tollund Man's 'kept body'. In this manner, the Tollund Man is identified with those saints who appear to have been incorruptible. The speaker tells us that he is willing to 'risk blasphemy' by venerating this pagan figure. This, he hopes, will result in a consecration of the land, which in turn will lead to a transformation of the 'cauldron bog' of internecine violence into a 'holy ground' of common purpose. In order to emphasise the religious significance of the Tollund Man, Heaney capitalised the 'h' in 'Him' in the sixth stanza. Given that the Tollund Man was sacrificed as part of a fertility ritual of renewal and revival, the speaker feels he can go so far as to hope for a miraculous germination of the dead victims of violence in his country. The parallels between these two parts of Europe, separated by culture, time and geography, are such that the poet feels 'at home' in the 'man-killing parishes'. In this sense, the poem does appear to offer a small amount of hope for an end to the violence that has plagued modern Ireland.

According to Andrew Foley:

> If Heaney's work generally emphasises the inefficacy of Christian symbols such as the cross to provide consolation or resolution of a conflict in which Christianity is after all a contributing factor, then a poem like 'The Tollund Man' may be regarded as Heaney's attempt to offer more 'befitting emblems of adversity' to help understand and counter the 'rage' of Irish religious and political enmity.

It is clear that Heaney is both repulsed and fascinated by the Tollund Man. The depiction of his persevered body, which at first seems to emphasise his restful nature, yields to the forensic, even voyeuristic, description of his innards:

> His last gruel of winter seeds
> Caked in his stomach,

The harsh *cacophonous* sound of words such as 'Caked' and 'stomach' stresses the disgust the poet feels. Furthermore, the idea that we are privy to this man's insides calls attention to the violation that is part of such violence. Other Northern Irish poets such as Michael Longley have made similar points about violence. It is as though human dignity is effaced by the cruelty of violence.

Finally, when one considers the historical changes that have swept aside the fertility rituals in which this man participated, his death seems particularly pointless. Could Heaney be suggesting that any violent death for any cause, religious or otherwise, is pointless?

3. Essay Writing

If you think that you would like to make reference to 'The Tollund Man' in any response to Heaney's poetry that you may be asked to make, you may wish to keep some of the following points in mind.

a. This is a complex poem that draws on the past in order to provide us with a powerful platform from which the poet attempts to identify central truths about the Irish experience.
b. This is one of two bog poems on the Leaving Certificate course. As such, it may be useful to devote a paragraph to a comparison with 'Bogland'.
c. Heaney's poetry frequently deals with violence and religion. It may be possible to devote an entire paragraph to these themes in his poetry and to draw some interesting parallels between 'A Constable Calls' and 'The Tollund Man'.

Critical Commentary: Mossbawn: Two Poems in Dedication (I) Sunlight

See the text of the poem on pp. 62–3.

1. Content

In this beautiful and heart-warming dedicatory poem, Heaney evokes a sense of genuine love, a connection with a passing way of life and a childlike sense of security. The poem opens with a depiction of the silence that the poet associates with Mossbawn. In the yard, the pump is warmed by the sunlight while the water in the 'slung bucket' is 'honeyed'. The timelessness of the scene is emphasised by the image of the sun standing like a 'griddle cooling I against the wall'. Once the scene is set, the poet moves into the interior of Mossbawn, where his aunt's 'hands scuffled I over the bakeboard, I the reddening stove'. As with the yard outside, the poet emphasises the warmth of the place. A 'plaque of heat' rises up against her as she stands 'in a floury apron I by the window'. In the fifth stanza, the poet's attention remains focused on his memories of his aunt performing her household chores:

Now she dusts the board
with a goose's wing,

While Mossbawn obviously occupies a special, even **mythical** place in Heaney's imagination, he does not seek to embellish or airbrush his memory of his aunt. She is described as being 'broad-lapped' and as having 'measling shins'. In the same stanza, the speaker again emphasises the peace and the 'space' that this place afforded him. The 'two clocks' that presumably symbolise the past and the present 'tick' in unison as past and present are unified by the poem's uplifting message.

The final stanza of the poem affirms Heaney's central belief that it is the ordinary, everyday, domestic quality of his love for Mossbawn and his aunt who lived there that makes it so special:

And here is love
like a tinsmith's scoop
sunk past its gleam
in the meal-bin.

The 'tinsmith's scoop', worn and in some respects unremarkable, becomes a **metaphor** for the warmth and love that Mossbawn represents.

2. Stylistic Features

Heaney grew up on a County Derry farm not far from Mossbawn. Mossbawn lies 30 miles north-west of Belfast, between Castledawson and Toome Bridge, along the Bann River just north of where it emerges from Lough Neagh. Mossbawn holds a vital place in Heaney's imagination. In *Preoccupations*, Heaney has described the place as a 'navel':

I would begin with the Greek word, omphalos, meaning the navel, and hence the stone that marked the centre of the world, and repeat it, omphalos, omphalos, omphalos, until its blunt and falling music becomes the music of somebody pumping water at the pump outside our back door.

In this poem, Heaney balances natural speech with a genuine dedication to what he has described as a 'musically satisfying order of sounds'. As a result, the reader feels that he or she is sharing in what is, in the words of the Swedish Academy, a moment of 'lyrical beauty and ethical depth'. The intimate domestic images that dominate the poem are matched by a rich and sensuous language that enables the reader to share fully in the experience. In particular, the **alliterative** combination of words such as 'helmeted', 'heated', 'honeyed', 'slung', 'sun', 'stood', 'scuffled' and 'stove' work to create an easygoing, relaxed sense of homely comfort. The naturalness of the language is mirrored in the sensuous **imagery** used by Heaney. The first two stanzas stress the elemental place that Mossbawn holds in the poet's imagination. In fact, images associated with two of the elements, water and sunlight, dominate the first stanza:

> There was a sunlit absence.
> The helmeted pump in the yard
> heated its iron,
> water honeyed

According to Michael Parker, Heaney's search for 'myth and **symbol** has caused him to return frequently to the Mossbawn pump as a source for his creative energy [...] It is a recurring fecund image in several volumes. With its phallic shape and life giving water, it symbolises the creative union of his parents, the male and female, the mysterious fusion of fixity and fluidity which gives the world and Art its shape; it is a south Derry equivalent of the Pieran spring.' The interior world at Mossbawn is no different in that it is also associated with a life-giving, creative energy. The heat that emanates from the stove is a reminder not only of the warmth that Heaney associates with Mossbawn, but of his aunt's creative spirit. The act of baking bread and the sight of the scones rising are obvious reminders of this creativity.

There are frequent references to time throughout the poem. In the first instance, the sun's movement is likened to a 'griddle cooling | against the wall | of each long afternoon'. Here, the long vowel sounds slow down the progression of the poem and create a lazy, hazy feeling that works to capture a sense of timelessness. As the poem reaches its conclusion, the speaker refers to the scones 'rising | to the tick of two clocks'. This is a difficult line to interpret. Heaney may have the notion of past and present in mind. Certainly, Mossbawn, with its water pump, 'goose's wing' duster and homemade baking, is a reminder of another time. However, the two clocks ticking may also refer to the beating of the two hearts of aunt and child. Whatever the case, it is clear that the poet is savouring his memories of the unspoken love and warmth that he experienced during this period in his life. In the final instance, this love is likened to a tinsmith's scoop:

> And here is love
> like a tinsmith's scoop
> sunk past its gleam
> in the meal-bin.

Tin is a soft metal that is relatively fragile. As such, it is a prefect **metaphor** for the unassuming, unspoken love that lies hidden, 'sunk […] | in the meal-bin'. The meal-bin links this metaphor to the kind of nurturing and sustaining love that Heaney associates with his aunt and Mossbawn.

3. Essay Writing

If you are thinking of making reference to 'Mossbawn', you may wish to keep some of the following points in mind.

a. In much of the poetry on the course, Heaney moves easily from the homely images of farm and village to larger issues of history, language and national identity, creating what he once called 'the music of what happens'. 'Mossbawn' is an obvious an example of Heaney's deep connection to his roots in Derry.
b. The language of the poem evokes the importance that Heaney attaches to Mossbawn in a beautiful manner.
c. Despite the almost mythical significance that Heaney affords the people and places surrounding Mossbawn, his depiction remains at all times believable and realistic.

Critical Commentary: A Constable Calls

See the text of the poem on pp. 64–5.

1. Content

Speaking of his sense of identity as a Catholic in an interview with Seamus Deane, Heaney had the following to say:

> Poetry is born out of the watermarks and colourings of the self. But that self in some ways takes its spiritual pulse from the inward spiritual structuring of the community to which it belongs: and the community to which I belong is Catholic and Nationalist. I believe that the poet's force now, and hopefully in the future, is to maintain the efficacy of his 'mythos', his own cultural and political colourings, rather than to serve any particular momentary strategy and his political leaders, his paramilitary organisation or his own liberal self might want him to serve. I think that poetry and politics are, in different ways, an articulation, an ordering, a giving form to inchoate pieties, prejudices, world-views, or whatever. And I think that my own poetry is a kind of slow, obstinate, papish burn, emanating from the ground I was brought up on.

Certainly it is difficult to read this poem without sensing the 'papish burn' of which Heaney speaks. The poem opens with a depiction of the constable's bike that stood at the 'window-sill'. While there is nothing unusual about any of its component parts, it is difficult not to feel that this bike constitutes a threat. A gun comes to mind when, in the second stanza, we learn that the '"spud" | Of the [bike's] dynamo' was 'cocked back'. A sense of the constable's presence is conveyed by the bike's pedal treads, which hang 'relieved | Of the boot of the law'.

In the next stanza, further information regarding this man's arrival is provided. Something of the quality of the welcome that this man has been afforded is conveyed when we are told that his cap lay 'upside down | On the floor, next his chair'. In the final **couplet**, Heaney intimates that the constable is a physically unappealing man. He is 'sweating' and the line of pressure on his head caused by the tightness of his cap suggests that he is overweight. As the child narrator looks on, the constable opens his ledger and his father makes his returns in imperial measurements:

He had unstrapped
The heavy ledger, and my father
Was making tillage returns
In acres, roods, and perches.

The opening line of the next stanza conveys the intensity of the scene. 'Fear' mingles with 'Arithmetic' and the inferences of violence that were suggested by the constable's bike in the previous stanzas now become overt. The speaker's attention is drawn to the 'polished holster' and the 'revolver butt'. In the next stanza, the speaker's apprehension leads him to wonder if his father is being entirely truthful when he answers 'No' to the constable's questions concerning root crops. His worry is heightened as he begins to fret about possible imprisonment and the 'black hole in the barracks'. Of course, the constable does not take any action. He simply closes his 'domesday book', places his 'cap' on his head and looks at the speaker as he says 'goodbye'. In the final stanza, the constable's shadow bobs in the window as he prepares to leave. The closing line of the poem, with the ticking of the constable's bike as it moves into the distance, is highly suggestive of the menace that he represents in the poet's imagination.

2. Stylistic Features

This poem, which first appeared in the collection *Singing School*, is one of six autobiographical works that detail Heaney's growing sense of identity both as a poet and a Northern Irish Catholic. 'A Constable Calls' is his most overtly political poem on the Leaving Certificate syllabus. The political agenda can first be seen in the poem's title. The word 'constable' is highly suggestive of British rule. The poem recalls the visit of an RUC man to his home in order to collect agricultural statistics. Told principally through the eyes of a child, the reader is also made aware of a second voice. Although it is not fully articulated, there is a sense of adult resentment for the law. To begin with, the constable's bike is representative of the repression that the poet associates with the Royal Ulster Constabulary. The 'rubber cowl' and 'fat black handlegrips' recall the batons and rubber bullets that were frequently used by the RUC during the Troubles. The association with violence is maintained in the description of the 'dynamo'. The fact that it lies 'cocked back' is strongly suggestive of a gun that is ready to fire. Similarly, the mention of the 'boot of the law' brings to mind the jackbooted policing that was often associated with the RUC.

One of the most interesting stylistic features of this poem is the manner in which Heaney manages to infer the nature of the deep-rooted divide that exists between the predominantly Protestant police force and the Catholic minority. The *cacophonous* 'g', 's' and 'k' sounds of the first two stanzas further add to the underlying tension of the constable's visit. The fact that the poet's parents do not afford the man anything nearing a hospitable welcome speaks volumes about the division that exists in this society. Rather than take his cap, as would normally happen with a visitor, it is left on the ground.

In the second movement, Heaney allows the child's voice to intrude. The sense of curiosity and wonder that should be a child's reaction to the arrival of a policeman is supplanted by apprehension and palpable tension. The description of the constable works to dehumanise him. Like his bike, he is described as series of separate components, reducing him to little more than an extension of his job. The 'uniform', the 'polished holster', the 'cap', 'braid cord' and, more ominously, the 'revolver butt' tell us nothing about this man himself except that he is a representative of the law. In the end, he is a 'shadow' that jeopardises the secure atmosphere of home. The fact that he represents British rule is **alluded** to in the imperial measurements used by him to quantify the farm's returns. The 'acres, roods, and perches' are more than just measurements – they are clear reminders of British rule and the Heaney family's place in the social hierarchy of Northern Ireland. Furthermore, there is an obvious incongruity between the routine nature of the constable's visit and the fact that he is armed.

It is interesting that the encounter with the constable should take place on a farm, especially when one considers that so much of the violence and tension that has been part of Ireland's history has centred on the struggle for land. One of the most upsetting aspects of the encounter with the constable is the manner in which it involves the emasculation of the father in the eyes of the son. The young speaker should never have had to witness his father's 'fear' that the farm's 'Arithmetic' might not satisfy the constable's inspection.

In the fourth movement of the poem, Heaney allows the tension to mount. The speaker is complicit in his father's lie and he imagines them being thrown in jail for not declaring the turnip patch:

> […] I assumed
> Small guilts and sat
> Imagining the black hole in the barracks.
> He stood up, shifted the baton-case

The repetition of the consonant sounds 'b' and 'ck' reinforces the sense of dread that this imagined place creates.

The fifth movement brings with it the relief at the constable's departure. However, we are afforded one last glimpse of the 'baton case', the belt and of course the 'domesday book'. The 'Small guilts' of the previous stanza seem to have pre-empted the mention of Doomsday. It is typical of Heaney's poetry that an *allusion* should be so multi-layered. Thoughts of guilt and Doomsday are not only suggestive of a Catholic mindset, but also hint at the history of the British Empire. The Domesday Book was commissioned in 1085 by William the Conqueror, who invaded England in 1066. As the poem closes, the menacing *alliteration* of the bicycle that 'ticked, ticked, ticked' hints at the troubling times to come in Northern Ireland.

According to Daniel Tobin, 'the poem ends with the haunting sound of the constable bicycle ticking down the road like a bomb about to go off. An air of oppression hovers about the scene, and while we know that neither the father nor the son will respond violently to that oppression, the poem nevertheless suggests that a violent reprisal will someday detonate in this explosive social climate'. Heaney is so successful in evoking tension and a sense of dread that we share in the speaker's relief at the constable's departure.

3. Essay Writing

If you are thinking of making reference to 'A Constable Calls' in any essay on Heaney's poetry that you may be asked to make, you may wish to consider some of the following points.

a. The poem provides us with an interesting perspective on the divisions that exist in Northern Irish society.
b. Heaney makes interesting use of sound devices such as alliteration and consonance to heighten the tension surrounding the constable's visit.

c. Many of Heaney's poems deal with the theme of violence. It may be interesting to consider a comparison between this poem and 'The Tollund Man'.

Critical Commentary: The Skunk

See the text of the poem on p. 67.

1. Content

The title of this poem is unusual if not mischievous. Very few people would see the skunk as being an appropriate symbol for love, yet in this humorous and tender poem Heaney has managed to link his memory of a skunk that used to enter his garden at night to the romantic love he feels for his wife. Heaney's marriage poems have been praised for their 'unromanticizing exactitude'. This description could certainly be applied to 'The Skunk'.

The poem opens with an interesting description of the skunk. In an unusual *simile*, its tail is likened to a 'chasuble', the loose garment worn by a priest at mass:

> Up, black, striped and damasked like the chasuble
> At a funeral Mass, the skunk's tail
> Paraded the skunk. [...]

By the poem's end we are led to feel that erotic separation and anticipation are interwoven with feelings of marital intimacy and completion in this wonderful simile. We learn that this creature used to visit the poet 'Night after night'. In the second stanza, the poet describes a familiar domestic setting. The refrigerator 'whinnied' into silence while the poet's desk light casts a soft light on the 'Small oranges' that lie 'beyond the verandah'. Sensing the approach of the skunk, the poet becomes 'tense as a voyeur'. Then, in the third stanza, the poet tells us that for the first time in 'eleven years [he] was composing | Love-letters again'. This fact causes him to meditate on his relationship with his wife. The word 'wife' holds his attention and he likens it to 'a stored cask'. In his imagination, the 'slender vowel' of the word is changed or mutated until it becomes part of the 'night earth and air | Of California'. As the poet thinks about his wife, it is as though everything reminds him of her absence. The 'Tang of eucalyptus' and the aftertaste 'of a mouthful of wine' are likened to 'inhaling' his wife's scent from 'a cold pillow'. This reverie is disturbed by the arrival of the skunk 'Snuffling the boards five feet beyond' him.

In the final stanza, the speaker's wife, who is absent in the first four stanzas, makes an appearance. In his description of his wife rooting through the bottom drawer of her dresser, Heaney achieves a mischievous comparison between her and the skunk.

2. Stylistic Features

'The Skunk' is one of a number of humorous, loving and passionate expressions of married life, such as 'The Otter', 'Homecomings' and 'A Dream of Jealousy', that Heaney has composed. While the poem belongs to the long tradition of the **Epithalamium**, it is an unusual marriage poem in that it celebrates a mature relationship. According to Neil Corcoran, 'The Skunk' provides 'a tender, loving comedy of the consolations of the habitual [... it is] tender without being cosy, personal without being embarrassingly self-revealing'. In fact, the lack of an obvious **rhyming** scheme lends to the poem's conversational manner and stresses the ordinary nature of the poet's relationship with his wife.

The poem's title and its **confessional** subject mater recall the poem 'Skunk Hour' by the American poet and Heaney's friend, Robert Lowell. However, unlike Lowell's poem, where the speaker is pained by isolation, Heaney's isolation in this poem affords him the chance to celebrate his love for his wife. In the speaker's imagination, his wife achieves a humorous, even erotic definition in the **image** of a skunk rooting around outside his house in California. Heaney ignores the offensive associations that the word 'skunk' connotes in favour of aspects of this creature's behaviour that remind him of his wife's absence. While the **onomatopoeic** depiction of the 'refrigerator' whining into silence evokes the familiar and domestic setting, the use of **assonance** and **consonance** emphasise the soft sense of longing that the speaker is experiencing:

> [...] The beautiful, useless
> Tang of eucalyptus spelt your absence.

The use of the word 'voyeur' is a deliberate attempt by Heaney to convey the fact that his imagination has conflated the arrival of the skunk with his wife's absence. In the final stanza, the connection between this animal's nightly visits to his house and his wife is made obvious. Here, the poet's wife finally makes a welcome appearance. We are afforded glimpses of what is an utterly normal but very private moment in the routine of any married couple. As his wife undresses and the 'plunge-line' of her 'nightdress' is revealed, the reader is cast in the role of voyeur. In the end, Heaney reminds us of both the comic and the erotic. In this manner, he refuses to *mythologise* marriage, preferring instead to highlight the humour and passion that are part of any good relationship:

> It all came back to me last night, stirred
> By the sootfall of your things at bedtime,
> Your head-down, tail-up hunt in a bottom drawer
> For the black plunge-line nightdress.

However, perhaps the most remarkable aspect of 'The Skunk' is the manner in which the *tone* of the poem strikes a balance between longing and honesty that is utterly without self-regard. Despite the unusual comparison at the heart of this poem, there is nothing pretentious or conceited about the emotions it expresses.

3. Essay Writing

If you think that you would like to refer to 'The Skunk' in any essay that you may be asked to write on Seamus Heaney's poetry, you may wish to keep some of the following points in mind.

a. This is one of a number of poems on the course by Heaney that deal with relationships. You may wish to devote an entire paragraph to this aspect of his poetry.

b. The humorous quality of the poem distinguishes it from many of the other poems on the course. In this respect, you may wish to compare 'The Skunk' to some of the other poems that you have studied.

c. There is a wonderfully open and honest quality to this poem. You may wish to consider the impact that the poem had on you as a reader in any personal response to Heaney's poetry that you may be asked to make.

Critical Commentary: The Harvest Bow

See the text of the poem on p. 69.

1. Content

This deeply personal poem explores the poet's memory of his father making a harvest bow. As the father works silently on the bow, it is as if aspects of his personality are incorporated into it:

> As you plaited the harvest bow
> You implicated the mellowed silence in you
> In wheat that does not rust

The 'wheat that does not rust' is a reminder of the way in which the bow is an enduring part of the natural cycle.

In the next line, the bow 'brightens', becoming transformed in the poet's imagination into a 'knowable corona, | A throwaway love-knot of straw'. The second stanza focuses on his father's hands, and the man's connection to the natural cycle is emphasised once again. These hands have worked on 'ashplants and cane sticks' and 'gamecocks'. Such was his father's skill that his 'fingers moved somnambulant' on the harvest bow. In the final *couplet* of this stanza, the poet takes the bow and holds in it his hand. Imagining that he is touching the item as a blind person would read 'braille', he manages to glean or gather unsaid truths.

In the third stanza, the poet looks through the 'golden loops' of the harvest bow and in the process a door into the past is opened. Images of his relationship with his father are brought to the fore. He can see the two of them walking 'between the railway slopes | Into an evening of long grass and midges'. On a general level, an auction notice on an outhouse wall reminds us of the type of change that the bow in his father's lapel seems to defy. However, this auction notice is also a reminder of a particularly painful moment in Heaney's early life. Following the death of his younger brother, Christopher, who was killed by a car when he ran out from behind a bus, the Heaneys sold the family home at Mossbawn. Heaney has said that the move from Mossbawn signalled the end of his childhood.

Warmer memories dominate the fourth stanza, where the poet remembers fishing trips with his father. The joy of these outings was such that the young speaker anticipated the longed-for lift to his spirits that he associated with these evenings. The poet then recalls the ticking sound of his father's stick as it 'Beats out of time'. In the closing couplet of the stanza, the speaker pictures his father once more as a quiet 'tongue-tied' man working on the straw of the harvest bow.

The italicised opening line of the final stanza alludes to the poet Coventry Patemore, who claimed that the purpose of art was 'to bring peace'. The speaker feels that this could be the 'motto' of this 'frail' yet obviously powerful harvest bow that he has 'pinned up' on the 'dresser'. In the final lines of the poem, the poet attempts to make concrete the relationship between the natural and human worlds. The bow is likened to 'the spirit of the corn' or rabbit that has slipped its 'snare' and eluded capture.

2. Stylistic Features

This beautiful memory poem is one of Heaney's most anthologised pieces of writing. The bow that occasions the poet's heartfelt tribute to his father also creates a number of tangible links with such varied themes as the passing of time, nature and the worth and purpose of artistic endeavour. In Robert F. Garratt's opinion, 'the poem draws its powerful effect from a delicate *conceit*, which develops throughout the piece from what it is in actuality – a woven badge of straw signifying the harvest – to what it represents symbolically'.

The bow is of course a powerful and interesting *metaphor*. Firstly, it represents a link with the traditions of the rural community. The bow was made in celebration of the bounty of the harvest and often hung above the kitchen door. The advent of intensive, mechanised farming and the waves of migrations from the land that have taken place since Heaney wrote the poem have threatened the way of life that the bow represents. For Heaney, the bow is a potent reminder of our connection to the land. In the poet's imagination, the art of making the bow provides a link to a time when the 'spirit of the corn' was an integral part of the rural community's life. Such pre-Christian rituals are of course now lost to us, but the bow, made from 'wheat that does not rust', is a symbol of our connection to such traditions.

Secondly, an interesting aspect of the bow is the manner in which it reveals aspects of Heaney's relationship with his father. Notice how the speaker never recalls any instance of direct communication with this father. The bow, however, allows the poet to form a connection with his father that transcends the spoken word. This 'frail device' communicates an 'unsaid' message of love and tradition. This message is likened by the poet to a form of 'braille' that, when understood, allows him to glean 'the unsaid off the palpable'. This 'unsaid' knowledge seems to speak of the enduring value of community and tradition. Despite the reminders of change that are present in the poem in the form of 'old beds', 'ploughs in hedges' and even 'An auction notice', the 'original townland' that inspires Heaney's imagination still exists. The separateness of the father and son, which is emphasised by the personal pronouns 'You' and 'Me', is countered in the end by the inclusiveness and warmth that the bow **symbolises**. This inclusiveness is further expressed by the fact that in its current incarnation, the bow seems to act as a symbol of the poet's love for his wife:

> *The end of art is peace*
> Could be the motto of this frail device
> That I have pinned up on our deal dresser –

An interesting aspect of the poem's stylistic features is the manner in which the casual nature of the poem's form creates the sense of the speaker's mind wandering back through time. While each of the five stanzas relies on three **rhyming couplets**, the **run-on lines** and lack of emphatic **rhymes** push the poem forward in a gentle, unforced manner. However, despite the meandering nature of the poem, its final message is clear. Artistic endeavour, whether spoken or not, has the ability to transcend division. The reference to Coventry Patmore's belief that the 'end of art is peace', which the poet feels 'Could be the motto of this frail device', is wonderfully uplifting.

3. Essay Writing

If you are thinking of making reference to 'The Harvest Bow' in any response to Heaney's poetry that you may be asked to make, try to keep the following points in mind.

a. This poem is one of a number on the course that deals with relationships. Given the predominance of this theme in Heaney's poetry, you may wish to devote an entire paragraph to this aspect of his work.
b. The poem's form works to create the impression that the speaker's mind is wandering back through the years.

c. It has been said of Heaney's poetry that he 'treats of nature with a lover's intensity'. This poem embodies Heaney's deep connection with the natural world.

Critical Commentary: The Underground

See the text of the poem on p. 71.

1. Content

This poem, which was first published in Heaney's 1969 collection, *Station Island*, has at its heart a clever **allusion** to the Greek myth of Orpheus and Eurydice. In this Greek myth, Orpheus married the nymph Eurydice. A snake bite that resulted in her death forced her to descend to the underworld. Orpheus was so distraught that he descended into the underworld in order to beg for her release. This descent into the underworld is something only a small number of mortals have successfully done in Greek **mythology**. When he was granted an audience with Hades and his wife Persephone, who ruled the underworld, Orpheus played a beautifully melancholy melody on his lyre that melted the hearts of the king and queen of the underworld. Hades allowed Orpheus to ascend from the underworld with his wife on the proviso that he not look at Eurydice directly. As the pair was leaving the underworld, Orpheus glanced over his shoulder in the direction of Eurydice in order to make sure that she was in fact accompanying him. She was instantly whisked away and condemned to remain forever in the underworld. When Orpheus made a second attempt at freeing his wife, the Thracian maidens drowned out his music and he was killed and his lyre was carried to the heavens to become a constellation. It may be possible that Heaney had Georges Franju's 1958 film *La Première Nuit* in mind when he wrote this poem. In this film, the story of Orpheus is retold through the eyes of a schoolboy in the modern setting of the Paris Métro.

In Heaney's poem 'The Underground', the speaker and his wife assume the roles of modern-day Orpheus and Eurydice. The poem opens with a description of the pair in the 'vaulted tunnel' of the Underground. The speaker's wife is described as wearing her 'going-away coat'. Then, in an unusual **simile**, the poet compares himself to a 'fleet god' gaining on her before she is 'turned to a reed'. Perhaps the poet is **alluding** to the Greek myth of Syrinx. Syrinx was the daughter of the minor deity and river god Ladon. She was chased by the god Pan, who was enamoured with her. Frightened, she called out to her father for help. In order to save her from Pan, he turned her into a water reed.

In the second *quatrain*, the poet describes how his wife's coat buttons fell off one by one 'in a trail | Between the Underground and the Albert Hall'. The third stanza provides us with glimpses of the honeymooners 'mooning around' London, 'late for the Proms'. There is a perceptible change in *tone* in the next line:

> Our echoes die in that corridor and now

The long vowel sounds of this line create a haunting quality that emphasises the passage of time. In the final *couplet* of the stanza, the poet sees himself as a Hansel-like figure who, following the buttons that his wife lost from her coat years earlier, retraces the path back to 'a draughty lamplit station'.

In the final lines of the final stanza, the poet describes himself as being tense as he waits for his wife to return. Unlike Orpheus in the underworld, he tells us that he is 'damned' if he looks back.

2. Stylistic Features

Heaney is fascinated by the *motif* of the journey to the underworld. The figures of Dante, Orpheus, Hermes and Virgil, all of whom are associated with the descent to the underworld, have featured in his poetry. Of course, this interest is also found in Heaney's bog poems, where the speaker undertakes an excavation that takes us down through layers of soil and history.

In 'The Underground', Heaney demonstrates his mastery of form and sound. The poem memorialises the Heaneys' honeymoon in London in 1965. From the outset, the sounds in the poem match the poet's *thematic* concerns. Notice how in the first line the long vowel sounds in the words 'vaulted' and 'tunnel' create an echo that draws the reader's imagination to an underground world of mystery:

> There we were in the vaulted tunnel running,

This haunting quality is balanced, however, by a sense of energy that suggests something important is going to happen. In fact, the first sentence of the poem takes the reader in a headlong rush through the first two quatrains. The sparse punctuation (just two commas in eight lines) barely gives us time to draw a breath. This sense of movement is further maintained by the sound patterns and clever use of present and past participles in the second stanza. The present participles 'running', 'speeding' and 'gaining' all create a sense of excitement and movement. Meanwhile, the past participles 'japed' and 'flapped' capture the sound of Heaney's wife's coat as the wind rushes against it. For anyone who has been in the London Underground, the sensation of rushing air that is created by the pressure of the trains as they enter the tunnel is immediately brought to mind. Of course, this unusual combination of present and past participles mirrors the poem's preoccupation with the passing of time.

An interesting stylistic feature of the poem is the manner in which Heaney mixes contemporary and even **colloquial** language with **allusions** to Greek mythology. Obviously, the poem references the myth of Orpheus and Eurydice, but there is also the erotic reference to Pan's pursuit of Syrinx. Yet Heaney chooses to couch these references in language that can be described as playful. ('There we were', 'And me, me then', 'damned if I look back').

For most readers, the most thought-provoking aspect of 'The Underground' is the manner in which the poem draws attention to the passing of time. The poem opens in the London Underground on the day of the speaker's honeymoon. As we have discussed, the poem's language captures the anticipation and excitement of that day. However, while the poem concludes in the same Underground station, we cannot help but feel that much has changed. The energy and vitality of the first stanza have faded like 'echoes' in a 'corridor'.

The inclusive personal pronouns 'we' and 'Our' are transformed in the final stanza to the individual 'I' as the poet ends up in a wet and 'draughty lamplit station'. As the poem draws to a close, Heaney reminds the reader of the original myth of Orpheus and Eurydice, though there is a tragic reversal of that myth in this poem. In the end, it is the poet who is damned if he looks back, not his lover.

3. Essay Writing

If you are thinking of referring to 'The Underground' in a personal response to Seamus Heaney's poetry, you may wish to keep some of the following points in mind.

a. It has been said of Heaney that for him, 'myth expresses the past's penetration of the present, the presentness of the past'. This poem provides us with an interesting example of Heaney's use of mythology.

b. The motif of the underground appears in many of Heaney's poems. As such, it may be interesting to compare this poem with 'The Tollund Man' or 'Bogland'.

c. Given that Heaney has written about his relationship with his wife in 'The Skunk', it might be worthwhile comparing or contrasting that poem with 'The Underground'.

Critical Commentary: Postscript

See the text of the poem on p. 73.

1. Content

The title of the poem, 'Postscript', gives us a clue as to how the opening line should be read. The poem opens with the word 'And', which suggests that the poem may be centred upon a clever *conceit*. It becomes clear to the reader that what the poet is saying may be an afterthought. As if he is advising someone who is about to go on a journey, Heaney suggests that the time should be taken to go to 'County Clare':

> In September or October, when the wind
> And the light are working off each other

The poet continues to describe the rugged beauty of the Clare landscape. Initially, the speaker draws our attention to the coastline that is 'wild I With foam and glitter'. He then moves 'inland among stones' and describes the arrival of a flock of swans on the 'surface of a slate-grey lake'. The description of the swans is accurate and memorable. The speaker then tells any would-be visitor that it is useless to try and 'capture' this event 'More thoroughly'. The quick and vigorous movement of these swans is captured in a series of unusual and muscular verbs:

> Their feathers roughed and ruffling, white on white,
> Their fully grown headstrong-looking heads
> Tucked or cresting or busy underwater.

In these memorable lines, Heaney manages to convey accurately the uniqueness of these creatures.

In line 14 there is a change in the direction of the poem. 'Postscript' begins by suggesting that a physical journey is about to be undertaken. Now, in the final lines of the poem, it becomes clear that this journey has been more than just a physical one. The speaker suggests that the landscape has the ability to bring about change. Just as the wind buffets the car, the beauty of the landscape can 'catch the heart off guard and blow it open'.

2. Stylistic Features

This poem was chosen by Heaney to conclude his 1996 collection, *The Spirit Level*. This warm-hearted collection of poetry consistently hints at the spiritual dimension to life. In many respects, 'Postscript' reiterates the central message of the *The Spirit Level* as a whole. Interestingly, it is possible to read this poem as providing a postscript to Heaney's 1969 poem 'The Peninsula', in which he advises the reader:

> When you have nothing more to say, just drive
> For a day all round the peninsula.
> The sky is tall as over a runway,
> The land without marks [...]

'Postscript' opens in a conversational fashion. It is as if Heaney purposefully attempts to dull the *imperative* verb 'make' by beginning the poem with 'And'. The unusual *syntax* of the opening line creates the impression that we have interrupted a conversation between two friends. However, while Heaney is very specific about the geographical location (County Clare), his descriptions of that part of the world are rather vague. The *imagery* used by the speaker seems to recommend the experience rather than any particular part of Clare or the West of Ireland.

As the poem progresses there is a distinct feeling that we are moving towards a moment of intense poetic perception. This is mirrored in the poem's form; the *blank verse* that dominates the first half of the poem is maintained until the final line. However, Heaney strengthens the stress patterns in the final lines in order to emphasise the importance of the spiritual experience that he is attempting to 'capture'. At the heart of the poem is an attempt by the poet to pay homage to the poetic powers of the imagination, which he sees as being able to depict a transitory moment in time. It is the effect of the scene on the imagination that Heaney is attempting to convey, not the actual scene itself. The three sentences in which the scene is depicted carry the reader along in a soft rush of thoughts and images. The high point of the poem is achieved when it becomes clear that the separate component parts of this scene appear to be working in unison to produce a uniquely memorable moment of natural beauty:

> […] when the wind
> And the light are working off each other
> So that the ocean on one side is wild
> With foam and glitter, and inland among stones
> The surface of a slate-grey lake is lit
> By the earthed lightning of a flock of swans,
> Their feathers roughed and ruffling, white on white,

However, despite the poet's attempts to convey the convergence of beauty that has taken place during this moment, it ultimately defies capture. The poet warns us that this experience must be lived, that it is 'Useless to think you'll park and capture it'. According to Wim Tigges:

> As so often, Heaney manages to convey the remarkable by way of an ordinary experience, in this case seeing a flock of swans on a windy day. The poetic power of the 'earthed lightning' resonates in the reader's ear and connects with the emotional force of having the 'heart' blown 'open'.

In fact, one of the most remarkable aspects of the poem is the way in which it captures not only the physical impact of this landscape on the poet, but also the emotional impact of visiting this place. Concrete adjectives such as 'wind', 'light', 'slate-grey' and 'white' convey the physical reality of the place, while the emotional experience is captured in such phrases as:

> catch the heart off guard and blow it open.

While the poem pays homage to the power of poetry to capture the indefinable, there is also a clear sense that Heaney is grateful to some of his literary forbears. The description of the swans as they rise bears a close resemblance to Yeats's depiction of the swans in 'The Wild Swans at Coole' and the poem also recalls Gerard Manley Hopkins's 'Hurrahing for Harvest'. Finally, the way in which the poem vaunts the poetic power of the imagination brings to mind Wordsworth's poetry.

3. Essay Writing

If you are thinking of using 'Postscript' in any response to Heaney's poetry that you may be asked to make, you should try to bear some of the following points in mind.

a. The poem describes nature in a realistic and beautiful manner that manages to capture both the physical and spiritual impact of the countryside.
b. The form of the poem provides the reader with the space and time that are necessary to consider the complex nature of the *epiphany* that lies at the heart of this poem.
c. The poem is packed full of sound and movement. It may be useful to describe the visceral effect that some of the descriptions had on you in any personal response that you may be asked to make.

Critical Commentary: A Call

See the text of the poem on p. 75.

1. Content

In this beautiful poem, Heaney manages to create a *tone* that is at once celebratory and *elegiac*. The poem opens with an utterly familiar scene. The speaker has just phoned his father, who is unable to come to the phone straight away as he is in the garden doing 'a bit of weeding'. In the time it takes his father to come to the phone, the speaker begins to imagine what the old man is doing in the garden. The poet envisions him:

> Down on his hands and knees beside the leek rig,
> Touching, inspecting, separating one

Stalk from the other, gently pulling up
Everything not tapered, frail and leafless,

The gentle, earthy quality of this man's character comes to the fore when the speaker pictures him being 'Pleased' yet 'rueful' at the thought of breaking the roots of the 'little' weeds.

The ellipses at the end of the second stanza seem to indicate a slight shift in the poet's thinking. As his thoughts wander, he finds himself 'listening to | The amplified grave ticking of hall clocks' on the other end of the phone. These ellipses, which are repeated at the end of the third stanza, indicate a significant change in the poem's tone. The speaker now wonders if in modern times 'Death would summon Everyman' through the use of the phone. *Everyman* is a well-known 15th-century morality play that seeks to answer important theological questions. In the play, God sends Death to summon Everyman, who represents all mankind. The play centres on an account of Everyman's journey to this final judgement. As he prepares to meet his maker, Everyman attempts to convince the other characters to join him. These other characters are allegorical representations of humankind, each of them representing a different abstract idea. Essentially the play dramatises the conflict between good and evil by examining the ways in which the different characters interact. The unknown author of *Everyman* attempts to show us not only how every man should face death, but how every man should live his life. It may be that Heaney subconsciously views his father as representing an example of how one should choose to live one's life.

As so often in Heaney's poetry, there is not any explicit communication between father and son. Despite this, however, the depth of the relationship is obvious:

Next thing he spoke and I nearly said I loved him.

2. Stylistic Features

'A Call', which first appeared in the 1996 collection *The Spirit Level*, focuses on a deeply personal account of a private phone call placed by the speaker to his family home. However, this private moment transcends Heaney's personal experience to achieve universal significance. In order to emphasise the significance of the moment in time, the poet slows down the poem's tempo. This is achieved by a reliance on broad vowel sounds. In particular, the **cadence** of the speaker's voice in the second stanza mirrors the idea that he has entered into an intense moment of meditation.

It is important to remember that the time span of the poem is limited to the length of time that it takes Heaney's father to come to the phone. However, the condensed nature of the thought and the vivid nature of the poet's description of his father at work make this interval seem much longer. In the words of the poem, it truly is as if the ticking of the clocks has become amplified.

In the poet's description of his father at work, we learn a lot about this man. As he touches and separates each 'stalk', we are led to believe that this man is intimately connected to the land and the natural cycle. Some of the adjectives used by Heaney to describe his father at work appear to function like **transferred epithets.** Words like 'gently' and 'frail' suggest a kind man nearing the end of his life. Meanwhile, the mention of the 'grave ticking of hall clocks' and 'pendulums' hint not only at the passing of time, but the ineluctable nature of death. These associations between the passing of time and his father's ageing lead the poet to create a subconscious link between his father and Everyman. This is a complex **allusion** that further casts light on how the speaker views his father. Given that *Everyman* is a morality play on how we should live our lives and prepare for the inevitability of death, the reference to this play places his father in the role of a representative figure whose life offers a model for how we all should live. If you choose this reading, then Heaney seems to be suggesting that a simple life in harmony with the natural cycle offers the best preparation for death.

Finally, the poem has much in common with another poem on the course, 'The Harvest Bow', in that the intense warmth and affection the speaker feels for his father remains unsaid. Obviously moved to feeling love for his father by the reminder that he is nearing death, the poet is tempted to verbalise his feelings. However, in the end he remains silent.

3. Essay Writing

If you are thinking of making reference to 'A Call', you may wish to keep some of the following points in mind.

a. Once again, Heaney examines the nature of his relationship with his father. Given that two other poems on the course, 'Pitchfork' and 'The Harvest Bow', also deal with this theme, you may wish to devote an entire paragraph to this aspect of his work.

b. The poem relates a relatively ordinary event that paves the way for deeper considerations concerning the nature of life and death. It is typical of Heaney's poetry that such ordinary descriptions lead to profound meditations.

c. The language of the poem combines concrete and vivid descriptions of his father at work with complex literary allusion.

Critical Commentary: Tate's Avenue

See the text of the poem on p. 77.

1. Content

'Tate's Avenue' is taken from Heaney's most recent collection, *District and Circle*. The central theme of this collection, which takes its title from the London Underground lines of the same names, is the need to cherish and nurture the memories of youth. 'Tate's Avenue' has been described by one reviewer as a love poem of 'deliciously understated discretion'. The poem is limned in terms of three different rugs spread out by the speaker in such a manner that they recall different stages of the couple's relationship. Heaney opens the poem with the speaker requesting that his partner not take the 'brown and fawn car rug'. Over the course of the next two stanzas, the poet continues to describe rugs. From these descriptions it is obvious that the speaker associates this first rug with the romantic and even the erotic. He speaks of its 'vestal', or chaste, folds and its 'comfort zone'. Further details about this first rug emerge in the final line of the first stanza. We learn that it is fringed by 'wool tails' that are 'sepia-coloured'.

The second stanza opens with another negative and a description of another rug. This time the poet asks his partner not to take the rug that was soiled from the remnants of so many previous picnics:

> Not the one scraggy with crusts and eggshells
> And olive stones and cheese and salami rinds

The speaker recalls laying this rug out by the Guadalquivir River in Spain. On this occasion, both he and his partner got drunk before going to see the bullfights, or 'corrida'. In the third stanza, the poet returns to Belfast and presumably the Tate's

Avenue of the poem's title. It is Sunday and the public parks of Belfast are closed. In a walled back yard where the 'dust-bins' lie 'high and silent', the speaker watches his partner. The mention of the silent dustbins is a reminder of the troubling times to come in Belfast. During the Troubles, the Catholic minority would frequently bag dustbin lids to warn of the approach of the security forces. As his lover 'twirls warm hair' in her hand and leafs through her book, the speaker remarks rather enigmatically that 'nothing gives on the rug or the ground beneath it'.

The final stanza provides us with an alternative perspective. Here, the speaker describes himself as lying with his legs outstretched. He feels that the discomfort he is experiencing because of the uneven ground or 'lumpy earth' has heightened his senses. The speaker then informs us that he never once 'shifted off the plaid square' of the rug. All the tension and passion that are associated with courtship are captured in the poem's final line:

When we moved I had your measure and you had mine.

2. Stylistic Features

There are three love poems by Heaney on the course. Whereas 'The Skunk' recounts Heaney's separation from his wife when he was living in California, 'The Underground' and 'Tate's Avenue' both examine the earlier stages of that same relationship. The idea for this poem came to Heaney during a recent series of interviews with Denis O'Driscoll when he was reminded of this period in his life. The title of the poem refers to Tate's Avenue in Belfast, where his wife-to-be, Marie, used to share a flat with friends during the 1960s. Throughout the poem, the speaker uses descriptions of rugs as a means to explore the changing nature of his relationship with his lover. In the opening stanza, the description of the first rug captures the nature of the early stages of that relationship. Snippets of these early outings emerge as we picture Heaney and his then girlfriend picnicking 'on sand by the sea'. The images and the geography in this stanza link this early stage of love with a natural openness. Furthermore, it is clear from the poet's rather unusual description of the rug that the relationship is a relatively innocent, unadventurous and even old-fashioned one. While the 'vestal folds' of the rug suggest chastity, its 'sepia-coloured wool tails' recall a turn-of-the-century photograph.

The rug that is described in the second stanza seems to suggest a later stage in the relationship. The *imagery* used to describe this rug is associated with passion.

Drunken picnics 'by the torrents of the Guadalquivir' and 'before the corrida' are a world apart from the 'fawn' and 'sepia-coloured' imagery of the first stanza. It is important to remember that 'olive stones and cheese and salami rinds' were relatively exotic foodstuffs in Ireland in the 1960s.

The return to Belfast signals a further progression in the relationship. There is a vivid contrast between the passionate descriptions of Spain and the dour reality of life in Belfast. As so often in Heaney's poetry, there are subtle **allusions** to the political realities in Northern Ireland. Together with the mention of the 'dust-bins high and silent', the description of 'locked-park Sunday Belfast' hints at Protestant hegemony in Northern Ireland. However, 'Tate's Avenue' is not a political poem; it is a beautiful love poem. In the final stanza, these lovers have reached a point where they have the 'measure' of each other. Perhaps the most remarkable feature of this poem is the manner in which Heaney manages to paint a picture of erotic love within a relationship that is not embarrassing or voyeuristic.

3. Essay Writing

If you are thinking of making reference to 'Tate's Avenue' in any essay that you may be asked to write on Heaney's poetry, you should try to bear the following points in mind.

a. This poem is one of three love poems on the course by Seamus Heaney. Given the predominance of this theme on the course, you may wish to devote a paragraph or two to Heaney's treatment of love and relationships.

b. Yet again, Heaney draws on memories of the past for inspiration. Memory plays a powerful role in Heaney's poetry, so you may wish to consider a paragraph that deals with this aspect of his work.

c. The poem contains subtle allusions to the political realities in Northern Ireland. In this respect, it may be possible to compare the poem to 'A Constable Calls'.

Critical Commentary: The Pitchfork

See the text of the poem on p. 79.

1. Content

Heaney wrote this poem during the summer when his father was dying, and the poem is certainly as much a reflection on his father's personality as on the composition of the pitchfork. While the poem concentrates on the physical object, it obviously hints at a much deeper purpose. 'The Pitchfork' opens with a straightforward statement of fact. We are told that:

> Of all implements, the pitchfork was the one
> That came near to an imagined perfection:
> When he tightened his raised hand and aimed with it,
> It felt like a javelin, accurate and light.

The speaker feels that this simple implement transcended its normal state when placed in his father's hands. It becomes transformed so that it felt like a 'javelin, accurate and light'.

The pitchfork is made from ash. The fact that this wood is also used to make weapons leads the speaker to liken his father to some Greek 'warrior' or 'athlete' who 'worked in earnest in the chaff and sweat'. Of course, in the context of Irish history, the pitchfork has long had associations with violence and the struggle for land. In one memorable line of Patrick Kavanagh's poem 'Epic', he speaks of 'our pitchfork-armed claims'. Perhaps Heaney is aware of the potential for violent use that the pitchfork has.

In the final two lines of the second **quatrain**, the speaker describes the 'grain' of the pitchfork's wood that had 'Grown satiny' from use. The third stanza is dominated by a marvellous series of adjectives that bring the object to life. Then, in the penultimate stanza, there is a distinct change in the poem's **tone**. In these somewhat cryptic lines, the poet attempts to view the pitchfork through his father's eyes. In the speaker's imagination, his father likened the probes that reached into space to the shaft of a 'pitchfork sailing past [...] | Its prongs starlit and absolutely soundless'. The final stanza of the poem concludes with a powerful **image** of the pitchfork or javelin sailing out of his father's hand into the infinite:

Past its own aim, out to an other side
Where perfection – or nearness to it – is imagined
Not in the aiming but the opening hand.

2. Stylistic Features

In an interview with Steven Ratiner, Seamus Heaney had the following to say about this poem:

> I've used the digging metaphor once in my life and it has followed me ever since. 'The Pitchfork' one was done for sheer pleasure, written when I was back at home a few years ago, in the house where I grew up. It was about the sensation of holding the fork again. But it's also about changing. I hoped the poem would carry beyond the pitchfork as a thing in itself. At the end, it says that the pitchfork wants to go to another side where perfection isn't in the perfect toolness of the thing, but in the way it can go beyond efficiency into a kind of opulent weightless elsewhere. Where it's not weaponly or forceful, but where it is generous, where it's the opening hand rather than the shut hand.

Heaney achieves two things in this poem. Firstly, his description of the pitchfork stands as testimony to his powers of observation and control of language. In particular, the lengthy string of adjectives used in the third stanza conveys the essence of this implement:

Riveted steel, turned timber, burnish, grain,
Smoothness, straightness, roundness, length and sheen.
Sweat-cured, sharpened, balanced, tested, fitted.
The springiness, the clip and dart of it.

Notice how Heaney manages to capture both the physical and metaphysical attributes of the pitchfork. Interestingly, many of the adjectives, such as, 'Smoothness', 'length' and 'balanced', could be applied to the art of writing poetry. It is as if Heaney appreciates this object from an artistic, even poetic point of view.

Secondly, the pitchfork tells us as much about Heaney's father as it does anything else. His stature and presence are inferred when Heaney compares him to an athlete or a javelin thrower. These *images* confer a *mythical* status on the poet's father because they recall the heroes of Greek poetry. In particular, Homer's Odysseus, who was a renowned javelin thrower, is brought to mind when we learn that when Heaney's father raised his hand and 'aimed' with the pitchfork, 'It felt like a javelin, accurate and light'. Of course, this is typical of Heaney's poetry in general in that the mythological and the actual worlds collide so as to illuminate deeper truths about life.

In the final two stanzas, the poet attempts to capture a moment of artistic perfection. As the pitchfork sails silently and 'imperturbably through space', he realises that real 'perfection' is attained by learning to follow the 'simple lead | Past its own aim'. In the final line of the poem, Heaney imaginatively transforms the pitchfork into a *symbol* of peaceful inclusion. In the end it is not the aiming that attracts the poet, but the 'opening hand'. The very ordinary yet inclusive gesture of an opened hand concludes the poem.

3. Essay Writing

If you are thinking of making reference to 'The Pitchfork', you may wish to keep the following points in mind.

a. This poem provides us with a marvellous example of Heaney's ability to capture and describe an object with beauty and precision.
b. Once again, Heaney's poetry is influenced by a rural way of life. You may wish to devote an entire paragraph to this aspect of his poetry. It may be possible to compare and contrast this poem with 'Mossbawn'.
c. Relationships play a major role in the poetry by Heaney on the Leaving Certificate syllabus. This poem is as much about Heaney's father as it is about the pitchfork.

Critical Commentary: Lightenings viii

See the text of the poem on p. 81.

1. Content

This wonderful short poem belongs to the second part of the collection *Seeing Things* and is one of four groupings of 12 poems, each consisting of 12 lines. Each of the poems in this collection explores the notion of shifting perspectives in a different manner. This poem is numbered eight in the first grouping and details the legendary account of an air ship that appeared to the monks in Clonmacnoise. The first *tercet* of the poem tells us that the monastic annals recount the arrival of a ship which appeared above them in the air during prayer time. In the second stanza, we learn that as the ship passed over the roof of the monastic site, its 'anchor dragged along', hooking the vessel to the 'altar rails'. Unable to move, the ship 'rocked to a standstill'. The next stanza describes how one of the crewmen of this miraculous ship 'grappled down the rope' and 'struggled to release' the ship. However, his actions were 'in vain'. In the final line of the stanza, what is presumably the voice of one of the monks warns the man that he will drown should he descend from the ship:

> A crewman shinned and grappled down the rope
> And struggled to release it. But in vain.
> 'This man can't bear our life here and will drown,'

In the poem's final tercet we are told that the abbot urged the monks to help the man. The ship is then freed and the crew member climbs back out of what, from his perspective, is the 'marvellous' realm of the monks.

2. Stylistic Features

When he was awarded the Nobel Prize for Literature in 1995, Heaney selected this poem to read to the members of the Swedish Academy. According to the Academy, 'A poem like "Lightenings viii", on the miracle at Clonmacnoise, is a crystallisation of much of Heaney's imaginative world: history and sensuality, myths and the day-to-day – all articulated in Heaney's rich language.' The poem is based on an account of a ship having appeared in the sky from the Annals of Ulster for 748 AD, of which there only exists a much later English translation. Apart from the specific reference to the appearance of a ship in the annals of Clonmacnoise, the idea of a ship sailing souls toward God goes back to the very early Church. The form of this poem – four tercets comprising 12 lines – recalls what the Irish poet Hopkins termed the **curtail sonnet**. Speaking specifically on this form, Heaney has said that to him:

> it felt arbitrary but it seemed to get me places swiftly. So I went with it, a sort of music of the arbitrary that's unpredictable, and can still up and catch a glimpse of the subject out the blue.

In this poem, Heaney outlines an account of a seemingly miraculous event. As a result, he forces us to reconsider our understanding of the relationship between the ordinary and the miraculous. From the monks' perspective, the arrival of the ship is truly a miraculous event. Yet for their part, these otherworldly visitors view the monks as dwelling in an extraordinary place. In reality, the monks do inhabit a realm that constitutes a strange convergence between our world and the metaphysical world. Their ascetic lifestyle and meditative prayer put them in contact with a spiritual dimension to life.

The poem seems to draw on the concept of a world consisting of three separate planes of existence. The anchor that the men cast seems to **symbolise** the links that exist between the various planes. However, in this instance it is difficult to ascertain whether Heaney is in fact referring to a purely religious experience or simply a moment of heightened awareness on behalf of the monks. Whatever the case, the miraculous nature of this event is captured in luxurious language that is the stuff of pure poetry. The **imagery** of the poem occupies, like the monks themselves, a place between the ordinary and the miraculous. The relatively ordinary diction is juxtaposed with a clear vision of a floating ship. Perhaps the poem's greatest achievement is the manner in which it forces the reader to question his or her perception of reality.

3. Essay Writing

If you think that you would like to refer to 'Lightenings viii' in any response to Heaney's poetry that you may be asked to make, please try to bear the following points in mind.

a. *Mythology* and tradition play important roles in Heaney's poetry. In this poem, the world of the miraculous is viewed from an entirely different perspective.

b. The language of the poem is rich and sensuous.

c. The poem's form is unusual compared to the other poems by Heaney on the course. The 12-line groupings of four tercets recalls the *terza rima* employed by the Renaissance poet Dante and the American poet Robert Frost as well as the curtail sonnet used by Hopkins.

Patrick Kavanagh (1904–67)

A Short Biography

> O commemorate me with no hero-courageous
> Tomb – just a canal-bank seat for the passer-by.

To say that Patrick Kavanagh's beginnings were humble is to understate the truth. He was born on 21 October 1904 in the townland of Mucker in the parish of Inniskeen, County Monaghan, the son of Bridget Quinn and James Kavanagh. His father owned a small, nine-acre farmstead and supplemented the family income by working as a cobbler. At the age of just 13, the young Kavanagh left mainstream education and followed in his father's footsteps. He was apprenticed as a shoemaker and also began to work the land. On the surface, his life was no different from thousands of other peasant farmers. He went to the local markets and played in the position of goalie for the local Gaelic football team. However, even at this young age Kavanagh was reading voraciously and was writing poems. After 15 months, he gave up his work as a shoemaker, admitting that he had never managed to make a pair of boots that was wearable. Towards the end of August 1925, while at a market in Dundalk, the young poet was exposed to a world of arts and letters beyond the narrow confines of his rather limited schooling. While browsing the magazines in a newsagents, he stumbled across the *New Statesman*, which was edited by the writer and leading member of the **Irish Literary Revival**, George Russell, Æ. This magazine contained poems by James Joyce and W.B. Yeats. For the next five years, until the magazine ceased publication in 1930, Kavanagh used the *New Statesman* to provide him with a window on the wider literary world. In 1929 he plucked up the courage to submit some of his own work. One of the submissions, 'Ploughman', was eventually published in a London literary magazine and was selected as one of the year's best poems. His fledgling career was now underway.

Æ took Kavanagh under his wing after the young poet had walked from Monaghan to Dublin to meet with him in the late winter of 1931. From the outset, Kavanagh was lauded as being a peasant poet. Yet while it is true to stay that he had a close attachment to the land, his relationship to rural Ireland was an extremely complicated one. His early poetry consisted of rather anodyne poems that hinted at his rural background but did little more than that. However, in many of his later poems, Kavanagh launched scathing attacks on rural Ireland. His most controversial poem, 'The Great Hunger', an excerpt from which is found in this anthology, amounts to a bitter attack on the spiritual, social and moral repression that he saw as lying at the heart of rural Ireland.

In 1939, at the age of 25, the young poet left his native Monaghan behind him and moved to Dublin. Whatever Kavanagh felt about rural life, he was viewed by the Dublin literary set as a country farmer with intellectual aspirations. Slowly, he began to establish an identity that challenged this view of him. As a poet growing up in rural Monaghan, he knew only too well what it meant to be an outsider. Now in Dublin, living the life he had chosen, Kavanagh was once again an outsider. Rather than idealise his rural background, he sought to document it. If this meant acknowledging the harsh realities of this way of life, then so be it. Fortunately for Kavanagh, a new publication, *The Bell*, was attempting to forge new ground. One of his best-known poems, 'Stony Grey Soil', was published in *The Bell* in 1940. Then, a year later, he began work on one of his most accomplished works, 'The Great Hunger'. The realism of this truly *epic* poem, combined with its modern style, established Kavanagh as one of the great poets of the 20th century.

When Yeats died in 1939, he issued a command to his poetic successors:

> Irish poets, learn your trade
> Sing whatever is well made
> Scorn the sort now growing up
> All out of shape from toe to top,
> Their unremembering hearts and heads
> Base-born products of base beds.

Although Kavanagh rejected many of the central aspects of Yeats's poetry, his poems were indeed 'well made'. In fact, by the late 1940s, Kavanagh was widely regarded as the most important Irish poet since Yeats. However, his lifestyle was increasingly unconventional and he found it difficult to integrate into normal life. He lost his job as a staff reporter on the *Standard* and began to lead a bohemian existence. His unkempt appearance and unusual behaviour marked him out as an eccentric character around the Baggot Street area of Dublin. He regularly approached complete strangers for money and was often seen holding conversations with himself. In particular, he showed more than a passing interest in good-looking women. One of his best-loved poems, 'On Raglan Road', which is included in this anthology, is inspired by one of these encounters.

In 1947, his first major collection, *A Soul for Sale*, was published. Then, in 1948, he published the novel *Tarry Flynn*, which centres on a small-time farmer who dreams of a different life as a writer and a poet.

The 1950s was a very difficult time for Kavanagh. For three months in 1952, he headed up a weekly newspaper, *Kavanagh's Weekly*. The paper was edited by his brother Peter and aimed to attack some of the pillars of Irish society. Kavanagh heaped scorn on what he perceived as the narrow-mindedness of the Fianna Fáil government and many of the state agencies involved in the arts. Two years later, in 1954, he became embroiled in a lengthy court case. Having accused *The Leader* newspaper of slander, he was not prepared for the fact that the paper would choose to fight this accusation in open court. Foolishly, Kavanagh decided to represent himself during the trial. His mistake was compounded by the fact that *The Leader* appointed the gifted John A. Costello as its senior council. Costello ran rings around Kavanagh in court and the case dragged on for over a year. All of this took a serious toll on the poet's health.

By now Kavanagh was, in many respects, a total outcast. His failed career as a newspaper publisher and his reputation for ill temper rendered him virtually unemployable. He became completely dependent on the charity of friends and strangers. He took refuge in alcohol and was frequently seen drunk around Dublin. Eating poorly or infrequently, he spent what little income he had on gambling. Any hope of stability in his personal life was dashed when his girlfriend of four years married someone else. Then, in 1955, he was diagnosed with lung cancer and had a lung removed. If, as his sonnet '1954' details, that year marked a low point in his life, then 1955 brought with it a complete change in his outlook. His brush with death and his slow convalescence in hospital rejuvenated him spiritually and artistically. Three of the poems on the Leaving Certificate course – 'Canal Bank Walk', 'The Hospital' and 'Lines Written on a Seat on the Grand Canal, Dublin' – were written during this extraordinary period of poetic inspiration. The poet himself described this time in his life as bringing about an artistic renaissance or poetic rebirth.

In many other respects, too, Kavanagh had turned the corner on the dark years of the early 1950s. University College Dublin created an extra-mural lectureship for him which, for the first time in many years, saw his return to gainful employment. The summer of 1955 was an exceptionally warm one and Kavanagh spent much of those summer months on the banks of the Royal Canal in Dublin. This tiny patch of nature in the heart of Dublin formed the backdrop to many of his later poems. The canal, its wildlife and the human traffic that he witnessed acted as a kind of emollient to a completely new way of looking at the world. In these aptly named 'canal poems', Kavanagh appeals to all the senses in order to convey his newfound understanding of life.

In 1957 he spent six months in New York and began writing many of the poems that would later appear in *Come Dancing with Kitty Stobling*, which was published in 1960. He met and fell in love with Katherine Barry Moloney. Kavanagh's final years were characterised by the kind of happiness that had eluded him for most of his adult life. His work was recognised and had an international readership, he had achieved relative financial security and was in love with the woman he would later marry in 1967. However, despite these welcome changes in his life, the poet continued to drink heavily and his health, which had been precarious since the removal of his lung, continued to worsen.

The poetry that he wrote in these final years has to be admired for the honest manner in which it details uncomfortable truths about his personal life. In this respect, Kavanagh had evolved from the peasant poet who dared to challenge the literary orthodoxy of his native country to a poet who was at the vanguard of artistic expression. In many respects, Kavanagh's reputation as a poet was assured by the poems he published in the late 1950s. Since then, generations of readers have found it impossible to ignore the lyrical quality of his work, his mastery of language and form and his ability to transform the parochial into something truly universal.

One of the great ironies of Kavanagh's life was that he, like so many other inspirational Irish writers, was never officially recognised by his own country. On 30 November 1967, suffering from a severe bout of bronchitis, Patrick Kavanagh died. He was buried in his native Inniskeen.

Critical Commentary: Inniskeen Road: July Evening

See the text of the poem on p. 88.

1. Content

In his early career, Kavanagh developed a near *Romantic* style of poetry that had at its heart an imaginative insistence on the importance of the poet's relationship with his homeland. As a result, his early poems tend not to yield readily to the normal rhythm and **cadence** of received English, preferring instead to mimic the dialect of his native Inniskeen. This is certainly true of 'Inniskeen Road: July Evening'.

This **sonnet** is rooted in a very particular time and place. From the 1920s through the 1950s, barn dances, as they became known, provided the only means for Ireland's young men and women to interact socially. These events were frowned upon by the Catholic Church. In fact, so strong was the Church's opposition to these gatherings that one priest saw fit to liken the dance floor at these dances to the hob of hell. In Kavanagh's imagination, these barn dances became symbols of sensuality. However, as a poet, he also felt excluded from the normal social activities of his peers and found it difficult to fit in at such events. According to Antoinette Quinn, in 'Inniskeen Road: July Evening', Kavanagh 'dares to write out of his peculiar personal circumstances, as a young Inniskeen man whose poetic gift excludes him from the normal pleasures enjoyed by his neighbours'.

The poem opens in a jaunty, carefree manner that captures both the atmosphere of the evening and the momentum of the bicycles as they 'go by in twos and threes'. We learn that there is to be 'a dance in Billy Brennan's barn tonight'. Despite the fact that it is apparent that Kavanagh is completely familiar with the world he is describing, it quickly becomes clear that he is also excluded from that world. He is an outsider and as such has to content himself with the status of an observer. In the fifth line, the reality of his isolation is underscored by silence. Time has moved on, the dance is presumably underway and the poet is left alone with his thoughts:

> Half-past eight and there is not a spot
> Upon a mile of road, no shadow thrown
> That might turn out a man or woman [...]

In the **sestet**, the poet takes the time to contemplate the significance of his 'plight'. He likens his situation to the British sailor Alexander Selkirk. The poet's need for solitude is a complex and at times **paradoxical** one. It confers on him the sovereignty over thoughts and emotions that he needs in order to write; however, it also isolates him from his fellow man.

In the final lines of the poem, Kavanagh expresses something of the frustration that he feels. As his peers enjoy each other's company in 'Billy Brennan's barn', he is left with the dubious distinction of being 'king | Of banks and stones and every blooming thing'.

2. Stylistic Features

In Robert Garratt's opinion, the 'purity of expression, the admission of realistic detail for its own sake, and the digression on the theoretical aspects of [Kavanagh's] poetic vision were never more clearly stated than in "Inniskeen Road: July Evening".' In light of this statement, the seeming simplicity of the poem's subject matter belies a far greater complexity. Put simply, this is a deceptive poem.

Running throughout 'Inniskeen Road: July Evening' is an **allusion** to Cowper's poem, 'The Solitude of Alexander Selkirk'. When one reads the first two stanzas of Cowper's poem, it becomes apparent how heavily influenced Kavanagh was by this poem:

> I am monarch of all I survey;
> My right there is none to dispute;
> From the centre all round to the sea
> I am lord of the fowl and the brute.
> O Solitude! where are the charms
> That sages have seen in thy face?
> Better dwell in the midst of alarms,
> Than reign in this horrible place.
> I am out of humanity's reach,
> I must finish my journey alone,
> Never hear the sweet music of speech;
> I start at the sound of my own.
> The beasts that roam over the plain
> My form with indifference see;
> They are so unacquainted with man,
> Their tameness is shocking to me.

The comparison to Selkirk's plight is, in fact, a particularly apt one because, much like Kavanagh, Selkirk's isolation was self-imposed. In Antoinette Quinn's words, it becomes clear that Kavanagh is 'fully conversant with the drama of local life yet denied any share in it'.

The language of the poem does not seek to hide the fact that the poet's roots are in the community that he is describing. The repetition of the word 'and' together with the use of 'There's' lends the first five lines of the **octave** a **colloquial** flavour.

This is reinforced with further colloquial expressions such as 'half-talk code' and 'wink-and-elbow language'.

However, by the sixth line, there is a slight change in the poem's *tone*. In the sestet, the poem's meaning shifts from a straightforward composition of *mood* and place to the subject of poetry itself. As a result of this shift in focus, the *rhythm* of the speech becomes more formal. The rise and fall of the words in the final stanza help to create a rhetorical effect that increases the emotional impact of the words on the reader. In fact, the entire poem is infused with a warm energy. This energetic momentum is sustained by the use of *enjambment*. Nearly every line in the poem depends on the following line in order for its meaning to be understood. In this manner, the poem is gently carried forward to its conclusion.

The poem is similar to many of the other poems by Kavanagh on your course in that it draws heavily on places and people that the poet knew. 'Inniskeen Road: July Evening' represents Kavanagh at his best, writing openly and honestly about things that he knew intimately.

3. Essay Writing

'Inniskeen Road: July Evening' has much in common with many of the poems by Kavanagh on the course. If you are thinking of referring to this poem in an essay on Kavanagh's poetry, you may wish to bear some of the following points in mind.

a. 'Inniskeen Road: July Evening' draws on local events for inspiration. This is a hallmark of Kavanagh's poetry. Indeed, it may be worthwhile devoting an entire paragraph to this aspect of his work.

b. The poem is technically accomplished. Here as elsewhere in the poetry on the course, Kavanagh makes use of *end rhymes*, *alliteration* and repetition. As a result, he is able to approximate the rhythm and cadence of everyday speech and incorporate it into the sonnet form.

c. The poem draws heavily on nature imagery. This is perhaps one of the most characteristic aspects of Kavanagh's poetic style.

Critical Commentary: Shancoduff

See the text of the poem on p. 90.

1. Content

According to Antoinette Quinn, this was Kavanagh's 'favourite poem among his thirties lyrics'. She goes on to describe the poem as a 'farmer-poet's love poem to his own fields … a complex love poem that questions the holiness of the heart's affections and allows worldly doubt to trouble poetic faith'.

'Shancoduff' opens with a bleak statement that captures the *mood* of the entire poem.

> My black hills have never seen the sun rising,
> Eternally they look north towards Armagh.

The constancy of the poet's hills is conveyed in an unusual *allusion* to the Bible. According to the Bible (Genesis 19:23), Lot's wife's curiosity got the better of her and despite being told not to, she looked back on the destruction of Sodom and Gomorrah. As a result, she was turned to a pillar of salt. The speaker feels that this would not have happened if she had been as 'Incurious as [his] black hills'. Although the landscape of Shancoduff is sombre and cold, it is also completely at ease. When Glassdrummond chapel is whitened by the arrival of dawn, the poet views this as a cause of happiness for his black hills.

In the second stanza, the speaker describes the frost that remains in Shancoduff in springtime as 'the bright shillings of March'. In an obvious example of *hyperbole*, the poet compares his hills to the Matterhorn. We learn that on many occasions he has climbed with 'a sheaf of hay for three perishing calves | In the field under the Big Forth of Rocksavage.'

In the *sestet* that comprises the final stanza, the poet completes his portrait of Shancoduff. Once again, the harsh, unforgiving nature of the climate is emphasised:

> The sleety winds fondle the rushy beards of Shancoduff
> While the cattle-drovers sheltering in the Featherna Bush
> Look up and say: 'Who owns them hungry hills

That the water-hen and snipe must have forsaken?

In the first two stanzas of the poem, the speaker is possessive and fond of the landscape he inhabits. While he does not seek to deny the austere ruggedness of Shancoduff, he is also deeply attached to this place. He sees in his hills a worth that goes beyond their commercial value. In the final two lines, this attitude is contrasted with the mercenary outlook of the cattle drovers. These low-minded men view the hills as hungry and their poet owner as poor:

> A poet? Then by heavens he must be poor'
> I hear and is my heart not badly shaken?

The reader is left with the clear impression that the poetic vision of the natural landscape as offered by Kavanagh is infinitely preferable to the narrowly materialistic outlook of the cattle drovers.

2. Stylistic Features

In this poem, Kavanagh depicts the wintry, cold and craggy landscape of Shancoduff. The adjectives that dominate the poem's narrative work to create a bleak and cold **atmosphere**. Yet despite the harsh nature of Shancoduff, the depth of the poet's feelings for the place is never in question. Kavanagh qualifies every mention of the hills with the possessive adjective 'my'. In this manner, it is obvious that Shancoduff is viewed by the speaker as being part of who he is. Once again, as with so many of the poems by Kavanagh on the course, the poet speaks about places that he knows intimately. 'Glassdrummond chapel', 'Featherna Bush' and 'Rocksavage' combine to create a wholly local feel. When the poet chooses to introduce the outside world by mentioning the 'Alps' and the 'Matterhorn', this is simply a means of emphasising the importance that Shancoduff holds for him.

Throughout the poem, there are a series of religious references that reinforce the notion that the poet's love of this place is an article of deep faith. The poem opens by stating that the poet's hills look northward 'towards Armagh'. Armagh is the ecclesiastical capital of Ireland and as such the centre of all faith in the country. Further religious references are to be found in the biblical allusion to 'Lot's wife' and the description of dawn whitening Glassdrummond chapel.

Then, in the second stanza, the poet gives us evidence of his physical commitment to his hills and his livestock. We learn that he has climbed Shancoduff in wintry weather in order to feed 'three perishing calves'. In the poet's imagination, this is a sacred place and this fact is recognised by nature itself. Even the normally harsh 'sleety winds fondle' the landscape of Shancoduff. Originally, Kavanagh had intended to include another stanza before the final one:

> My hills have never seen the sun rising,
> With the faith of an illiterate peasant they await
> The final Resurrection when all hills
> Will face the East.

Reading this omitted stanza, it becomes clear that the poet's attachment to Shancoduff is a deeply spiritual one.

In the final stanza, the logic of the poem's narrative looks downward to the cattle drovers. Physically, the hills of Shancoduff are situated above these men. However, it is also obvious that the speaker's love for this place transcends the low-minded attitude of men who fail to look beyond its monetary value. In many respects, this poem offers the reader a clear example of the poetic imagination's ability to transform its environment. The frost and cold of the second stanza become 'shillings' when viewed through the poet's eyes. Similarly, his imagination takes flight in a series of hyperbolic phrases where Monaghan becomes the Alps and his hills the Matterhorn. It is important that you bear in mind that the transformative power of the poetic imagination is one of the hallmarks of Kavanagh's poetry.

3. Essay Writing

'Shancoduff' has much in common with many of the other poems by Kavanagh on your course. If you are thinking of referring to this poem in an essay on Kavanagh's poetry, you may wish to bear some of the following points in mind.

a. Here as elsewhere ('The Hospital', 'Canal Bank Walk', 'A Christmas Childhood', etc.), Kavanagh transforms the bland into something that provokes 'spirit shocking I Wonder.'
b. Once again, the natural landscape of Monaghan plays a central role in this poem.
c. In 'Shancoduff', Kavanagh acknowledges his role as a poet. This is a common feature of his poetry in general and of the Leaving Certificate selection in particular. 'On Raglan Road' and 'Inniskeen Road: July Evening' both deal with the role of the poet.

Critical Commentary: The Great Hunger

See the text of the poem on pp. 92–4.

1. Content

The publication of 'The Great Hunger' sparked a wave of controversy. In his note to the collected poems published in 1946, Kavanagh had the following to say about this poem:

> In 1942 I wrote 'The Great Hunger'. Shortly after it was published a couple of hefty lads came to my lonely shieling on Pembroke Road. One of them had a copy of the poem behind his back. He brought it to the front and he asked me, 'Did you write that?' He was a policeman. It may seem shocking to the devotee of liberalism if I say that the police were right. For a poet in his true detachment is impervious to policemen. There is something wrong with a work of art, some kinetic vulgarity in it when it is visible to policemen. 'The Great Hunger' is concerned with the woes of the poor. A true poet is selfish and implacable. A poet merely states the position and does not care whether his words change anything or not. 'The Great Hunger' is tragedy and Tragedy is underdeveloped Comedy, not fully born.

The entire poem comprises 14 sections written in 756 lines. The style of 'The Great Hunger' is in fact quite varied. Some stanzas contain long, free-flowing lines, while others are written in rhyming **couplets** or *free verse*. **Assonance, alliteration, colloquialisms** and **half-rhymes** also figure prominently. In the extract selected for study for the Leaving Certificate, we are introduced to the anti-heroic Patrick Maguire. Maguire represents the stereotypical Irish bachelor farmer whose life is sterile and empty. Traditionally, many Irish farmers often postponed marriage and children in order to improve the financial resources of the farm holding. According to Eamonn Wall, 'Maguire is the Irish farmer personified, the man Kavanagh has plucked from the mass of unhappy Irish farmers. The land he works is neither warm nor welcoming: it has no spirit of its own which rubs off on the farmer. On the contrary, it seems dead and the farmer who comes into contact with it is deadened by the experience.'

This extract opens with an obvious biblical **allusion**. From the opening line, the atmosphere is dark, foreboding and even hellish. Although the men are engaged in harvesting the fruits of their labour, there is little to suggest that this is going to be a life-affirming poem. The 'potato-gatherers [move] like mechanized scare-crows', 'crows gabble' and the speaker mentions the 'Book I Of Death'. The opening stanza contains a series of interrogatives and as a result the reader is made to feel that this is going to be an enquiry into Maguire's existence. The narrator asks us which of the men was devoted to the Virgin Mary, or 'the queen'.

It quickly becomes apparent that the passing of time is central to the drama unfolding before our eyes. The narrator wonders which of the men:

> […] promised
> 　　marriage to himself
> Before apples were hung from the ceilings for Hallowe'en?

However, before this question is answered, the speaker tells us to wait and 'watch the tragedy' of Maguire's life. In the meantime, the narrator continues to paint a bleak picture of life on this farm.

Then, in line 29, we are given the first direct insight into Maguire's thoughts. We learn that as a young man he believed himself 'wiser than any man in the townland' to have escaped the trap of marriage. However, even back then Maguire needed to deceive his soul in order to believe 'That children are tedious in hurrying fields of April'. Rather than dwell on the significance of the decisions that Patrick Maguire made in his early life, the speaker returns to the mundane details of Maguire's working day:

> 'Move forward the basket and balance it steady
> In this hollow. Pull down the shafts of that cart, Joe,
> And straddle the horse,' Maguire calls.
> 'The wind's over Brannagan's, now that means rain.

We then return to Maguire's private thoughts and learn that 'he is not so sure now if his mother was right I When she praised the man who made his field his bride'. As we read on, it becomes apparent that there is a tension between the fertility of the land and the sterility of Maguire's existence. It is now becoming clear that his commitment to the land has resulted in an unfulilled, barren life. However, it is also clear that Maguire is not completely unaware of this fact. In the next section, we are asked to 'watch' this man again who exists so 'that his little fields may stay fertile'.

In the next section that begins with line 68, the narrator provides us with some further background detail about Patrick Maguire. We are told that 'He was suspicious in his youth as a rat near strange bread' and that his attraction to young girls was not enough to break the grip of the land. Then, in line 78, we return to the present and Maguire's sinking realisation that his foolish commitment to the land has resulted in empty despair:

> 'O God if I had been wiser!'
> That was his sigh like the brown breeze in the thistles.
> He looks towards his house and haggard. 'O God if I had been
> wiser!'

This moment of anguish leads to Maguire's bitter *epiphany* in line 85:

> And he knows that his own heart is calling his mother a liar.
> God's truth is life – even the grotesque shapes of its foulest fire.

While these lines are life affirming, there is no escaping the depressing reality of Maguire's situation.

In the final three sections of the poem, Kavanagh returns to the natural world. We see a horse lifting its head and crashing through the 'whins and stones'. Opposed to this is the crushing morality of the human world that has contributed to Maguire's spiritual desolation. In the final stanza, the speaker appeals directly to the 'Imagination', asking it to aid him in his telling of Maguire's story. The final lines end in hushed silence as the speaker addresses the normally harsh month of October, beseeching it to 'Be easy'.

2. Stylistic Features

'The Great Hunger' has not only become part of our national culture, but is widely regarded as belonging to the world's store of truly great poems. The poem's title plays a vital role in our understanding of Kavanagh's intent. The title alludes to the Great Famine. However, the hunger in this poem is not for food, or even for land – it is a hunger for a fulfilled and meaningful life. According to Anthony Cronin, this poem charts 'the life of an old peasant in a poor country where late marriages are universal, lifelong bachelordom is not rare, nor, being a puritan country, is lifelong virginity. It is a tragedy of loneliness and frustration, something, some rare promise of life and fulfilment vanishing from Maguire as his farm and his religion cheat and defeat him.'

Despite the fact that the **protagonist** is in many respects a typically Irish character, Maguire's plight is a universal one. From the opening lines, which Seamus Heaney has described as 'gravid, powerful and rough-cast', the reader is drawn into the hopeless world of Maguire and his men. The poem opens with a sombre depiction of the monotonous toil of the potato-gatherers:

> Clay is the word and clay is the flesh
> Where the potato-gatherers like mechanized scare-crows move
> Along the side-fall of the hill – Maguire and his men.
> If we watch them an hour is there anything we can prove
> Of life as it is broken-backed over the Book
> Of Death? [...]

The first line, 'Clay is the word and clay is the flesh', announces the central theme of the poem, the perversion of the Catholic teaching on sex and marriage, as evidenced in the life of Patrick Maguire. The idea that the word is made flesh is one of the central truths of Christianity as perceived by Catholics. However, this truth has become perverted into something unrecognisable. The cycle of love, marriage and birth has become substituted by 'the passion that never needs a wife'. In every respect, Patrick Maguire, the man who made 'a field his bride', becomes the **symbol** for this depressing mindset. He exists that his small farm holding may stay fertile when his own body 'Is spread in the bottom of a ditch under two coulters crossed in I Christ's Name.'

In fact, throughout the poem, Kavanagh makes clever use of religious *imagery* in order to enrich our understanding of Maguire's predicament. For the most part, this imagery highlights the tension between Maguire's natural physical desires and the denial of these impulses that his religion demands of him. As the speaker looks at the potato-gatherers, he asks:

> If we watch them an hour is there anything we can prove
> Of life as it is broken-backed over the Book
> Of Death? [...]

The poet himself had gone a long way to answering this question in his autobiographical work, *The Green Fool*. In a passage which closely resembles the opening section of 'The Great Hunger', Kavanagh wrote:

> As we picked up the tubers the smells rising from the dry brown clay were a tonic to revive the weariest body, the loneliest spirit. Turning over the soil our fingers were turning the pages in the Book of Life. We could dream as we gathered the potatoes, we could enter in the secret places where all unwritten poems lie.

Similarly, Patrick Maguire wonders if there is 'some light of imagination in these wet clods?'

As we read 'The Great Hunger', it becomes increasingly clear that what Maguire experiences in this poem is a shuddering moment of clarity, or **epiphany**, during which he is free to contemplate the awful reality of his life. He has glimpsed the possibility of a fuller life, but the dawning of his imagination only deepens his misery. For the most part, this misery finds its expression in sexual frustration. In the poem, the passing of time is closely linked to marriage prospects that were dismissed in favour of the land and religious devotion:

> Which of these men
> Loved the light and the queen
> Too long virgin? Yesterday was summer. Who was it promised
>   marriage to himself
> Before apples were hung from the ceilings for Hallowe'en?

Juxtaposed with this is the inevitability of Maguire's death. However, rather than the prospect of eternal salvation, the reader is presented with the image of Maguire's soul rolling down the sides of the hill 'like a bag of wet clay'. This stark reality causes Maguire to admit that:

> [...] his own heart is calling his mother a liar.
> God's truth is life – even the grotesque shapes of its foulest fire.

The 'foulest fire' that Kavanagh refers to is the perversion of Christianity that equates all sexuality with sin. Many critics feel that there are obvious clues to Maguire's confused sense of his own sexuality throughout the poem. In one passage, the narrator calls on the protagonist to 'Turn over the weedy clods and tease out the tangled skeins'. The speaker then goes on to tell us that Patrick Maguire 'thinks it is a potato, but we know better | Than his mud-gloved fingers probe in this insensitive hair'. Most commentators feel that this is an allusion to sexual fantasies. Other lines in the poem echo this:

> Lost in the passion that never needs a wife –
> The pricks that pricked were the pointed pins of harrows.

Of course, none of this is fully developed or explained. This is because Maguire lacks the vocabulary needed to understand this side to his being. His sexuality has become sublimated in the language of farming. This is all that he knows.

As the poem continues to move back and forth in time, we realise that there really is no hope for the protagonist. He is doomed. Nothing but winter faces Maguire. According to Brendan Kennelly, 'Maguire is a tragic figure. He is a man who, sentenced to a horribly lingering death, is compelled to watch the natural world reproduce itself with spendthrift fertility while he shrivels into barren anonymity.' In the end, the speaker is left with nothing to say about Maguire, choosing instead to address the month of October. This is because the awful truth of this man's life has already been given to the reader. We know that in his life, Maguire was dominated by his mother, servile to Catholicism and devoted to the land. His existence is in every respect a sad mockery of dehumanising physical labour, with little to look forward to but the depressing and inevitable advance towards old age. In the end, we instinctively feel that the bitter irony of his existence is that he is devoted to a shocking lie that began in his childhood and will end only with his death.

Taken as a whole, this is a profoundly moving extract written in taut and resonant language that combines a ***colloquial*** ease with flashes of vivid and thought-provoking imagery. As with so many of the poems by Kavanagh on the course, 'The Great Hunger' brilliantly catches the turns and ***tones*** of rural language and thought processes. There is a roughcast, guttural quality to many lines, such as:

> 'The wind's over Brannagan's, now that means rain.
> Graip up some withered stalks and see that no potato falls
> Over the tail-board going down the ruckety pass –
> And *that's* a job we'll have to do in December,
> Gravel it and build a kerb on the bog-side. Is that Cassidy's ass
> Out in my clover? Curse o' God –
> Where is that dog?

This extract from 'The Great Hunger', as with the poem as a whole, is carefully structured.

- Section one, in which the landscape of Maguire's world is described in all its gloom, can be found between lines 1 to 19.
- The second section of the poem details the dawning of Maguire's understanding of his predicament. In this section, the poet also outlines the passing of time. This serves to add to the urgency of Maguire's dilemma.
- In the third section, the speaker attempts to understand Maguire's despair.
- In the fourth section of the poem, Maguire openly questions his past decisions. At the same time, he continues to toil on the very land that has contributed to his despair.
- In the fifth section, the narrator becomes more emotionally involved in Maguire's predicament.
- In the sixth section, the poet provides us with a retrospective account of Maguire's youth. It becomes apparent that his personality traits and decisions have contributed to his present despair.
- In the seventh section, the narrator once again describes the landscape of Donaghmoyne.
- Then, in the eighth and final section, the speaker makes an invocation to October, asking the normally cruel month to be kind:

Be easy, October. No cackle hen, horse neigh, tree sough, duck quack.

3. Essay Writing

'The Great Hunger' is widely held to be Patrick Kavanagh's most important poem. As such, it is difficult to ignore in any personal response to Kavanagh's poetry you may be asked to make. If you are thinking of mentioning this poem, you may wish to include some of the following points.

a. The poem is different from the other poems by Kavanagh on the Leaving Certificate course in that its outlook is entirely despairing. In this sense, it might be worth contrasting this poem with the other poetry by Kavanagh that you have studied.

b. The imagery in the poem is dark, brooding and unforgettable. In a personal response-type essay, it might be worthwhile considering the impact that this imagery had on you.

c. Once again, Kavanagh draws heavily on imagery from the natural world.

Critical Commentary: Advent

See the text of the poem on p. 97.

1. Content

In this poem, Kavanagh undertakes a dialogue with his own soul. This dialogue is prompted by the beginning of Advent. According to the Roman Catholic Church, the feast of Advent exists in order to prepare Christians to celebrate the anniversary of the Lord's coming into the world as the incarnate God of love. The opening line of the poem contains a frank admission of corruption:

We have tested and tasted too much, lover—

In this line, Kavanagh acknowledges that his fall from a state of grace or innocence has been caused by tasting and testing 'too much'. In other words, he has become too worldly wise. His curiosity and greed have removed any sense of innocent joy from the world. In the next line, the speaker informs us that 'Through a chink too wide there comes in no wonder'. These two lines set up the premise for the entire poem, namely, that experience and knowledge lead to the corruption of the soul. However, by the third line Kavanagh offers an alternative to this moral rot. The 'Advent-darkened room' and associated 'penance' will, he tells us, 'charm back the luxury | Of a child's soul'. As a result, the poet feels confident that he will be able to 'return to Doom' the useless knowledge that has resulted in his present state of moral decay.

In the second stanza, the poet focuses on the childlike state of innocence that he hopes to recreate. It is a state of being where 'stale thing[s]' look new and fresh and nature appears 'spirit-shocking'. Even the 'tedious talking | Of an old fool' will, if he enters into the spirit of Advent, appear 'prophetic'. Then, in the final lines of the second stanza, 'the whins | And the bog-holes' of rural Ireland are transformed in the poet's imagination into the Bethlehem of Christ's nativity.

In the third stanza, the poet continues to examine the changes that Advent will cause. We learn that 'after Christmas' he will no longer need to search for logical meaning in old religious phrases. Instead of searching for rational meaning, he will instead look to the wonder and mystery to be found in the sound that churning butter makes. The speaker then continues to list the places where such 'difference' or regained innocence can been found:

> [...] in the streets where the village boys are lurching.
> And we'll hear it among decent men too
> Who barrow dung in gardens under trees,
> Wherever life pours ordinary plenty.

Now that the poet has accepted that the ordinary things in life lead to spiritual fulfilment, he feels justified in feeling genuinely 'rich'. The type of spiritual impoverishment that characterised his life before Advent has been transformed into a simple, unquestioning acceptance of God's presence in the world. The key to this new state of being is to be obtained by rejecting 'pleasure, knowledge and the conscious hour'. Having done this, the poet is now ready to greet Christ, who 'comes with a January flower'.

2. Stylistic Features

The critic Anthony Cronin has said of Patrick Kavanagh's poetry that in it, 'things are seen with not only with the intensity of vision which is a characteristic of many children ... but also with an emotional intensity which comes from the fact that the poet is an adult looking back through the complexity of adult experience to what is possible to see again only by shedding the confusion we call experience'. This is certainly true of 'Advent'. This poem, first published in the collection *A Soul for Sale*, is in fact a meditation in three distinct movements. In the first movement of the poem, we witness a return to the Advent of Kavanagh's childhood, to the 'dry black bread and the sugarless tea', and to the penitent path to redemption that ends in a vision of God's light. However, the poet also manages to combine this vision with a clear sense that he has become corrupt and unfulfilled. The harsh 't' sounds in the opening line emphasise his feelings of disgust and distaste at this fact:

> We have tested and tasted too much, lover—

The second movement of the poem takes us through the darkened storeroom of childhood memories, the 'newness' in 'stale thing[s]', the 'spirit-shocking | Wonder' of black Ulster hills and the 'tedious talking | Of an old fool'. Suddenly, as a result of those memories, the world becomes transformed in the poet's eyes until we are greeted with the vision of 'old stables where Time begins.'

In the final movement of the poem, the poet attempts to articulate the difference between faith and reason. We learn that in the churning of butter, where village boys lurch and in the actions of 'decent men', it is possible to glimpse 'God's breath in common statement'. Here the poet suggests that once we have shed the 'clay-minted wages', we are ready to bear witness to Christ's coming 'with a January flower'. The message at the end of the poem is simple. Once faith has been embraced in favour of conscious knowledge, then the 'chink' of worldly experience becomes narrowed to the point that the miraculous truth of God's presence in the natural world is suddenly made visible.

On a technical level, 'Advent' is a highly accomplished poem. In fact, the poem is composed of two separate **sonnets.** Rather than adopt the conventions of sonnet writing, the first sonnet is divided into two distinct halves, which stress in equal measure the importance of penance to spiritual rebirth. In this manner, the moment of **epiphany** that dominates the poem is not only found on a thematic level, but is also contained in the poem's structure. In this poem, Kavanagh manages to suggest simultaneously the promise of Christ's birth and the belief that Christ has been born. As a result, the **imagery** in the poem is designed in such a way as to point to the imminent presence of Christ in the world. The **symbolism** of Christmas is used in conjunction with biblical **allusions** to magnify the importance and indeed some of the **paradoxes** of penance and luxury, newness and staleness, tedium and astonishment that lie at the heart of the poet's fall from grace.

These complex notions are put forward in three carefully structured movements. In the first two seven-line stanzas, Kavanagh moves from a subconscious meditation to a conscious expression of faith. Then, in the third stanza, the poet undertakes a deeply philosophical consideration of the eternal nature of God. As a result, the poem moves from a series of definite images that are grounded in reality to a series of spiritual images or from imagery set in a specific time to infinite and timeless imagery. This change is mirrored somewhat in the poem's **rhyming** scheme. The second and third sections that comprise the two sonnets that go to make up the poem contain more **end rhymes** than the first section. In this manner, the poem's form attempts to capture something of the happy expectation that the poet feels at the advent of Christ's birth.

3. Essay Writing

'Advent' shares much in common stylistically and thematically with many of the other poems by Kavanagh on your course. As such, it may be worthwhile including it in any response to Kavanagh's poetry that you may be asked to write.

a. 'Advent' is a Christmas poem and in this respect you can use 'Advent' in conjunction with 'A Christmas Childhood'. In fact, it may be possible to devote a paragraph to these two poems.

b. In this poem, Kavanagh is preoccupied with the search for spiritual renewal. In his later sonnets in general and the so-called 'canal poems' in particular, the poet regains the sense of innocence that he craves in this poem. As such, you may want to compare and contrast 'Advent' with poems like 'Canal Bank Walk'.

c. Once again, Kavanagh draws heavily on religious imagery and allusions. You may wish to devote an entire paragraph to this stylistic feature of Kavanagh's poetry. Furthermore, the poem is technically accomplished. It comprises two sonnets unified into a single poem. Given that Kavanagh relies heavily on the sonnet form, you may wish to give consideration to this fact in any essay that you write.

Critical Commentary: A Christmas Childhood

See the text of the poem on pp. 99–100.

1. Content

This wonderful poem achieves much of its impact through its unabashed sentimentality. The opening *quatrain* of the poem presents the reader with a Christmas card tableau of winter in Monaghan. We learn that 'One side of the potato-pits was white with frost' and that wind played a 'magical' 'music' on the 'paling-post'. In the second quatrain, the poet turns his attention to the 'light between the ricks of hay', which he believed was emanating from a 'hole in Heaven's gable'. The *run-on line* that links the second and third stanzas is of vital importance to our understanding of this poem. Here the speaker informs us that the 'December-glinting' of an 'apple tree' *symbolises* the temptations of the world that would later erode his sense of childhood innocence. In the final stanza of the first section, the speaker cuts short his meditation on lost innocence and returns to his childhood memories. It is a place where a 'green stone lying sideways in a ditch | Or any common sight' provided the poet with a vision of untouched 'beauty'.

The second section of the poem opens with a very specific memory of the poet's father playing the 'melodeon | Outside [… the] gate'. Here again, the specificity of this memory yields to the poet's sense of imaginative wonder. When viewed through the speaker's eyes, even the 'stars in the morning east' are seen to 'dance' to his father's music.

In the second stanza of the second section, the poet conveys something of the anticipation and excitement that he felt on Christmas morning:

> As I pulled on my trousers in a hurry
> I knew some strange thing had happened.

The seventh stanza of the poem presents us with a nativity scene. Here, the poet's mother is busy milking the family cow. The light from her 'stable-lamp' is transformed into a star. The magical nature of this recollection is interrupted by the screeching of 'A water-hen' and the sound of 'Mass-going feet' as they crunch 'the wafer-ice on the pot-holes'.

We are reminded in the eighth stanza that even as a child, Kavanagh was already viewing the world through a poet's eyes:

> My child poet picked out the letters
> On the grey stone,
> In silver the wonder of a Christmas townland,
> The winking glitter of a frosty dawn.

The poetic impulse to transform the landscape is witnessed once again in the next stanza. Viewing the constellation of Cassiopeia that lay over 'Cassidy's hanging hill', the poet is suddenly confronted with a vision of 'the Three Wise Kings' on their way to worship Jesus Christ. The poet's reverie is interrupted by an old man who comments on his father's skill as a 'melodeon' player as he passes. In the next stanza, we learn that the young poet was 'six Christmases of age'. This beautiful poem ends with one last glimpse of Kavanagh's childhood. It is a world that Kavanagh embraces with enthusiasm, a world of innocent certainties in which:

> My father played the melodeon,
> My mother milked the cows,
> And I had a prayer like a white rose pinned
> On the Virgin Mary's blouse.

2. Stylistic Features

This poem, first published in the collection *A Soul for Sale* (1947) but written much earlier, provides us with yet another example of Kavanagh's ability to transform the ordinary into something wonderful. In essence, this is a memory poem that is heavily grounded in the tradition of ***pastoral*** poetry. In other words, the poet draws heavily on his childhood memories in order to present us with a vision of rural innocence. An atmosphere of childhood enthusiasm pervades the poem from beginning to end and while the narrator obviously deals with past events, there is nevertheless an overwhelming sense of immediacy to 'A Christmas Childhood'. This is largely achieved by mixing tenses. At regular intervals throughout the poem, the past definite and past imperfect tenses yield to the present continuous tense. Aside from drawing the reader into the narrative, this also has the effect of lending the poem an air of childish enthusiasm. Other effects in the poem contribute to this sense of innocent childishness. According to Antoinette Quinn, 'detail is picked out with a crisp, frosty clarity; yet the apparent arbitrariness of its ordering, the limpid simplicity of the spoken language, the brief quatrains with their unobtrusive assonantal rhymes, sustain the illusion of childhood experience'.

The sense of movement in the poem is also very interesting. The various locations are wholly determined by the child's limited understanding of the world. The speaker takes us from the domesticity of the farmhouse, to the 'cow-house', out the gate and along the 'pot-holes' of a country road until we reach a 'townland' waking to the magic of Christmas morning. Even the distant constellation of Cassiopeia is viewed as being an extension of a local place name:

> Cassiopeia was over
> Cassidy's hanging hill,

Another remarkable aspect of this poem is the manner in which Kavanagh manages to transform rural Monaghan into an imaginative and poetic rendering of the original nativity scene. The people and places from Kavanagh's childhood become intertwined with *images* from the Bible. The cow shed becomes the stable where Jesus Christ was born, gorse bushes become the Three Wise Men and finally, the poet's mother is likened to the Virgin Mary. In the final lines, which contain the only full *rhyme* in the poem, memory mixes with spiritual and filial devotion in order to produce a beautiful evocation of childhood happiness.

3. Essay Writing

If you are thinking of making reference to 'A Christmas Childhood', you may wish to consider some of the following points.

a. Once again, Kavanagh draws on childhood memories in order to recapture something of its innocence. The search for lost innocence preoccupies Kavanagh in many of the poems on your course. You may consider devoting an entire paragraph to this aspect of his poetry.

b. Religious imagery and *allusions* dominate this poem. The use of such imagery is a key stylistic feature of Kavanagh's poetry on the course. It may be possible to unify a single paragraph around the poet's use of religious imagery in any response to Kavanagh's poetry that you may be asked to make.

c. The ordinary and the banal are once again transformed into the magical. In this case, the parish of Inniskeen becomes Bethlehem on the morning of the nativity. In many of the poems by Kavanagh on your course, commonplace settings are seen as sources of poetic inspiration.

Critical Commentary: Epic

See the text of the poem on p. 102.

1. Content

'Epic' first appeared in a volume of poetry called *Come Dance with Kitty Stobling*, which was published in 1960 and reprinted three times within the next year. This **sonnet** is a playful but extremely perceptive celebration of rural Ireland, where the land has always held a central place and disputes over it have been frequent. This sonnet presents the reader with a mini comic drama and opens with the narrator's affirmation that he has 'lived in important places, [and] times'. In the third and fourth lines the narrator describes one of the important 'events' that he has witnessed. This event centred upon 'a half rood of rock [in …] no-man's land' that was laid claim to by men armed with pitchforks. The poet tells us that during the confrontations concerning this land, he heard the Duffys shouting 'Damn your soul' and saw old McCabe stripped to the waist as he defied the 'blue cast-steel' pitchforks of his enemies. In the eighth line, it becomes clear that this is a border dispute. One of the parties concerned announces his territorial claim by defiantly stating that the border, or 'march', lies 'along these iron stones'. Then, in the first line of the **sestet**, the narrator tells us that this local dispute took place during the year of the 'Munich bother'. Interestingly, in the first part, or **octave**, of the sonnet, Kavanagh inflates the importance of a local dispute while in the **sestet** he seeks to diminish the significance of one of the events that contributed to the outbreak of the Second World War. The narrator then poses an interesting question:

> [...] Which
> Was more important?

On the face of it, the Munich Crisis, which was a precursor to one of the most significant events in human history, obviously overshadows a 'local row' over land. The poet, too, is inclined to believe this until 'Homer's ghost came whispering to [his] mind'. The father of Western literature tells him that he created his great *epic*, the *Iliad*, from a parochial dispute.

2. Stylistic Features

Despite its seeming simplicity, this is a complex poem. In Antoinette Quinn's estimation, '"Epic" is a tactical triumph, encouraging the reader to indulge a disdainful smile at the simple annals of the poor only to wipe the supercilious grin off his face in the closing line.' In this poem, Kavanagh returns to Inniskeen, the original source of his poetic inspiration, and attempts to explain his attachment to this place. Elsewhere, in a section of 'The Great Hunger' not included on the Leaving Certificate syllabus, Kavanagh describes peasant culture in the following terms:

> *There* is the source from which all cultures rise,
> And all religions,
> There is the pool in which the poet dips
> And the musician.
> Without the peasant base civilization must die,
> Unless the clay is in the mouth the singer's singing is useless.
> [...] The peasant is the unspoiled child of prophecy,

In many ways, 'Epic' is an attempt to salute the importance of the peasant. However, the strategy that Kavanagh adopts in the poem is a peculiar one. In the *octave*, he deliberately calls into question his choice of subject matter by over-inflating the importance of the land dispute. The adjectives chosen by the speaker – 'great', 'important', the description of pitchforks as 'blue cast-steel' and the border as a 'march' – work to create an *ironic*, even mocking *tone* when one considers the nature of the dispute at issue. Then, in the *sestet*, Kavanagh deflates the importance of the Munich Crisis. It is unusual that Kavanagh should apply the epithet 'bother' to the events of September 1938, which directly contributed to a war that saw the mobilisation of more than 100 million military personal and brought about over 45 million civilian casualties.

In the final lines, Kavanagh's intention becomes clear and the sonnet's title is assured. As the ghost of Homer whispers in his ear, Kavanagh is reminded that he should not fear provincialism. The *Iliad*, one of the most important poems in the Western canon, was 'made' from such 'A local row'. It is worth bearing in mind that the poem also amounts to a commentary on the power of poetry to transform the here and now. Even though Kavanagh gives centre stage to a very parochial dispute and sets Ballyrush and Gortin in the balance against the crisis in Munich, these events gain transcendental significance only through poetry.

3. Essay Writing

If you are thinking of making reference to 'Epic' in an essay on Kavanagh that you may be asked to write, you might consider the following points.

a. Once again, Kavanagh makes use of the sonnet form. Given that so many of the poems on the course by Kavanagh make use of this form, you may wish to devote an entire paragraph to this stylistic feature of his work.
b. Many of the poems on the course stress the importance of the poet's intimate relationship with his own home and parish. As with 'Inniskeen Road: July Evening', 'Epic' approximates the dialect of Kavanagh's native Monaghan and draws heavily on local place names.
c. As with many of the poems on the course by Kavanagh, 'Epic' emphasises the role of the poet and the poetic process.

Critical Commentary: Canal Bank Walk

See the text of the poem on p. 104.

1. Content

This extraordinary poem has its genesis in Kavanagh's recovery from lung cancer. In *Self-Portrait*, a television documentary first broadcast on 30 October 1962, Kavanagh tells us:

So it was that on the banks of the Grand Canal between Baggot and Lesson Street Bridges in the warm summer of 1955, I lay and watched the green waters of the canal. I had just come out of hospital [...] that the poet is born, not made, is well known. But this does not mean that he was a poet the day he was physically born. For many a good-looking year I wrought hard at versing but I could say that, as a poet, I was born in or about 1955, the place of my birth being the banks of the Grand Canal. Thirty years earlier Shancoduff's watery hills could have done the trick but I was too thick to take the hint.

The poem opens with one of Kavanagh's favourite poetic techniques, the *neologism*. The banks of the Grand Canal in Dublin are described as being 'Leafy-with-love'. As elsewhere in Kavanagh's poetry, nature is seen as reflecting God's will. In this case, the 'will of God' is that the poet should 'wallow in the habitual, the banal' and 'Grow with nature again as before I grew'.

Then, in the fifth line, the poet provides us with the first in a series of examples of the ordinary, everyday occurrences that he wishes to celebrate. The sight of a 'bright stick trapped' in the canal waters is a joyous one for the poet. Similarly, a 'couple kissing on an old seat' and a 'bird gathering materials for the nest' add to the feeling of joyful exuberance at the heart of the poem. In the seventh line, it becomes clear that this joy is explicitly linked to a sense of spiritual renewal. The bird gathering building material is viewed by the poet as doing God's work. In the eleventh line, the poet makes a heartfelt demand that the 'gaping need of [his] senses' be fed so that he can 'pray unselfconsciously with overflowing speech'. In the final lines of the *sonnet*, the poet hopes that he will embrace an unquestioning faith that obtains its inspiration from the natural world:

> For this soul needs to be honoured with a new dress woven
> From green and blue things and arguments that cannot be proven.

2. Stylistic Features

In this sonnet, Kavanagh combines his deep spiritual conviction that God's presence can be glimpsed in the natural world with a longing to be born again. From the outset, the poem is infused with religious *imagery*. The waters of the canal offer the poet redemption and in this sense recall the baptismal waters of Christian belief. In

Christian baptisms, one is named and, according to the liturgy, reborn 'to a new innocence by water and the Holy Spirit'. In this respect, the waters of the canal are central to this poem. Elsewhere, in his poem 'Is', Kavanagh restates the importance of water as a spiritual symbol:

> Mention water again
> Always virginal,
> Always original,
> It washes out Original Sin.

If you have already studied 'Advent', you will remember that in that poem the poet prayed for a renewal and spiritual rebirth. Now, in 'Canal Bank Walk', Kavanagh achieves his desire.

The hyphenated opening, which employs an unusual neologism, establishes the **mood** and **tone** of the poem. The poet literally does not have the language to express his feelings adequately, so he invents the words that he needs. Passionate appreciation of the natural world combines with a heartfelt longing to appreciate God's beauty in an unconscious manner. It is important to realise that the imagery employed by Kavanagh in the poem reflects his own state of being. The stick that is 'trapped' but glowing recalls his present incapacity. Similarly, the bird that gathers 'materials for the nest for the Word' is strangely reminiscent of the poetic process in general and Kavanagh in particular. Like Kavanagh, the bird is busy at work creating a fresh and original sound. It is 'Eloquently new and abandoned to its delirious beat'. The free-flowing, melodious sound of this line matches the fluid nature of the water itself.

This is obviously a highly emotional poem where the poet has great difficultly in containing his exuberance. However, rather than let the poem descend into an unconnected series of joyful outbursts, Kavanagh once again makes use of the sonnet. This highly structured form allows him to arrange his thoughts to present a situation and then to reflect on it. This is precisely what happens in 'Canal Bank Walk'. In the **octave** he sets the scene and then in the **sestet** he reflects on this scene in an intense manner. In fact, this reflection is more akin to a prayer or religious hymn. However, while the poem draws heavily on Christian imagery in its outlook, this is not a traditional prayer to God. Many critics have pointed out that the poem is almost pantheistic in its outlook. According to Antoinette Quinn:

this sonnet is never orthodoxly Christian. It finds its religion out of doors, not in church or bible or creed. It divinises or sacramentalises the natural, turning the earth into an Eden where eternal voices are heard among the trees. It is a 'coloured sonnet,' in which the poet wants to forego logic and weave a worldly garment for the soul out of things sensual and natural, the greenness of beech leaves, grass and canal waters, the blue of the sky.

As with so many other of Kavanagh's poems on the course, 'Canal Bank Walk' addresses the complex issue of poetic inspiration. There is an interesting **paradox** at work in the poem. Kavanagh pleads with God to grant him the very thing that he has managed to conjure up in this poem. Even on a first reading it is readily apparent that this poem is free flowing and fluid. **Run-on lines** combine with **assonance, rhymes** and **half-rhymes** and impel the poem forward in a joyful rush of sensual delight.

3. Essay Writing

If you are thinking of making reference to 'Canal Bank Walk', you may wish to refer to some of the following points.

a. Given that two poems on the course are directly inspired by the Grand Canal in Dublin, it might be worthwhile comparing and contrasting 'Canal Bank Walk' with 'Lines Written on a Seat on the Grand Canal, Dublin'.

b. In this poem, Kavanagh achieves the sense of spiritual renewal that he craves elsewhere in his poetry. You may wish to devote a paragraph to Kavanagh's search for innocence.

c. Nature and religious imagery are once again to the fore in this poem. The waters of the canal symbolise baptismal waters. As in 'Advent', the idea of redemption and regained innocence dominates this poem.

Critical Commentary: Lines Written on a Seat on the Grand Canal, Dublin

See the text of the poem on p. 106.

1. Content

This is yet another poem by Kavanagh that results from his life-threatening illness in 1955, which led to the removal of a cancerous lung. This illness was looked upon by Kavanagh as a turning point in his life, when he felt he was born as a poet. It is important that you read 'Canal Bank Walk' in order to understand the importance of the Grand Canal to Patrick Kavanagh.

'Lines Written on a Seat on the Grand Canal, Dublin' opens with baptismal *imagery* that captures the poet's new lease on life:

> O commemorate me where there is water,
> Canal water, preferably, so stilly
> Greeny at the heart of summer. [...]

Once again, a joyful and exuberant *mood* is established in the opening lines. In a series of gentle *imperatives*, Kavanagh requests that his brother commemorate him by the canal banks. This is a place that the poet associates with beauty and peace. The sound of the water as it pours over the 'lock' drowns out the noise of the city and creates a 'tremendous silence'. The transformative power of the canal is such that 'no one' who witnesses its beauty 'will speak in prose'. The Grand Canal suddenly becomes a 'Parnassian island' where everyday events take on a 'fantastic' aspect:

> A swan goes by head low with many apologies,
> Fantastic light looks through the eyes of bridges –

As the sun sets, it passes under the bridge until it resembles an eye. The poet's sense of childish wonderment is captured in the next line, which begins with an exclamatory 'And look!' That the reason for such excitement is the arrival of a 'barge' 'from Athy' adds to the sense of innocence that dominates this *sonnet*. Here as elsewhere in Kavanagh's poetry, the importance of ordinary people and places in the creation of poetry is acknowledged. The undeniable link between local culture and *mythology* is reflected in the precious cargo of the barge from Athy.

In the final lines of the poem, the speaker reiterates his wish that he be commemorated by a seat on the banks of the Grand Canal:

> O commemorate me with no hero-courageous
> Tomb – just a canal-bank seat for the passer-by.

2. Stylistic Features

This is another exuberant exploration of the poet's connection to the natural world. While 'Lines Written on a Seat on the Grand Canal, Dublin' has much in common with 'Canal Bank Walk', it is in fact a very different poem. Whereas its companion piece is overflowing in its energetic appreciation of the natural world, the *mood* of this poem is serene. In many respects, the tone of the poem captures the essence of the monument that Kavanagh wishes to be erected in his memory. In other words, the pace and *rhythm* of the poem reinforce the idea that this seat will be a place of quiet and peaceful contemplation.

Similarly, the *imagery* in the poem is straightforward and uncomplicated. Hyphenated words such as 'canal-bank' and 'mid-July' create a clear impression in the reader's mind of both time and setting. Kavanagh once described the time he spent on the Grand Canal in the following terms:

> I lay on that grass in an antenatal role ... and because that grass and sun and canal were good to me they were a particular, personal grass, sun and canal. Nobody else in the world knew that place as I knew it. There is a branch in the water and it is still in the immortal water in my mind and the dent in the bank can never be changed ...

With skilful ease, Kavanagh employs such phrases and *neologisms* as 'stilly | Greeny' and 'Niagarously' in order to convey the sense of joy, tranquillity and peace that he receives from this place. This is an important feature of Kavanagh's poetic style. He simply does not have the vocabulary to convey his new outlook on life.

As you read 'Lines Written on a Seat on the Grand Canal, Dublin', it is important to bear in mind that Kavanagh was acutely aware of his own mortality when writing this sonnet. His near brush with death, occasioned by the removal of a lung due to lung cancer, forced him to look again at familiar surroundings. So, in this respect, although the poem celebrates the ordinary plenty of everyday life, there is, at its heart, an awareness of the mutability of the human condition. This consciousness of approaching death is first suggested in the title. The inscription that inspired Kavanagh's poem is obviously intended to memorialise the dead 'Mrs Dermod O'Brien'. This sentiment is followed through in Kavanagh's gentle imperative to his brother to 'commemorate' him.

Yet for all the static poise of this gentle poem, it abounds with life. **Half-rhymes** and **internal rhymes** combine with **assonance** to create a soft and musical energy in the poem that matches the watery oasis that Kavanagh is describing. As with so many of Kavanagh's poems on the course, 'Lines Written on a Seat on the Grand Canal, Dublin' adverts to the transformative power of the poetic imagination. In this sonnet, the often unattractive Dublin canal is transformed into a 'Parnassian island'. This most urban of settings becomes a rural ideal where ordinary, everyday scenery is lit up by the 'fantastic light' of the poetic imagination. The **allusion** to Greek **mythology** is a rich one. The waters of Mount Parnassus were said to confer the powers of poetic inspiration on those who drank from it. The poet John Milton, for example, ascribed the waters as having the power to inspire poetic inspiration. Here in Kavanagh's poem, the prosaic and parochial take on a mythical aspect. Athy, in nearby Kildare, is seen as being a far-flung place when viewed through the lens of the poetic imagination.

3. Essay Writing

Given the importance of the Grand Canal in Dublin to Kavanagh's sense of poetic rebirth, you may wish to consider mentioning this poem in an essay on Kavanagh. Should you do so, try to bear some of the following points in mind.

a. Here, as in 'Canal Bank Walk', the poet is restored by the beauty of the canal.

b. Once again, Kavanagh addresses the poetic process. The canal waters are likened to the Castalian spring on Mount Parnassus. In other words, the canal is a source of poetic inspiration.

c. In this poem, Kavanagh imaginatively transforms the Grand Canal into a place of mythical significance. In 'Shancoduff', 'Canal Bank Walk', 'A Christmas Childhood' and 'Advent', the poet views the ordinary and the banal as being sources of wonder.

Critical Commentary: The Hospital

See the text of the poem on p. 108.

1. Content

This *sonnet* opens with an unusual statement. The speaker informs us that a year ago he fell in love with the 'functional ward | Of a chest hospital'. The poet then describes this place in order to stress its purely functional nature. 'Square cubicles' lie in a 'row' and 'wash basins' are housed in 'Plain concrete'. The entire place is, he tells us, an 'art lover's woe'. In order to reinforce the mundane banality of this place, the speaker informs us that the 'fellow in the next bed' snores.

Then, in the next line, we are told that love has the ability to embrace and transform even the humdrum reality of a cold hospital ward:

> But nothing whatever is by love debarred,
> The common and banal her heat can know.

The ability of love to transform the 'banal' is witnessed again in the next line. An ordinary 'gravelled yard' can become a place of 'inexhaustible adventure' when viewed in a certain light. The poet then tells us in the *sestet* that this is 'what love does to things'. The 'Rialto Bridge', The 'main gate' and the 'seat at the back of a shed' are transformed because they are loved by the speaker. He tells us that:

> Naming these things is the love-act and its pledge;

His message is a simple yet important one. It is imperative that the mysterious ability of love to transform the ordinary be recorded 'without claptrap'. Once this is done, something lasting can be salvaged from the transitory nature of existence.

2. Stylistic Features

This is another poem that Kavanagh wrote while recovering from illness. His brush with death as a result of lung cancer brought about a complete change in Kavanagh's outlook. This sonnet, like so many of the poems that Kavanagh published in the

1950s, is not only masterly in its control of speech **rhythms**, but is most moving as a declaration of newfound faith in life. The poet had more than enough reason to love this chest hospital – it was where he survived the removal of a cancerous lung. He was, as it were, born again into the common world of human experience. It is as if following his brush with death, his soul has risen phoenix-like from the ashes, newly inspired and newly dedicated to the pursuit of real meaning in the world. As a result, he is now ready to embrace the stark beauty of a functional hospital ward in a manner that rejects artistic orthodoxy.

As with so many of Kavanagh's poems on the course, this sonnet contains a heartfelt appreciation of the banal that challenges widely held concepts of beauty. In the poet's estimation, 'square cubicles', 'Plain concrete' and 'wash basins' can have aesthetic value. They may have been ignored by poets and they may be an 'art lover's woe', but in this poet's opinion, they are worthy of appreciation. Kavanagh's biographer, Antoinette Quinn, feels that the poet is 'taking a radical aesthetic stance, breaking ranks with orthodox art-lovers, making art out of anti-art'. This process commences with the title, which is almost anti-poetic, and continues throughout the next two **quatrains** of the **octave** until we reach the **volta**, or turn, in the **sestet**. In this respect, the poem is typical of the traditional **Petrarchan sonnet** in that it makes its series of observations in the octave and employs the sestet as the vehicle for clarification. The clarification is a simple yet profound one. The reason that the ordinary and normally unattractive things of everyday life are worthy of the poet's attention is that they have been transformed by 'love'. The poet never specifies the exact nature of this love. However, it is obviously closely linked to his newfound lease on life. These objects may be ordinary, but the experience is anything but commonplace. The language used by Kavanagh reflects this fact. The vernacular words and phrases that dominate the octave yield to a deeply philosophical, formal and rhetorical mode of expression in the sestet. As the poem moves outward from the confines of the hospital ward to the 'gravelled yard' and beyond 'Rialto Bridge', it eventually transcends the ephemeral nature of life itself. All of this is made possible by the transformative power of love to 'Snatch out of time the passionate transitory'.

3. Essay Writing

If you are considering referring to 'The Hospital' in an essay, you may want to consider some of the following points.

a. 'The Hospital' is important to our understanding of Kavanagh's rebirth as a poet. In this respect, the poem can be compared to and contrasted with 'Advent' and the 'canal poems'.
b. Once again, Kavanagh transforms an ordinary setting. In this case, 'a gravelled yard' becomes a source of 'inexhaustible adventure'.
c. Here, as with so many of the poems on the course by Kavanagh, the poet relies on the sonnet form. You may wish to devote an entire paragraph to the poet's use of this poetic form.

Critical Commentary: On Raglan Road

See the text of the poem on p. 110.

1. Content

The background to this poem is very interesting. In 1944, Patrick Kavanagh met Hilda Moriarty. She was a 22-year-old medical student from Kerry who was studying at University College Dublin. The poet, who was 20 years older, became obsessed with Hilda Moriarty, who was reputedly one of the most beautiful women of her day. In fact, such was her beauty that fashion designers offered her their new collections to wear. At the time of the meeting, Patrick Kavanagh was in deep need of inspiration. He was entering one of the darker periods of his life. He was unemployed and relied on charity donations from friends and patrons, including the Archbishop of Dublin, Archbishop McQuaid. In 1944, the poet wrote to McQuaid about this encounter with Hilda Moriarty, which he described as a special grace. While Hilda never reciprocated Kavanagh's feelings for her, she did tolerate him. However, it has to be said that the poet's continued pursuit of this woman was strange at best. In Christmas of 1944, he chose to follow Hilda to Kerry. However, Kavanagh was not invited by the Moriarty family to spend the holidays with them. As a result, he checked into a local guesthouse and wrote a piece for the *Irish Press* entitled 'A Christmas in Kerry' so as to defray the costs. Back in Dublin, he attempted to transform himself into the type of person he felt Hilda would admire. However, his love was unrequited and she later married Donogh O'Malley, the Fianna Fáil Minister for Education. Kavanagh still had difficulty accepting the obvious end of their relationship, such as it was, and was said to have chaperoned Moriarty and O'Malley on dates. By the end of 1945, Kavanagh felt that he needed to express his complex feelings regarding his failed pursuit of Hilda. The couple met only once again at a social function. However, Hilda did send a wreath of red roses in the form of an 'H' when Kavanagh died in 1967.

When one considers the unrequited nature of Kavanagh's love for Hilda Moriarty, the opening of the poem is rather ominous. The poet's first encounter with this beautiful woman takes place on an 'autumn day'. Traditionally, autumn has been used by poets as a **metaphor** for death or decay. The speaker acknowledges that when he met her he knew:

> That her dark hair would weave a snare that [he] might one day rue;

Yet despite seeing the 'danger' of pursuing this beautiful woman, the poet decides to walk along the 'enchanted way' that presumably leads to love. The final line of the first stanza hints that this relationship is indeed doomed from the outset:

> And I said, let grief be a fallen leaf at the dawning of the day.

In the second stanza, we move ahead in time to November. The dangers inherent in pursuing this woman are once again **alluded** to. Grafton Street, where the poet's courtship of Hilda takes place, is transformed into 'the ledge | Of [a] deep ravine'. Then, in the third stanza, the speaker outlines some of the gifts that he has bestowed on the object of his desire. We learn that he has given her artistic 'gifts of the mind' such as 'poems' that have been named after her. Once again, in the closing lines of this stanza, the speaker alludes to the danger that this woman poses. Her hair casts a cloud 'over fields of May'.

In the final stanza of the poem, we move forward to a point in time when the poet's courtship has ended. On 'a quiet street' the poet is confronted by the memories, or 'ghosts', of the past. The woman he once pursued so vigorously now hurries past him and as a result he is forced to concede that he lavished his attention on someone who was not worthy of him:

> [...] I had wooed not as I should a creature made of clay –
> When the angel woos the clay he'd lose his wings at the dawn of day.

2. Stylistic Features

Kavanagh wrote this poem around one year after his courtship of Hilda Moriarty had ended. From the beginning of the poem, it is apparent that the poet was acutely aware that this relationship was doomed to failure. Autumn, which forms the backdrop to the beginning of the poem, has widely been used by poets as a metaphor for decay. Similarly, the description of the woman recalls the *femme fatale* of *Romantic* literature. Her hair is a 'dark', foreboding colour that forms a 'snare' from which he cannot free himself.

One of the more interesting aspects of this poem is the manner in which Dublin is transformed into a nostalgic storehouse of memory. Grafton Street, where Kavanagh often watched Hilda Moriarty and her friends drinking coffee in Mitchels Café, and Raglan Road, where he first saw her, become the loci for a magical journey of the heart that ends in bitterness and regret.

It is difficult to ignore the musicality of this poem. 'On Raglan Road' has a hauntingly beautiful sound to it that is enhanced when combined with the air 'The Dawning of the Day.' Intricate *internal rhymes* combine with *assonance* and *alliteration* to produce an unforgettably poignant evocation of unrequited love. Many of the more memorable lines in the poem rely on internal rhyme even at the expense of meaning in order to enhance the sound. Consider the following lines:

> The Queen of Hearts still making tarts and I not making hay –
> O I loved too much and by such, by such, is happiness thrown away.

Here Kavanagh borrows from a well-known children's nursery rhyme:

> The Queen of Hearts she made some tarts all on a summer's day;
> The Knave of Hearts he stole the tarts and took them clean away.
> The King of Hearts called for the tarts and beat the Knave full sore
> The Knave of Hearts brought back the tarts and vowed he'd steal no more.

The poet maintains much of the intricate internal rhymes of the original, which are well suited to his purpose in this poem.

As with so many of the poems by Kavanagh on the Leaving Certificate course, 'On Raglan Road' has at its heart an awareness of the role of the writer. When it becomes apparent that his pursuit is pointless, the speaker defensively argues that he, being a poet, was wrong in wooing 'a creature made of clay'.

3. Essay Writing

If you intend to refer to 'On Raglan Road' in an essay that you are writing, you might want to bear some of the following points in mind.

a. This is perhaps Kavanagh's most popular poem. You may wish to assess the reasons (its beautiful imagery, the haunting melody, etc.) for this popularity.
b. Once again, the ordinary is transformed by Kavanagh. Raglan Road and Grafton Street become dangerous places where the poet risks his happiness in the pursuit of his beloved.
c. This is a highly crafted poem. You may wish to mention 'On Raglan Road' in a paragraph that outlines Kavanagh's technical ability. Haunting sounds combine with carefully chosen imagery to produce a remarkable and unforgettable poem.

Thomas Kinsella (1928–)

A Short Biography

Thomas Kinsella was born on 4 May 1928 in Inchicore, Dublin. He was the eldest child of John Kinsella and Agnes Casserly. His father had what the poet would later describe as an 'untypical interest in literature and classical music'. John Kinsella worked for Guinness and was instrumental in establishing the trade union there. It is not surprising that so much of Kinsella's inspiration for his poetry should come from what can be described as old Dublin. His maternal grandparents lived in Bow Lane in the Liberties, where they ran a small local shop. Kinsella has fond memories of his early childhood in Phoenix Street, Dublin 10. He attended primary school and was taught through Irish at the Model School in Inchicore. His teachers, Miss Kearney and Mr Brown, are celebrated in his poem 'Extract 38 Phoenix Street'. At the age of 12 he entered the well-known O'Connells School on Dublin's north side, and in his own words, this was a 'tough place' to study. At this stage in his schooling, there was little to indicate that Kinsella would later become a poet. Although he recalls enjoying poetry, he felt that he misunderstood it. He has also stated that the way poetry was taught to him actively destroyed the material of the poem. It was not until much later in life, when he chanced upon a book of poetry by the English poet W.H. Auden, that he realised ordinary human experience, and more importantly, speech, could be adapted to poetry.

Following his Leaving Certificate, Kinsella entered University College Dublin on a scholarship to study science. However, he quickly felt that physics and chemistry held little interest for him, and when the opportunity arose to join the civil service, he abandoned his degree and took up employment at the Congested District's Board, though he did continue to study languages at UCD on a part-time basis. It was around this time that he met his future wife, Eleanor, in the library of UCD. The relationship flourished, and when Eleanor contracted tuberculosis, Kinsella visited her every Wednesday and Sunday during her protracted stay in St Mary's Sanatorium in the Phoenix Park. During the summer of 1954 he wrote many love letters to Eleanor, some of which include first draughts of some of his most famous poems. According to Dr Andrew Fitzsimons of Gakushuin University, Tokyo, Eleanor has always acted as Kinsella's muse and continues to occupy a central place in his life and work. The extract from 'The Familiar', which is included for study in this anthology, reflects the depth and importance of his relationship with Eleanor to his poetry.

Following their marriage, the couple moved to Baggot Street, where Kinsella met the influential Irish composer Seán Ó Riada and the publisher and founder of the Dolmen Press, Liam Miller. In particular, the meeting with Miller was to have a dramatic impact on the direction that his career would take. Kinsella had been writing and publishing poetry in University College Dublin's literary magazine, *The National Student*, and was beginning to make a name for himself in Dublin literary circles of the 1950s. However, it was Miller's decision to publish a volume of Kinsella's poetry in book form that brought his work to the attention of a much wider readership. His first collection, *Poems* (1956), was nominated for a Poetry Book Society Award. This first publication was followed by a succession of highly acclaimed collections: *Another September* (1958), *Moralities* (1960), *Downstream* (1962), *Wormwood* (1966) and *Nightwalker* (1967). These collections won the recognition they deserved. Kinsella won the Poetry Book Society Award twice – in 1958 and 1962 – and in 1967 he was awarded the Denis Devlin Memorial Award.

He also held directorships on both the Cuala and Dolmen Presses and in 1972 founded his own publishing press, the Peppercanister Press. His *Collected Poems 1956–1973* was published by Oxford University Press. *Notes from the Land of the Dead* appeared in 1972 and was followed by *New Poems* in 1973 and *Fifteen Dead* and *One and Other Poems* in 1979. There then followed a seven-year hiatus in publishing new material, which was broken by the publication of *An Duanaire: 1600–1900, Poems of the Dispossessed*, translated by Kinsella and edited by Seán Ó Tuama, and *The New Oxford Book of Irish Verse* (1986), edited by Kinsella.

Around this time, Kinsella also began to translate Irish literature into English. Perhaps his most notable achievement in this field is his 1969 translation of the ancient Irish epic *The Táin*. This book, which is included for study on the Irish Leaving Certificate Classics syllabus, was published by the Oxford University Press in 1970.

Throughout this time, Kinsella continued to rise through the ranks in the civil service, reaching the position of assistant principal officer in the Department of Finance. In 1965, he left this job and made the move to the Southern Illinois University, where he became writer-in-residence. Five years later, he left for Philadelphia's Temple University. Between 1965 and the late 1970s, Kinsella was awarded three Guggenheim Fellowships. These awards allowed him to divide his time between Philadelphia and his native Dublin. His daughter, Sara, who continued to study in Dublin's Pembroke School on Leeson Street, recalls how he visited the school and how he was a 'bit of a celebrity'. At the time, Kinsella was the only living poet on the Leaving Certificate course, and he came to speak to the class about his poetry. He also recorded for her readings and critical analyses of many of the other poets on the course, including Keats and Dickinson. His interpretations of the poems stressed the importance of the language and form of poetry.

Despite the astonishing early success and recognition that Kinsella received both at home and abroad, his career began to falter somewhat in the late 1970s. Speaking on RTÉ's *Arts Lives* in March 2009, Kinsella attributes this decline in his popularity to the publication of his poem 'Butcher's Dozen'. This scathing poem is a *satire* on the now discredited Widgery Report's exoneration of the British Army's actions on 30 January 1972. On what has now become known as the Bloody Sunday massacre, 13 unarmed civilians were shot dead in Derry. According to Kinsella, this poem lost him '90 percent of his British audience and it has stayed that way ever since'. However, it has to be noted that the 1970s saw the emergence of a new group of Irish poets from the North of Ireland. Heaney, Mahon, Longley and Muldoon captured the zeitgeist of the time and in many ways eclipsed Kinsella.

Nevertheless, Kinsella has continued to write, publish and translate poetry. Throughout the 1980s and into the 1990s, Kinsella wrote often obscure and difficult pieces that combine observations on contemporary Ireland with *allusions* to Irish *mythology*, contemporary politics, classical music, ancient Greek thinking and 20th-century philosophy. Speaking on the occasion of his eightieth birthday in 2008, Kinsella said, 'I feel I should be dead, but I've never felt so much alive.'

Critical Commentary: Thinking of Mr D.

See the text of the poem on p. 116.

1. Content

This rather bleak poem concluded Kinsella's 1958 collection, *Another September*. However, Kinsella has made significant alterations to the poem since it first appeared. The version of the poem in this anthology is the one chosen by Kinsella for inclusion in his 2001 *Collected Poems*. The poem centres on the poet's recollections of Mr D., who many critics believe may be a veiled reference to the Irish poet Austin Clarke. In the opening line, the speaker concentrates on Mr D.'s physical appearance. We learn that he was a man 'light of foot, but ageing'. He 'took | An hour to drink his glass' and delighted in what the poet calls 'cheerful slander'. Another dimension to Mr D.'s character emerges in the next stanza. We learn that he had a 'scathing smile' and that when he was sober, he used to nod in such a manner as to withhold his 'assent'.

While the opening line of the third stanza announces the death of Mr D., it is not until we read the line that follows that its full meaning becomes clear. Despite the fact that Mr D. is now dead, we learn that the speaker claims to have seen him on two separate occasions since he passed away. On the first occasion, the poet remembers seeing him as he once looked retiring from company on a night out. On the second occasion that the poet was visited by a ghostly reminder of Mr D., the man looked like a 'priest-like figure turning, wolfish-slim'. The poem concludes with this second vision of Mr D., which took place under the light of the 'wharf- | Lamps':

> A priest-like figure turning, wolfish-slim,
> Quickly aside from pain, in a bodily plight,
> To note the oiled reflections chime and swim.

2. Stylistic Features

In an interview with Peter Orr in 1962, Kinsella described death and the passing of time as numbering amongst his most pressing concerns.

> I think they can all be summed up in the 'passing of time' and its various effects; I think, in particular, death, the death of individual people. Some of the poems which I like most of mine are the cold-blooded lamentations for individuals whom I've known and liked and who have died.

In this case, the individual, or Mr D., that Kinsella describes may be the Irish poet Austin Clarke. According to the critic Donatella Abbate Badin, 'Thinking of Mr D.' is 'a portrait of Clarke, whose anger against Irish society is seen as alienating and damaging for his poetry'. Kinsella, who edited an edition of Clarke's collected poems, has written more than one poem that centres on Clarke and his place in Irish literature. In such poems as 'Magnanimity' and 'Brothers in Craft', the poet emphasises both the sharpness of Clarke's tongue and his role as an outsider. In the original version of the poem, Kinsella compares Mr D. to the Renaissance poet Dante Alighieri, who was born in 1265 and is widely regarded as one of the greatest poets of world literature. In one episode of Dante's most famous poem, the *Divine Comedy*, Dante describes a journey by the poet figure into hell. Dante's writings earned him the enmity of the establishment and eventually led to his banishment. If we keep this comparison from the original version of the poem in mind, it could be that Kinsella is making a parallel between the treatment that Dante received and the fact that Clarke was shunned by literary establishment figures such as W.B. Yeats.

However, if this poem is indeed a veiled portrait of Austin Clarke, it is not without its criticisms. In fact, on more than one occasion, Kinsella has levelled criticism at Clarke. In his 1956 review of *Ancient Lights*, which at the time was Clarke's first collection in almost 20 years, Kinsella viewed the **satirical** views of Irish society contained in the collection as unproductive, describing Clarke's poetry as the 'product of an angry mind that ranted and raved', only to 'beat the wall'. While the **tone** of 'Thinking of Mr D.' underscores the sentiments contained in the review of Clarke's poetry, it is also possible to read this poem as an act of self-criticism or self-warning. For the larger part of Kinsella's early career, the poet felt out of step with and even alienated from modern Ireland. Taking this view of the poem, Kinsella may be reminding himself that any attempt at social satire, or 'cheerful slander', is dangerous in that it can lead to a lack of perspective, which can in turn result in the isolation of the poet figure. In the original 1958 version of this poem, Kinsella included the following lines:

> Yet his look
> Was narrowed to an angry ember the young
> Would pity, if they noticed – rage barred in
> By age [...]

In this version, Mr D.'s bitterness and rage lead to his words going unnoticed by the young.

While 'Thinking of Mr D.' may amount to a criticism of either Austin Clarke specifically or indeed Kinsella himself, it can also be seen as providing us with an intense meditation on the nature of death and the passing of time. In the first half of this poem, the isolated and lonely Mr D. appears on the brink of death. In the third stanza, he seems to have made the transition from life to death:

> When he died I saw him twice.

The movement from life to death, however, has not freed Mr D. from the pain that dogged him in life:

> A priest-like figure turning, wolfish-slim,
> Quickly aside from pain, in a bodily plight,
> To note the oiled reflections chime and swim.

The vision of the afterlife in this poem is a bleak, even hellish one.

3. Essay Writing

If you are making reference to 'Thinking of Mr D.' in an essay, you may wish to include some of the following points.

a. Once again, Kinsella meditates on the passing of time and death.
b. The poem may be read as a portrait of the dead Irish poet Austin Clarke.
c. 'Thinking of Mr D.' can be read as a critique of the writer in society in general and more specifically of those poets like Clarke and indeed Kinsella himself who chose to stand apart from their compatriots.

Critical Commentary: Dick King

See the text of the poem on pp. 118–19.

1. Content

'Dick King' was first published in Kinsella's 1962 collection *Downstream*. This complex and thought-provoking memory poem centres on a figure from Kinsella's childhood. In the opening stanza of the poem, the 'ghost' of Dick King comes back to haunt the speaker. The 'phantom vowels' are a ghostly reminder of the sound of his dead neighbour's voice that ignites the speaker's fond memories of this man and provokes the meditation on life, death and the passing of time that follows.

In the second stanza, the haunting recollection of his dead neighbour's voice causes the poet to remember the 'rain on the cobbles' of his native Dublin. From here, we are transported to the 'iron trough, and the horses' dipped | Faces under the Fountain in James's Street'. As the poet remembers sheltering under the buttons of the old man's coat, a darker note is introduced into the poem. In the final line of the second stanza, we are told rather ominously that Dick King's 'dread years were to come'.

In the third stanza, the poet recalls the hushed voice of Dick King when he 'named the dead' of Dublin's past. The young poet's response at the time was a purely physical one: he 'squeezed' the man's 'fingers' until Dick King 'found again | [his] hand hidden' in his. The repetition of the line 'I squeezed your fingers' announces the transition from the first half the poem to the six shorter **quatrains** that comprise the second half of 'Dick King'. Each one of these quatrains provides the reader with additional information about Dick King's life.

In the fourth stanza, we learn that Dick King was an 'upright man' who now is now 'Fifteen' years dead. Originally from the West of Ireland, or the 'salt seaboard', he moved east to bring the 'dying' Irish 'language' to Dublin and eventually came to dwell in Basin Lane. As the poem progresses, the speaker tells us that he worked by the Southern Railway, while in the seventh stanza, we learn that Dick King married an 'invalid' who 'prayed her life away', whose whispering prayers:

> [...] filled the whitewashed yard
> Until her dying day.

In the penultimate stanza, the poet emphasises the passing of time, and in the final line he announces the death of Dick King. In the closing stanza, the speaker describes the final moments of this man's life. We are told that he clasped his hands 'in a Union ward | To hear St James's bell'. Even though the poet was 'young', he understood the significance of this event:

> I searched his eyes though I was young,
> The last to wish him well.

2. Stylistic Features

It is central to our understanding of this poem that we bear in mind that Kinsella's memories of Dick King are intrinsically linked to his growth and development as a writer. In fact, throughout the poem, the speaker makes numerous references to language and sound. This process begins with his recollection of his neighbour's 'phantom vowels', but is also seen in the poet's memories of Dick King's low voice, his hushed tones, the language he spoke and even in his wife's whispered prayers. Finally, this poetic awareness of sound culminates with the St James's bell tolling the end of Dick King's life. As we read the poem, it becomes obvious that Dick King has served as a kind of inspiration for Kinsella in his development as a poet. It is not surprising, therefore, that the speaker should refer to himself as being 'Bemused' by this old man's accounts of Dublin's past. In Greek *mythology*, the Muses were the nine daughters of Zeus and Mnemosyne, goddess of memory. The Muses were believed to inspire poets in particular and to preside over the creative arts in general.

Dick King's presence is a vital one in the narrative of Kinsella's early life. The place names that the poet associates with Dick King are obviously very important to the poet in terms of both his family history and his identity as a Dubliner. Basin Lane and the areas surrounding James Street, the Liberties and Coomb feature frequently in Kinsella's poetry because his maternal grandfather ran a shop there. However, beyond the intimate personal associations that the poet had with this area, this part of Dublin is also rich in tradition. Jonathan Swift lived on Patrick Street and the area also has strong associations with Robert Emmet's 1803 rising. Emmet was executed opposite St Catherine's Church on Thomas Street. Although it is impossible to know exactly if the speaker is referring to Emmet and Swift, it does not require a huge leap of the imagination to picture Dick King whispering the names of these dead Irish men to the young Kinsella:

> And your voice, in a pause of softness, named the dead,
> Hushed as though the city had died by fire,
> Bemused, discovering ... discovering

In the second half of the poem, the poet acknowledges the impact this man had on the development of his imagination by making a sudden shift in the poem's form and *rhythm*. In the fourth stanza, Kinsella changes abruptly to the balladic form and rhythm. The *ballad* is a song or poem that is particularly associated with tradition. In choosing to make use of this form, Kinsella is acknowledging the key role Dick King played in opening his mind to the wealth of tradition that surrounded him in his youth.

According to the poet and critic Dennis O'Driscoll, if 'James Joyce is the quintessential Dublin novelist', then 'Thomas Kinsella must be viewed as being the quintessential Dublin poet'. More than one critic has pointed out that there is an extraordinary intensity to Kinsella's childhood poems that recalls the sense of immediacy one gets from reading Joyce. In fact, on more than one occasion, the accounts of Dublin found in this poem evoke similar episodes in Joyce's *Dubliners*:

> Clearly now I remember rain on the cobbles,
> Ripples in the iron trough, and the horses' dipped
> Faces under the Fountain in James's Street,
> When I sheltered my nine years against your buttons
> And your own dread years were to come:

Kinsella's poetry has been praised for its ability to explore the power of the imagination and its capacity to understand the profound nature of human relationships. However, at the heart of Kinsella's understanding of relationships is the often depressing realisation that death is the inevitable lot of all mankind. Yet in his poetry, this disheartening reality is often mitigated by the enduring power of love. Here in this poem, the warmth and love that the poet feels for his now-dead friend causes Dick King to live again in a very real sense. His rough West of Ireland accent is reborn in the 'phantom vowels' that haunt the poet. Finally, the manner in which the old man inspired the young Kinsella's imagination is mirrored by the way Dick King's memory has now inspired this poem. In this respect, Dick King lives on.

3. Essay Writing

If you are making reference to 'Dick King' in any essay on Kinsella, you may wish to include some of the following points.

a. This is a memory poem. Many of Kinsella's poems centre on his memory of his early life in Dublin. In this poem, we are given an intimate and open account of his relationship with Dick King and how it affected his growth as a poet.

b. The poem makes use of the ballad form in such a way that it stresses the role that Dick King played in introducing the poet's imagination to the history and tradition of Dublin.

c. As with many of Kinsella's poems on the course, this poem acknowledges the inevitability of death. However, the warm affection that the poet feels for Dick King mitigates the depressing reality of his death.

Critical Commentary: Mirror in February

See the text of the poem on p. 121.

1. Content

This short poem, which was included for study on the former Leaving Certificate English syllabus, is familiar to generations of Irish schoolgoers. The poem, which first appeared in the 1963 collection *Downstream,* is in many ways typical of Kinsella's poetry in general. 'Mirror in February' opens with a highly memorable, if depressing, depiction of the dank and dreary February weather:

> The day dawns with scent of must and rain,
> Of opened soil, dark trees, dry bedroom air.

The speaker has just woken and his mind, not yet fully alert, is 'Idling on some compulsive fantasy'. The scene is an entirely familiar one. However, as he towels his 'shaven jaw and stop[s], and stare[s]', the poet experiences a moment of **epiphany** that rivets him to the spot. The source of this startling moment of revelation is his appearance. His 'dark exhausted eye' and 'dry downturning mouth' force upon him an acknowledgement of his own mortality. This in turn leads to the admission at the beginning of the second stanza that it is 'again [...] time to learn'.

Many readers find the next line, where Kinsella speaks of this 'untiring, crumbling place of growth', difficult to decipher. In order to understand this line, it is necessary to appreciate the full context of the poem. The awareness that Kinsella experiences is informed and directed as much by the natural world as by his own thoughts. Outside it is February and the natural world is slowly beginning to wake and renew itself. This fact is uppermost in Kinsella's mind when he looks into the mirror. The 'opened soil' and 'dark trees' of the previous stanza are reminders of the natural cycle at work. In contrast to the renewal taking place outside his window, the poet confronts the uncomfortable reality that he is ageing. Looking 'plainly in the mirror of [his] soul', he understands that he has looked his last 'on youth'. However, in the final lines of the second stanza, he acknowledges that despite having reached 'the age of Christ', or 33, he has not yet completed his life's work. According to the Bible, Christ died having fulfilled the covenant between man and God, but the poet accepts that he has not yet been 'made whole'.

In the final stanza, the link between the poet's altered perception of his physical state and the natural cycle is made explicit:

> Below my window the awakening trees,
> Hacked clean for better bearing, stand defaced
> Suffering their brute necessities,

In order for the trees to bear more fruit, they need to be pruned, or 'Hacked clean'. Such suffering is a necessary price to pay for the trees' growth. The parallels between this and human existence are obvious. In order for human beings to experience growth, suffering is not only inevitable, but perhaps necessary:

> And how should the flesh not quail that span for span
> Is mutilated more? [...]

In slow distaste at the realisation of this fact, the speaker folds his towel. It is of course significant that he does not throw in the towel, choosing instead to put it aside with 'what grace [he] can'.

The final **couplet** of the poem is both an acknowledgement of the fragility of the human condition and a triumphant testimony to the power of the human spirit to endure:

> I fold my towel with what grace I can,
> Not young and not renewable, but man.

2. Stylistic Features

This deeply thought-provoking poem opens in a manner that recalls a moment from Irish literature. In the famous opening sequence of James Joyce's novel *Ulysses*, Stephen Daedalus stares into the mirror as he shaves. Here in this poem, the bedroom, which is normally associated with rest and comfort, becomes the location for an extraordinary event. In the course of this poem, the speaker experiences an unsettling **epiphany** that alters his understanding of his place in the world. The mirror into which the poet stares – 'the mirror of [his] soul' – is an appropriate **metaphor** for the exploration of self that he undertakes. In many of Kinsella's poems, a male figure is forced to reassess his self-image while staring at the actual image. Kinsella is a fluent Irish speaker and the critic Brian John has asserted that it 'is hardly coincidental, that the Irish for mirror (*scáthán*) and for shadow (*scáth*) are commonly derived'. In other words, in this poem the poet examines his reflection and is confronted by a shadow image of himself. Mirrors reflect and this mirror provokes a moment of intense reflection. Looking in the mirror, he not only sees his 'dark exhausted eye, I A dry downturning mouth', but his own soul:

> Now plainly in the mirror of my soul
> I read that I have looked my last on youth
> And little more; for they are not made whole
> That reach the age of Christ.

In other respects, this poem is typical of Kinsella's poetry in general. Many of Kinsella's poems take place at dawn, centre on the importance of self-awareness and self-revelation and examine man's place in terms of the broader natural cycle. Another interesting aspect of the poem is that for the greater part of 'Mirror in February', Kinsella employs **rhyme** in such a way as to reinforce the mirror metaphor. The uneven rhyme in the final lines of the first two stanzas is resolved in the final two lines of the third stanza, where 'can' rhymes with 'man'.

'Mirror in February' opens in a dramatic way that manages to capture both the physical reality of his surroundings (the 'dry bedroom air') and his mood. Dawn is often associated with hope, yet any sense of hope in this poem is obscured by the dark and gloomy atmosphere. St Brigid's Day, the first of February, has traditionally marked the beginning of spring in Ireland, but any sense of renewal that one would normally associate with spring is lessened by the sense of existential malaise that dominates the poem. Outside his bedroom, there are reminders both of growth and the inevitability of decay. While the 'opened soil' may hint at the process of planting and renewal, it may also point to the ineluctability of death or the certainty of the grave. Furthermore, the long vowels coupled with the repetition of the consonant 'd' sounds create a heavy, plodding and oppressive effect.

Yet despite all this, the predominant **mood** in the opening stanza remains one of startled awareness. The short verb 'Riveted' captures the sudden jolt that the speaker experiences once he is confronted by the image of his own mortality. Yet the triumph of this poem lies in Kinsella's ability to overcome his own feelings of distaste concerning his ageing. By the poem's end, the speaker accepts the fact that he is no longer a young man and that change is unavoidable. This confers a certain dignity not only on him, but on the human condition. The *image* of the poet folding and not throwing in the towel is a simple yet profoundly thought-provoking one.

Earlier in the poem, the poet refers to having reached 'the age of Christ' and not being whole. It is possible to interpret the poet's failure to dwell more deeply on Christian spirituality as a rejection of traditional religion in favour of more humanist or secular solutions to the dilemmas posed by life and death. At the end of the poem, the poet relies on his humanity, not some higher power, to provide him with the strength necessary to carry on.

Finally, the poem centres on a number of obvious contrasts. Throughout the poem there are implied contrasts between light and darkness, winter and spring, life and death, reflection and reality, sleeping and waking, renewal and decay and youth and ageing. These contrasts create tension and force the reader to think more deeply about the poem's themes.

3. Essay Writing

If you are going to include 'Mirror in February' in an essay, you may want to mention some of the following points.

a. Nature and the natural cycle play a significant role in many of the poems by Kinsella on the course. Here in this poem, nature forms the backdrop to his consideration of the human condition.
b. The poem's rhyming scheme reinforces the central metaphor of the mirror.
c. 'Mirror in February' is constructed around a series of powerful and thought-provoking contrasts.

Critical Commentary: Chrysalides

See the text of the poem on p. 123.

1. Content

This short narrative poem centres on the poet's recollections of a bicycling holiday during what he describes as his 'last free summer'. In the opening stanza of the poem, the speaker describes how he and his companion pedalled slowly through 'country towns, stopping to eat I Chocolate and fruit'. In the second stanza, the poet describes how later, at night, they watched the 'crunching boots of countrymen' to the backdrop of 'melodeon music'. In the speaker's imagination, these men appeared 'huge and weightless' as they twirled and leapt over the 'yellow concrete'.

The poet's carefree depiction of this holiday continues in the third stanza, where he describes how they 'awoke at noon' and were mocked by their friends when they poked their faces into the kitchen. There is a slight change in **tone** in the fourth stanza, when the poet singles out the ephemeral or fleeting nature of this happiness, describing the carefree joy as a happiness and a 'tolerance' that they would 'never know again'. According to the poet, during this period of their life, both he and his partner confused the 'licit', or what was lawful, with 'the familiar'. As the couple grew closer, the speaker claims that their 'instincts blurred' and that 'a strange wakefulness I Sapped [their] energies'. During these intensely passionate moments, the couple was brought into the 'extremes of feeling'. In the penultimate stanza, the **imagery** of high romance dominates the poet's recollection of those 'youthful midnights':

> When by a window ablaze softly with the virgin moon
> Dry scones and jugs of milk awaited us in the dark,

There is a sharp change in the poem's tone in the final stanza. As with so many of Kinsella's poems, his memories of the past are clouded by a realisation of mortality. Here in the final stanza, the beautiful images of romance that have dominated the previous six stanzas are replaced by a sense of 'lasting horror'. On the face of it this sense of horror is provoked by a mass death of a 'flight of ants', which die in such numbers that they glisten 'like drops of copper' in the path of the young lovers.

2. Stylistic Features

This poem first appeared in Kinsella's 1962 collection *Downstream*. As with so many of the other poems in this collection, 'Chrysalides' consists of a short narrative that is interspersed with moments of intense meditation. The title of the poem is pivotal to our understanding of its central message. A chrysalid is the stage between the larva and the adult in an insect. More than anything else, this poem is about change, growth and the inevitability of death. While the poem centres on the speaker's memories of a summer of innocent joy and passionate discovery, it is the speaker's awareness of how much he has changed since that summer that really interests him. The idyllic scene that Kinsella presents to us forms little more than the backdrop to his shuddering realisation later on in life that death is the ineluctable lot of all living things.

If one looks closely, it is possible to see that Kinsella qualifies his recollection of that carefree summer. In the opening line, we are told that this was to be the 'last free summer', which suggests the inevitable changes that are about to occur in the speaker's life. As a younger man he was 'insensitive' to both the extraordinary gift of that 'unique succession of our youthful midnights' and to the significance that lay beyond his discovery of the dying ants. The use of the adjective 'unique' is suggestive of the precious nature of time that this couple spent together. However, it is important to bear in mind that it is the mature speaker who qualifies the experience. At the time, the young couple was blissfully unaware of the significance of their time together. This lack of sensitivity or awareness is also reflected in the manner in which they fail to see any real significance in the death of so many flying ants. The mature narrator, however, has the capacity to see these ants as acting as a *metaphor* for the inevitability of death and decay:

> Or to lasting horror: a wedding flight of ants
> Spawning to its death, a mute perspiration
> Glistening like drops of copper, agonised, in our path.

This sense of the inevitability of transformation and of course decay is what lends the poem its title. This is an interesting and thought-provoking poem that, like so many of the other poems in *Downstream*, forces the reader to acknowledge the fragility of life and the ephemeral nature of all human experience.

3. Essay Writing

If you are thinking of referring to 'Chrysalides' in any essay on Kinsella's poetry that you may be asked to write, try to bear the following points in mind.

a. The title of the poem is central to our understanding of Kinsella's thematic intent.

b. In another poem, 'Downstream', which is not on the Leaving Certificate syllabus, Kinsella speaks of his 'lasting horror' of mortality. At the heart of this poem is an attempt by the adult narrator to come to terms with his first intimation of mortality.

c. There is a duality to this poem. The beauty and youthful passion that dominate most of the poem are replaced by the darker *imagery* in the final stanza.

Critical Commentary: from Glenmacnass VI: Littlebody

See the text of the poem on pp. 125–7.

1. Content

This unusual poem centres on an encounter that is strongly reminiscent of many *mythological* stories. The poem opens with a description of the landscape where this encounter takes place. The place seems particularly Irish. The 'black bog channels I dug down in the water' contain 'white cottonheads'. While the shining car in the distance reminds us that the narrative takes place in a contemporary setting, this landscape is rich in history. Behind a rocky 'prow', 'stones on top' form 'an old mark'.

In the next section of the poem, the voice of the narrator intrudes as the speaker tells us that he was 'climbing up, making no noise' when the music mentioned in the second stanza 'stopped'. Then:

> There was a hard inhale,
> a base growl,
> and it started again, in a guttural dance.

As the speaker looks around, he recognises the figure of 'Littlebody', 'Hugging his bag I under his left arm, with his eyes closed'. Taken aback, the speaker loses his footing and then their eyes meet. Littlebody scuttles 'up the slope with his gear', resembling some sort of fairytale bogeyman, with 'his hump, elbows out and neck back'. In a series of commands that are strongly reminiscent of a children's bedtime story, the speaker demands of Littlebody that he stop:

> 'Stop, Littlebody!
> I found you fair and I want my due.'

When Littlebody obeys and drops his pipes, the poet reacts by reciting the following admonition:

> 'Demon dwarf
> with the German jaw,
> surrender your purse
> with the ghostly gold.'

The incantation has its desired effect and Littlebody accedes to the poet's demand. In a somewhat surreal voice that is 'too big for his body', Littlebody reminds the speaker that they will 'meet again' when he dances in the poet's ashes. Then, 'looking off to one side', this unusual figure tells us that he thought that he was 'safe' in this place from the attention of people such as the poet. Then, running his fingers 'up and down the stops', Littlebody squeezes the bag one last time and 'a slow air' played 'out across the valley'. In an act of gracious magnanimity, the speaker leaves Littlebody and the purse of gold where it was. The poem concludes with the speaker turning his back on Littlebody and making his 'way down to the main road', happy in the knowledge that he has not taken any 'unnecessary risks'.

2. Stylistic Features

This unusual poem, which appears in Kinsella's Peppercanister series, stands apart from the other poems by Kinsella selected for inclusion on the Leaving Certificate syllabus. In order to come to terms with this poem, it is necessary to assign some *symbolic* value to the encounter with the demonic leprechaun, Littlebody. In more than one poem in the Peppercanister series, Kinsella bemoans the prostitution of art for commercial gain. Bearing this in mind, it is possible to read this poem as offering a rebuke to those who would seek to profit from art. While the setting of the poem is obviously an Irish one, it appears far removed from many of the traditional images of Ireland found in popular poetry. It may be that Kinsella views this isolated and almost primeval landscape as offering a clearer vision of poetic inspiration from an Irish perspective:

> From a stony slope half way, behind a rock prow
> with the stones on top for an old mark,
> the music of pipes, distant and clear.

The music that holds the poet's attention may be 'distant', but it also 'clear'. As the poet draws closer to the source of this music, he sights the leprechaun, Littlebody. European folklore contains many stories of treasure-hoarding faeries, but the leprechaun is particular to Ireland. Although versions of the leprechaun myth vary, he is commonly seen to guard a pot of gold, which is in fact a cauldron associated with the crone goddess. According to the myth, if one can gain control of the leprechaun, one is entitled to three wishes and the cauldron of gold. It is believed that the origin of this myth is rooted in crone worship and that the gold is symbolic of spiritual attainment. While Kinsella draws heavily on the traditions of the myth, the leprechaun's gold seems to symbolise artistic integrity rather than spiritual attainment:

> You have to give the music a while to itself sometimes,
> up out of the huckstering
>
> – jumping around in your green top hat
> and showing your skills
> with your eye on your income.'

The 'huckstering' to which Kinsella refers is the compromises that many artists make in order to appeal to a wider audience and increase their material gain. In many respects, Kinsella has always felt isolated from his contemporaries. Speaking about Irish poets writing in either Irish or English, he has said:

> The word 'colleagues' fades on the lips before the reality: a scattering of incoherent lives ... I can learn nothing from them except that I am isolated.

Although obviously impressed by Littlebody's skill as an artist, the poet decides to leave the creature be. In the final two three-line stanzas, the speaker acknowledges that artistic independence comes at a price and that sometimes it is best not to take risks:

I left him to himself.

And left the purse where it was.

I have all I need for the while I have left

without taking unnecessary risks.

And made my way down to the main road

with my mind on our next meeting.

The 'main road' must be viewed as a **_metaphor_** for mainstream artistic endeavour. In the end, the poet returns from the heights of the mountaintop to level ground.

3. Essay Writing

If you choose to mention 'Littlebody' in any essay on Thomas Kinsella that you may be asked to write, you may wish to keep some of the following points in mind.

a. This poem stands apart from the other poems by Kinsella on the course. In this respect, it may be possible to contrast the poem with many of the other poems that you have studied.

b. In this poem, Kinsella hints at the price he has paid for refusing to compromise his artistic integrity.

c. Once again, Kinsella blurs the lines between mythology and reality. The encounter with Littlebody recalls many of the other quasi-mythological encounters in Kinsella's poetry.

Critical Commentary: Tear

See the text of the poem on pp. 128–31.

1. Content

This is yet another poem by Kinsella that confronts the uncomfortable theme of death. The poem centres on the young speaker's painful recollection of his grandmother's death. This depressing event is complicated further because as the poet witnesses his father's reaction to his grandmother's passing, he is reminded of this man's suffering and tears over the earlier death of an infant daughter.

The poem opens with the child being 'sent in to see' the dying woman. In the second stanza, the speaker describes how his 'heart shrank' as he was swallowed in the 'chambery dusk'. In order to emphasise the all-encompassing nature of this experience, the speaker describes the smell of 'disused | organs and sour kidney'. In the third stanza, the speaker's attention is drawn to his grandmother's 'black aprons', which lie 'folded at the foot of the bed'. Standing in the 'last watery light' of dusk, the poet's memories of this woman are interrupted by someone urging him to 'Go in and say goodbye to her'. At this point in the poem, the speaker stresses the intense nature of this experience by telling us that he felt as if he had been 'carried off | to unfathomable depths'. In the final line of the fourth stanza, we are told that he 'turned to look at' his grandmother. The dying woman looked 'distracted' and appeared to be 'resting for the next attack'.

In the sixth stanza, the poet reveals something of her personality when he tells us that lines on her mouth were marks of her 'ill-temper'. Despite the fact that her 'hair | was loosened out like a young woman's', the poet reminds us of her impending death by describing the strands of shadow 'criss-crossing her forehead'. Ominously, these appear to tie her down, dragging her towards the larger shadows that cover the floor. Unusually, the poet describes himself as being fearful that the dying woman might tempt him with some 'fierce wheedling whisper':

> to hide myself one last time
> against her, and bury my
> self in her drying mud.

In the eleventh stanza, the young speaker betrays his immaturity by describing his uncertainty as to how to proceed. Wondering if he should kiss her, he admits that he would rather kiss 'the damp that crept | in the flowered walls' of the room. Realising that he 'had to kiss' her and kneeling by the 'bulk of the death bed', the young speaker sank his face into the old woman's black aprons. At this point, the poet feels carried away into what he describes as a 'derelict place', and in the process memories of an earlier loss that befell the family begin to surface. This painful memory centres upon the death of his younger sister, when his normally harsh grandmother attempted to soothe the poet's grieving father:

but her voice, soft, talking to someone
about my father: 'God help him, he cried
big tears over there by the machine
for the poor little thing.' [...]

The speaker describes his own incoherent attempts to express his sadness for this child as a primitive 'wail of child-animal grief'. The pain he felt then is reawakened by his presence in his dying grandmother's room. When the dying woman 'shuddered tiredly', the speaker manages to break free and leave the room. Realising that his embrace was less than whole hearted, the poet promises to himself that he would 'really kiss' her 'when she was really dead'.

Although the poet has clearly been marked by this experience, the adults, such as his grandfather, barely seem to notice his re-emergence from his grandmother's room. Feeling awkward, the poet fidgeted for a while before leaving the house. Outside, he 'felt better able to breathe'. In the final two stanzas of the poem, the poet attempts to gain perspective on his experience at his grandmother's deathbed. He sees old age as a type of appetite that 'can digest I anything'. The entirety of one's life must eventually be consumed by death. For the old, the journey to death and heaven is a 'long and hard' one. However, in the tragic case of his little sister Agnes, she vanished 'with early tears'.

2. Stylistic Features

In this complex poem, Kinsella relives his first understanding of death. All the fear, confusion and even repulsion associated with this event are clearly evident. It is important to bear in mind that the journey into his grandmother's death chamber is a **metaphor** for the inner journey of understanding and awareness that the poet undertakes. Extreme fear takes hold of the young child as he makes this difficult journey downward into the depths of knowing:

I couldn't stir at first, nor wished to,
for fear she might turn and tempt me
(my own father's mother)
with open mouth

– with some fierce wheedling whisper –
to hide myself one last time
against her, and bury my
self in her drying mud.

If you have read 'Hen Woman', which is also contained in this anthology, you should already be familiar with the significance of this grandmother figure to Kinsella's poetry. Kinsella's poetry is heavily influenced by the writings of the Swiss psychiatrist Carl Jung. This revolutionary and extremely influential thinker founded a type of psychoanalysis known as analytical psychology. Jung was virtually alone amongst 19th-century thinkers in believing that human beings had placed far too much emphasis on science and needed to return to the realms of the *mythological* and the spiritual in order to obtain a true understanding of what defines our humanity. In particular, Jung believed that certain innate universal archetypes had the profoundest influence on human thinking. He identified numerous such archetypes, including the woman figure. In many of Kinsella's poems, the women of his childhood are representative archetypal feminine figures that are strongly influenced by Jungian thinking. In Jungian psychology, the male needs to struggle with, understand and eventually accommodate the feminine element of his masculine identity in order to achieve a sense of balance. Jung also believed that there were numerous ways in which such archetypes could be analysed and understood. In particular, he emphasised the importance of dreams but also stressed the necessity of examining our fantasies, memories, imaginative and creative projects and the events of our daily lives. This is essentially what Kinsella does in this poem. He takes a powerful memory of a transformative event that occurred during his childhood and analyses it in the deepest possible manner so as to cast light on his understanding of death. In many respects, the grandmother figure in this poem is a Jungian archetype. In the poem, she becomes a representative of a version of femininity that recalls the Cailleach of Irish mythology.

Similar to Hecate in Greek myth, the Cailleach is one of the most intriguing and significant figures in Irish mythology. Some tales portray her as a benevolent and primal figure who, from the dawn of time, has shaped the land and controlled the forces of nature, while others depict her as the harsh spirit of winter. According to the critic Brian John, the *epiphanic* moment that occurs in this poem is brought about 'through contact with the grandmother-cailleach, just as in Irish myth union with the cailleach brings illumination and, in certain instances, sovereignty'. If we accept that the grandmother figure in this poem is representative of the mythological Cailleach, then the illumination and understanding that the speaker receives is the knowledge centring on death and decay. The farewell kiss that he forces himself to bestow carries the speaker to a 'derelict' place in his imagination that smells of 'ash'.

There are constant reminders in the poem of the youth and life that once characterised this dying woman. The speaker emphasises the grandmother's hair 'loosened out like a young woman's I all over the pillow', 'her mouth and eyes' and his unreasoned fear that she might 'tempt' him. While her youthful femininity is now all but consumed by the shadowy tangles of death, it does remind the poet of a kinder, softer aspect to his grandmother's being. Thus, having tasted the ash and decay of death, what the speaker now experiences is the compassion of his dying grandmother that once moved her to tears over her own son's loss.

In this respect, the grandmother has a dual function in the poem. On the one hand, she represents a dark and rather sinister temptation that draws the boy towards her. This aspect of her persona is closely linked to the speaker's awareness of decay and impending death. The 'smell of disused I organs and sour kidney' that overwhelms the young speaker is a disturbing reminder of how close the old woman is to death. Yet the grandmother also represents a deep and comforting wisdom that can at least ease some of the harsh realities of death. This aspect of the grandmother persona is conveyed through the speaker's memory of her kind words to his father following the death of his daughter:

> [...] And I found
> what I was looking for
> – not heat nor fire,
> not any comfort,
>
> but her voice, soft, talking to someone
> about my father: 'God help him, he cried
> big tears over there by the machine
> for the poor little thing.' [...]

According to Maurice Harmon, the speaker's understanding is gained by 'facing the aged woman and the fears associated with her, an understanding of life's cruel ordeals, a wider sense of life and death, and a respect for the capacity of old people to "digest" experience'. Interestingly, both the speaker and the grandmother never actually communicate in this poem, but instead concentrate on their own experience. It could be that Kinsella is attempting to emphasise the uncomfortable truth of the solitary nature of understanding.

Perhaps the most remarkable stylistic feature of this poem is the manner in which Kinsella manages to explore profound ideas concerning life and death in language that is wholly ordinary and unremarkable. The **rhythms** and **cadences** of everyday speech are combined with a very commonplace **metre**. In this manner, Kinsella lends a simple authority to his narrative. The memories of the child are faithfully recreated with chilling clarity. As with all good poetry, it is left to the reader to provide perspective on and interpret the significance of the speaker's recollections.

3. Essay Writing

If you are thinking of making reference to 'Tear' in any essay by Kinsella that you may be asked to write, you may want to consider some of the following key points.

a. Once again, Kinsella concentrates on the theme of death and decay. This theme is central to many of the poems by Kinsella on the course. In this respect, it is possible to compare and contrast 'Tear' with many of the other poems that you have studied.

b. The grandmother is a powerful figure in Kinsella's poetry. In many of his poems, his grandmother serves a symbolic function that is closely linked to mythology. In nearly every poem that features his grandmother, she plays a pivotal role in guiding the poet to greater understanding.

c. 'Tear' presents us with extremely complex and thought-provoking ideas in language that is clear and readily understandable.

Critical Commentary: Hen Woman

See the text of the poem on pp. 132–4.

1. Content

This complex poem first appeared in Kinsella's 1973 collection *New Poems: Notes from the Land of the Dead*. 'Hen Woman' purports to tell the story of the young speaker as he watched an old woman (named as Mrs Delaney in an earlier version of the poem) rush from her cottage to pick up a hen about to lay an egg. The poem opens with an atmospheric depiction of his grandmother's yard that appeals to all the senses:

> The noon heat in the yard
> smelled of stillness and coming thunder.
> A hen scratched and picked at the shore.

As the hen stopped and crouched its body, the 'brooding silence' in the yard 'seemed to say "Hush…"'. Meanwhile, the 'cottage door opened' and the contrast between the bright light outside and the darkness of the dwelling creates the appearance of 'a black hole'. In fact, the light thrown off the whitewashed wall was so bright as to cause the speaker's eyes to narrow. In the closing line of the second stanza, a clock sounds, and then in the next one-line stanza, the speaker emphasises the utter familiarity of the scene:

> (I had felt all this before.)

Then, in the fourth stanza, the speaker's grandmother rushes 'out in her slippers | muttering, her face dark with anger'. Although she moves quickly to gather up the hen before it lays its egg, the old woman is 'Too late'.

In the fifth stanza, the young speaker is transfixed by the hen's 'pebble eyes'. Then a 'white egg showed in the sphincter' and the creature's mouth and beak open in unison. From the speaker's point of view, time appeared to stand still and 'Nothing moved' as both hen and woman remained 'locked' in a strange form of embrace. This sensation of time having been slowed down continues in the seventh stanza, where the speaker makes a 'tiny movement' and notices that:

> A beetle like a bronze leaf
> was inching across the cement,
> clasping with small tarsi
> a ball of dung bigger than its body.

The poet's perception of the scene is intense and magnified. He notices the 'serrated brow' of the beetle, which he imagines as pressing the 'ground humbly'. For the rest of this stanza, the poet continues to trace the slow progress of the beetle as it advanced 'minutely, | losing a few fragments' of the ball of dung.

In the ninth stanza, a 'mutter of thunder' in the far distance reminds the poet that 'time [has] not quite stopped'. Meanwhile, it appears that the egg had moved a fraction, and in the tenth stanza, as the speaker continues to observe the hen, the 'mystery [is] completed':

> The black zero of the orifice
> close to a point
> and the white zero of the egg hung free,
> flecked with greenish brown oils.

As the egg falls free, it turns slowly and drops 'to the shore'.

There is a sharp change in the poem's **tone** in the twelfth stanza. The voice of the mature narrator intrudes to inform us that he still feeds on this egg. This is puzzling at first, until we realise that he is referring to the manner in which this event has nourished his imagination, which he describes as the 'yolk of one's being'. Once the event that he has just described became lodged in his imagination, it grew. Over the course of the next few lines, the way in which this event fed and fired the poet's imagination is likened to the growth of a living organism:

> dividing blindly, twitching, packed with will,
> searching in its own tissue
> for the structure in which it may wake.

Over the course of 'what seemed a whole year', the events of that day in his grandmother's yard took shape in the poet's inner mind. In fact, such was the power of this event on the poet's imagination that he believes it will probably continue to influence his thinking until the day he dies:

> As it will continue to fall, probably, until I die,
> through the vast indifferent spaces
> with which I am empty.

Then, in the penultimate stanza, we return to the hen laying its egg. The egg has now fallen through the hands of the speaker's grandmother and the entire event is 'over in a comical flash'. For a moment, the 'soft mucous shell clung' to the sides of the drain and then disappeared. His grandmother 'stood staring, in blank anger'. However, this anger does not last for long as the old woman laughingly admits that there are plenty more eggs 'where that [one] came from'.

2. Stylistic Features

'Hen Woman' is the first poem in the subsection of Kinsella's collection *Notes from the Land of the Dead* entitled 'An Egg of Being'. All five poems in this part of the collection focus on early childhood experiences that are grounded in reality. On a cursory reading, this poem can appear as nothing more than a straightforward, even simplistic narration of an event that impressed itself on the speaker's imagination. However, upon closer inspection it becomes clear that this is a complex and difficult poem that rewards our close attention. Throughout the subsection 'An Egg of Being', strands of **imagery** appear and reappear in such a way as to create connections that deepen our understanding of both this poem and the other poems in the sequence.

More than one critic has noticed that 'Hen Woman' is heavily influenced by the writings of Carl Jung. Jung was a Swiss psychiatrist and influential thinker who founded a type of psychoanalysis known as analytical psychology. Jung was virtually alone amongst 19th-century thinkers in believing that human beings had placed far too much emphasis on science and needed to return to the realms of the **mythological** and the spiritual in order to obtain a true understanding of what defines our humanity. In particular, Jung believed that certain innate universal archetypes had the profoundest influence on human thinking. He identified numerous such archetypes, including the woman figure, and symbols of fertility such as the egg. In many of Kinsella's poems, the women of his childhood are representative archetypal feminine figures that are strongly influenced by Jungian thinking. In Jungian psychology, the male needs to struggle with, understand and eventually accommodate the feminine element of his masculine identity in order to achieve a sense of balance. Jung also believed that there were numerous ways in which such archetypes could be analysed and understood. In particular, he emphasised the importance of dreams, but also stressed the necessity of examining our fantasies, memories, imaginative and creative projects and the events of our daily lives. This is essentially what Kinsella does in this poem. He takes an ordinary moment that occurred during his childhood and analyses it in the deepest possible manner so as to cast light on his growth as an individual.

The poem opens with a hyper-realistic and painstaking depiction of an egg emerging out the darkness of the hen's 'sphincter'. This event coincides with the emergence of an old woman from the 'dark hole' that is her cottage. In the first section of the poem, the events are narrated entirely by the voice of child. In this manner, it is possible to conclude that this event had a profound effect on the young Kinsella. In an earlier version of the poem which was first published in the *Irish Press*, Kinsella described the event in a more straightforward, less emblematic fashion:

> One day of midsummer,
> when I was ten years old,
> the noon stillness seemed heavier
> than I had ever known it.
> The silent heat
> Smelled of dryness and coming thunder.
> Mrs Delaney's cottage door was open
> like a black cave-mouth
> in a whitewashed wall so bright
> the eyes narrowed.
> In the middle of the yard
> near the shore a hen scratched
> and picked at the cement.
> The brooding silence seemed to say 'Hush!'
> Inside, a clock murmured 'Gong...'
> (To this day that sound will bring it back to me:
> the hot cement around the iron grating,
> the stale cool breath from the underworld.)

Only two lines survived the revisions that Kinsella made to the version that is included on the Leaving Certificate syllabus. However, from the revisions that Kinsella made to this earlier version, it is clear that he intended to concentrate more on the symbolic importance of the event than on his actual recollection of that day. For this reason, in the finished version of the poem, Kinsella chooses to interrupt the child's narrative with a series of meditations that seek to cast light on the significance of this event.

The **symbol** of the egg is of course a rich one. In this poem, Kinsella uses the egg symbol to signify the way ideas grow and contribute to our sense of identity. The egg emerging from the sphincter and the woman emerging from the doorway are both associated with growth and transformation. It is possible to read this poem as an attempt by the poet to trace the progress to what Carl Jung described as 'individuation'. In Jungian psychology, individuation is the development of the self, achieved by resolving the conflicts arising at life's key stages. In particular, Jung stressed the transition from adolescence to adulthood. Jung believed this process could not be completed until middle age. This is why the older voice of the mature poet orders and directs the recollection of the younger narrator. If we take this reading of the poem, then it is possible to conclude that this event is both a key one in the development of the poet's being and a symbolic representation of that development. Watching the egg being laid, the poet is forced to meditate on the processes of creation, which is an unknowable mystery that defies analysis. For this reason, later in life the poet draws from this event and attempts to understand its significance:

> I feed upon it still, as you see;
> there is no end to that which, not understood,
> may yet be hoarded in the imagination,

Another significant event that took place on that day is the poet's recollection of the beetle struggling to carry a ball of dung. The beetle may be an **allusion** to the Egyptian scarab, which is a long-standing symbol for renewal and rebirth. Notice how the beetle, in its slow progress, is forming and shaping a circle of sorts. In this manner, the speaker again reminds us of the process of creation. Thus, three relatively ordinary events (the emergence of the old woman from the shadows, the laying of an egg and the rolling of a ball of dung) initiate the young child into mysteries of creation. Interestingly, the **imagery** is also suggestive of the undeniable fact that creation implies destruction. The egg is destroyed, the woman is old and nearing death and the beetle is an uncomfortable image that has often been associated with rotting flesh. The mysterious aspect of this process is emphasised by the fact that the we do not know which came first, the poet's recollection of the vision or the actual event, as the poem stresses that the speaker 'had felt all this before'. In its barest form, then, the emergence of the egg becomes the entire mystery of birth and death in general and the poet's sense of who he is in particular.

Essentially, this poem amounts to a deep and complex reflection on the mystery of creation. This creation takes place on two levels in the poem. Firstly, we have the egg and the dung beetle, each struggling with creation. Then, on a deeper level, we have the emergence of the speaker's identity as a poet and his growing awareness of the creative process. In the twelfth stanza, the poet attempts to describe this process at work. As the memory of the events of that day lay 'hoarded in [his] imagination', it grew in an almost organic fashion:

> dividing blindly, twitching, packed with will,
> searching in its own tissue
> for the structure in which it may wake.

Towards the end of his meditation, the poet hints at the fact that this event is central to his growth as a creative being:

> […] it will continue to fall, probably, until I die,
> through the vast indifferent spaces
> with which I am empty.

In a pervious version of the poem, the speaker translates the old woman's dismissive cry of indifference 'It's all the one. | There's plenty more where that came from!' into what at first seems like a childlike slogan:

> Hen to pan!
> It was a simple world.

In this version of the poem, 'Hen to pan' is an ***allusion*** to the Greek *Hen tō pan*, which is an ancient Greek alchemical formula meaning 'one in all'. Kinsella must have known that this inscription is regularly found alongside some interpretations of the ancient Greek Ouroboros. The Ouroboros is commonly depicted by a snake devouring its own tail so as to form a circle. For the Greeks, the Ouroboros represented self-reflexivity, or the cyclical nature of existence, especially in the sense of something constantly re-creating itself. Thus (depending on which version you read), in the concluding line of this complex and thought-provoking poem, the poet returns to the idea of the cycle or circle of creation.

3. Essay Writing

If you are going to include 'Hen Woman' in an essay, you may want to mention some of the following points.

a. This poem is very deceptive. On a first reading, it appears straightforward, but further exploration reveals that this is a complex poem.
b. The poem is rich in ***allusion*** to Greek mythology and Jungian thinking.
c. This is a deep and thought-provoking poem that rewards the reader's efforts.

Critical Commentary: His Father's Hands

See the text of the poem on pp. 136–9.

1. Content

In this long poem, Kinsella evokes family traditions. The poem centres on the poet's recollection of his father's ***hyperbolic*** narration of the Kinsella family lineage. Taking the form of a conversation between the poet and his father, the poem opens with the narrator telling us that he 'drank firmly I and set the glass down [...] firmly'. The poet stresses his father's hyperbole when he says that:

> His finger prodded and prodded,
> marring his point. Emphas-
> emphasemphasis.

At this point in the poem, the poet is reminded of the family similarities that exist between the generations. The manner in which the speaker's grandfather used to cup and tighten 'the black Plug' of tobacco 'between knife and thumb' is recalled by the sight of his father's hands.

In the course of the next three stanzas, the narrator provides us with instances of his grandfather's skill as an artisan. Kinsella's grandfather, who originally worked for Guinness, became a cobbler in his retirement. It is the poet's memories of this period in his grandfather's life that dominate this section of the poem:

> carving off little curlicues
> to rub them in the dark of his palms,
>
> or cutting into new leather at his bench,
> levering a groove open with his thumb,
> insinuating wet sprigs for the hammer.
>
> He kept the sprigs in mouthfuls
> and brought them out in silvery
> units between his lips.

These vivid recollections of his grandfather's skill as an artisan cause the poet to recognise the connections that exist between the generations of the wider Kinsella family.

In the ninth stanza, the poet recalls his grandfather's skill as a musician. Such was his ability as a fiddle player that it seemed as if 'his bow hand [was] scarcely moving'. The poet then tells us that whenever he hears folk songs such as 'The Wind That Shakes the Barley', his memories of his grandfather are so strong that they manage to bridge the 'void' of time and even death.

A distinct shift in the poem occurs in the thirteenth stanza. The poet's memory of the lyrics of 'The Wind That Shakes the Barley' causes him to delve further back into his family history. This famous ballad, penned by Robert Dwyer Joyce, is written from the perspective of a doomed young Wexford rebel. In the song, this young man's involvement with the 1798 Rebellion causes him to turn his back on his relationship with a young woman. As the poet moves beyond his grandfather's generation, he is brought back through the years to a time when members of his family 'met with and helped | many of the Croppies in hiding from the Yeos'. The Croppies were so called because many of the rebels wore their hair in a closely cropped fashion. This hairstyle was an act of defiance, as it was seen by the authorities as sympathising with the anti-wig and consequently anti-aristocrat French revolutionaries. According to the narrator in this poem, his family ancestors sheltered such Croppies as 'the Laceys', who were 'later hanged on the Bridge in Ballinglen | between Tinahely and Anacorra'.

In the course of the next two stanzas, the poet continues his potted history of his family ancestors. We learn that they worked as 'Stone Cutters | or masons' and then in the '18 | and late 1700s' they became farmers. Tracing his family history even further back, the poet suggests that his ancestors originally lived in 'Farnese among a Colony | of North of Ireland or Scotch settlers'.

In the third section of the poem, a shift occurs in the temporal perspective of the narrator. As in the previous section, this movement further back in time is signalled by the words 'Beyond that'. As the poet moves further back in time, we are brought to a primeval, even hellish landscape. This is a threatening place:

> Littered uplands. Dense grass. Rocks everywhere,
> wet underneath, retaining memory of the long cold.
>
> First, a prow of land
> chosen, and webbed with tracks;
> then boulders chosen
> and sloped together, stabilized in menace.

The speaker tells us that he is frightened by this place and instinctively feels that 'Terrible things happened' here.

In the fourth and penultimate movement of the poem, the poet contemplates the interconnections that have been created by the various 'Dispersals or migrations'. He cites the evolutions or accidents that eventually resulted in his grandfather playing the fiddle 'by the fireside'. In the next stanza of the fourth section of the poem, as the speaker works on the very bench his grandfather used, he recalls the old man at work as a cobbler:

> That serene pause, with the slashing knife,
> in kindly mockery,

In the final two stanzas of this section of the poem, the speaker meditates on the links that exist from generation to generation. The blood that advances from family member to family member carries with it similarities that are modulated or changed slightly in the succeeding generations.

In the final stanza, the speaker focuses his attention on his grandfather's 'block'. The sight of this 'Extraordinary' 'big block' has given rise to the intense meditation on the poet's family history. This wooden instrument is transformed in the speaker's imagination into an organic living thing:

> it turned under my hands, an axis
> of light flashing down its length,
> and the wood's soft flesh broke open,
> countless little nails
> squirming and dropping out of it.

2. Stylistic Features

In his personal account of his own family history, Kinsella included the following preface to 'His Father's Hands':

> It was later in life, when I was on equal terms with my father, that something else important out of that early time became clear: the dignity and quiet of his own father, remembered as we talked about him. With an awareness of the generations as they succeed each other. That process, with the accompanying awareness, recorded and understood, are a vital element in life as I see it now.

This complex poem draws heavily on the poet's uncle Jack Brophy's handwritten history of the Kinsella family. According to Brophy, the menfolk in the family were either:

> Stone Cutters or Masons or probably both. in the 17 and late 1800s even the Farmers had some other trade to make a living. The Kinsellas lived in Farnese (it's now White Rock) among a colony of North of Ireland or Scotch settlers left there in some of the dispersals, or migrations which occurred in this Area of Wicklow, Wexford and Carlow. [...] The Kinsellas met with and helped many of the Croppies in hiding from the

Yeos or on their way home after the defeat in south Wexford. And some years before that time the Family came from somewhere round Tullow.

In the course of the poem, Kinsella moves from a conversation over drinks between father and adult son, through a series of vivid reminiscences of his grandfather cutting tobacco, working as a cobbler and playing traditional music, to an examination of the family history, and finally to a meditation on the nature of generational and even race memory.

The title contains the dominant **metaphor** running throughout this poem and indeed much of Kinsella's poetry. The hands that the title speaks of are **symbolic** of the physical similarities that exist between generations. However, hands are also symbolic of the way we communicate with each other. They imply touch, trust and symbolise the skills that men such as his grandfather pass down to succeeding generations.

Perhaps the most remarkable stylistic feature of this poem is the manner in which Kinsella manages to blend history with intense meditation. Although the poem moves across the span of time, it is neither sentimental nor nostalgic. In a series of fragmentary sentences, Kinsella presents the reader with a succession of tactile images that eventually lead to a complex and thought-provoking abstraction. However, even as the poem draws to a close and reaches its most abstract point, Kinsella never loses touch with the primary tactile reality that provoked his mediation. The poem ends in a profound **epiphany**:

> Extraordinary … The big block – I found it
> years afterward in a corner of the yard
> in sunlight after rain
> and stood it up, wet and black:
> it turned under my hands, an axis
> of light flashing down its length,
> and the wood's soft flesh broke open,
> countless little nails
> squirming and dropping out of it.

According to Donatella Abate Baddin, this is a 'luminous moment of writing in which imagination assimilates the past and sets itself up as the basis of the emergent self'.

This poem first appeared in the 1979 collection *One*. Throughout this collection (and indeed Kinsella's wider body of work), the **motifs** of the phoenix and the snake shedding its golden skin appear. These are obviously metaphors for renewal and regeneration. As the speaker listens intently to tales of his family from back in the day when they worked as 'Stone Cutters' or helped fleeing 'Croppies', he is led back beyond this point to a primeval imagining of his origins. In this sense, Kinsella's aim in this poem is to attempt to understand the process of generation and regeneration and how it culminates in himself. The cold and threatening place that the poet imagines as being the location for the genesis of his family line gives way to the peace and 'gentleness' that he associates with his grandfather. In the words of Brian John, 'despite his sense of evil, the poet has been brought to peace, patience and gentleness, which also constitute the inheritance and have moulded his self'.

His grandfather's wooden block, which forms the centre of the final powerful and epiphanic stanza, symbolises the poet's profound sense of himself as an individual linked but separate from the previous generations. The form and structure of these final lines, with their reliance on **dactyls** (stressed syllables followed by unstressed syllables), create a sense of the moment's importance. Closely resembling embryonic cells or spermatozoa, the nails break free of the womb-like block and begin their existence separate from but always linked to the wood that housed them. In this manner, they resemble the poet's own existence and journey towards selfhood, individuation and independence. Thus, while the poem acknowledges the powerful influences that place and shared history have on forming our identities, it ends with a compelling assertion of the very human need for individual identity.

3. Essay Writing

If you are thinking of making reference to 'His Father's Hands' in any response to Kinsella's poetry that you may be asked to make, try to bear the following points in mind.

a. Once again, Kinsella draws on the people and places of his native Dublin for inspiration.
b. The poem manages to combine concrete imagery with complex and abstract notions concerning identity and race memory.
c. In more than one poem, Kinsella examines his emerging sense of his own identity. As such, it may be useful to compare and contrast this poem with 'Hen Woman'.

Critical Commentary: Model School, Inchicore

See the text of the poem on pp. 141–2.

1. Content

In his preface to 'Model School, Inchicore' in the 2006 collection *A Dublin Documentary*, Kinsella had the following to say:

> Toward Inchicore; 'island of berries'. Where the main road divided. To the left, toward the midlands, and Naas of the Kings. To the right, toward Chapelizod, on the River Liffey. On the angle of division, the triangular playground of the Model School, with the old chestnut trees; where once, when the weather was very satisfactory — and probably something else — our very good school-teacher, Mr. Brown, took us out into the sun and sat us down to share his pleasure.

It is obvious from reading this poem that Kinsella has fond memories of his time in Inchicore. The opening stanza, with its talk of 'blank paper and marla' and 'plasticine', should be familiar to anyone who attended a national school in the Republic of Ireland. In these stanzas, Kinsella adopts the voice of a young child as he recalls the classroom activities at Inchicore Model School. In the third stanza, the poet remembers the childish pleasure that he and his friends took when they recited 'the adding-up table in Irish' and came to Miss Carney's name. When said in quick succession or repeated quickly, the Irish words for 'four' and 'nine' sound like 'Carney':

> Cúig is a dó, Seacht
> Cúig is a trí, Ocht
> Cúig is a Ceathair, Naoi (*CEARNOAI*).

In the next stanza, the poet moves on in time to 'the second school', where he had 'Mr Browne'. The childish description of this man is charming and endears the reader to him:

He had white teeth in his brown man's face.

He stood in front of the black board
and chalked a white dot.

The final two-line stanza of the first section of the poem, where the speaker tells us that he is 'going to know | everything', hints at its central theme – knowledge.

The next section of the poem centres on Kinsella's recollection of one particularly fine day when Mr Browne said, '"Out into the sun!"' The children were 'delighted' and the idyllic location of this impromptu classroom is more in keeping with a pastoral setting than an inner-city school.

The fourth section of the poem focuses on the passing of time and a clear change in the season. In quick succession, the childish narrative voice recalls heaping the 'big chestnut leaves', 'jumping over the heaps' and racing his classmates. The next section of the poem provides us with a glimpse of the young poet as a solitary figure contemplating 'the draught | blowing the papers | around the wheels of the bicycles'. This meditative moment is interrupted by the overtly religious language of a more adult voice. Echoing the words of the Catechism of Trent, the young boy wonders if 'God will judge | our most secret thoughts and actions'.

In the poem closes with a powerful *gustatory image*:

The taste
of ink off
the nib shrank your
mouth.

The bitter taste of knowledge is obviously associated with the fall from innocence that the mention of the Catechism implies.

2. Stylistic Features

Perhaps the most impressive stylistic feature of this memory poem is the manner in which the poet recreates a child's view of the world. Through the language, diction and *imagery*, Kinsella provides us with a vivid recreation of his childhood in Inchicore. As with many of the other poems on the Leaving Certificate syllabus, 'Model School, Inchicore' traces the slow emergence of Kinsella's consciousness.

This poem was originally chosen by Kinsella to open his 1985 collection, *Songs from the Psyche*. Contained under the subsection 'Settings', 'Model School, Inchicore' examines the way in which knowledge transforms the psyche and plays a pivotal role in determining who we become.

The poem opens with the poet's earliest memories of his most formative years. At the same time, the poem's language captures the subtle social changes that have occurred in Ireland since Kinsella's time in school. The use of the word 'marla' and the rote learning of mathematical tables in Irish demonstrate clearly just how embedded the Irish language was in the primary education system. In the next stanza, the same 'marla' is transformed by the poet into a snake:

> You started with a ball of it
> and rolled it into a snake curling
> around your hand, and kept rolling it
> in one place until it wore down into two
> with a stain on the paper.

Throughout Kinsella's wider body of work, **motifs** of the snake appear. In 'His Father's Hands' and in some versions of 'Hen Woman', snake-like images represent self-reflexivity or the cyclical nature of existence, especially in the sense of something constantly recreating itself. In this sense, the reference to the chid remoulding the 'marla' into the shape of a snake is more than just a passing coincidence, for this is exactly what lies at the heart of this poem: as the speaker journeys through his school years, he remakes and reforms his sense of who he actually is. This journey embraces his sense of himself as an Irishman (the impromptu history lessons of Mr Browne) and culminates in his reassessment of his relationship with God (the recitation of the Catechism).

In the final two movements of the poem, the poet recalls the time before his Confirmation. In the Catholic religion, as a child prepares for Confirmation, he or she is encouraged to see the Holy Spirit working in their own lives. During the Sacrament of Confirmation, children renew the baptismal promises made by their parents on their behalf when they were infants. Thus, in a clever manner the **image** of the snake and the strong connections with renewal that it holds in Kinsella's poetry are recalled in the closing moments of the poem. It should also be pointed out that the poem makes it clear that judgement, and the fall from grace that it often implies, are inextricably bound up with our thirst for knowledge. It is difficult not to recall the Garden of Eden, where a snake tempted mankind to eat from the Tree of Knowledge. This simply written yet thought-provoking poem examines the role that knowledge plays in our growth as individuals and our development as spiritual beings. However, the poem also hints that knowledge can be bitter in that it implies a loss of innocence.

3. Essay Writing

If you are thinking of making reference to 'Model School, Inchicore', you may wish to keep the following points in mind.

a. Yet again, Kinsella draws on his memories of the people and places of Dublin for inspiration. Given that Dublin forms the backdrop to so many of the poems by Kinsella on the course, you may wish to devote an entire paragraph to this aspect of his work.

b. Once again, Kinsella addresses the process of learning and growth. In more than one poem on the course ('Hen Woman', 'Mirror in February'), Kinsella examines the process of change.

c. Despite the complex nature of the poem's theme, the manner in which Kinsella expresses his ideas is straightforward and accessible.

Critical Commentary: from The Familiar: VII

See the text of the poem on pp. 144–5.

1. Content

Kinsella's wife, Eleanor, is a profoundly important presence in the poet's life. For over 40 years, she has acted as his muse and partner. His relationship with 'Fair Ellinor', as he has described her, has provided him with the stability needed to undertake the painful explorations of his own psyche that have dominated much of his later verse. One critic has pointed out that 'the void that Kinsella's poetic explorations find at the centre of human existence becomes tolerable in the knowledge that he shares his time on this earth with a woman whom he truly loves'. The extract chosen for study for the Leaving Certificate course is the final section of a much longer poem. Here in this poem, Kinsella presents us with an intimate glimpse into a breakfast rite. The opening stanza presents the speaker as a solitary figure 'looking out through the frost on the window'. Outside the warmth of the kitchen on 'the hill opposite', 'the sheets of frost' lie 'scattered down among the rocks'. A watchful cat completes this domestic tableau. As the poet prepares the breakfast, one cannot help but feel that the scene is reminiscent of a priest preparing a sacrament:

> A chilled grapefruit
> – thin-skinned, with that little gloss.
> I took a mouthful, looking up along the edge of the wood [...]
>
> I sliced the tomatoes in thin discs
> in damp sequence into their dish;
> scalded the kettle; made the tea,
>
> and rang the little brazen bell.

In the final two-stanza movement of the poem, the speaker appears in his dressing gown with his arms extended as the subject of his efforts comes into view. Like some divine apparition, his wife's 'shade showed in the door' and praises his efforts.

2. Stylistic Features

The language and *imagery* in this poem are firmly rooted in the domestic. Perhaps the most interesting stylistic feature of the poem is the manner in which Kinsella draws heavily from a well-known episode of James Joyce's *Ulysses*. In the 'Calypso' episode, Leopold Bloom fixes breakfast for his wife, Molly, and feeds his cat:

> The coals were reddening.
>
> Another slice of bread and butter: three, four: right. She didn't like her plate full. Right. He turned from the tray, lifted the kettle off the hob and set it sideways on the fire. It sat there, dull and squat, its spout stuck out. Cup of tea soon. Good. Mouth dry. The cat walked stiffly round a leg of the table with tail on high.

It is easy to see the extent to which Joyce has influenced Kinsella in this poem. Much like Bloom in Joyce's 'Calypso' episode, the speaker in this poem is enthralled and captivated by his wife's presence. Joyce named his episode of the book 'Calypso' after the Greek goddess Calypso, who detained the Great hero Odysseus on her island. In Kinsella's poem, the manner in which the speaker prepares breakfast is likened to a sacramental offering fit for a goddess. The slow, deliberate preparation of the 'chilled grapefruit', the 'tomatoes in thin discs', 'the tea' and the ringing of 'the little brazen bell' and the speaker's appearance in his 'dressing gown | with [his] arms extended' do much to reinforce the notion that we are witnessing a sacrament of sorts.

In the final stanza, the link to Greek *mythology* is made stronger when the speaker describes the apparition of his wife at the door:

> Her shade showed in the door.
> Her voice responded:
> 'You are very good. You always made it nice.'

In this final *tercet*, the *image* of the wife as a 'shade' places her firmly in the realm of the afterlife. In the poet's imagination, she is an otherworldly figure haunting and inspiring him.

3. Essay Writing

If you are thinking of making reference to this poem, you may wish to keep some of the following points in mind.

a. So many of Kinsella's poems on the course are inspired by people and places from his background. In this poem, the speaker imaginatively transforms his wife into an almost mythological figure.

b. Mythology plays a central role in many of Kinsella's poems on the course. In this poem, Kinsella *alludes* to Greek mythology as well as pays homage to Joyce's *Ulysses*.

c. Once again, Kinsella uses ordinary language to present complex and thought-provoking ideas.

Critical Commentary: Echo

See the text of the poem on p. 146.

1. Content

This short poem was first published as part of Kinsella's Peppercanister series in 2007. There is a fairytale quality to this poem that recalls childhood stories of old. The opening stanza outlines a journey past a broken gate. An unnamed man has to clear thorns for his lover in order to make it 'through the heart of the wood'. Then, in the second stanza, we learn that the couple 'revealed their names' to each other and 'told their tales'. This journey seems to be the culmination of a promise that was made on the day when 'their love began'. The poem concludes with the *image* of both lovers moving down to the water and the woman whispering a 'final secret'.

2. Stylistic Features

It is difficult to know what to make of this poem. The poem was first published in 2007 by the Peppercanister Press, which Kinsella founded in 1972. Over the course of the past 20 years, Kinsella's Peppercanister poems have changed dramatically in form and content. To begin with, they were heavily influenced by the Anglo-American poet W.H. Auden. Over time, however, Kinsella began to read the writings of the Swiss psychiatrist Carl Jung. Jung was a revolutionary and extremely influential thinker who founded a type of psychoanalysis known as analytical psychology. Jung was virtually alone amongst 19th-century thinkers in believing that human beings had placed far too much emphasis on science and needed to return to the realms of the *mythological* and the spiritual in order to obtain a true understanding of what defines our humanity. Reading 'Echo', it is easy to see the extent to which it draws on the stock images of myth and fairytales. The 'gate', the 'holy well' and the 'heart of the wood' are all familiar ingredients of any good childhood fairytale. Of course, it is possible to look on this simple tale as being a *metaphor* for the progression that takes place in any relationship. If one assigns this reading to the poem, then 'the heart of the wood' becomes *symbolic* of the mystery and even risk that are present when two people begin to trust each other. The sharing of secrets and the telling of tales are also familiar aspects of any love story. As the poem concludes and the couple move closer to one another, Kinsella presents us with a image of renewal or rebirth in the form of water:

> And hand in hand
> they turned to leave.
> When she stopped and whispered
> a final secret
> down to the water.

3. Essay Writing

If you are thinking of referring to 'Echo' in an essay on Kinsella, you may wish to keep the following points in mind.

a. This is yet another example of the role that myth plays in Kinsella's poetry. Given the predominance of this aspect of his work on the syllabus, you may wish to devote an entire paragraph to Kinsella's treatment of myth.
b. The imagery in the poem is archetypal and familiar on a first reading. This makes the poem accessible and memorable.
c. It is possible to assign a metaphorical reading to this poem.

Philip Larkin (1922–85)

A Short Biography

When Philip Larkin died in 1985, England mourned the passing of one of its best-loved poets. He was born on 9 August 1922, the son of Sydney and Eva Larkin. His relationship with his parents is reflected in his lifelong distaste for married life. Although the poet did form close attachments to women, he felt himself incapable of marriage. His father was an extremely bizarre man who displayed a small statue of Hitler on the mantelpiece of their home. Its arm rose in a salute at the press of a button! In his most famous poem, 'This Be the Verse', Larkin outlines, in forceful and common language, his feelings towards his parents:

> They fuck you up, your mum and dad.
>   They may not mean to, but they do.
> They fill you with the faults they had
>   And add some extra, just for you.
>
> But they were fucked up in their turn
>   By fools in old-style hats and coats,
> Who half the time were soppy-stern
>   And half at one another's throats.
>
> Man hands on misery to man.
>   It deepens like a coastal shelf.
> Get out as early as you can,
>   And don't have any kids yourself.

Larkin spent his formative years in Coventry, which was heavily bombed during World War Two. The England of Larkin's youth was a depressing place in which to grow up. Economically devastated by the war, Great Britain was rapidly losing the central role it had once played in world affairs. His memories of this time in his life are reflected in the poem 'I Remember, I Remember':

> [...] I suppose it's not the place's fault,' I said.
>
> 'Nothing, like something, happens anywhere.'

The young poet attended King Henry VIII school in Coventry, where he was, by his own admission, good at nothing but English and where he spent most of his time reading. He completed his A levels and went to Oxford in 1940. Here, he became friendly with the new generation of writers that was beginning to emerge in the post-war years. This group of novelists and poets would later be known as the 'angry young men'. Larkin received a first-class honours degree in 1943, but remained aimless and fell into a job as a librarian at the public library in Wellington. At the same time, he published his first collection of poetry, *The North Ship*. He published two novels in 1946 and 1947. His next collection of poems, *The Less Deceived*, appeared a decade later. In this collection, Larkin began to exhibit the poetic style that we now associate with him: **irony** mixed with precise, detailed descriptions of everyday objects, places, people and events. The collection's melancholic, ironic digs at everyday life and his perceived lack of social etiquette earned the poet the nickname the 'Hermit of Humberside'.

Larkin's 1964 poetry collection, *The Whitsun Weddings*, received the Queen's Gold Medal for Poetry. In 1973, Larkin edited the *Oxford Book of Twentieth Century English Verse*. This anthology of poetry broke with the past by including many new voices in poetry. Well-known poets such as W.H. Auden and Sir John Betjeman lauded Larkin's attempts to modernise the public's perception of poetry, while other critics with a more traditional outlook attacked it. He published his last poetry collection, *High Windows*, in 1974 and his last major poem, 'Aubade', in 1977. During this period, he also worked as jazz correspondent for the *Daily Telegraph*. Following the death of Sir John Betjeman, Larkin was offered the poet laureateship in 1984, which he turned down because he felt he was unlikely to write any more poetry. Philip Larkin died in 1985, aged 63. In his biography, *Philip Larkin: A Writer's Life*, Andrew Motion describes the effect of Larkin's memorial service on the congregation:

> Some felt the service had drawn Larkin too easily into the Christian fold. Some thought the ceremony suited a man who so evidently loved tradition. Some pondered a deep personal loss. Some marvelled that a poet they had never met could have spoken to them so intimately. Some remembered whole poems. Some thought of individual lines: 'the one about mum and dad', 'Nothing, like something, happens anywhere', 'What will survive of us is love'. The procession thickened, flooding out into the cold, blustery afternoon. It was Valentine's Day.

Contrary to Larkin's wishes, previously unseen writing, such as *Collected Poems* (1988) and *The Selected Letters* (1992), was published posthumously. They revealed a man riven by petty prejudices. Ever since, critics have debated the worth of these publications. However, notwithstanding the controversy that has surrounded Larkin since his death, his poetry still remains extremely popular.

Critical Commentary: Wedding-Wind

See the text of the poem on p. 151.

1. Content

In 'Wedding-Wind' Larkin speaks in the fictional voice of a young woman on the night of her wedding and on the morning following it. Larkin hated marriage and abhorred the idea of lifelong commitment. According to his biographer, Andrew Motion, the poet once wrote the following in his diary:

> Let me remember that the only married state I intimately know (i.e. that of my parents) is bloody hell. Never must it be forgotten.

The self-contained narrative in 'Wedding-Wind' opens with a straightforward statement of fact:

> The wind blew all my wedding-day,
> And my wedding-night was the night of the high wind;

The wind affects the immediate environment and a stable door is 'banging, again and again'. The speaker's husband must leave in order to shut the door and she is left alone and feeling 'Stupid'. In the 'candlelight' her face is reflected in the 'twisted candlestick'. On his return, her new husband informs her that the horses were restless. It saddens the speaker:

> That any man or beast that night should lack
> The happiness [she] had.

In the second stanza, we move forward in time. It is now daytime and all becomes clear in the sunlight. Her husband has 'gone to look at the floods', while she carries 'a chipped pail to the chicken-run'. The woman stops, places the pail on the ground and stares at the scene in front of her. The wind is still blowing. It rushes through the clouds and the forests. The wind thrashes against her apron and the clothes on her washing-line. Meanwhile, she continues to meditate on her situation. She wonders if this powerful wind could possibly give expression to the joyful emotions that her marriage has awakened in her. She would like this joy to be borne on the wind and 'like a thread | Carrying beads' to become connected to every other facet of her life. The experience of marriage is like an everlasting morning. Her life is so infused with hope and brightness that she feels that nothing, not even death, can challenge how she feels. The poem concludes with an *image* of abundance and life. On her farm, on this morning after her wedding night, her cattle kneel down and drink from 'delighted lakes'.

2. Stylistic Features

Speaking about 'Wedding-Wind', Larkin has commented:

> I write poems to preserve things I have seen/thought/felt both for myself and for others, though I feel that my prime responsibility is to the experience itself, which I am trying to keep from oblivion for its own sake. Why I should do this I have no idea, but I think the impulse to preserve lies at the bottom of all art. Generally my poems are related, therefore to my personal life, but by no means always, since I can imagine the emotions of a bride [in 'Wedding-Wind'] without ever having been a woman or married. As a guiding principal, I believe that every poem must be its own sole freshly created universe.

In this poem, the poet adopts the narrative voice of a newly married woman in order to convey something of the joy she feels about marriage. In typical Larkin fashion, the language of the poem is simple and effective. Even though this *lyrical* poem opens in the middle of the night, it looks forward to the morning. The morning in literature has long been used as a *symbol* of hope. This poem is no different in that it is infused with a sense of brightness and the emotional language of the poem suggests a new beginning. 'Wedding-Wind' relies heavily on nature imagery in order to convey the extent of the speaker's emotions. The wind that rages on the night of her wedding is indicative of her passion. According to Conrad Brunström, in his essay in *Making it New: Essays on the Revised Leaving Certificate English Syllabus*, 'this poem describes the merging sexual energies within the larger cosmic forces in an affirmative way'. The force of the storm is captured by the *onomatopoeic* sound of the 'door [...] banging, again and again'.

Similarly, in the second stanza, the natural world seems to be in harmony with the woman's feelings. The wind continues to blow and in the process all is 'ravelled under the sun'. The wind rushes through the forest and hunts the clouds and morning itself shares the speaker's bed. The poem ends in a beautiful *transferred epithet*. The lakes in the speaker's view are 'delighted' and their waters are 'all-generous'. A transferred epithet occurs when a figure of speech is applied to one thing but is more suited to another. Here, in the last two lines of this poem, the words 'delighted' and 'all-generous' are used to describe the lake and its waters. However, they are really intended to convey the speaker's emotional state.

This is a beautiful poem that precisely captures the speaker's delight and passion at being married. This poem lacks the cynicism of 'The Whitsun Weddings' or the realism of 'An Arundel Tomb'. What is interesting, however, in this case is the fact that Larkin felt the need to adopt a *persona* in order to voice positive feelings about marriage. It is as if the poet finds it necessary to distance himself from the emotions expressed by the female speaker in this poem.

3. Essay Writing

If you are thinking of including 'Wedding-Wind' in your essay, you may wish to consider the following points.

a. The poem is unusual in that Larkin adopts a female persona. You could make this point in a paragraph dealing with Larkin's style.

b. The poem is positive in its outlook and lacks the cynical tone of voice present in so many of Larkin's poems on the course. You may wish to devote a single paragraph to the tone of Larkin's poetry. Should you do so, it might be worthwhile contrasting 'Wedding-Wind' with many of the other poems on the course.

c. The poem seems to be set in the past. This is true of many of Larkin's poems on the course.

Critical Commentary: At Grass

See the text of the poem on p. 153.

1. Content

'At Grass' is a beautiful, gentle and contemplative poem that describes two racehorses in retirement. This poem opens by presenting the reader with a view of the horses in the distance. We learn that:

> The eye can hardly pick them out
> From the cold shade they shelter in,

It is only when the wind ruffles their tails and manes that their shape becomes more defined. One of the horses then moves to eat some grass, while the other seems to look on. Strangely, the speaker ends the first stanza by claiming that the horses now are anonymous.

In the second stanza, the poet explains why the horses have achieved anonymity. Fifteen years ago, all that was needed to win them fame on 'afternoons | Of Cups and Stakes and Handicaps' was a mere 'Two dozen distances'. It becomes clear that these two animals are retired racehorses. In the poet's imagination, their names have become part of the faded fabric of 'classic Junes'. In the third stanza, the poet begins to describe the atmosphere of race days. His recollections are crowded with ***images*** of the jockeys' 'Silks', 'Numbers', 'parasols', 'littered grass' and the sounds of long cries 'Hanging unhushed'. In the fourth stanza, the poet wonders if the horses are plagued by similar memories:

> Do memories plague their ears like flies?
> They shake their heads. Dusk brims the shadows.

The pace of the poem slows down markedly. The crowds fade away and we return to the present-day meadows, where the horses now remain unmolested. Their names live on in various sports directories or almanacs. However, they have managed to free themselves from this past life. They now 'stand at ease'. Rather than being forced to race, they 'gallop for [...] joy'. The crowds that once cheered them on have vanished and there are no stopwatches to measure their pace.

> Only the groom, and the groom's boy,
> With bridles in the evening come.

2. Stylistic Features

'At Grass' was inspired by a short film that Larkin saw about a famous racehorse called Brown Jack. According to Larkin's biographer, Andrew Motion:

> As Larkin walked home that evening he found the story of the horse had for some reason impressed him very strongly, and when he reached his room he wrote about it. The result was the poem 'At Grass', which for its filmic re-creation of actual details, its formal melancholy and its graceful swoop into familiar experience has become one of his most admired and best-liked poems.

The fact that the poem was inspired by a film is apparent from its construction. The opening lines of 'At Grass' bring the horses slowly into focus. This cinematic technique gives the reader time to adjust to the *image* of the horses in the field. This poem moves from a series of realistic details that define the world of horse-racing to an implicit comparison between horses and people. In the process, Larkin raises questions about man's ability to adjust to the later stages of life.

The horses in the poem not only 'stand at ease', but they stand outside the hectic excitement of their early lives. The horses seem happy and secure. While their past achievements are commented on, the poet does not seek to explain why they are now so happy in their retirement. Their contentment is almost beyond explanation. Rather than explain the horses' feelings of peace and freedom, the poet relies on long vowel sounds to slow down the pace of the poem. The stanzas run gently into one another until the poem's final and gentle conclusion.

At the end of the poem, the horses' eventual death is prefigured in the arrival of the groom's boy. However, rather than the traditional Grim Reaper of literature, the person that greets these animals seems kind and gentle. 'At Grass' offers us a glimpse of happiness at the end of a long and successful career. While Larkin never seeks to explain how this happiness is achieved, it does seem to be linked to the idea that these once famous horses 'Have slipped their names, and stand at ease'. Could the poem be suggesting that real happiness in old age is linked to letting go of one's past? Of course, it is possible to read this poem as a simple evocation of two graceful animals in retirement. Whatever reading you choose to accept, 'At Grass' is undeniably a beautiful poem.

3. Essay Writing

'At Grass' is a warm and inviting poem. It is easy to see why you might be tempted to include the poem in any personal response to Larkin's poetry. If you do so, you might want to include some of the following points.

a. The poem can be read as a ***metaphor*** for the ageing process.
b. Once again, Larkin draws on images associated with the natural world.
c. The ***tone*** of the poem is gentle and contemplative. In this sense, it is in keeping with such poems as 'The Trees' and 'Cut Grass'. You might want to consider devoting a paragraph to the tone of voice in Larkin's poetry. Remember, this tends to be either warm and inclusive or cynical.

Critical Commentary: Church Going

See the text of the poem on pp. 155–6.

1. Content

In a manner typical of Larkin's poetic style, 'Church Going' opens in a modest, understated fashion:

> Once I am sure there's nothing going on
> I step inside, letting the door thud shut.

From the outset, it is clear this is going to be a ***monologue*** of a personal nature. To begin with, the poet adopts the ***persona*** of an interloper or trespasser. Once inside the church, the speaker takes in all the paraphernalia of the church. There are 'little books' and 'sprawlings of flowers' which were cut for Sunday's mass but have now gone brownish in colour. In the front of the church, which the speaker describes as being the 'holy end', there is a 'small neat organ'. The entire church is infused with a 'tense, musty, unignorable silence'. It is customary for men to remove their hats upon entering a church. However, not wearing a hat, the poet feels compelled to make some gesture that will demonstrate respect. He chooses to remove his cycle-clips in 'awkward reverence'.

In the second stanza, the poet begins to interact with the church. He runs his hand around the font and wonders about the condition of the roof as one would wonder about the condition of the soul: 'Cleaned, or restored?' He moves forward and mounts the lectern. The speaker begins to peruse the scripture and proclaims the words '"Here endeth" much more loudly' than he intended. He feels a little silly and the echo from his own voice appears to 'snigger' at him. Moving back towards the exit, he signs the visitors' book and 'donate[s] an Irish sixpence' to the church collection box. Of course, this is not legal tender in Great Britain. He then reflects on his visit and decides that the place was 'not worth stopping for'.

In the third stanza, the poet begins to wonder about his decision to stop in the first place. He tells us that he often stops to visit churches like this one. Curiously, he is left with the same feelings of uncertainty each time the visit is over. The speaker then begins to examine the role that churches play in a world that is becoming increasingly secular. He wonders what will become of church buildings once they have fallen completely out of use. Will some of them become museum pieces 'chronically on show', but no longer functional? In the final lines of the third stanza, the speaker compares a disused church to the religious ruins of our pagan past. He wonders if in the future, when church buildings have fallen into complete ruin, they will be considered unlucky places, as is the case with pagan ruins.

The third and fourth stanzas are linked by a *run-on line*. In keeping with the previous stanza, the fourth stanza opens with the poet wondering whether church grounds will eventually become the haunt of witches or 'dubious women'. These women, he imagines, will:

> [...] make their children touch a particular stone;
> Pick simples for a cancer; or on some
> Advised night see walking a dead one?

However, even these superstitious activities will fade with time. He then looks forward to a time when the site of the church has become completely dissociated from spirituality or belief. The ruins will become less recognisable each week as they succumb to the ravages of time. This leads the poet to speculate about who will be the last person 'to seek | This place for what it was'. He suggests it may well be someone who specialises in ruins, such as an archaeologist or 'Some ruin-bibber, randy for antique'. This stanza ends with the poet speculating that a future visitor to this place may well be some:

> [...] Christmas-addict, counting on a whiff
> Of gown-and-bands and organ-pipes and myrrh?

2. Stylistic Features

This poem contains two of Larkin's favourite themes: spirituality and the passing of time. In the poem, the poet takes on the *persona* of an ordinary man trying to understand the role of the Church in an increasingly secular world. However, the poem really contains two interlaced voices. Firstly, there is the **colloquial**, workaday voice of the speaker. This voice emerges clearly in such phrases as 'I don't' and 'I've no idea'. Since the poem is written in *iambic pentameter* (a metre particularly suited to normal voice patterns), the speaker's voice sounds natural. Yet despite all this, a more scholarly voice intrudes from time to time. At various points in the poem, the speaker's knowledge of religious vocabulary goes beyond that of the layman. By allowing this aspect of the speaker's voice to encroach on the narrative, Larkin manages to convey something of the mystique of the traditional Church. At the same time, we are made to feel that words like 'pyx', 'font' and 'plate' are really no longer significant to the common man. The notion that the Church is no longer completely relevant is, of course, at the heart of this poem.

The **ambiguous** title hints at the poem's central thesis, the idea that the 'Church [is] Going'. In order to grasp the significance of this, it is important to comprehend the crucial role that church buildings have played in European culture. In social, legal, artistic and, of course, religious terms, the Church literally lay at the heart of Western society for nearly two thousand years. This fact remained largely unchanged until the latter half of the last century. Yet 'Church Going' does not articulate the central role that the Church played in the past. Rather, the poem looks to the future and imagines a world without the Church. In so doing, Larkin reveals (albeit in a subtle manner) the important role that traditions play. If this poem had ended after the second stanza, it would have been very easy to dismiss the speaker as deprecating the importance of the Church. However, once the speaker leaves the church, it becomes apparent that this is not the first time that he has visited such a building. This honest admission reveals that the Church still holds an important place in the poet's life. Even when the poet imagines the disappearance of this church, he still envisages people being drawn to this site.

Although Larkin was an agnostic member of the Anglican Church, he once pointed out (commenting on the decline of the Church of England) that 'the Catholic Church would be better than nothing'. While 'Church Going' does look forward to a time when the formal Church will lose its relevance to everyday life, the poem also celebrates, in an understated manner, the traditions of the Church. The speaker in this poem is evidently a person without faith, but the *tone* of the speaker's voice betrays his need to recover something of the comfort that faith provides. When first published, this poem helped to establish Larkin's reputation as an important post-war poet. Most critics agree that 'Church Going' incorporates into its very structure the openness and self-scrutiny that came to be hallmarks of Larkin's style.

3. Essay Writing

'Church Going' is one of Larkin's best-known poems. It also exhibits many stylistic features typical of his poetry. If you are considering including the poem in a response to Larkin's poetry, you might want to consider some of the following points.

a. The poem deals with loss and the passing of time. These are recurrent themes in Larkin's work. You might want to devote an entire paragraph to this aspect of his poetry.
b. Once again, Larkin adopts a persona. This is a typical feature of his work.
c. The tone of the speaker's voice changes during the course of the poem. This matches the change in his understanding of the role of the Church. Larkin tends to make subtle use of tone to enhance the overall effect of his poems.

Critical Commentary: An Arundel Tomb

See the text of the poem on pp. 158–9.

1. Content

'An Arundel Tomb' opens with the depiction of an engraving on the surface of a tomb. We learn that the couple lie 'Side by side' and that their faces have become 'blurred' by the passing of time. The speaker then describes pleats on the couple's garments, their 'jointed armour' and the carved 'little dogs under their feet'. In the second six-line stanza, we learn that this carving is ordinary and plain. Etched in the 'pre-baroque' style, which is known for its plainness, this carving 'Hardly involves' the poet's eye. However, in the ninth line the speaker hints at why this statue fascinates him. The 'left-hand gauntlet' is empty because the figure has removed it in order to hold his wife's hand. This detail comes as a 'sharp tender shock' to the poet.

Commenting further on the couple, the speaker points out that they would never have imagined lying together for so long. The poet then wonders whether the couple had ever intended such a detailed statue to be seen by anyone other then their friends. The speaker imagines that this couple and the sculptor they commissioned would have viewed the statue as merely being a device to 'prolong' the family name.

In the fourth stanza, we learn that there is no way, in the early days of their long 'supine stationary voyage', that the couple could have understood how much the world would change. They would have been ignorant of the extent to which their tomb would be affected by the processes of weathering. Similarly, they would have been surprised at the social changes that have occurred. The 'old tenantry' have all but disappeared and people can no longer read Latin:

> Turn the old tenantry away;
> How soon succeeding eyes begin
> To look, not read. [...]

The fourth and fifth stanzas run on into one another. Here, we learn that this couple has 'Persisted, linked, through lengths and breadths | Of time'. The poet imagines the changing of the seasons that have gone unrecorded. In the last line of the fifth stanza, we return to the present age of mass tourism:

> [...] And up the paths
> The endless altered people came,

The sheer number of people visiting the tomb has helped to erode the engravings on its surface. In this sense, they are 'Washing at their identity'. The couple have come down through history and now lie 'helpless in the hollow of | An unarmorial age'. Today, there is little interest in coats of arms or family history. In the final stanza, we learn that this couple have become 'transfigured [...] into | Untruth'. Cast in stone, they have achieved a level of fidelity they could never have intended. This accident of time, by which the couple have come to *symbolise* lasting love, is viewed by the poet as being highly significant. However, while the statue reminds us that love can endure, it also reminds us that nothing, including love itself, is completely free from the ravages of time.

2. Stylistic Features

This is a complex poem that poses some interesting questions. The structure of 'An Arundel Tomb' is simple and straightforward. This construction mirrors the ordinary, 'pre-baroque' style of the tomb itself. The poem opens with a strong visual *image* of the stone worn away by the passing of time. It has been 'blurred' by the agents of erosion. However, this process has taken place at an almost imperceptibly slow pace. An impression of this slow passing of time is achieved through the use of *alliteration* and soft *sibilant* 's' sounds. Notice how the 'f' sound in 'faithfulness' is picked up again in the word 'effigy'. This whispering sound is captured again in such lines as 'sweet commissioned grace'. The flow of the poem continues uninterrupted until the fifth stanza. Here, the use of *caesura* breaks the lines up and interrupts the progression of thought. In this manner, the destructive effects of the passing of time are reflected in the poem's structure.

One of the more interesting features of this poem is its overall lack of clarity. At times, it is as if the poet is not quite sure what to make of the statue. This lack of clarity is first introduced in the opening line with the word 'blurred'. In the first stanza, the poet tells us that:

> The earl and countess lie in stone,
> Their proper habits vaguely shown

The use of the word 'lie' is interesting here. The speaker exploits the ambiguity between the two meanings of the word. 'Lie' can mean to rest or to tell an untruth. So, from the outset, the speaker may be suggesting that the statue lies to us about the notion of never-ending love. Similarly, words such as 'faint', 'hint', 'Hardly', 'almost' and 'vaguely' all suggest a lack of purpose. These words, when taken into consideration with the equivocal final line of the poem, lead the reader to question the central message of 'An Arundel Tomb'. Does Larkin really believe that love can see off the ravages of time? At the end of the manuscript draft of the poem, the poet wrote:

> [...] love isn't stronger than death just because statues hold hands for 600 years.

According to his biographer, Andrew Motion, this is 'a remark which reinforced, privately, the sense of futility that hovers around the poem's conclusion in words like "helpless", "scrap", "attitude", "Untruth" and "almost"'. In fact, the poem is purposely ambiguous. On the one hand, its language suggests a lasting, even timeless, relationship, but on the other hand, the poem recognises that the lovers are dead. Words like 'pleat' and 'jointed' lead us to the central image of the two figures with their hands clasped together. However, the reader is never allowed to forget that this pair of lovers is dead and the world they knew has long since faded away.

The visitors to the tomb *symbolise* the extent to which the world has changed. The old hierarchies of social order have vanished and people can no longer read Latin. One of the most profound changes that has taken place in the world is implied but never stated explicitly by the poet: our attitude to love has been radically altered since this couple commissioned their statue. Marriage is no longer seen as being for life and the idea of unending love is widely disparaged in the modern world. Conrad Brunström believes that the final stanza of 'An Arundel Tomb' is often misread, even by literary critics (see *Making it New: Essays on the Revised Leaving Certificate English Syllabus*):

> The 'almost-instinct almost true' does not demonstrate that love lasts for all eternity but only that love can *seem* to last. The fact that 'love' does not quite rhyme with 'prove' is illustrative of this deceptive seeming.

This is a memorable poem that forces its readers to rethink deeply held beliefs about love, death and the passing of time.

3. Essay Writing

'An Arundel Tomb' has much in common with many of the poems by Larkin on the course. As such, you might want to consider using the poem in an overall response to Larkin's poetry. If you decide to use the poem in an essay, you might want to consider some of the following points.

a. Once again, Larkin deals with the passing of time. In this sense, it is possible to compare and contrast 'An Arundel Tomb' and 'Church Going'.
b. The notion of enduring love is a source of fascination to the poet. Here, again, Larkin examines this theme. Consider a comparison between this poem and 'The Whitsun Weddings'.
c. The poem reveals Larkin's keen eye for detail.

Critical Commentary: The Whitsun Weddings

See the text of the poem on pp. 161–3.

1. Content

'The Whitsun Weddings' is the title poem from Larkin's best-known collection of poems. On the day on which Larkin was inspired to write this poem, he tells us that he caught:

> A very slow train that stopped at every station and I hadn't realised that, of course, this was the train that all the wedding couples would get on and go to London for their honeymoon; it was an eye-opener to me. Every part was different but the same somehow. They all looked different but they were all doing the same things and sort of feeling the same things. I suppose the train stopped at about four, five, six stations between Hull and

London and there was a sense of gathering emotional momentum. Every time you stopped fresh emotion climbed aboard. And finally between Peterborough and London when you hurtle on, you felt the whole thing was being aimed like a bullet — at the heart of things, you know. All this fresh, open life. Incredible experience. I've never forgotten it.

The poem opens with a very personal and direct statement of fact. The speaker tells us that on 'That Whitsun, [he] was late getting away'. The details are very specific; it was about 'One-twenty on [a] sunlit Saturday'. The **mood** in the opening stanza is relaxed. All 'sense | Of being in a hurry [is] gone'. The train moves behind the backs of the houses and, as its momentum gathers, the scenery changes. As the train passes by the fish docks and the river, the Lincolnshire countryside begins to stretch out before the poet.

In the second stanza, we learn that the train followed a southward curve. 'Wide farms' dotted with 'short-shadowed cattle' come in and out of view. Slowly, the countryside gives way to the small towns. 'Canals with floatings of industrial froth' signal the approach of a more urban landscape. The area between towns is indicated by hedgerows and the smell of cut grass. In the poet's estimation, these small towns are nondescript. The second stanza closes with the ugly **image** of 'acres of dismantled cars'.

The speaker reasserts his presence in the third stanza. He informs us that 'At first, [he] didn't notice what a noise | The weddings made'. This is the first mention of the weddings referred to in the title. The powerful sun shining down on each of the stations that the train stops at hides 'what's happening in the shade'. The speaker admits that he had heard 'whoops and skirls' of excitement coming from the platforms. However, he had mistakenly believed that this noise came from the porters messing and joking. He now realises that the commotion was coming from wedding parties gathered on the station platforms. The sight of grinning and pomaded 'girls | In parodies of fashion, heels and veils' grabs the speaker's attention. These girls stand on the platform and wave tentatively at the train. Anticipating a similar scene at the next station, the poet leans:

> More promptly out next time, more curiously,
> And saw it all again in different terms:

In great detail, the poet describes the scene that greets him. There is an 'uncle shouting smut' and women wearing 'nylon gloves' and 'jewellery-substitutes'. The colours of their clothes are bright, even garish, and 'Marked [them off] unreally' from the rest of the crowd on the platform. The poet imagines that these wedding parties have come from the surrounding cafés and 'banquet-halls' and then remarks that the 'wedding-days | Were coming to an end'.

Meanwhile, 'Fresh couples' continue to climb on board the train. As they do so, these newly married men and women move away from the crowds in the station. The poet sees different things etched on the faces of the people who are there to see the newlyweds off. The children 'frowned' while the fathers 'had never known | Success so huge and wholly farcical'. The women view the wedding couple in a different light. The look on their faces implies a recognition of the pain that marriage can bring. Their experience of watching their daughters depart is described as being akin to attending a funeral. The younger girls anticipate the physical pain of the sexual act. The poem picks up momentum slightly towards the end of the sixth stanza:

> We hurried towards London, shuffling gouts of steam.
> Now fields were building-plots, and poplars cast
> Long shadows over major roads, and for
> Some fifty minutes, [...]

The sixth stanza runs into the seventh and, in this manner, the poem maintains its impetus. The women settle their hats and the uniformity of their experience is expressed when they are all seen to exclaim: '*I nearly died*'. The landscape continues to go by and couples remain fixated on one another. They give little thought to those other newlyweds on the train whose 'lives would all contain this hour'. Suddenly, towards the end of the stanza, the poet begins to think of 'London spread out in the sun, | Its postal districts packed like squares of wheat'. London is the final destination of this journey and in the final stanza, it becomes clear that the poet has been changed by his experience on the train. The last two lines of the poem reveal something of the power of this experience. The poet is overwhelmed by:

> A sense of falling, like an arrow-shower
> Sent out of sight, somewhere becoming rain.

The poem itself is also transformed from a simple commentary on a train ride to a profound meditation on the many paths that life can take.

2. Stylistic Features

The **persona** adopted by Larkin in this poem echoes many of his own heartfelt reservations about love and marriage. Confronted by the sights and sounds of wedding parties, the poet is forced to meditate on the concept of marriage and the new beginning that it implies. The **rhythms** and **metre** of the poem create a sensation of movement and progression. And while such movement reflects the momentum of the train, it also captures something of the progress of the couples as the journey of their married life begins. The broad vowel sounds in the opening stanzas create an impression of openness that is mirrored in the descriptions of the countryside, but they also suggest the sense of hopefulness associated with marriage.

In stark contrast to all of this is the attitude of the speaker. He is, unlike the couples, completely alone. The opening line of the poem emphasises his isolation by stressing the personal pronoun 'I'. At times in the poem, it seems as if the speaker is contemptuous of the people who are taking part in the wedding ceremony. The hope and belief in a future life together, symbolised by the newlyweds' commitment to marriage, is contrasted with the failings of the older generation. The fathers with 'seamy foreheads', the 'mothers loud and fat' and the 'uncle shouting smut' remind us that the idealism of marriage fades quickly into an ugly reality. Are we meant to suppose that these young, hopeful couples will eventually become as unappealing as the families that are there to wave them off?

In any case, the poem contains many crude generalisations. The girls who wait on the platform are adorned in cheap clothing that imitates the fashions of the time. The pastel shades of their dresses were chosen because they are fashionable, but instead they appear brash and common. The weddings, which were intended to celebrate the special uniqueness of each relationship, become indistinguishable from one another. As they board the train, the poet has the newlyweds uttering the same exclamations. There is a darker side also to the poem. The women should be entering into a new life. However, the reality is different. Their subjugation and repression is indicated by the expressions on the faces of their mothers.

As with many of Larkin's poems, in 'The Whitsun Weddings' it is often quite difficult to determine where the speaker stands. Given that the **tone** of the poem hints at a cynical attitude to marriage, the final lines seem curiously out of place. According to Andrew Motion:

> All the paradoxes which govern Larkin's thoughts about love are collected here in an image adapted from a film he had seen as a young man during the war.

The arrow has been *symbolic* of love since the earliest days of Greek literature. Here, at the end of the poem, the speaker is confronted with the joy, excitement and hope of married life. It is a joy, however, from which he is excluded.

> [...] We slowed again,
> And as the tightened brakes took hold, there swelled
> A sense of falling, like an arrow-shower
> Sent out of sight, somewhere becoming rain.

Despite his undoubted scepticism concerning marriage, the speaker has been marked by his encounter with the wedding couples. One suspects that he will leave the train a different person.

3. Essay Writing

This complex poem is considered by many to typify Larkin's poetic style. This fact alone makes it worthy of inclusion in any personal response that you may be required to write on Larkin's poetry. When preparing an essay that mentions 'The Whitsun Weddings', you might want to include some of the following points.

a. The tone of the speaker's voice is cynical at times.
b. The language of the poem is infused with an energy that gathers and grows until the couples reach their final destination.
c. Once again, Larkin examines the notion of love and marriage. In this respect, the poem can be compared to 'An Arundel Tomb' and 'Wedding-Wind'.

Critical Commentary: MCMXIV

See the text of the poem on p. 165.

1. Content

'MCMXIV' captures a moment in time before the onset of one of the most horrendous episodes in human history – World War One. In the opening lines, we are presented with the sight of long queues of men:

> Standing as patiently
> As if they were stretched outside
> The Oval or Villa Park,

The disturbing reality, however, is that these men are not queuing for a football match or a game of cricket. They are, in fact, standing in line to enlist in a war from which most of them will not return. Their innocence is captured in the ***image*** of their 'archaic faces | Grinning as if it were all | An August Bank Holiday lark'.

In the second stanza, the holiday atmosphere continues to prevail. The shops are closed for the long weekend and the children are at play. Throughout this stanza, a number of images highlight the extent to which this world has vanished. The currency ('farthings and sovereigns') has passed into history. The clothes that the children wear are no longer fashionable and their names no longer popular. What is not stated, however, is the fact that World War One will accelerate the pace of this change.

In the third stanza, there is a shift in location. We move from the city to the 'countryside'. There is a lazy, hazy feel to the poet's depiction of these final days of summer in 1914:

> And the countryside not caring:
> The place-names all hazed over
> With flowering grasses, and fields

In the fourth line of this stanza, we receive our first indication that all is not well. The mention of 'Domesday lines' casts a shadow over the poet's beautiful description of the countryside. The absence of human voices is replaced by the sound of 'wheat's restless silence'. In the closing lines of the third stanza, we are reminded once again of the class differences that existed in England before the war. Houses with 'differently-dressed servants' are a thing of the past. The final stanza expresses in clear terms what was previously implied. The speaker reminds us that there was:

> Never such innocence,
> Never before or since,
> As changed itself to past

The innocent world that the speaker refers to vanished with the onset of World War One. In these final days before the war in August 1914, the men remain ignorant of the fact that their marriages will only '[last] a little while longer'.

2. Stylistic Features

Most critics agree that 'MCMXIV' is a nostalgic poem that laments the passing of a way of life. The first two stanzas rely on a number of *images* and quietly stated *allusions* to achieve their effect. In particular, the mention of 'Villa Park' and 'The Oval' highlights the extent to which Britain was divided along class lines before the war. World War One changed all that. The upper classes suffered as much as the working class. In fact, the life expectancy of a middle-ranked officer was less than that of an enlisted soldier. Furthermore, the drain on manpower and the social chaos created by the war put an end to the servant–master relationship that had dominated British life up to 1914. The image of 'archaic faces' with moustaches seems, at first, to refer to specific photographs, but on closer inspection it proves to be a representation of our collective image of the time. We have all seen the silent newsreels of the era and the images in the first two stanzas are representative of how we imagine the men of that period looked.

This nostalgic recollection of a world that no longer exists extends into the third stanza. The depiction of the English countryside in this stanza is, in Andrew Motion's opinion, 'part of a vanished ideal, a better world than ours, marooned on the wrong side of a colossal war'. The poem moves slowly, but inevitably, towards the final stanza. The extensive use of the *present participle* – 'Standing', 'Grinning', 'caring', 'flowering' and 'Leaving' – suggests an easy, flowing sense of permanence and stability. The poem does not contain a main verb; this fact, coupled with the lack of intrusive punctuation, reinforces this smooth, flowing sense of continuity. However, all the while, the spectre of war hangs over the poem. The lives that those men took for granted are going to be much shorter than the grammar of the poem would suggest. The men who stand in the queues in the first stanza would later form what became known as the 'pals' battalions'. Most of these men were to die in the insanity of the British advances on the German lines in 1916. The Great War was a horrific fault line in European history.

'MCMXIV' is more than a nostalgic trip down memory lane. It is a poem that memorialises a generation that was virtually wiped out. The roman numerals, along with the shape of the poem, evoke images of a cenotaph or commemorative monument. Much of the imagery in the poem is bright and cheerful. However, on closer examination, you should notice that dark colours, shades and shadows are present in nearly every stanza. There is also an eerie and foreboding lack of human voices throughout the poem.

3. Essay Writing

If you are thinking of including 'MCMXIV' in your essay, you may wish to consider the following points.

a. The poem amounts to a powerful and emotional depiction of a vanished world. Nostalgia is a common feature of Larkin's poetry and you may wish to devote a paragraph to this aspect of his writing.
b. Unlike many of the poems on the course, Larkin chooses not to adopt the voice of a persona.
c. The poem is honest and realistic. It does not seek to glorify the patriotism of those about to die.

Critical Commentary: Ambulances

See the text of the poem on p. 167.

1. Content

'Ambulances' evokes a familiar and uncomfortable sight – that of an ambulance stopped at the side of a kerb. In the opening line, ambulances are made to seem secretive and closed off from the ordinary world. The glass on their windshields is dark:

[…] giving back
None of the glances they absorb.

The ambulances are a light, glossy grey colour and on them is a coat of arms. Ominously,

They come to rest at any kerb:
All streets in time are visited.

In the second stanza, the speaker concentrates on the onlookers' reactions to the arrival of the ambulance. From the children playing on the road to the women coming from the shops, this event interferes with the normal course of the day. They stop to see the 'wild white face that overtops I Red stretcher-blankets'. This random event brings people closer to some uncomfortable truths concerning life and death. In the third stanza, the speaker begins to outline just what these truths are. The gathering crowd begins to sense 'the solving emptiness I That lies just under all we do'. In a blinding flash of insight into their own mortality, the onlookers begin to perceive how fragile life is. Witnessing the sick person's plight, the people whisper 'Poor soul'. However, the speaker feels that these bystanders are really distressed because they recognise that one day, they too will end up like the person on the stretcher:

The fastened doors recede. *Poor soul,*
They whisper at their own distress;

In the fourth stanza, the victim is 'borne away' and the speaker begins to meditate on the circumstances of that person's life. Like all of us, this person is the product of a 'unique random blend'. To his 'families' and friends this person is irreplaceable. There is a depressing sense of inevitability to the final stanza. The ambulance moves away from the kerbside and, in the process, the bonds that tied this person to his life and family become loosened. He is brought to a place where he is 'Unreachable'. Where this place is, is never stated explicitly. In the closing lines of the final stanza, the ambulance moves away into the traffic. In the course of its journey it:

Brings closer what is left to come,
And dulls to distance all we are.

2. Stylistic Features

The most interesting aspect of Larkin's description of the ambulance is the fact that he provides us with so much detail, while actually telling us very little about the vehicle. The ambulance is not open to enquiry or scrutiny. Inside, it is secretive and mysterious. In this respect, it strongly resembles a coffin. The *half-rhyme* between 'noons' and 'None' captures the sound of the siren as the ambulance comes 'to rest at any kerb'. In this short sentence, something of Larkin's genius as a poet is revealed. The idea that the arrival of the ambulance is random and indiscriminate is one that is central to our understanding of the poem. In 'Ambulances', the vehicle becomes *symbolic* of death. The speaker's assurance that 'All streets in time are visited' clearly indicates that death is the inescapable lot of all humankind. As the person is taken away on the stretcher, the language of the poem suggests that his or her life, personality and individuality are being effaced. Notice how the poet uses the pronoun 'it' rather than 'he' or 'she' to describe the person being taken away. The speaker employs the verb 'to stow' to describe the victim being taken away on the stretcher. This is not a verb that one would normally use to describe the placing of a person inside a vehicle. The verb is suggestive of baggage or cargo, and in this manner, the person becomes less human. It is typical of Larkin's style that complex ideas are suggested to the reader in a subtle fashion.

In a real sense, the entire poem centres on a depressing moment of insight into our own mortality. The onlookers, confronted by the image of the white, frightened face of the victim, do not really sympathise with this person. They retreat into 'their own distress'. However selfish this retreat may be, it also forces those present to acknowledge that life is fragile and fleeting. 'Ambulances' opens with the word 'Closed' and the idea of permanent closure or a final end is central to this poem. Much of the language of 'Ambulances' hints at the finality of death. The doors on the vehicle are 'fastened' and, as the person is taken away, there is a 'sudden shut of loss'. This is a complex poem that forces us to take account of the unpredictable nature of life and death. The language is ordinary and straightforward. This simplicity adds force to the poem's bleak message.

3. Essay Writing

If you are thinking of including 'Ambulances' in your essay, you may wish to consider the following points.

a. Once again, Larkin meditates on the transience of life. This means that you can compare and contrast the poem with 'The Explosion', 'MCMXIV', 'The Trees', 'Cut Grass' and 'An Arundel Tomb'. In fact, this theme is so dominant in Larkin's poetry that you might want to devote one or more paragraphs to it in your essay.

b. In typical Larkin fashion, 'Ambulances' uses familiar *imagery* and symbolism to explore complex ideas.

c. This poem is not afraid to confront an unpleasant reality.

Critical Commentary: The Trees

See the text of the poem on p. 169.

1. Content

'The Trees' is a beautiful and simple meditation on the transience of life. Consisting of three perfectly rhymed stanzas, 'The Trees' opens with a straightforward statement of fact:

> The trees are coming into leaf

The poet compares this natural process to 'something almost being said'. The buds of the trees relax and spread open to reveal a fresh greenness. Curiously, the poet likens this greenness to a 'kind of grief'.

In the second stanza, the speaker wonders whether or not the trees have been born again. He quickly dismisses this idea because trees do, in fact, age and die. The poet sees the growth of early summer as being a 'trick' that is possible to measure in the rings of the tree. In the final stanza, the speaker chooses to view the arrival of the new leaves as a message from the trees. This message tells him to begin 'afresh'.

2. Stylistic Features

This is a beautiful *lyrical* poem that evokes, through nature, a powerful sense of continuity. The eloquent and harmonious construction of the poem is in keeping with its central message. At the heart of the poem lies a desire for permanence. The speaker views the trees as offering a glimpse of the continuity that can be found in the natural world. 'The Trees' opens in the present continuous and remains in this tense from start to finish. However, while the poem is written in the present tense, the poet manages to convey to the reader the idea that the process of the trees coming into leaf has not yet fully taken place. In order to do this, the speaker makes use of an unusual *simile*. We are told that it is 'Like something almost being said'. In this comparison, something of the whispering, restless energy of the trees is captured. While the poem is infused with the vitality and energy of a spring day, its *tone* is relaxed and peaceful.

The poem does, however, admit the possibility of death and in this sense the speaker is not self-deceiving. He acknowledges that the trees 'die too'. The inclusion of this simple word 'too' broadens the scope of the poem so that it addresses human mortality. The fact that the trees are renewed each year is viewed by the poet as being a sleight of hand or a 'trick'. The poet does not try to convince us that the trees are immortal. However, the poem does end with an extremely uplifting message. The trees in springtime remind the speaker that it is possible to begin 'afresh'. The repetition of the word 'afresh' stresses the importance of the process of renewal to the poet. Unlike most of the poems by Larkin on the course, 'The Trees' does not contain a personal pronoun. This has the effect of making the poem's message seem less personal and more universal.

3. Essay Writing

If you are thinking of mentioning 'The Trees' in your essay, you may wish to consider the following.

a. This is another lyric poem by Larkin that addresses the transience of life. In this sense, you can compare and contrast 'The Trees' with many of the poems on the course.

b. Unusually for Larkin's poetry on the course, 'The Trees' does not contain a *persona* or personal pronoun. This makes the poem appear more universal.

c. Once again, Larkin turns to the natural world in order to evoke complex ideas. You might want to devote a single paragraph to this facet of Larkin's poetry.

Critical Commentary: The Explosion

See the text of the poem on p. 170.

1. Content

Larkin was prompted to write 'The Explosion' after watching a television documentary about the mining industry in 1969. The poem opens with a stark statement of fact. We learn that 'On the day of the explosion I Shadows pointed towards the pithead'. The mention of shadows alongside the word 'explosion' creates a sense of foreboding. In the first stanza, there is an uneasy silence, which is only broken by the arrival of the 'men in pitboots' in the second *tercet*. These men are lively; they cough 'oath-edged talk and pipe-smoke'. In the fourth stanza, the men pass through the tall gates of the pithead wearing 'moleskins'.

By the fifth tercet, it becomes apparent that time has moved on. The men are now below the surface. It is noon and the first indication that something has gone horribly wrong is felt when a 'tremor' reaches the surface. The cows stop 'chewing for a second'. However, at this distance from the explosion, these animals are 'Scarfed' or protected from any harm. In the sixth stanza, which is set off from the rest of the poem by italics, we are then given an extract from what is presumably the funeral sermon of these men. Instead of dwelling on the men's deaths, this sermon is life-affirming. We are promised that the men

> *Are sitting in God's house in comfort,*
> *We shall see them face to face—*

In the seventh stanza, the speaker assures us that this message is unambiguous, that it is as 'Plain as lettering in the chapels'. Mysteriously, the wives of the men see the 'men of the explosion I Larger than in life'. The *imagery* in the last three lines of the poem is bright and, in this manner, it reaffirms the notion of life after death. The men are surrounded by light and they walk towards their wives while one of them holds the unbroken lark's eggs.

2. Stylistic Features

This beautiful poem evokes a sense of community that manages to transcend death. The men at the heart of the poem are 'Fathers' and 'brothers'. They are working men, and this aspect of their characters is suggested by a number of indicators. They wear 'pitboots', 'moleskins' and cough 'oath-edged talk and pipe-smoke'. However, for all these rough edges, the men are made to appear connected to their environment. The **image** of the young man taking the lark's nest only to return it safely is a moving and tender evocation of gentleness and care. Furthermore, the egg itself has long been **symbolic** of the cycle of life. Notice how, when the man returns, these eggs remain unharmed and unbroken. In this respect, we are assured in a subtle manner that despite the impending disaster, life goes on.

The poem manages to suggest that something awful is about to happen through a number of symbolic associations. The shadows that point towards the pithead are ominous. In a similar fashion, the tall gates that stand open can be read as an **allusion** to the gates of heaven. In a more obvious fashion, the tremor that disturbs the cows chewing the grass indicates a powerful, yet distant, explosion. The distant nature of this explosion not only makes it seem mysterious but, more importantly, it stresses the inexplicable nature of the women's vision of their dead husbands walking towards them. The poet makes no effort to explain how or why the women could have seen their husbands, but this vision does seem to be linked to the message that is given during the funeral sermon. In this sermon, we are assured that the '*dead go on before us*' and that '*We shall see them face to face*'. And, indeed, this is what happens in the final movement of the poem. 'Plain as lettering in the chapels', the wives see their husbands. In death, the men are completely transformed. Normally covered in coal dust, the men are now bathed in light. In a final gesture, one of the men shows the unbroken eggs. The fragility of the eggs not only suggests the fragility of life itself, but also hints at the frailty of the bonds of family, society and love that linked the men to this mining community.

Interestingly, the poem's construction mirrors its theme. The poet's use of tense is, according to the critic Andrew Swarbrick, very effective. He believes that:

> ... the manipulation of tenses (from the continuous present tense of the pastor's quoted words to the past 'it was said' and the 'wives saw men', and forward to the **present participles** of the momentary vision) creates the logic by which the men walk 'Somehow from the sun', at

the very moment it has 'dimmed' for the underground explosion. The effect of this is quite miraculously to annihilate the moment of death not by meekly editing it out of the poem, but by building it in to what survives that moment of death. The men are unbroken like the eggs. They have simply passed 'Through the tall gates standing open'.

While the use of tenses in the poem works to cancel out the deaths of the men, Larkin's use of **rhythm** creates a solemn, funereal feeling. This continues until the final line, when suddenly the poet employs a completely different rhythm. While this creates a sudden and jarring sense of loss, it also suggests that the men have moved on to a different plane. In this fashion, the reader is made to feel the full impact of the men's deaths. 'The Explosion' is unlike most of the other poems by Larkin on the Leaving Certificate course. It treats a mysterious and spiritual moment of profound loss in a respectful and unquestioning manner. The ***ironic tone*** that dominates so much of Larkin's work is absent. In short, this is a profoundly emotional poem that acknowledges the possibility of life after death.

3. Essay Writing

If you are thinking of including 'The Explosion' in your essay, you may wish to consider the following points.

a. The poem is a powerful and emotional depiction of the fragility of human life. Death, the passing of time and loss are major themes in Larkin's poetry. As such, you may wish to devote an entire paragraph to this aspect of his poetry.
b. The language devices employed by Larkin greatly enhance the overall effect of the poem.
c. The poet chooses not to include a personal statement or the voice of a ***persona*** in this poem. In this respect, it might be worthwhile comparing and contrasting 'The Explosion' and 'MCMXIV'.

Critical Commentary: Cut Grass

See the text of the poem on p. 172.

1. Content

'Cut Grass' is another short, lyrical poem in which Larkin addresses the theme of transience. The opening **quatrain** tells us that cut grass lies on the ground. These lines suggest that the brevity of the cut grass's life is in sharp contrast to the 'Long, long [...] death' that awaits it. In the second four-line stanza, the death of the grass is juxtaposed with 'young-leafed June', where chestnut flowers and hedgerows are in full bloom. The final quatrain continues in much the same vein. **Images** of 'lilac', 'Queen Anne's lace' and 'summer' clouds crowd this short stanza.

2. Stylistic Features

This short, elegant **lyric** is defined by its opening line. The image of the cut grass breathing its last breath is contrasted with the images of early summer that dominate the rest of the poem. While most of the imagery in the poem is life-affirming, the reader is not allowed to forget the sight of the cut grass. In this manner, the poem reminds us of the brevity of life. This message is made more powerful because it is given at the beginning of summer in 'young-leafed June'. There is a beautiful musicality to this poem. In fact, Larkin once complained that the music of the poem took over and supplanted the impact of the words. Certainly, it is difficult for any reader to ignore the sounds of the poem.

3. Essay Writing

If you are thinking of including 'Cut Grass' in your essay, you may wish to consider the following points.

a. This poem provides us with another short, lyrical meditation on the passing of time.
b. The sound effects in the poem add to its overall meaning.
c. Unlike so many of Larkin's poems, 'Cut Grass' does not contain the voice of a **persona**. This lends the poem's central message the air of an objective truth.

Sylvia Plath (1932–63)

A Short Biography

Sylvia Plath was born in Boston's Memorial Hospital on 27 October 1932, the daughter of Aurelia and Otto Plath. Her father was a biology professor and an authority on entomology at Boston University. He would later figure as a major image of persecution in some of his daughter's best-known poems. His death in 1940 had a profound effect on Plath. In fact, this event would continue to haunt her for the rest of her life. However, on the surface of things, there was little to indicate how badly Sylvia had taken the news of her father's death. In school, she excelled at every undertaking and dazzled her teachers with her brilliance. She was barely nine years of age when her first poem was published in the *Boston Sunday Herald*. Two years after her father's death, the family moved to Wellesley. To begin with, Plath appeared to settle well into this middle-class, conservative community and, in many respects, was regarded as an all-American girl. Plath even had stories published in *Seventeen* magazine and began to plan diligently for her writing career. However, she was deeply troubled, though she seems to have been largely unaware of this fact, and at the end of her junior year at Smith College, she tried to take her own life. Following a slow recovery, she eventually graduated from Smith and won a Fulbright scholarship to study in Cambridge in England. Continuing to write, she filled her notebooks with stories, **villanelles**, **sonnets** and **rondels**, shaping and reshaping her poems with studious precision and winning many awards.

Plath's life entered a new phase when she met the English poet Ted Hughes. The pair were married in London on 16 June 1956 (to coincide with Bloomsday). After obtaining her graduate degree, Plath returned to America and accepted a teaching job at Smith College for the academic year of 1957–58. She left the position after only one year and returned to England, where she settled in rural Devon. Her first volume of poetry, *The Colossus*, appeared in 1960 and was well received by critics. These early poems were well-crafted, contained potent **symbolism** and evinced a brooding sense of danger and lurking dread. Unlike her later work, the poems published in *The Colossus* did not contain an overtly personal voice. It was not until Plath wrote her radio play *Three Women: A Monologue for Three Voices* in 1962 that evidence of her later style began to emerge. The play foreshadows some of Plath's later poetry in that its structure is dramatic and it explores highly personal themes. The year 1962 was,

.er, a difficult year for Plath. Her husband was seeing another woman and ↲ left her in the autumn of that year. Plath and her two children stayed on in the house in Devon for a while and she wrote furiously. More than any other period in her short life, it was this highly productive time that would make her famous. In October, she was writing almost one poem a day. On 12 October, she claimed that she was 'writing like mad' and four days later, she felt that she was 'writing the best poems of [her] life'.

Most of these poems appeared in her collection *Ariel* and it is generally accepted that the speaker is, in fact, Plath. The poems are violent and frighteningly vivid in their depiction of suicide, loss, disfigurement and cruelty. *Ariel* shocked and excited its readers. Although Plath had written about such things before, the manner in which she expressed her thoughts had changed completely. The formal, measured, even traditional approach of her earlier poems gave way in *Ariel* to a fast-moving, energetic style. One of the great tragedies of Plath's life is that she never lived to enjoy fully the rewards of her work. She was ambitious, highly talented and she craved recognition. However, she was simply unable to escape the tragedy that invaded her personal life.

By February of 1963, her marriage had broken down irretrievably. She was living in a small flat in London and was nervous, edgy and deeply depressed. That winter was one of the coldest in living memory and Plath was unable to leave the confines of the apartment. In this claustrophobic atmosphere, her condition worsened and on Monday, 11 February, she took her own life.

The theme of motherhood figures prominently in Plath's poetry and one of her final acts as a mother was to prepare two mugs of milk and a plate of buttered bread for her children. In many respects, Plath died completely alone and unable to cope with her inner demons. In one particularly eerie passage in her poem 'Elm', the tree says:

> I am inhabited by a cry.
> Nightly it flaps out
> Looking, with its hooks, for something to love.

The **metaphors** and **images** in so many of Plath's poems suggest violence and suffering. Unfortunately, these disturbing aspects of her art found a tragic correspondence in her life.

Critical Commentary: Black Rook in Ra'
Weather

See the text of the poem on p. 177.

1. Content

As with most of Plath's poetry, it is difficult to discern a clear narrative structure in 'Black Rook in Rainy Weather'. The poem opens with an objective description of a black rook as it 'Hunches' in a tree 'Arranging and rearranging its feathers'. The speaker then becomes subjective by telling us that she does not expect a miraculous change in situation:

> I do not expect a miracle
> Or an accident
>
> To set the sight on fire

She then goes on to tell us that she will no longer look for some design in the 'desultory weather' and that the falling leaves should go unnoticed. At this point in the narrative, the speaker admits that from time to time she would like to receive some sign or 'backtalk | From the mute sky'. Yet despite this longing for a deeper meaning or purpose to the world, she feels that she really shouldn't complain. The poet then states that:

> A certain minor light may still
> Lean incandescent
>
> Out of kitchen table or chair

Although, the speaker's meaning is not completely clear, the transformation that these ordinary objects undergo is directly linked to what the poet perceives as a 'celestial burning'. In her view, this heavenly light has the power to take 'Possession of the most obtuse objects'. As a result, the manner in which we view these objects is altered.

In the third stanza, the poet tells us that such moments of altered perception are unique. They are near-religious intervals that are unlike ordinary, run-of-the-mill experiences. In the speaker's estimation, these glimpses of objects that have been transformed bestow 'largesse', 'honor', even 'love' on the person who notices them. The poet then breaks off her meditation and returns to her present situation. As she walks warily through the 'dull, ruinous landscape' of the countryside, she looks for further examples of the altered states of perception that she described in the previous two stanzas.

She approaches the landscape in a slow, hesitant manner, unable to see any sign of the light that previously transformed her kitchen table and chair. Then, suddenly, she acknowledges that the rook preening its 'black feathers' also has the ability to 'shine' and 'seize [her] senses'. In so doing, this bird grants the poet a 'brief respite from fear I Of total neutrality'. Towards the end of the third stanza, a slight change occurs in the **tone** of the poem. The poet tells us that her journey through the countryside will allow her to patch together a sense of contentment. The poem ends with an admission that:

> [...] Miracles occur,
> If you care to call those spasmodic
> Tricks of radiance miracles. [...]

The poet views these intermittent 'Tricks' of the light that have the ability to alter her perception of the world as miraculous. At the end of the poem, the speaker hints that these altered states of perception are transitory and unpredictable. The moment that allowed her to view the black rook in a different light has passed and, in the final lines of the poem, she acknowledges that:

> [...] The wait's begun again,
> The long wait for the angel,
> For that rare, random descent.

2. Stylistic Features

In this poem, the speaker's observation of the rook arranging its feathers in the rain prompts a much deeper examination of the nature of perception. The introduction of the personal pronoun 'I' in the fourth line signals that this enquiry is to be a deeply personal and subjective one. In a moment that strongly recalls Robert Frost's poem 'Design', the speaker attempts to attach some significance to the falling leaves of autumn. Her claim that the weather is 'desultory' or random is immediately countered by her admission that she often seeks inspiration or recognition from God. It is as if she is looking for a sign in nature that will link her quest for inspiration to a sympathetic God.

Many critics have pointed out that this poem can be read as an extended **metaphor** for the artistic process. In the poem, the altered states of perception that allow the poet to view the world in a completely different light are transitory. The fleeting and unpredictable nature of these moments can be likened to poetic inspiration. Given that Plath was a poet who struggled with her art, she would, of course, have been painfully aware of this fact. By describing the weather as aimless, random and lacking in design, the poet may well be hinting at her own lack of purpose. Plath often had to force herself to write. Poetic inspiration did not come to her as a matter of course. Most serious writers identify their ability to write as being essential to their very existence. In this poem, Plath tells us that the sight of the rook provides her with a momentary 'respite from fear | Of total neutrality'. This neutral state that she fears may well be the inability to write or produce poetry.

You should take the time to examine the language of the poem. Notice how many of the words are associated with faith. Words like 'miracle', 'sky', 'angel', 'hallowing' and 'celestial' reinforce the idea that the experience that the poet longs for is a unique and almost religious one. However, the poem also links this religious vocabulary with the language of doubt and uncertainty. Words and phrases such as 'accident', 'luck', 'fall as they fall', 'spasmodic', 'random', 'occasionally' and 'it could happen' hint at hesitation, a lack of conviction and indecision. If the experience that Plath is looking for is indeed a near-religious one, then it seems that she is not completely convinced that it will actually occur.

3. Essay Writing

'Black Rook in Rainy Weather' is typical of Plath's poetry. In this respect, it is very useful when it comes to writing essays. If you are thinking of including this poem in an essay, you may want to bear some of the following points in mind.

a. It is difficult to establish a clear narrative structure in the poem. Given that Plath explores the subconscious mind, it is often hard to discern a logical pattern to her poetry. 'Black Rook in Rainy Weather' can be used in any paragraph that addresses this difficulty in reading Plath's poetry.

b. The observations that Plath makes in this poem are unusual and intense.

c. The inclusion of the personal pronoun 'I' lends the poem a **confessional** feeling. Many of the poems by Plath on the course are deeply personal.

d. As with so many of the poems by Sylvia Plath in this anthology, 'Black Rook in Rainy Weather' uses the natural world as a vehicle for exploring deeper concerns.

Critical Commentary: The Times Are Tidy

See the text of the poem on p. 179.

1. Content

'The Times Are Tidy' presents us with a series of generalised observations on both the past and the present. The opening line of the first five-line stanza begins with a weary remark on the nature of the world as the speaker sees it. Any hero born into this society is 'Unlucky'. Like a stuck record, it is a place where little changes. In the next line, the poet makes a political comment. In doing so, she employs an unusual **metaphor** to highlight her point. She describes those who are innovative and daring as being like unemployed cooks at the mayor's barbeque.

In the legends of old, great heroes would often fight a dragon in order to win fame and protect their community. Here, in the second stanza, the giant dragon of folklore is reduced to the size of a small lizard. The speaker informs us that there is no sense of adventure to be gained in riding against such a creature. The passing of time in the form of 'History' has withered the once-giant dragon and, in the process, any epic threats or hazards have been diminished and 'beaten'.

In the closing stanza, the speaker tells us that the 'last crone got burnt up I More than eight decades back'. The death of this witch and the danger she once posed are juxtaposed with the safety and luxurious comfort of the present. In the past, children had to contend with dragons and witches. Now, they live in a predictable world where 'The cow milks cream an inch thick'.

2. Stylistic Features

Plath believed that 'the poet must be an expert packer of suitcases', and must be able to convey ideas and emotions in telling detail and striking images. This poem certainly remains true to those convictions. Neatly packed into three five-line stanzas, the poem perfectly captures a sense of world-weariness. Unlike many of Plath's poems on the course, 'The Times Are Tidy' does not contain the personal pronoun 'I'. Yet it is possible to detect a clear, unambiguous **tone** in this poem. The voice in 'The Times Are Tidy' is a cynical and reproachful one. The poem's vocabulary matches this disparaging tone. The speaker opposes the notion that the past was heroic and interesting with the dull, boring and uneventful language of the present.

3. Essay Writing

'The Times Are Tidy' is unlike many of the poems by Plath on the Leaving Certificate course. This means that you can contrast the poem with many of the other poems that you have studied. If you are thinking of using 'The Times Are Tidy' in an essay, some of the following points may be helpful.

a. The poem does not contain the personal pronoun 'I'. This is unusual as it is not in keeping with Plath's confessional style.
b. Once again, the poem contains strange and arresting images and comparisons.
c. The poem's theme is unlike that of any of the poems in this anthology.

Critical Commentary: Morning Song

See the text of the poem on p. 181.

1. Content

'Morning Song' was first published in Plath's most famous collection of poems, *Ariel*. In the words of Al Alvarez, this collection of poetry contains poems that are 'despairing, vengeful and destructive'. However, it also contains pieces that are warm, tender and unusually clever. While 'Morning Song' contains moments of insecurity, it is basically an optimistic poem. It opens with a direct and warmly inclusive statement:

> Love set you going like a fat gold watch.

We learn that the midwife slapped the child's feet in order to prompt it to take its first breath. As a result, the baby's 'bald cry | Took its place among the elements'. In the second *tercet*, the narrative takes on a slightly surreal aspect. This is most likely a conscious attempt on Plath's part to mirror her feelings of disorientation following the birth. The baby is likened to a museum piece. What are presumably the adults are seen to be shadowed by this naked, newborn baby. The poet then reveals her insecurity and uncertainty by proclaiming in the third stanza:

> I'm no more your mother
> Than the cloud that distills a mirror to reflect its own slow
> Effacement at the wind's hand.

Here, the poet compares the complex relationship between mother and child to that between a cloud and a pool of water. The cloud produces water that forms a pool, and the pool, in turn, reflects the cloud.

In the fourth stanza, the speaker's attention focuses on her child. The child's breath is described as being like the fluttering of a moth. Its lips are likened to pink roses. In many of Plath's poems, flowers are, at best, viewed in an ambiguous light and, at worst, as being threatening. However, here, the roses act as **symbols** of maternal warmth. Lying awake, the poet listens and is reminded of a 'far sea' moving in her 'ear'. Alerted by the baby's cry, she stumbles (despite the fact that she is 'cow-heavy') in its direction. The baby responds to her arrival by opening its mouth. 'The window square | Whitens and swallows its dull stars'. As the poet contemplates this sight, her child begins to cry once again, '[its] handful of notes | [...] rise like balloons'.

2. Stylistic Features

Plath wrote 'Morning Song' after the arrival of her first child, Frieda. This poem makes use of detailed and beautiful imagery in order to evoke the mother–child relationship. So many of Plath's poems are dark and disturbing, but 'Morning Song' is different in that it is a genuine and tender expression of love. The poem opens in a direct and inclusive manner that draws the reader into the narrative and invites him or her to share in the beauty of the scene. The descriptive language employed by the poet to illustrate her feelings on becoming a mother is as precise as it is original. For the most part, she concentrates on the sounds that the child makes. Its cry is described as being 'bald' and its breathing is likened to the fluttering of a moth. These unusual associations underline the newness of this experience for the poet. She cannot rely on the traditional or standard *images* of poetry to describe how she feels. In order to convey to the reader the idea that her baby is an entirely different and new person, the speaker makes use of a captivating *simile*. The baby's mouth 'opens clean as a cat's'. Her baby, having left the womb, is no longer a part of her. It is a new and unique individual.

However, the child does reflect aspects of the poet. In order to convey this aspect of their relationship, Plath relies on the unusual natural imagery of rainwater and clouds. The intensity of the mother's feelings is captured by the surreal description of the adults in the room standing 'round blankly as walls'. Notice how the echo of the adult voices seems to magnify the importance of the child's arrival. However, while the poet is expressly joyous in her outlook, she also has the honesty to admit to feelings of unease. The baby is described as shadowing the safety of its parents. This line reflects the poet's sense of disquiet and uncertainty. A way of life that was safe and established is obviously about to be turned on its head. It would be wrong, however, to read this poem in a negative light. It is, above all, a celebration – an honest celebration of the single most important event in the lives of most parents.

3. Essay Writing

'Morning Song' provides us with a welcome respite from the darker aspects of Plath's poetry. Motherhood is a major theme in her poetry and you may want to consider devoting a paragraph to this theme. If you are going to use 'Morning Song' in an essay, you may wish to use some of the following points in your paragraph.

roud and protective of her newborn child. The **tone** of the poem is
lusive.

play an important role in the poem. This is, of course, true of many
's poems. You may wish to devote an entire paragraph to her use of
col r.

c. The arrangement of the stanzas in six tercets is controlled and measured. This
prevents the poem from becoming over-sentimental.

Critical Commentary: Finisterre

See the text of the poem on pp. 183–4.

1. Content

'Finisterre' is a dark and somewhat disturbing poem that opens with a statement in
the past tense. Referring to the place named in the title, the poet says 'This was the
land's end'. This landscape is likened to the hand of a rheumatoid arthritis sufferer.
It is 'knuckled and [...] | Cramped on nothing'. The dark cliffs overlook what seems
to be a bottomless sea. In a disturbing moment, the water appears as if it has been
whitened by the faces of the drowned. The dull and ominous rocks are seen as
being akin to 'Leftover soldiers from old, messy wars'. For a brief moment, the poet
considers what might lie under the water but then draws back.

In the second stanza, she returns to the cliff edges. They have been embroidered
with 'trefoils, stars and bells'. In her imagination, the speaker sees the decorative
covering of clover that adorns the cliff edge as being embroidered by fingers close to
death. She then returns her gaze to the sea. The mist seems unconcerned with this
imaginary figure who is nearing death. In Western literature, the mists of the sea
have long been associated with the souls of the dead. Plath can now see these souls
as they roll in the 'doom-noise of the sea'. When they do manage to break free, their
only action is to:

> [...] bruise the rocks out of existence, then resurrect them.
> They go up without hope, like sighs.

As the wind lashes the coast, the poet feels as if she is walking among these souls. They 'stuff [her] mouth with cotton' and when they free her, she is 'beaded with tears'.

In the third stanza, the poem becomes even more disconnected from the actual world as the speaker imagines that:

> Our Lady of the Shipwrecked is striding toward the horizon,
> Her marble skirts blown back in two pink wings.

This is most likely intended to be a description of a statue of the Virgin Mary. At the foot of this figure, a 'marble sailor kneels'. 'A peasant woman in black' is also 'praying to the monument'. However, it is the statue of the Virgin Mary that keeps the speaker's attention. She is 'three times life size' and her 'lips [are] sweet with divinity'. Worryingly, she appears to ignore the prayers of the people at her feet:

> She does not hear what the sailor or the peasant is saying—
> She is in love with the beautiful formlessness of the sea.

For most of 'Finisterre', the speaker has the courage to face the dark and dangerous sea on her own. However, in the closing movement of the poem, she makes a marked withdrawal from the cliff's edge. The surreal seascape that has dominated the poem now yields to the more human landscape of 'postcard stalls', 'pretty trinkets', 'necklaces' and 'toy ladies'. In a final reference to the dark, watery world she has just visited, the speaker reminds us that these seaside souvenirs 'do not come from the Bay of the Dead down there'. They come from 'another place, tropical and blue'. In the final line of the poem, a human voice interrupts the speaker's thoughts. She is told to eat her pancakes before they go cold.

2. Stylistic Features

The disturbing **tone** of Plath's poetry underscores a depth of feeling that can be attributed to few other poets. Writing in *The Observer*, Al Alvarez described her work as being 'of great artistic purity'. Her obsession with death and her near-suicidal attempts to communicate a frightening vision of the world often overshadow all discussion of stylistic technique. Nevertheless, it is possible to detect stylistic features in 'Finisterre' that are also present in much of Plath's other poetry on the course.

In her poems, the sea is often associated with death by drowning. In this respect, 'Finisterre' is no different. The title of the poem is suggestive of death or the end of a journey. Interestingly, the poem opens in the past tense. This unusual choice of tense (given that the place still exists) hints at the *symbolic* meaning of the poem. The opening *image* of old, rheumatic fingers clinging desperately to the land is a disturbing one. The cliffs that these fingers cling to warn of danger and, far below, the sea explodes angrily. Many of Plath's seascape poems depict a turbulent sea that is, in fact, a reflection of the poet's troubled state of mind. The world of this poem is reminiscent of the images contained in a surreal painting. It is a world that has been 'Whitened by the faces of the drowned'. By the end of the first stanza, the poet has succeeded in establishing a threatening, sinister and uneasy *atmosphere* through her use of *personification*. A battle is being waged between the sea and the rocks. At times, the souls of the dead, in the form of mist, appear to break free from their watery graves only to be drawn back into the water again. This seems to be an endless struggle.

You should pay attention to the visual quality of the poem. The colours black and white appear in many of Plath's later poems. When she uses these colours, black is usually used to convey despair and gloom, while white symbolises emptiness and deadness. The introduction of 'Our Lady of the Shipwrecked' does little to lessen this dark and gloomy atmosphere. Normally a *symbol* of hope and comfort, in this poem Our Lady turns her back on those looking for her help.

In the closing stanza of the poem, the dark atmosphere continues to prevail. As the poet moves away from the daunting seascape of Finisterre, she returns to the human world of commerce, 'crêpes' and 'pretty trinkets'. The fact that none of these comes from the place that she has just been to reinforces in the reader's mind the idea that Finisterre is a dark and disturbing place. In fact, throughout this poem, human concerns seem trivial when one considers the darkly powerful and elemental conflict that takes place between land and sea. The sea has often been used as a *metaphor* for the subconscious in literature and it is entirely possible to read the sea as acting as such in this poem. In any case, this poem deals with extremes and extreme states. The act of reaching the edge of a cliff is strongly suggestive of a mental breakdown. While the jerky and jagged appearance of the stanzas mirrors the physical landscape of Finisterre, it may also be suggestive of the poet's state of mind. If the sea does represent her subconscious, then it is obviously meant to depict a troubled mind.

3. Essay Writing

'Finisterre' is one of the most memorable poems by Plath on the course. This fact alone merits its inclusion in any response to Plath's poetry that you may be asked to make. If you wish to include 'Finisterre' in a response to her poetry, you may wish to include some of the following points.

a. The imagery in the poem is dark and powerful.
b. The sea can be interpreted as a metaphor for Plath's subconscious mind. This fact may provide you with an opportunity to link your discussion of the poem to other poems on the course.
c. Once again, Plath turns to nature in order to make concrete the inner workings of her mind.

Critical Commentary: Mirror

See the text of the poem on p. 185.

1. Content

'Mirror' opens with two short, clipped sentences that capture the mirror's essence perfectly:

> I am silver and exact. I have no preconceptions.

The voice of the mirror goes on to tell us that whatever it sees, it swallows 'immediately'. The mirror does not seek to alter the image that it reflects. It is 'unmisted by love or dislike'. As this series of statements may appear harsh, the mirror quickly seeks to reassure us that it is 'not cruel, only truthful'. The *tone* of the mirror's voice changes slightly in the fifth line. It tells us that it is like:

> The eye of a little god, four-cornered.

When no one passes in front of the mirror, it 'meditate[s] on the opposite wall'. In fact, this mirror has spent so much time contemplating the 'pink' and speckled wall that it believes the wall to be part of its heart.

There is a sudden shift in the narrative in the second stanza. The mirror now sees itself as a lake over which a woman is leaning:

> Searching my reaches for what she really is.

The woman then turns to the 'candles' and the 'moon'. The mirror views these traditional **symbols** of romance as being 'liars'. Suddenly, the looking-glass takes on a sinister aspect. It feels rewarded by the woman's tears and the shaking of her hands. It feels that it occupies an important place in the woman's life. In this mirror, the woman has watched herself change from a young girl to an old woman:

> In me she has drowned a young girl, and in me an old woman
> Rises toward her day after day, like a terrible fish.

2. Stylistic Features

In order to capture the essence of the mirror, the poet endows it with human characteristics. This use of **personification** renders the mirror more interesting and sinister. The opening statement by the mirror suggests that it is honest and open. However, its short, clipped sentences and its metallic appearance lead us to believe that this mirror is cold and harsh:

> I am silver and exact. I have no preconceptions.
> Whatever I see I swallow immediately
> Just as it is, unmisted by love or dislike.
> I am not cruel, only truthful—

Something of the mirror's sinister ego is revealed when it likens itself to 'The eye of a little god'. The mirror's **tone** of voice is smug and disturbing.

Even more troubling is the manner in which the woman rewards its behaviour. She searches its 'reaches' for who she really is and, in the process, gratifies it. By including a human figure, Plath expands the scope of the poem. In this manner, the shallow belief that surface appearances can reveal deeper truths is exposed for what it is. The foolhardy trust that the woman seems to place in superficial, outward appearances feeds the mirror's monstrous ego. Whenever she attempts to seek comfort elsewhere, such as from 'those liars, the candles or the moon', the mirror's resentment is almost palpable.

The other noticeable aspect of the poem is the manner in which it charts the woman's ageing. In a disturbingly *ironic* moment, the woman is swallowed up as a result of her own egotism. Her desperate need to be reassured by what she sees leads her to worship her own self-image. However, this act results in the complete annihilation of her personality. She literally drowns in her ego and, in the process, is transformed into a 'terrible fish'. Ageing is seen to lead to a difficult and even frightening transformation. As we have said, this is a process that gratifies the cold mirror.

3. Essay Writing

'Mirror' is a fascinating poem and worthy of inclusion in a personal response to Plath's poetry. If you are considering writing about 'Mirror' in an essay, you may want to include some of the following points.

a. The poet's language captures the essence of the mirror in chilling detail.
b. The poem is structured in such a manner so as to appear symmetrical. Both stanzas are carefully measured and, in this sense, the form of the poem mirrors the subject matter.
c. Once again, Plath draws on unusual and memorable imagery so as to retain the reader's attention.

Critical Commentary: Pheasant

See the text of the poem on p. 187.

1. Content

The speaker in 'Pheasant' opens the poem with a plea that the pheasant should not be killed:

> You said you would kill it this morning.
> Do not kill it. It startles me still,

Although the appearance of the pheasant (its jerky movements and its 'odd, dark head') startles the speaker, she feels privileged to be 'visited' by this bird. In the third **tercet**, the poet tells us that she does not assign any spiritual significance to the arrival of the pheasant. She simply views the bird as being 'in its element'. This bird has a stately or kingly bearing. Her first encounter with the pheasant dates back to last winter, when she witnessed 'The print of its big foot [...] | [...] on the snow'. Now, she can see it through the 'crosshatch of sparrow and starling'. The speaker then wonders if it is the rareness of the bird that she finds attractive. In the sixth tercet, she even goes so far as to suggest that she would like to see:

> A hundred, on that hill—green and red,
> Crossing and recrossing: a fine thing!

The poet's admiration for the physical form of the pheasant emerges in the next stanza. She feels it has a 'good shape' and that its form is clear. In the final stanza of the poem, there is a shift in the poet's perception. She now sees herself as being the trespasser. This bird is 'in its element' and it is the speaker who has entered this environment 'stupidly'. She ends the poem feeling that she should 'Let be, let be'.

2. Stylistic Features

'Pheasant' belongs to a series that has become known as the 'April group'. During this extraordinarily creative period, Plath began to explore the countryside around her. In many of the poems written during this time, Plath uses nature to undertake journeys of self-exploration.

This poem is constructed in a series of tercets. This carefully formed arrangement of stanzas traces the speaker's changing attitude towards the pheasant. The *rhyming* scheme, *terza rima*, is a very formal arrangement that implies continual progression.

In many respects, the poet undertakes a journey in this poem. 'Pheasant' charts her changing attitude to the natural world. In the opening stanza, the *tone* of the speaker is urgent. She implores the unnamed addressee not to kill the bird and then goes on to consider the bird. The staccato, or jerky, third line of the first stanza captures something of the pheasant's movement. By making use of *enjambment*, or the run-on line, to join the first and second stanzas, Plath approximates the fluid progress of the bird 'Through the uncut grass'. This urgent, even nervous, tone of the opening stanzas slowly yields to a calmer, more contemplative *mood* in the latter half of the poem. Here, the poet sees the bird as representing abundance and plenty. In her eyes, it becomes 'a little cornucopia'. This subjective description of the bird is matched by an objective observation of nature's abundance. The sun, the elm tree and the narcissi, along with the colours of spring, all suggest a world in full growth. The critic Tim Kendall believes that 'the bird represents vibrant life: it is "red" and "vivid", a "good shape", "a little cornucopia", it "unclaps, brown leaf, and loud", and it suns itself among the narcissi'.

Finally, the ending of the poem leads us to feel hopeful. The reader is made to realise that the speaker's attitude to the bird has been altered and, as result, the pheasant will live.

3. Essay Writing

'Pheasant' clearly demonstrates Plath's powers of perception. You may wish to devote a paragraph to this aspect of Plath's ability as a poet. If you are going to include this poem in an essay, you should consider the following points.

a. Plath's poetry tends to be dark and troubling, yet the language of the poem is vivid and lively. This means that you can contrast 'Pheasant' with many of the poems by Plath on the course.

b. The poet's observation of the bird is intense and the language she uses to convey her thoughts is unusual.

c. Once again, colour plays an important role in the poem. You may want to consider devoting a paragraph to Plath's use of colour.

Critical Commentary: Elm

See the text of the poem on pp. 189–90.

1. Content

'Elm' is a complex, even confusing, poem. The poem takes the form of a dialogue between the speaker and an elm tree. Because both voices in the poem employ the personal pronoun 'I', many readers find it difficult to make sense of the narrative structure of 'Elm'.

The poem opens with a startling statement from the tree:

> I know the bottom, she says. I know it with my great tap root:
> It is what you fear.

It is possible to read the next line as a reply from the speaker to what the elm has just said. Here, the speaker refutes the tree's suggestion that she is afraid of the bottom:

> I do not fear it: I have been there.

In the second three-line stanza, the elm questions the speaker. It asks her whether or not she hears echoes of her own 'dissatisfactions' or 'madness' in the movement of the tree. In the third stanza, the voice of the speaker claims that 'Love is a shadow'. The elm reminds her that she still yearns for love, but the speaker replies that love has disappeared:

> Listen: these are its hooves: it has gone off, like a horse.

What is presumably meant to be the voice of the elm then tells the speaker that it intends to 'gallop [...] impetuously | Till [her] head is a stone'. In the fifth stanza, the voice of the elm offers to bring the speaker 'the sound of poisons'. In the sixth stanza, we are made aware that the tree has 'suffered' terribly. The 'atrocity of sunsets' that the elm refers to has 'Scorched [it] to the root'.

The abrupt change in action in the seventh stanza is signalled when the elm tells us that it 'break[s] up in pieces that fly about like clubs'. This scattering effect refers to the physical action of the wind on the trees, but it also hints at a troubling break-up of the tree's being. In the eighth stanza, the elm tells us that the 'moon, also, is merciless'. The *imagery* becomes even more troubling. In the eyes of the elm, the moon is a sinister figure. It is 'barren' and its 'radiance scathes' the tree. For a moment, the tree feels that it has caught the moon in the tangle of its branches. However, it quickly lets the moon go. For its part, the moon has been disfigured by the encounter with the tree. It is as if it has been forced to undergo a mastectomy or some other form of 'radical surgery'.

At this point in the poem, it becomes difficult to separate the voice of the speaker from that of the tree. The tree tells us that it feels 'inhabited by a cry'. This 'dark thing | That sleeps' in her a is soft and its 'feathery turnings' are described as being malign. Meanwhile, the 'Clouds pass and disperse'. These fleeting images are likened to the faces of past loves. They, too, have been changed radically and can never be restored to the way they once were. The fact that these 'faces of love' are irretrievable is a source of pain and agitation for the speaker:

Is it for such I agitate my heart?

In the final two stanzas, the poem becomes more difficult to decipher. The imagery is increasingly surreal and it is no longer clear who is speaking. Perhaps the narrative voice is meant to represent both speakers in the poem. In any case, the speaker tells us that it is 'incapable of more knowledge'. A face appears in the 'strangle of branches' and its 'snaky acids kiss' literally 'petrifies the will' of the speaker. The final words of the poem are disturbing. In language that is violent, both speakers are effaced, or erased. The physical assaults that it has been subjected to take their toll on the elm. Similarly, the emotional damage that the female speaker has suffered destroys her. These 'faults', both physical and emotional, are seen as being the ones:

That kill, that kill, that kill.

2. Stylistic Features

The critic Tim Kendall feels that, while it is given the single date of 19 April, 'Elm' 'perfects themes and images with which Plath had been struggling for weeks'. During the five months preceding her suicide, Plath wrote almost the entire body of poems that were to be collected two years later and published as *Ariel*. These poems amount to a personal catalogue of the loneliness and insecurity that plagued her.

Crowded with desolate, disturbing imagery, *Ariel* lays bare her fixation with death. 'Elm' was first published in this collection. Plath's early drafts of the poem were published by her husband, Ted Hughes, in her *Collected Poems*. The notes to this early version of the poem reveal that Plath intended 'Elm' to capture a disturbed psychic state. Plath's first draft opened with the line, 'She is not easy she is not peaceful.' The final version, which appears in this anthology, also contains an uneasy attempt to express the pain of a mind in torment. While there seem to be two speakers in the poem, at times it is as if their identities merge. 'Elm' contains some of Plath's favourite images: trees at night and the icy pallor of the moon. It is typical of Plath's poetry that nature mirrors the emotions of the poet and this is certainly the case here.

The voice of the elm empathises with the female speaker in the poem. It shares her emotions and recognises her fears and insecurities. The ***personification*** of the tree leads us to believe that the elm really can empathise with the speaker's troubled emotional state. This process begins in the second stanza. The **onomatopoeic** effect of the word 'dissatisfactions' not only approximates the sound of the leaves rustling, but also creates an uneasy, restless sound. This sound is echoed in the fifth stanza by the rain, which falls in a 'big hush'. This is another restless sound that may be intended to mirror the speaker's emotional state. In the sixth stanza, the tree informs us that it has:

> [...] suffered the atrocity of sunsets.
> Scorched to the root
> My red filaments burn and stand, a hand of wires.

This may well be an **allusion** to electro-convulsive shock therapy. This treatment is used on patients who suffer from depression and other mental illnesses. Plath underwent shock treatment at Valley Head Hospital following a serious mental breakdown and attempted suicide in 1952. It seems more than coincidental that the voice of the tree should articulate a sensation that closely resembles being electrocuted. It is important to realise that the central image here is not a hopeful one. The image of a sunset suggests an end, not a beginning. Furthermore, this sunset is not natural: it is over-bright and worryingly intense.

If the elm has suffered, it is also capable of empathy. It senses the speaker's own suffering and pain. It understands how she has been tormented by 'love' and 'madness'. In response to this suffering, the elm offers to assuage the speaker's pain with the 'sound of poisons'. As we have already discussed, sounds are very important to the overall feelings of unease in this poem. In the second half of 'Elm', these feelings are reinforced by some strange and unsettling imagery. The moon is linked to a cold, barren vision of a mutilated femininity. Could this be a projection of the poet/speaker's self-image?

In the final stanzas of the poem, death appears to close in as fear turns to numbness. As the poem draws to a close, both personae adopted by the poet become submerged. Neither the tree nor the speaker emerges fully in the final stanza. It is as if both speakers have been destroyed by their encounter with one another. It is impossible to provide an accurate description of what takes place in this poem. The lack of logic and loose narrative structure in 'Elm' reflect the speaker's own troubled state of mind. This is a dark poem that offers us a glimpse into the violent, uneasy and ultimately tragic mental condition of the poet.

3. Essay Writing

'Elm' embodies many of the qualities that make Plath's poetry so memorable. If you are writing a paragraph that makes use of this poem, you might want to include some of the following points.

a. The language of the poem is haunting and troubling, yet it is also very beautiful.
b. The poem reveals to us the extent of Plath's disturbed mental state.
c. Once again, the poet draws on nature to make her innermost feelings intelligible to her readership.

Critical Commentary: Poppies in July

See the text of the poem on p. 192.

1. Content

A concise and powerful poem, 'Poppies in July' opens with an unusual description of the poppies. From her hospital bed, the speaker views the flowers as 'little hell flames'. She then addresses the poppies directly, asking them if they do any harm. In the second *couplet*, the poet continues to gaze at the flowers. She cannot touch them. They flicker like flames but, importantly, they do not burn. The experience of staring at the flowers so intently 'exhausts' the poet. The petals of these small, red flowers remind the speaker of the 'skin of a mouth'. The *image* is extended in the fourth couplet. Here, the speaker tells us that she views the poppies as being like a 'mouth just bloodied'. She goes on to say that these flowers remind her of 'little bloody skirts'.

As the speaker's senses become increasingly dulled, she continues to stress the fact that she cannot touch these flowers. Aware of the poppies' scent, the poet now searches for their 'opiates' and 'nauseous capsules'. In the sixth couplet, the imagery becomes more disturbing. The speaker longs for release from her numbed state:

> If I could bleed, or sleep!—
> If my mouth could marry a hurt like that!

The juices of the poppy (from which opiates are derived) continue to seep into her. As a result, the speaker feels that her senses have been dulled. Eventually, everything becomes 'colorless'.

2. Stylistic Features

'Poppies in July' is another darkly disturbing poem. The *tone* of the speaker's voice suggests a masochistic desire for self-harm. At the centre of the poem is the belief, on the speaker's part, that sleeping and bleeding are solutions to her present state of mind. Interestingly, the flowers refuse to co-operate with the speaker. They might be 'little hell flames', but they refuse to burn the speaker even when she puts her hands amongst them.

This poem was written during a period of great emotional turmoil for Plath and it captures the poet's desperate desire, loneliness and confusion. The speaker uses *synaesthesia* in the poem in order to convey her bewildered state. She attempts to touch the 'fumes', yet the imagined flames fail to burn her. Notice how the predominance of broad vowel sounds mirrors the poet's lethargic and numbed state of being. Yet Plath manages to juxtapose these broad vowel sounds with the more lively, slender sounds used to describe the flowers. The 'Little poppies' 'flicker' and dance in front of her. Their movement and energy are in sharp contrast to the stupor of the poet. Despite the speaker's attempts to capture the poppies' negative power, they remain *symbolic* of life.

At the end of the poem, the poet views the world as being 'colorless'. However, the vivid blood-red of the poppies lingers on in the memory of the reader. They refuse to yield to the speaker's harmful impulses and seem to insist on life. 'Poppies in July' is another disturbing and exhilarating poem that manages to convey something of the poet's troubled mental state.

3. Essay Writing

'Poppies in July' is another one of the poems by Plath on the course that offers us a glimpse into the poet's troubled mental state. If you are going to use this poem in an essay on Plath, you might want to make use of some of the following points.

a. The poem illustrates Plath's obsession with self-harm.

b. The use of colour in the poem reveals the intensity of Plat︶

c. As its title suggests, 'Poppies in July' draws on the natural wo.
   sense of the poet's troubled mental state.

Critical Commentary: The Arrival of the Bee Box

See the text of the poem on pp. 194–5.

1. Content

In 'The Arrival of the Bee Box', the opening statement by the speaker is arresting. She tells us that she has ordered a 'clean wood box'. It is 'Square as a chair and almost too heavy to lift'. Considering the box further, the poet feels that it could be the 'coffin of a midget' or even a 'square baby'. This disturbing association with death is temporarily countered by the lively sounds that come from the box. However, in the second five-line stanza, the poet sees the box as being 'dangerous'. Drawn to this danger, she says that she simply 'can't keep away from it'. She moves closer to the bee box in the third stanza and puts her 'eye to the grid'. The place is dark, angry and claustrophobic. In the fourth stanza, the speaker believes that she will never be able to let these creatures out. The noise they make 'appalls' her. She is shocked by the incoherent buzzing, which she likens to the noise a 'Roman mob' might have made. The thought of all these bees acting with a single purpose unnerves her:

> Small, taken one by one, but my god, together!

In the fifth stanza, the poet compares the sounds of the bees to a furious form of Latin. Then, she develops the *allusion* to ancient Rome. While she views the bees as being akin to a 'Roman mob', she, as their owner, does not believe she is Caesar:

> I am not a Caesar.
> I have simply ordered a box of maniacs.
> They can be sent back.
> They can die, I need feed them nothing, I am the owner.

There is a change in the *tone* of the speaker's voice here. As she asserts her own will, she reveals a darker side to her own persona. There is a cruel selfishness to her assertion that she can 'feed them nothing'. In the sixth stanza, the poet wonders how the bees would react if she 'undid the locks and stood back and turned into a tree'. Dressed in her beekeeper's 'moon suit', she feels that the bees would 'ignore' her. She is not a 'source of honey'. In the final lines of the poem, the speaker promises to be sweet and to set them free. In her eyes, 'The box is only temporary'.

2. Stylistic Features

At the heart of 'The Arrival of the Bee Box' lies an exploration of the concept of control. As the poem opens, the speaker attempts to describe her first impressions of the bee box. The first *simile* that she uses compares it to a 'chair' that is 'too heavy to lift'. The poet quickly dismisses this *comparison* in favour of the disturbing *metaphors* that follow. Firstly, the box is likened to the 'coffin of a midget' and then to that of 'a square baby'. The point here is that the language of the poem is unable to control or label the bees correctly. In the words of Tim Kendall, the 'specificity of the box resists comparisons'. Inside the box is a dark and 'dangerous' world. This danger is captured by carefully constructed sound effects. *Onomatopoeic* words and phrases, such as the 'din in it' and 'noise', hint at the sound of the bees. This buzzing, swarming sound adds to our impression that the atmosphere in the bee box is claustrophobic and angry. Meanwhile, outside the box, the speaker remains nervous and jumpy.

In 'The Arrival of the Bee Box', the poet attempts to assert her identity and, in the process, control this buzzing, maniacal mass. Notice how the poet uses the personal pronoun 'I' 18 times. It is as if her ownership of the bees causes her to become hyper-aware of her own sense of self. This intense consideration of her relationship with the world is, of course, typical of Plath's poetry. However, the speaker is not entirely at ease with her new role as a god. The comparison with 'African hands' alludes to the slave trade, where the strong controlled the weak. The speaker says that she can control this mass of bees by not feeding them. However, by comparing them to a 'Roman mob', this control is called into doubt. In fact, her frantic proclamation that she is 'not a Caesar' almost sounds defensive. Julius Caesar met a bloody end at the hands of the people he tried to control. The poem ends with the speaker promising to liberate the bees. She releases her control over them. Strangely enough, Plath never fully articulates what these bees are meant to *symbolise*. At the end of the poem, the very box that provoked such concentrated and intense consideration of identity and control is viewed by the speaker as being only 'temporary'.

3. Essay Writing

If you are thinking of including 'The Arrival of the Bee Box' in one of your essay's paragraphs, you may want to consider some of the following points.

a. The nervous and edgy tone of voice adopted by the speaker mirrors the poet's uneasy mental state.

b. On the face of it, the arrival of a box of bees is a run-of-the-mill event. However, when viewed from Plath's unique perspective, the event is transformed.

c. The language of the poem is intense and works to create a claustrophobic atmosphere.

Critical Commentary: Child

See the text of the poem on p. 196.

1. Content

'Child' is a dark, yet beautiful, poem which captures Plath's growing sense of insecurity concerning her marriage and her mixed feelings at being a mother again. In January 1962, Plath's son, Nicholas, was born. Unfortunately, the birth of the child coincided with a very painful time for Plath, during which her marriage broke up. Ted Hughes, her husband, who was in love with someone else, moved to London, leaving a bitter and beleaguered Plath with the two children in Devon; she wrote to her mother in August that she wanted a legal separation because:

> I simply cannot go on living the degraded and agonized life I have been living, which has stopped my writing and just about ruined my sleep and my health.

Struggling with her desolation and disenchantment, she kept herself occupied with beekeeping, took up horse-riding and wrote passionate and often violent poems. In this poem, she outlines her first impressions of her new son. She says that his 'clear eye is the one absolutely beautiful thing'. Her journal entry, written the day after Nicholas was born, echoes these sentiments:

> I felt very proud of Nicholas, and fond. It had taken a night to be sure I liked him – his head shaped up beautifully ... a handsome, male head with a back brain-shelf. Dark, black blue eyes, a furze of hair like a crewcut.

In the second line of 'Child', the speaker says she wants to fill the baby's clear eye with 'color and ducks'. In playful, childlike language, she describes this new arrangement of colours and ducks as being 'The zoo of the new'. In her estimation, her new baby is like an 'April snowdrop'. Its beautiful eyes should reflect noble and grandiose images, not the nervous agitation of its mother. The poem ends in a sombre, troubling manner. The child's eye now reflects a 'dark I Ceiling without a star'.

2. Stylistic Features

'Child' charts the poet's confused state following the birth of her child. To begin with, the poem suggests a hopeful and joyous *mood*. Colour is extremely important in Plath's poetry and this poem opens with the speaker longing to fill the clear eye of her child with colour. The language of the poem is childlike and deliberately attempts to simulate the sounds a mother makes when talking to her child. Likewise, the lilting *rhythm* and simplistic *rhyming* scheme of the poem work to create an almost nursery rhyme effect. The poem's narrative is related in four *tercets*. This three-line structure is normally used by Plath to contain separate viewpoints. However, in 'Child', the tercets are linked together by a series of *run-on lines*. The use of *enjambment* allows Plath to maintain its gentle momentum. In the fourth stanza, the *tone* and mood of the poem darken. The actions of the troubled mother are seen through the eyes of the child. A poem that began in a hopeful manner is utterly transformed in the final stanza. The brightness and hope that we associated with the clarity of the child's eye is now replaced by a dark despondency.

3. Essay Writing

Motherhood is an extremely important theme in the poetry of Sylvia Plath. Bearing this in mind, you may wish to include 'Child' in a response to the poetry of Plath that you have studied. Consider some of the following points.

a. Unlike 'Morning Song', this poem has a darker tone.
b. The poem reveals intimate details about the poet's private life.
c. Notice the contrast between dark and light in the poem. As we have mentioned previously, colour is extremely important in Plath's poetry.

Adrienne Rich (1929–)

A Short Biography

The following is an extract from the title essay of Adrienne Rich's poetic autobiography *Blood, Bread, and Poetry*, in which she outlines the factors in her life that influenced her most as a person and as a poet.

I was born at the brink of the Great Depression; I reached sixteen the year of Nagasaki and Hiroshima. The daughter of a Jewish father and Protestant mother, I learned about the Holocaust first from newsreels of the liberation of the death camps. I was a young, white woman who had never known hunger or homelessness, growing up in the suburbs of a deeply segregated city in which neighborhoods were also dictated along religious lines: Christian and Jewish. I lived sixteen years of my life secure in the belief that though cities could be bombed and civilian populations killed, the earth stood in its old indestructible way. The process through which nuclear annihilation was to become a part of all human calculation had already begun, but we did not live with that knowledge during the first sixteen years of my life. And a recurrent theme in much poetry I read was the indestructibility of poetry, the poem as a vehicle for personal immortality.

I had grown up hearing and reading poems from a very young age, first as sounds, repeated, musical, rhythmically satisfying in themselves, and the power of concrete, sensuously compelling images.

But poetry soon became more than music and images; it was also revelation, information, a kind of teaching. I believed I could learn from it – an unusual idea for a United States citizen, even a child. I thought it could offer clues, intimations, keys to questions that already stalked me, questions I could not even frame yet: *What is possible in this life? What does "love" mean, this thing that is so important? What is this other thing called "freedom" or "liberty"—is it like love, a feeling? How am I going to live my life?* The fact that poets contradicted themselves and each other didn't baffle or alarm me. I was avid for everything I could get; my child's mind did not shut down for the sake of consistency.

I thought that the poets in anthologies were the only real poets, that their being in the anthologies was proof of this, though some were classified as "great" and others as "minor." I owed much to these anthologies: *Silver Pennies*; the constant outflow of volumes edited by Louis Untermeyer; *The Cambridge Book of Poetry for Children*; Palgrave's *Golden Treasury*; the *Oxford Book of English Verse*. But I had no idea that they reflected the taste of a particular time or of particular kinds of people. I still believed that poets were inspired by some transcendent authority and spoke from some extraordinary height. I thought that the capacity to hook syllables together in a way that heated the blood was the sign of a universal vision.

I was in college during the late 1940s and early 1950s. The thirties, a decade of economic desperation, social unrest, war and also of affirmed political art, was receding behind the fogs of the Cold War, the selling of the nuclear family with the mother at home as its core, heightened activity by the FBI and CIA, a retreat by many artists from so-called "protest" art, witch-hunting among artists and intellectuals as well as in the State Department, anti-Semitism, scapegoating of homosexual men and lesbians, and with a symbolic victory for the Cold War crusade in the 1953 electrocution of Ethel and Julius Rosenberg.

Francis Otto Matthiessen, a socialist and a homosexual, was teaching literature at Harvard when I came there. One semester he lectured on five poets: Blake, Keats, Byron, Yeats and Stevens. That class perhaps affected my life as a poet more than anything else that happened to me in college. Matthiessen had a passion for language, and he read aloud, made us memorize poems and recite them to him as part of the course. He also actually alluded to events in the outside world, the hope that eastern Europe could survive as an independent socialist force between the United States and the Soviet Union; he spoke of the current European youth movements as if they should matter to us. Poetry, in his classroom, never remained in the realm of pure textual criticism. Remember that this was in 1947 or 1948, that it was a rare teacher of literature at Harvard who referred to a world beyond the text, even though the classrooms were full of World War II veterans studying on the G.I. Bill of Rights—men who might otherwise never have gone to college, let alone Harvard, at all. Matthiessen committed suicide in the spring of my sophomore year.

Because of Yeats, who by then had become my idea of the Great Poet, the one who more than others could hook syllables together in a way that heated my blood, I took a course in Irish history. It was taught by a Boston Irish professor of Celtic, one of Harvard's tokens, whose father, it was said, had been a Boston policeman. He read poetry aloud in Gaelic and in English, sang us political ballads, gave us what amounted to a mini-education on British racism and imperialism, though the words were never mentioned. He also slashed at Irish self-romanticizing. People laughed about the Irish history course, said it must be full of football players. In and out of the Harvard Yard, the racism of Yankee Brahmin toward Boston Irish was never questioned, laced as it was with equally unquestioned class arrogance. Today, Irish Boston both acts out and takes the weight of New England racism against Black and Hispanic people. It was, strangely enough, through poetry that I first began to try to make sense of these things.

I could hazard the guess that all the most impassioned, seductive arguments against the artist's involvement in politics can be found in Yeats. It was this dialogue between art and politics that excited me in his work, along with the sound of his language—never his elaborate mythological systems. A poet—one who was apparently certified—could actually write about political themes, could weave the names of political activists into a poem:

> MacDonagh and MacBride
> And Connolly and Pearse
> Now and in time to be
> Wherever green is worn
> Are changed, changed utterly:
> A terrible beauty is born.

As we all do when young and searching for what we can't even name yet, I took what I could use where I could find it. When the ideas or forms we need are banished, we seek their residues wherever we can trace them. But there was one major problem with this. I had been born a woman, and I was trying to think and act as if poetry— and the possibility of making poems—were a universal—a gender-neutral—realm.

But at the middle of the fifties I had no very clear idea of my positioning in the world or even that such an idea was an important resource for a writer to have. I knew that marriage and motherhood, experiences which were supposed to be truly womanly, often left me feeling unfit, disempowered, adrift.

The idea of freedom—so much invoked during World War II—had become pretty abstract politically in the fifties. Freedom—then as now—was supposed to be what the Western democracies believed in and the "Iron Curtain" Soviet-bloc countries were deprived of. The existentialist philosophers who were beginning to be read and discussed among young American intellectuals spoke of freedom as something connected with revolt. But in reading de Beauvoir and Baldwin, I began to taste the concrete reality of being unfree, how continuous and permeating and corrosive a condition it is, and how it is maintained through culture as much as through the use of force.

I am telling you this from a backward perspective, from where I stand now. At the time, I could not have summed up the effect these writers had on me. I only knew that I was reading them with the same passion and need that I brought to poetry, that they were beginning to penetrate my life; I was beginning to feel as never before that I had some foothold, some way of seeing, which helped me to ask the questions I needed to ask.

Many white North Americans fear an overtly political art because it might persuade us emotionally of what we think we are "rationally" against; it might get to us on a level we have lost touch with, undermine the safety we have built for ourselves, remind us of what is better left forgotten. This fear attributes real power to the voices of passion and of poetry which connect us with all that is not simply white chauvinist/male supremacist/straight/puritanical—with what is "dark," "effeminate," "inverted," "primitive," "volatile," "sinister." Yet we are told that political poetry, for example, is doomed to grind down into mere rhetoric and jargon, to become one-dimensional, simplistic, vituperative; that in writing "protest literature"—that is, writing from a perspective which may not be male, or white, or heterosexual, or middle-class—we sacrifice the "universal"; that in writing of injustice we are limiting our scope, "grinding a political axe." So political poetry is suspected of immense subversive power, yet accused of being, by definition, bad writing, impotent, lacking in breadth. No wonder if the North American poet finds herself or himself slightly crazed by the double messages.

By 1956, I had begun dating each of my poems by year. I did this because I was finished with the idea of a poem as a single, encapsulated event, a work of art complete in itself; I knew my life was changing, my work was changing and I needed to indicate to readers my sense of being engaged in a long, continuing process.

In my own case, as soon as I had published—in 1963—a book of poems which was informed by any conscious sexual politics, I was told, in print, that this work was "bitter," "personal;" that I had sacrificed the sweetly flowing measures of my earlier books for a ragged line and a coarsened voice. It took me a long time not to hear those voices internally whenever I picked up my pen. But I was writing at the beginning of a decade of political revolt and hope and activism. The external conditions for becoming a consciously, self-affirmingly political poet were there, as they had not been when I had begun to publish a decade earlier. Out of the Black Civil Rights movement, amid the marches and sit-ins in the streets and on campuses, a new generation of Black writers began to speak—and older generations to be reprinted and reread; poetry readings were infused with the spirit of collective rage and hope. As part of the movement against United States militarism and imperialism, white poets also were writing and reading aloud poems addressing the war in Southeast Asia. In many of these poems you sensed the poet's desperation in trying to encompass in words the reality of napalm, the "pacification" of villages, trying to make vivid in poetry what seemed to have minimal effect when shown on television. But there was little location of the self, the poet's own identity as a man or woman.

By the end of the 1960s an autonomous movement of women was declaring that "the personal is political." That statement was necessary because in other political movements of that decade the power relation of men to women, the question of women's roles and men's roles, had been dismissed—often contemptuously—as the sphere of personal life. Sex itself was not seen as political, except for interracial sex. Women were now talking about domination, not just in terms of economic exploitation, militarism, colonialism, imperialism, but within the family, in marriage, in child rearing, in the heterosexual act itself. Breaking the mental barrier that separated private from public life felt in itself like an enormous surge toward liberation. For a woman thus engaged, every aspect of her life was on the line.

To write directly and overtly as a woman, out of a woman's body and experience, to take women seriously as theme and source for art, was something I had been hungering to do, needing to do, all my writing life.

Women have understood that we needed an art of our own: to remind us of our history and what we might be; to show us our true faces—all of them, including the unacceptable; to speak of what has been muffled in code or silence; to make concrete the values our movement was bringing forth out of consciousness raising, speakouts, and activism. But we were—and are—living and writing not only within a women's community. We are trying to build a political and cultural movement in the heart of capitalism, in a country where racism assumes every form of physical, institutional, and psychic violence, and in which more than one person in seven lives below the poverty line. The United States feminist movement is rooted in the United States, a nation with a particular history of hostility both to art and to socialism, where art has been encapsulated as a commodity, a salable artifact, something to be taught in MFA programs, that requires a special staff of "arts administrators;" something you "gotta have" without exactly knowing why. As a lesbian-feminist poet and writer, I need to understand how this *location* affects me, along with the realities of blood and bread within this nation.

Critical Commentary: Aunt Jennifer's Tigers

See the text of the poem on p. 202.

1. Content

'Aunt Jennifer's Tigers' appeared in Rich's first volume of poetry, *A Change of World*, published when she was only 21. This collection has been noted for its highly *formalistic* poems that fashion an objective, intensely individualised and detached voice. In his introduction to the collection, the famous English poet W.H. Auden praised Rich for poems that 'speak quietly but do not mumble, respect their elders but are not cowed by them, and do not tell fibs'.

This poem amounts to an overtly *feminist* commentary on the male-dominated world that has oppressed Aunt Jennifer. The woman at the centre of the poem has been forced to create an alternative world in order to express her innermost desires. Aunt Jennifer's imagination provides her with her only outlet in a world in which her voice has been silenced. In the opening *quatrain*, or first four lines, of the poem, we are presented with a vivid depiction of the 'tigers' that Aunt Jennifer has created. The colours used to describe the tigers are vivid and suggestive of exotic adventure. These tigers are 'Bright topaz denizens of a world of green'. Their movement, suggested by the verb 'prance', is energetic and playful. Thomas B. Byars has suggested that 'the tigers display in art the values that Aunt Jennifer must repress or displace in life: strength, assertion, fearlessness, fluidity of motion'. However, Aunt Jennifer's fearlessness is only allowed to express itself through these tigers. This, in turn, suggests that in her ordinary, everyday existence, she is made to feel afraid. What she fears is never articulated fully in the poem. Yet it is entirely plausible to imagine that, unlike the tigers of her imagination, Aunt Jennifer is made to fear 'men'.

In the second quatrain, the focus of the poem switches from Aunt Jennifer's imaginative creation to the aunt herself. The idea that she is a nervous woman is captured in the *image* of her 'fingers fluttering through her wool'. She carries with her the 'massive weight of Uncle's wedding band'. This weight is an emotional one and the wedding ring, which is normally a *symbol* of unity and love, is suddenly made to represent Aunt Jennifer's subjugation.

In the final quatrain, the speaker looks ahead to when her aunt is dead. Rather than providing the woman with a release from those 'ordeals she was mastered by', 'her terrified hands' still seem scared of those undefined fears that subjugated her in life. The poem ends with the promise that Aunt Jennifer's tigers will 'go on prancing, proud and unafraid'. Her imagination, symbolised by the tigers, lives on in 'the panel that she made'.

2. Stylistic Features

This simple *lyric poem,* written in three quatrains, is more complex than either its form or straightforward, regular *rhyming* scheme would suggest. The poem is formalistic in its composition. In fact, the rigid structure of the poem mirrors its *theme*. The steady *rhythms* and *iambic pentameter*, especially in those lines that speak of wedding rings, heighten the aunt's feelings of constraint. Writing about this poem, Rich has said that:

> It was important to me that Aunt Jennifer was a person as distinct from myself as possible, distanced by the formalism of the poem, by its objective, observant tone ... In those years, formalism was part of the strategy like asbestos gloves, it allowed me to handle materials I couldn't pick up barehanded.

It is important when reading 'Aunt Jennifer's Tigers' to realise that despite its objective tone, it is an ideological poem written from a *feminist* viewpoint. In this respect, the poem presents us with a somewhat polarised view of the conflict between the sexes. In the poem, Aunt Jennifer is completely victimised and the absent 'Uncle', represented only by his wedding band, is demonised. Another aspect of the poem worth considering is the fact that the portrait of the aunt is presented in an economic fashion through the tension of opposing images. The nervous condition of Aunt Jennifer herself, her 'fingers fluttering through her wool', stands in contrast to her choice of subject for the tapestry:

> The tigers in the panel that she made
> Will go on prancing, proud and unafraid.

In order to convey its message, the poem makes use of a number of symbols. Aunt Jennifer's repressed imagination is symbolised by the tigers. This particularly effective image is suggestive of fierceness and nobility. However, it is also worth bearing in mind that although the tiger is a predatory animal, it has been hunted to the point of extinction. The colours used to describe the embroidered tigers are not those normally associated with these animals. Instead, they evoke a vibrant, active, even exotic imagination. The next major symbol in the poem is that of the 'wedding band'. A wedding ring is normally associated with inclusion and love, yet here the symbol is inverted so that it is made to represent oppression. While the oppressor is obviously the anonymous uncle whose heavy presence is almost palpable, the aunt is also oppressed by society in general. The wedding ceremony represented by the ring is a social and religious contract, sanctioned by state and Church. In this sense, the symbol of the ring moves beyond suggesting the uncle's domination and hints at society's subjugation of women.

3. Essay Writing

If you are thinking of including 'Aunt Jennifer's Tigers' in your essay, you may wish to consider the following points.

a. As with so many of Rich's poems, 'Aunt Jennifer's Tigers' can be read as a metaphor for the subjugation of women.
b. The metre and rhythm reinforce the central message of the poem. This makes the poem far more complex than it might at first appear.
c. The imagery in the poem is colourful and memorable.

Critical Commentary: The Uncle Speaks in the Drawing Room

See the text of the poem on p. 204.

1. Content

'The Uncle Speaks in the Drawing Room' opens with the voice of the uncle telling us that he has 'seen the mob of late'. This mob has gathered in the square. There is a restless and threatening attitude to this gathering. They talk in 'bitter tones' and finger 'stones'. In the second stanza, the uncle assures us that this type of foolish behaviour will subside. However, despite these assurances, the uncle does admit to fearing for his valuables. Given the fragility of glass, he feels his 'crystal vase' and 'chandelier' are in particular danger. In the third stanza, the speaker reassures us further that no missiles will be thrown. However, despite this, he is aware that the scene in front of him is reminiscent of a storm brewing. This, in turn, causes him to recall how one of his ancestors lost a valuable 'ruby bowl' during a storm. In the final stanza, the poet reminds us that such treasures have been passed down from a calmer age. It now lies with the present generation to protect such treasures from any harm:

> We stand between the dead glass-blowers
> And murmurings of missile-throwers.

2. Stylistic Features

'The Uncle Speaks in the Drawing Room' first appeared in Rich's collection *A Change of World*. This collection was praised for its broad range and control of **rhyme** and **metre**. Such control is readily apparent in this poem. On first reading, the poem can appear confusing, yet if you read it through several times, it quickly becomes apparent that it is very straightforward.

The poem presents us with the figure of the uncle, who responds to the social unrest taking place outside his window. In the poem, the uncle acts as a **metaphor** for conservative values. From his balcony (which in itself is suggestive of wealth), the uncle views the growing unrest on the streets below. His concern is not for the underlying tensions that have resulted in this unrest, but rather for his material possessions. These are **symbolised** in the poem by the 'chandelier' and 'crystal vase'. This choice is significant in that both the chandelier and the crystal vase are very fragile. Rich is probably hinting at the fragility of accepted social values in the face of great upheaval. The final stanza opens with an **imperative**. Here, the uncle warns us that the valuables that have been passed down from generation to generation are under threat. The uncle views himself as the present custodian of these valuables. It is his job to come between them and any harm, represented by the 'murmurings of missile-throwers'. It is interesting to note that the uncle's value system is never allowed to extend beyond the narrow confines of material concerns.

3. Essay Writing

If you are thinking of including 'The Uncle Speaks in the Drawing Room' in an essay, you may wish to consider the following points.

a. The poem is carefully measured both in rhyme and metre.
b. Once again, this is another poem by Rich that is overtly political.
c. The character and images in the poem can be viewed as representations of the poet's social concerns.

Critical Commentary: Power

See the text of the poem on p. 206.

1. Content

The title of 'Power' hints that this is another **metaphorical** piece. In other words, it is open to more than one reading. In the opening line of the poem, the speaker tells us that the earth contains 'earth-deposits of our history'. In the second stanza, the speaker explains why she has been reminded of this fact:

> Today a backhoe divulged   out of a crumbling flank of earth
> one bottle   amber   perfect   a hundred-year-old

When the mechanical digger removes the hundred-year-old bottle, the past is brought straight into conflict with the present. The bottle in question is a medicine bottle, a tonic that was used as a 'cure' for depression and fever. The poet's examination of this bottle reminds her that she has been 'reading about Marie Curie'.

In the third stanza, she begins to examine the life of this famous physicist. The speaker believes that Curie must have been aware of the fact that she was suffering from radiation sickness. Her body was, after all, 'bombarded' by the very 'element' that she helped to identify. Blinded by the radiation, she refused to believe that it was the source of her illness, even though her skin had become 'cracked' and was leaking puss:

She died   a famous woman   denying
her wounds
denying
her wounds   came   from the same source as her power

Thus, Marie Curie went to her grave in denial. The power source she had helped to identify was killing her and she refused to accept this fact.

2. Stylistic Features

This poem uses the story of Marie Curie's scientific discoveries and her subsequent death to make an overtly political point. Written in a stream of consciousness, 'Power' takes the form of a meditation on nature and on the role of women in a male-dominated world. The starting point for Rich's stream of consciousness is the unearthing of an old bottle of medicine for the treatment of depression. Perhaps this is meant to hint at the speaker's present state of mind.

In the second stanza, there is a sudden shift in the logic of the poem as the speaker's thoughts wander back and forth. The poet tells us that she is reminded of the life of Marie Curie. It becomes obvious that Curie stands as a *symbol* for women's struggle.

Cut off from traditionally male-dominated power structures, women have had to endure difficulties and hardships in order to be taken seriously. The visual *imagery* in the second stanza is arresting. The 'cracked and suppurating skin' amounts to a powerful physical representation of the difficulties women have had to endure.

The *tone* in the final stanza is pessimistic. Curie's death is a direct result of her achievements. In order to access traditional power structures, this woman had to pay a very high price. The fact that Curie was in denial of this truth makes the poem seem even more depressing.

3. Essay Writing

If you are thinking of including 'Power' in your essay, you may wish to consider the following points.

a. Once again, the poem makes a political statement concerning the subjugation of women.

b. The life of Marie Curie acts a metaphor for the wider treatment of women.

c. Unlike many of the poems on the course, this is not a *confessional* poem. This means that you could contrast 'Power' with many of the other poems by Rich on the course.

Critical Commentary: Storm Warnings

See the text of the poem on p. 208.

1. Content

'Storm Warnings' is typical of Rich's confessional style. On the face of it, the speaker describes the onset of a storm as it approaches her house. However, it is important to realise that this poem also details an internal or *metaphorical* storm. The opening line is ominous and foreboding. We learn that the 'glass has been falling all the afternoon'. The drop in atmospheric pressure is indicated on the barometer and suggests that a storm is coming. Once the speaker is aware of the likelihood of the storm, she moves from room to room and looks outside to gauge its intensity.

In the second stanza, the poet admits that the change in weather has forced her to 'think again'. It becomes clear that the speaker is describing an internal process. She tells us that she needs to move 'inward toward a silent core of waiting'. It is becoming increasingly difficult to distinguish between the storm brewing outside and the speaker's sense of an approaching emotional struggle. The reader realises that the internal and metaphorical storm, which represents the speaker's inner conflict, is about to take a similar path to the storm outside. Nothing can prevent these storms from raging and the speaker is aware of this:

> [...] Weather abroad
> And weather in the heart alike come on
> Regardless of prediction.

Although the speaker knows that an internal storm is brewing, this knowledge does little to ease her sense of apprehension. With 'a single purpose time' continues to pass and she examines and studies these final moments of calm.

In the third stanza, the speaker acknowledges that even though there are certain scientific devices to help forecast when a storm may strike, in reality, these appliances cannot predict the storm any better than the 'shattered fragments of an instrument'. Though the storm may give warnings, such as dark clouds and rumbles of thunder, its progress cannot be altered, nor can it be stopped. The storm must run its course, and the speaker realises that she must seek shelter and 'close the shutters'.

In the fourth stanza, the speaker takes the only viable course of action open to her: she 'draw[s] the curtains'. Her reaction is to seek shelter against the elements. She attempts to create a safe place that offers hope. She lights a candle, which, of course, is a long-standing literary **symbol** for hope. However, such is the intensity of the gale outside that this candle also needs protection from the 'insistent whine | Of weather'. The storm has not gone away, but the speaker has succeeded in maintaining a sense of calm. This is her 'sole defense against' the ravages of the storm. On a metaphorical level, she has managed to guard herself from the damaging effects of inner turmoil. The storm outside may have overtaken the natural world, but her inner storm must not be allowed to sweep aside her defences. She has come to understand that all she can do is fall back on what she has 'learned to do'. Just as those who occupy the world's 'troubled regions' instinctively seek shelter from the elements, she, too, has learned to shelter her soul from any harm:

> These are the things that we have learned to do
> Who live in troubled regions.

2. Stylistic Features

This poem uses the extended metaphor of an approaching storm to examine the onset of an inner emotional conflict. The precise nature of this conflict is never made entirely clear. The use of **pathetic fallacy** in the opening line hints at a disturbing event in nature. It soon becomes clear that this disturbance in the natural world mirrors a more worrying inner turmoil within the speaker. The poem uses a number of concrete **images** to explore the emotional turmoil that the speaker is about to experience. The physical weather conditions outside act as metaphors for the poet's emotional state.

The poem is organised and structured in such a manner as to guide us through the speaker's state of mind. The natural progression of the poem's stanzas may not seem altogether important, but the four **sestets** represent something extremely significant. The storm takes a steady and unwavering path. A less formal or more disorganised construction would have disrupted the way in which the inevitable progress of the storm parallels the symbolic and metaphorical meanings of the poem. In other words, the progress of her own disturbed state of mind is every bit as inevitable as the progression of the storm. The speaker states that 'The glass has been falling all the afternoon', 'winds are walking overhead', 'gray unrest is moving across the land' and 'Boughs strain against the sky'.

The storm that is now raging outside has been gathering in intensity all day. It has, however, not reached its climax. Therefore, the first stanza reveals the initial warning signs of a fierce inner storm that has yet to begin. The storm reaches its peak of intensity in the second and third stanzas and the speaker is forced to move 'inward toward a silent core of waiting' in order to protect herself. In other words, she needs to ready herself mentally for the conflict that she senses is approaching. The language here is measured and contemplative.

In the final stanza, the speaker 'draw[s] the curtains as the sky goes black | And set[s] a match to candles sheathed in glass'. In order to convey the need she feels to protect and nourish her sense of hope, the poet uses the symbol of the lighted candle. The image of the sky turning black is a disturbing visual representation of the poet's turmoil. In order to convey fully the sense of unease that she feels, the speaker appeals to our sense of hearing. The wind whistles outside and we instinctively feel that the poet is about to encounter the climax of the storm. Living in 'troubled regions', the poet has learned to anticipate and accept the onset of bad weather. As the poem draws to a close, it would seem that she has also accepted the necessity of preparing for and surviving the arrival of emotional conflict.

3. Essay Writing

If you are thinking of including 'Storm Warnings' in an essay, you may wish to consider the following points.

a. The language of the poem evokes powerful emotions in a darkly beautiful manner.
b. Once again, Rich uses form to reinforce a poem's message. If you are making a point like this, try to mention the manner in which the progression of the stanzas mirrors the progress of the storm.
c. The poem draws on nature imagery to convey its message. By making this point, you can draw a comparison between this poem and 'Diving into the Wreck'. Remember, such comparisons enrich your paragraphs.

Critical Commentary: Living in Sin

See the text of the poem on p. 210.

1. Content

'Living in Sin' first appeared in *The Diamond Cutters and Other Poems*, which was published in 1955 and received the Ridgely Torrence Memorial Award. The poem depicts a woman's growing dissatisfaction with her lover and with her living situation. In the opening line of the poem, something of the woman's naïvety is revealed:

> She had thought the studio would keep itself;
> no dust upon the furniture of love.

We are led to imagine the young woman in love and blissfully unaware of the realities of living with someone. Her love is seen as a near-religious experience, separate from the mundane chores of daily existence. Any suggestion that disagrees with this is viewed as being 'Half heresy' that profanes her relationship. The studio is revealed to us in vivid detail. Leaking taps, grimy windows, dusty furniture, a piano and a 'Persian shawl' depicting a cat and mouse all help us to envisage the place. There is nothing glamorous or romantic about this studio. One imagines a young couple with little money, prompted by their love for one another to break with the rules of society to 'live in sin'. It is important to remember that we are not getting an outsider's account of the studio. The poem opens with the words 'She had thought', thus it is made clear from the outset that the speaker intends us to view events from the woman's point of view.

In the second movement of the poem, it is made very clear that the woman is disturbed by the circumstances in which she now finds herself. The fact that she wakes at five each morning is indicative of a troubled mind or even depression. The heavy footfall of the 'milkman' is yet another indication of the humdrum, workaday reality of her relationship. In the thin 'morning light', 'the scraps | of last night's cheese and three sepulchral bottles' are somehow rendered more vivid. They remind the woman of the squalid nature of their living quarters and, of course, of the choices that she has made. The *image* of the 'beetle-eyes' staring back at her from behind the kitchen shelf is particularly unpleasant, and again captures the depressing gloom of the apartment in the morning light.

Meanwhile, her partner stirs and:

> [...] with a yawn,
> sounded a dozen notes upon the keyboard,
> declared it out of tune, shrugged at the mirror,
> rubbed at his beard, went out for cigarettes;

If the woman is painfully aware of the true nature of her surroundings, there is little to suggest that the man shares in this awareness. His indifference to the woman's concerns is perfectly captured in these lines. Notice how he leaves to satisfy his own needs. His concern extends only to the relatively unimportant fact that the piano is 'out of tune'. These little details reveal a great deal about the relationship and help to explain the woman's state of mind.

The woman in this poem expresses feelings of fatigue and disillusionment. She is tired with, and frustrated by, the course her life has taken. Her life contains little of the romance that must once have characterised her relationship with this man and which must have contributed to her decision to 'live in sin'. She makes the bed and dusts the 'table-top'. When the man leaves, the woman is 'jeered by the minor demons'. No doubt her inner voice mocks her for her stupidity in believing that 'the studio would keep itself' clean. Lost in her thoughts, she 'let[s] the coffee-pot boil over'.

In the final movement of the poem, we come full circle. The poem began at dawn and draws to a close as night approaches. Although the woman is 'back in love again', the reader is left with the feeling that the relationship has been forever tainted by her sinking realisation that her life has not followed the course she had hoped it would. Her love is not as complete as it once was and the night-time is no longer associated with passion and lovemaking. Rather, she is haunted by the fact that the day has to begin all over again. The thought is one that causes her anxiety and disturbs her sleep. We are told that 'she woke sometimes to feel the daylight coming'. The mundane, frustrating and depressing reality of her life in the studio is seen as being as relentless and as inevitable as the milkman's arrival each morning.

2. Stylistic Features

As we have seen, 'Living in Sin' examines how one woman's perception of her physical environment, her motive for entering into the relationship and the tone of the relationship are altered when she compares the life she expected to life as it actually is.

Even though this is an emotionally charged poem, its language is restrained and measured. The poem opens at dawn, but this is an **aubade** with a difference. As dawn is announced, there is a sinking realisation on the woman's part that she has made a mistake in choosing to 'live in sin'. The poet's use of the **pluperfect** tense suggests the woman's feelings of regret in a subtle manner. She 'had thought' that life would be very different, but now realises the truth. The depiction of the studio is extremely effective in conveying the reality of the woman's new life. Notice how the Persian shawl seems particularly out of place in these surroundings. Of course, the implication here is that the woman might have found a suitable surrounding for such a shawl if only she had chosen not to 'live in sin'.

The poem is crowded with unpleasant **images**. The scraps of 'last night's cheese' and the 'beetle-eyes' that stare back at the young woman add to the squalid **atmosphere** in this studio. There is also a claustrophobic feeling created in the depiction of the room. The movement from the bedroom to the living area through to the kitchen is achieved without the intervals necessary to create a sense of space. This feeling of claustrophobia naturally extends to the woman herself. She feels trapped and confined, not only by the studio, but also by the choices that led her to this place.

These feelings of regret are suggested by the 'minor demons' that jeer at her. The voices that mock her come, of course, from within, but they can also be seen as representing the outside world. The reality of her present circumstances now forces her to recognise that she may have been wrong in her choice of lover. The language used to describe the man is not particularly detailed, yet it manages to convey his complete lack of understanding of his partner's feelings. His concerns extend no further than the piano being out of tune and his next packet of cigarettes.

The poem is circular in its movement: from dawn to dusk, the woman's day is explored completely. She never leaves the studio and her work never extends further than the confines of her squalid surroundings. The final, unusual **simile** in the poem captures the inevitable arrival of a new day. It is likened to the arrival of the milkman; it is a routine, unremarkable event.

3. Essay Writing

If you are thinking of including 'Living in Sin' in your essay, you may wish to consider the following points.

a. The narrative of the poem engages the reader. As such, 'Living in Sin' is a memorable poem. This fact alone is worth mentioning in any personal response that you may be asked to frame on this poem.

b. Once again, the poem deals with the relationship between a man and a woman. Given that many of Rich's poems focus on this *theme*, you might want to devote one paragraph to this aspect of her work.

c. The language of the poem is poised and restrained. This prevents 'Living in Sin' from becoming too sentimental.

Critical Commentary: The Roofwalker

See the text of the poem on pp. 212–13.

1. Content

'The Roofwalker' first appeared in the collection *Snapshots of a Daughter-in-Law*. Like so much of Adrienne Rich's work, this collection challenged assumptions about women in Western society and gave many women the vocabulary to talk about their experiences. In this book, she helped to popularise the idea that the personal is political, meaning that the way we live our personal lives has public consequences and social ramifications that affect and shape the world around us. This poem is dedicated to the post-war, Anglo-American poet Denise Levertov. Levertov's activism and *feminism* became a prominent part of her poetry in later years. Her work is noted for its natural *rhythms* and its ability to capture intense feelings by relating them to everyday life. Rich had much in common with Levertov. Both poets were active feminists, politically aware and willing to break new ground. By dedicating the poem to Levertov, Rich is making a political statement.

In the poem, the act of walking on an unstable rooftop becomes a **metaphor** for the poet's experience of being a woman writer. This explains the dedication to Levertov: both poets overcame similar obstacles and prejudices. The poem opens with a description of 'half-finished houses'. Building sites have traditionally been the preserve of men. However, the poet describes the construction site as being incomplete. It is not difficult to see that this is a veiled criticism of the male-dominated world of writing and academia.

The 'Giants' that she refers to in the first stanza represent the giants of world literature. Of course, these important literary figures have been predominantly male. Suddenly, the rooftop becomes unstable. The difficulty the men experience in remaining upright is likened to the sensation of being on board a ship. The poet imagines this ship as housing the ghosts or shadows of the past. However, the world they knew, the world of male domination, is on fire.

There is a sharp change in focus in the short, three-line second stanza. The speaker tells us that she feels like the men on the roof. She feels 'exposed' to unspecified dangers that threaten to 'break [her] neck'.

In the third stanza, the **tone** of the poem becomes increasingly **confessional**. The poet asks some searching questions:

> Was it worth while to lay—
> with infinite exertion—
> a roof I can't live under?
> —All those blueprints,
> closings of gaps,
> measurings, calculations?
> A life I didn't choose
> chose me [...]

Here, the poet questions the very course her life has taken. She wonders if the 'exertion' and strain necessarily involved in being a writer have been 'worth while'. Furthermore, she also realises that her work as a writer has helped to support (however unwittingly) the very establishment that she is criticising. The role that she is forced to play as a woman writer is 'a roof [she] can't live under'. The poet acknowledges the vocational aspect of her life as a poet. It is, she tells us, something that she did not choose to be. While she feels unable to follow any other path in life, she also feels particularly ill-equipped to be a writer. Her 'tools are the wrong ones

I for what [she has] to do'. Her feelings of insecurity mount until she declares that she feels 'naked [and] ignorant'. It is as if she is completely exposed and open to examination by all and sundry. When Adrienne Rich first began to make her name as a poet, equality between men and women was still, to a large extent, equated with sameness. At that time, it was assumed that being a liberated woman meant being able to be the same as a man. There was little understanding of, or room for, a distinctly female perspective, experience or voice.

Thus, as a young writer, Rich found it difficult to define herself by writing a type of poetry that was based on styles perfected by men. In the final moments of the closing stanza, she acknowledges this fact. She feels that the unstable edifice (the 'roof' which is a metaphor for the act of writing) that the men are constructing is no different from the work that she has produced. The speaker recognises that all literary endeavour involves risk. She now sees that the works that she has read and even criticised must have necessarily made their creators feel vulnerable and exposed. In this respect, the poem can be read as an attempt on the part of the poet to understand her role as a female writer in a male-dominated world. The experience is a confusing one. While she can empathise with the difficulties and dangers experienced by all writers, regardless of their sex, she also feels it is necessary to point out that the literary establishment has largely ignored women.

2. Stylistic Features

As late as the 1990s, Adrienne Rich felt that she still needed to struggle to be accepted as a woman writer. In an interview in 1994 with *The Progressive* magazine, she outlined her difficulties in finding a place for a *feminist* voice in her poetry:

> Recently, I was sent a clipping from The Irish Times in which the Irish poet, Derek Mahon, refers to me as 'cold, dishonest, and wicked'. He deplores the 'victimology' of my ideas, which he says have seduced younger women poets. When I read that, I was sort of astounded, because we are in 1993. But then I thought, what this man is afraid of is the growing feminism in Ireland and the growing energy and strength of Irish women poets.

The need to be accepted on equal terms with men is obviously a pressing one for Rich. 'The Roofwalker' is dedicated to Denise Levertov and this is an important clue to the poet's intention. Levertov was a politically active female poet. Her poetic style often renders complex ideas more accessible by comparing them to everyday occurrences. Of course, this is precisely what Rich manages to do in this poem. Furthermore, Levertov's poetry is also noted for making use of the natural *rhythms* of everyday speech. Notice how 'The Roofwalker' also embraces the energetic rhythms of speech. In the poem, the speaker examines her feelings about being a woman writer in what is, after all, a male-dominated career.

In order to do this, Rich uses the idea of a roof under construction as a metaphor for creative writing. This is a complex and clever *allusion*. Firstly, much like writing, the building trade has historically been, and continues to be, a male-dominated activity. Secondly, the physical act of making a roof is not without its dangers. This again is very like writing. To put something down on paper is to expose oneself to the glare of public criticism. This explains why the poet feels 'naked' and 'exposed'. One of the more interesting aspects of this poem is the sense of empathy that the speaker feels with the workers on the roof.

As a writer, she recognises the difficulty that other writers experience. However, as a woman writer, she feels the need to challenge the patriarchal (male-dominated) world of literature. She may have contributed to this world, but she also feels that she 'can't live' under the same roof as those men that have dominated and suppressed women. This need to re-evaluate the relationship between women and their cultural inheritance is a common one in Rich's poetry. In 'Diving into the Wreck', she challenges our perception of *mythology* and calls for a completely new type of literature. On a more localised level, 'Aunt Jennifer's Tigers' explores the stifling of a woman's creative impulses. In a similar fashion, this poem also questions the role open to women in the world of literature.

3. Essay Writing

There are many interesting points that can be made about 'The Roofwalker' in any essay on Rich's work. If you are thinking of mentioning this poem in your essay, you may wish to consider the following points.

a. In this poem, Rich challenges assumptions made about women in society.
b. 'The Roofwalker' is confessional in that it draws on Rich's own life experience.

c. This poem takes a complex idea and renders it more accessible by comparing it to an everyday experience. Many of Rich's poems on the course do this, so you might want to consider devoting a paragraph to this aspect of her work.

Critical Commentary: Our Whole Life

See the text of the poem on p. 214.

1. Content

'Our Whole Life' is another overtly political poem that seeks to examine the relationship between language and oppression. The poem opens with a broad, sweeping and inclusive statement:

> Our whole life a translation
> the permissible fibs

While it is difficult to untangle the speaker's thought processes, the poem seems to be suggesting that language is a 'knot of lies'. The poet views language as containing 'Words bitten thru words', where real meaning has been 'burnt-off like paint | under the blowtorch'.

In her imagination, the 'dead letters' and 'burnt-off' words have been gathered up to form the oppressor's language. Presumably, the oppressor that Rich is referring to is men. Suddenly, in the penultimate stanza, there is a shift in the logical progression of the poem. We are presented with an unusual *simile*. The speaker tells us that trying to find a remedy for the situation that she has described is pointless. It is like 'the Algerian | who walked from his village, burning'. There are no words for this 'cloud of pain' because it has been self-inflicted. The point here is that the only way to free oneself from the 'oppressor's language' is through discussion. However, this necessarily means that the very language that has been used to oppress is now used to liberate. This is a *paradox* from which there is no escape.

2. Stylistic Features

This short poem first appeared in Rich's collection *A Will to Change*, published in 1969. Many of Rich's poems explore the relationship between language and political status, and in this respect, 'Our Whole Life' is no different. The poem declares the language of the oppressor to be a burnt-out collection of dead words. However, the speaker is unable to forward any alternative to this language. There is, of course, a deep *irony* running through the poem: the speaker is criticising the oppressor in his own language. In order to convey her argument, Rich employs two particularly vivid *images*. The first is that of a blowtorch burning paint. Here, the words of the language that she despises are burnt away. The second image is that of the Algerian on fire, walking from his village. Both of these images are associated with burning. This is a measure of the poet's seething anger and her resentment of the oppressor's language.

Perhaps one of the most interesting stylistic features employed by Rich in this poem is the manner in which she forces her own words to become almost incoherent. The poem contains only two punctuation marks; there is an absence of verbs and words are abbreviated. The opening line of the poem is difficult to read, as it is missing its verb. In this sense, Rich is attempting to show her rejection of the language that she is criticising.

3. Essay Writing

If you are thinking of mentioning 'Our Whole Life' in your essay, you may wish to consider the following points.

a. In this poem, Rich directly attacks what she views as the oppressor's language. In this respect, 'Our Whole Life' must be read as an overtly political poem. Given that so many of the poems on the course by Rich are political, you might want to consider devoting an entire paragraph to this aspect of her work.

b. Once again, Rich links the idea of oppression to language. This means that you can link this poem to other pieces by Rich on the course, such as 'Diving into the Wreck'.

c. This poem is very loosely structured. Given that Rich has displayed such control in her poetry, one has to assume that this is intentional. This would be a very interesting point to make in an essay.

Critical Commentary: Trying to Talk with a Man

See the text of the poem on pp. 216–17.

1. Content

In 'Trying to Talk with a Man', Rich outlines a visit to a nuclear test site. However, the title and the language point not to the landscape of this test site, but to the intimacy of a failing relationship. This is yet another poem that is open to more than one reading. In the opening lines, the speaker makes an unusual statement:

> Out in this desert we are testing bombs,
> that's why we came here.

By using the personal pronoun 'we', the poet includes herself in this process. This is the first hint in the poem that she may be referring to something other than the actual act of exploding a bomb. Despite the arid landscape, she sometimes 'feel[s] an underground river'. If we take the desert to represent her relationship, then the river may be viewed as being *symbolic* of the woman's feelings of hope. The visit to the desert was intended to 'change the face' of their relationship. However, the ghosts of the past are never allowed to fade away. The attempt to recreate and restructure the relationship fails. Towards the end of the third stanza, the poet recognises the similarities between the physical landscape and the state of affairs in which she now finds herself. The place they are in is a ghost town; this is a particularly apt *metaphor* for her failing relationship. In a measure of how strained their relationship has become, the poet tells us that the heavy silence that has descended on the place emanates from the couple.

This silence is something with which they have become 'familiar'. In this desolate, barren and naturally silent place, set as it is against the backdrop of nuclear devastation, the speaker accepts her own inability to communicate with her lover. Then, in the seventh stanza, the speaker makes a startling admission. She tells us that out here she feels 'more helpless' with her partner than 'without' him. Given the unusual and potentially dangerous setting of the poem, this is a damning indictment of the state of their relationship. Her partner reminds her of the danger outside. They speak about the need for companionship, especially in an emergency. Following a nuclear explosion, any survivors would, of course, suffer from lacerations and thirst. The poet uses these as metaphors for the situation the lovers find themselves in following the breakdown of their relationship. They feel hurt, even cut, by what has happened. The 'thirst' that she speaks of *alludes* to the fact that she stills needs her lover. This need is not, however, strong enough to prevent their break-up. It is becoming increasingly clear that this poem is meant to be read as an intense, metaphorical commentary on a failing relationship. The poet and novelist Margaret Atwood has pointed out that:

> 'Trying to Talk with a Man' occurs in a desert, a desert which is not only a place of deprivation and sterility, the place where everything except the essentials has been discarded, but the place where bombs are tested. The 'I' and the 'You' have given up all the frivolities of their previous lives, 'suicide notes' as well as 'love-letters', in order to undertake the risk of changing the desert; but it becomes clear that the scenery is already 'condemned,' that the bombs are not external threats but internal ones.

In the penultimate stanza, the poet addresses her lover directly. The sound of his voice has become a destructive force and his 'dry heat feels like power'. She tells him:

> your eyes are stars of a different magnitude
> they reflect lights that spell out: EXIT
> when you get up and pace the floor

As she stares into the eyes of her partner, the reflected exit sign tells her what to do in a clear and unambiguous fashion. Simply put, their relationship is over and she needs to leave. As her lover gets up and paces to and fro, the danger posed by the nuclear tests recedes. For the entire day they have talked about the risks and perils associated with nuclear weapons. They have examined the technical aspects of the bombs and even speculated about the aftermath of a nuclear war. In the end, it becomes clear that, all along, they were simply testing their own relationship.

2. Stylistic Features

In 'Trying to Talk with a Man', Rich uses the arid, 'condemned scenery' of a Nevada test site as a metaphor for her deteriorating relationship. The location of the poem is extremely important. The Nevada test sites are synonymous with the horror of nuclear weapons. The poem uses our shared understanding of the dangers of nuclear war to highlight the tension and danger in a failing relationship. The poem is remarkable for the manner in which it manages to interlace a clearly personal, yet broadly human, experience into the deep cultural dread associated with nuclear annihilation. In this manner, Rich manages to broaden the *figurative* scope of her *lyric* and the poem becomes thoroughly modern. Of course, the poem also mirrors our fear of the breakdown in personal relationships. Once the poet establishes the unusual and complicated link between these two different fears, the poem's message becomes clear.

'Trying to Talk with a Man' employs some unusual *images* to convey its message. We have already mentioned the poem's setting. The sterile, barren desert is a particularly fitting metaphor for a relationship that is no longer flowering. Similarly, the terrible, self-destructive urge that humankind has displayed in developing nuclear weapons finds a correspondence in the breakdown of the couple's relationship. This couple are responsible for the situation that they find themselves in, just as the men who have developed such terrible weapons are responsible for bringing the world to the brink of annihilation. The apprehensive and tense *atmosphere* that dominates the poem is cleverly linked to images associated with nuclear weapons. The testing of bombs has deformed the landscape. The heat and scorching sun bring the terrible heat of a thermonuclear detonation to mind. The mention of the ghost town provides us with a ghastly reminder of the awful results of a nuclear war.

It is also possible to apply a *feminist* reading to the poem. The title does seem to lay some blame at the feet of the man. Furthermore, it must not escape our notice that the nuclear weapons industry is dominated by men.

3. Essay Writing

'Trying to Talk with a Man' is typical of many of Rich's poems on the course. In this sense, it is worth including in any response to her poetry. If you do so, you may want to consider some of the following points.

a. As with many of Rich's poems on the course, 'Trying to Talk with a Man' addresses the relationship between a man and a woman.

b. The setting of the poem acts as a metaphor for deeper concerns. This is typical of Rich's style.

c. Yet again, this is a **confessional** poem in that it draws on details from Rich's private life.

Critical Commentary: Diving into the Wreck

See the text of the poem on pp. 219–21.

1. Content

Writing in the *New York Review of Books* in 1973, the famous novelist and poet Margaret Atwood had the following to say about 'Diving into the Wreck':

> The wreck she is diving into, is the wreck of obsolete myths, particularly myths about men and women. She is journeying to something that is already in the past, in order to discover for herself the reality behind the myth, 'the wreck and not the story of the wreck/the thing itself and not the myth.' What she finds is part treasure and part corpse, and she also finds that she herself is part of it, a 'half-destroyed instrument.'

Throughout the 1970s, Rich's work continued to reflect her growing commitment to **feminism**, to the environment and to community involvement. Her collection *Diving into the Wreck*, which won her a National Book Award in 1973, reflects these **themes**. Most critics agree, however, that the title poem 'Diving into the Wreck' transcends any easy thematic classification because of its absolute artistic beauty and **metaphorical** intensity. In this poem, the speaker recounts her experience as she dives down to explore a sunken ship. In the opening stanza, the poet tells us that she first encountered the wreck through a 'book of myths'. However, she chooses to experience the wreck first-hand. All the paraphernalia of the dive is assembled in preparation for the event. The speaker tells us that she:

> [...] loaded the camera,
> and checked the edge of the knife-blade,
> I put on
> the body-armor [...]

Her depiction of the material needed suggests that this is going to be a hazardous process. The verb 'loaded' is suggestive of a weapon being readied. The 'knife-blade' and 'the body-armor' add to the feelings of apprehension in this first stanza.

Most commentators accept that this dive is into the unconscious. If you accept this reading, the speaker's aim must be to touch the dark, powerful, elemental forces of life and to bring knowledge back into the conscious mind. In the second stanza, the poet tells us that, unlike the famous explorer Jacques Cousteau, she does not have the benefit of a back-up team. Her dive is a solitary affair. This is extremely important to realise when considering the poem. The sea has long been used by writers as a literary *symbol* for the unconscious. Bearing this in mind, the speaker's solitary dive can be read as an attempt to probe beneath the surface for hidden meanings and unconscious desires. The speaker still remains connected to the surface by the ladder that hangs 'innocently | close to the side of the schooner'. This process of becoming submerged is a slow and measured one:

> I go down.
> Rung after rung and still
> the oxygen immerses me

It is also a painful and bewildering experience; the 'flippers cripple' her and the speaker feels alone and confused. As she submerges herself into the water, no one can tell her 'when the ocean | will begin'. She tells us that she is like an insect. It is almost as if she is devolving. Remember that all life on earth originated from the sea; as the speaker enters the ocean, she becomes like a more primitive life form.

In the fourth stanza, the experience of entering the water is described in detail. Her sense impression of the experience is primarily visual and is relayed to the reader through her description of changing colours. The air that she breathes is described as being:

> [...] blue and then
> it is bluer and then green and then
> black [...]

The speaker is overwhelmed by the situation and feels that she is 'blacking out'. However, her 'mask is powerful' and it screens her from the pressure that the sea exerts. Towards the end of the fourth stanza, as she moves deeper and deeper into the ocean, she reminds us once again that this is a solitary experience. She has 'to learn alone I to turn [her] body without force I in the deep element'.

In the fifth and sixth stanzas, the speaker signals her arrival in the ocean's depths and feels the need to remind herself what she 'came for'. The experience may have prompted a personal exploration, but she initially came to explore the wreck and see the creatures that live there. This place is seen as being different and separate from the world above. It is a place where you 'breathe differently' and is inhabited by strange, exotic creatures. In the sixth stanza, she feels the need to remind herself again that she 'came to explore the wreck'. This damaged, underwater wreck contains treasures that have managed to 'prevail'. The light from the speaker's lamp illuminates the wreck that has remained hidden for so long. Slowly, she begins to perceive something 'more permanent' than the 'fish' that inhabit this place.

In the seventh stanza, 'the thing [she] came for' becomes a real presence in the poem. The 'wreck' is no longer the stuff of **myth** and stories; it is now the physical 'thing itself'. The atmosphere in this stanza is peaceful and the speaker's depiction of the wreck is hauntingly beautiful. A reminder of the world above is provided by the sunlight that streams in the direction of the wreck. It has, according to the poet, a 'threadbare beauty' that houses the ghosts of the past. In this environment, the speaker's perception of herself becomes altered. In the eighth stanza, she sees herself as a 'mermaid whose dark hair I streams black'. However, such is the unique quality of this underwater place that her identity and sense of self become blurred until, suddenly, she is no longer a mermaid but a 'merman in his armored body'. It is almost as if, in this underwater environment, the speaker is freed of the normal classifications that apply in the world above. She is neither male nor female. The process continues as the poet circles silently around the wreck until she admits that 'I am she: I am he'. Her perception of who she is has been changed radically and her identity as she knew it on the surface has become erased. Suddenly, she finds it difficult to distinguish her own identity from that of the sunken vessel. In an almost surreal turn of events, the poet sees herself as actually becoming the shipwreck:

> whose drowned face sleeps with open eyes
> whose breasts still bear the stress
> whose silver, copper, vermeil cargo lies

It is extremely difficult to apply a literal meaning to this poem. It is possible, of course, to see the poem simply as being about a dive into the ocean. However, this does not really provide us with a satisfactory reading of 'Diving into the Wreck'. It would seem, then, that by delving into the depths of the wreck, the diver uncovers hitherto hidden depths in her own submerged consciousness. This process continues and the diver views herself not only as the boat and its cargo, as a figurehead, an observer and an explorer, but also as a participant in the disaster:

> we are the half-destroyed instruments
> that once held to a course
> the water-eaten log
> the fouled compass

She has lost her bearings and, in this state, she uncovers new truths about her personality. What these truths are is never made explicitly clear in the poem, but they appear to be connected to her sense of gender. It is noteworthy that 'he' and 'she' become interchangeable until the speaker attempts to assert her identity as 'we'. In the final stanza, the speaker admits that 'We are, I am, you are'.

The poet has undoubtedly uncovered something worthwhile or valuable about herself and perhaps even about the role of women in society. The implicit question is, can she carry out a salvage operation? Can the treasures she has found, 'the silver, copper, vermeil cargo' that she speaks of in the previous stanza, be saved? The poem chooses not to answer this question. Instead, in the final stanza, the diver recapitulates the story of her arrival in order to explain how she found her way to this point. This process of discovery began by preparing for the dive. This preparation on the surface allowed her to move beyond the world of books and mythology and come face to face with a real and lived experience. 'Diving into the Wreck' has long been recognised as one of the most important poems of the 20th century. Whether or not you accept this view of the poem, it is difficult to deny that it is a memorable read.

2. Stylistic Features

At the time that she wrote this poem, Rich was learning and writing about the experience of the modern woman in the Western world. Before the women's movement took flight in the 1960s, it was very difficult for women writers to express themselves. Rich was one of the pioneers in the exploration of a woman's place in society. In 1971, she wrote an essay entitled 'When We Dead Awaken: Writing as Re-Vision'. In the essay, she wrote about an awakening of women's consciousness, their 'drive to self-knowledge'. In the same essay, she wrote that 'language has trapped as well as liberated us'. She urged women to re-examine their history, to learn 'to see—and therefore live—afresh'.

In many ways, this poem can be read as an extended metaphor that outlines the experience of examining one's consciousness. The sea has long been used as a symbol for the unconscious mind. In the poem, it is likely that Rich intended the sea to represent her subconscious. The dive then becomes symbolic of the process of self-examination. Every human being has spent some time examining his or her existence. This is an essential part of being alive. Such acts of reflection and contemplation are often uncomfortable and difficult to undertake. The speaker in this poem moves beyond examining her own identity and begins to question the role of women in society. In preparing for her dive, the poet first chooses to consult a book of mythology. This is interesting, as the **theme** of descent in order to obtain knowledge is a common one in Western literature. In Homer's *Odyssey*, the hero Odysseus descends into the underworld in order to garner information that will help him to return home. In Virgil's *Aeneid*, the hero Aeneas undertakes a similar journey. The poet recognises the significance of these myths and understands the valuable knowledge that can be obtained from reading these stories. However, during the dive, she chooses to leave this book of mythology behind. This is an important piece of information. The speaker recognises that neither language nor culture can prepare her for the real and lived experience that she is about to undergo. In the opening stanza, the poet acknowledges that this is going to be a difficult, if not dangerous, process. She mentions 'body armor' and knives.

As she descends into the depths of the ocean, her perception of her own identity becomes radically altered. This altered perception causes her to view her femininity in a completely different light. Remember that the book of mythology that she has left behind was written about men, by a man. This is another important element of the poem that has to be taken on board. Literature that was written from a male point of view cannot adequately convey the poet's experience. The myth that was the starting point of her journey is not enough. Its 'words' fail to acknowledge the role of women in the modern world. She must therefore return to tell her own tale. The dive becomes the metaphorical equivalent of a search, or quest, to retell the old myths, so that they make sense from a modern, female point of view. The new knowledge that the poet seeks is likened to a treasure:

> whose silver, copper, vermeil cargo lies
> obscurely inside barrels

In order to salvage this treasure, it is suggested that the male-dominated world of language and culture will need to be rewritten to include the points of view of women.

During the dive and the quest for a new mythology, she transforms herself into a new kind of creature. The dive into the ocean is, of course, interesting from a symbolic point of view. We have already said that the ocean has long been used as a metaphor for human consciousness. However, the ocean is also the place where all life originated. In her descent into the depths of the ocean, the speaker at first becomes a 'mermaid' and then becomes a 'merman'.

When Rich was writing this poem, she was aware of the need for Western civilisation to make room for the creativity and vitality of women. In fact, when *Diving into the Wreck* was awarded the National Book Award in 1973, Rich rejected the prize as an individual but accepted it, with a statement co-authored by Audre Lorde and Alice Walker, on behalf of all unknown women writers.

This is a difficult, but extremely interesting, poem that forces us to examine the place of women in society. In a subtle and complex fashion, it questions and undermines a patriarchal culture that devalues anything female or feminine. The best way to look on this poem is as an attempt to search for new meanings that will transform our understanding of the world.

3. Essay Writing

'Diving into the Wreck' is perhaps Adrienne Rich's best-known and most memorable poem. As such, it is worthy of inclusion in any personal response to Rich that you may be asked to make. If you decide to include this poem, bear the following points in mind.

a. The poem can be read as a commentary on the experience of being a woman in Western society. In this sense, it can be read as a political poem. Given that so many of the poems by Rich on the course are political in their outlook, you might want to consider devoting one paragraph to this aspect of her work.

b. The *rhythms*, repetition and layered imagery add to the mythical atmosphere in the poem.

c. 'Diving into the Wreck' can be read as an exploration of the subconscious mind.

Critical Commentary: From a Survivor

See the text of the poem on p. 223.

1. Content

Rich had to cope with her father's death in 1968 and her husband's suicide in 1970. 'From a Survivor' can be read as a response to the death of her husband.

In the opening stanza, the poet tells us that, initially, the commitment that they made to one another was almost expected of them. Put simply, it was the done thing to get married:

> The pact that we made was the ordinary pact
> of men & women in those days

She then highlights the fact that they were somewhat naïve in believing that they were different from any other couple. Their personalities were prone to the same human failings as anyone else. In the third stanza, the speaker tells us that she cannot decide whether or not they were fortunate to have been so innocent:

> Lucky or unlucky, we didn't know
> the race had failures of that order
> and that we were going to share them

The pair really thought of themselves as being 'special'. The poet can still remember the physical presence of her husband. His 'body' is still 'as vivid' to her as it was then.

With the passing of the years, the speaker has had time to reassess her feelings for her husband. The physical aspects of their relationship now seem less significant to her. She now understands what her husband's body 'could and could not do'. With the benefit of hindsight, she no longer views her husband as having 'the body of a god'. In the eighth stanza, the speaker informs us that next year would have been their twentieth wedding anniversary. They got married in 1953 and Rich wrote this poem in 1972. The speaker still feels the need to reflect on what might have been. Her husband, too, might have 'made the leap' that they 'talked, too late, of making'. It is never precisely clear what the speaker is *alluding* to here. However, it seems to be connected to the life that she now leads. She has achieved a sense of contentment and fulfilment, not through one leap, but through 'a succession of brief, amazing movements | each one making possible the next'.

2. Stylistic Features

'From a Survivor' amounts to a straightforward and honest reassessment of the poet's marriage. Given Rich's Jewish background, the poem's title is an emotive one. 'Survivor' is a term often applied to those Jews who survived the horrors of the Nazi concentration camps. Her personal experience of marriage cannot, of course, be compared to the Holocaust. However, the twentieth anniversary of the breakdown of their relationship does provoke strong emotions in the poet. The erratic arrangement of the stanzas demonstrates the poet's difficulty in containing her emotions. Notice how the length of the ninth line calls attention to the poet's naïvety in the early days of her relationship with her husband. The use of the conditional tense in the eighth stanza hints at her genuine belief that things may have been different. These feelings are, of course, negated in the following line, when the poet informs us that her husband is 'wastefully dead'.

3. Essay Writing

If you are thinking of including 'From a Survivor' in your essay, you may wish to consider the following points.

a. The poem is a highly charged, emotional exploration of very private concerns.
b. While the poem is deeply personal, it can also be read as a political statement. This is typical of many of Rich's poems. You might want to give some thought to constructing a paragraph on this aspect of her work.
c. Once again, the poem addresses the troubled relationships that can exist between men and women.

Examination Technique

Poetry is worth 70 marks on the Higher Level paper. Fifty marks are available for seen poetry and 20 marks for unseen poetry. It is extremely important that you do everything you can to maximise your chances on the day of the examination. The first thing that you need to do is to become familiar with the marking scheme. When your questions are being graded, the corrector will be using a number of guidelines. Your ability to write a response to a poet or a poem in accordance with the demands of the marking scheme will largely determine your final grade.

Qualities the Examiner Looks For

On a general level, the corrector will be looking for four different qualities in your answer.

1. The first of these is *Clarity of Purpose*. Here, the corrector will want to see that your answer engages with the question asked. This is worth 30 per cent of the available marks.
2. The second area that the corrector will consider is the *Coherence of Delivery*. Here, the corrector wants to see an ability to sustain your response throughout the entire answer. This is worth 30 per cent of the available marks. We will look at how this might be best achieved later.
3. The third area that the corrector will concern him/herself with is *Efficiency of Language* use. The corrector will want to see clear evidence of your ability to manage and control your language so as to achieve clear communication. This is worth 30 per cent of the available marks.
4. The final area that the marking scheme addresses is called *Accuracy of Mechanics*. This is basically spelling and grammar. Ten per cent of the available marks are given for this.

In the future, you should try to shape your answer with these four areas in mind. Remember, your essays must satisfy the demands of the marking scheme in order to meet the requirements set down by the State Examinations Commission.

Now that we have seen what the corrector is looking for, it is time to consider how to go about achieving these in an essay.

Clarity of Purpose

In order to achieve *Clarity of Purpose* in an answer, it is important that your essay is completely focused on the question asked. This means that you *must* address the key words in the question. In 2004, the following question appeared on the paper.

> **Imagine you were asked to select one or more of Patrick Kavanagh's poems for inclusion in a short anthology entitled *The Essential Kavanagh*. Give reasons for your choice, quoting from or referring to the poem or poems you have chosen.**

In order to get the full 15 marks available for *Clarity of Purpose*, you would have to:

- Provide an original and fresh answer. (Slavishly learned-off material can often damage your prospects in the exam.)
- Show that you understand the genre of poetry. This means that you demonstrate a technical knowledge of poetry as evidenced in Kavanagh's work.
- Focus on your experience of reading Patrick Kavanagh's poetry. In other words, you would have to state explicitly how you felt about Kavanagh's poetry. It would not be acceptable simply to say, 'I liked his poetry.' You must always justify your statements by providing examples from the poems on the course.

You would lose marks for *Clarity of Purpose* by:

- Retelling what each poem that you have studied is about. This is known as paraphrasing. Remember, you are expected to know the content of the poems. The content of a poem is only useful in so far as it illustrates a point that addresses the question asked. The chief examiner's report in 2001 specifically mentioned this point, saying that candidates should be aware that while questions on poetry will require them to come to terms with the content of poems, they may also require them to deal with the language of poetry. The easiest way to avoid paraphrasing is to deal with the poetry in a global sense. Paragraphs that deal with the poetry on a poem-by-poem basis lend themselves to paraphrasing.
- Reproducing an essay that you learned off by heart that does not address the question fully.
- Failing to show an awareness of the genre of poetry. Remember, it should always be blatantly clear to the corrector that your essay is a response to poetry.

Coherence of Delivery

In order to gain the full 15 marks available for *Coherence of Delivery*, you need to sustain your essay in a manner that demonstrates:

- **Continuity of argument:** In other words, your ideas need to follow on from one another.
- **Management of ideas:** You must control the manner in which you present your ideas in an essay. The easiest way to ensure this is to write in focused paragraphs. A focused paragraph deals with one aspect of the poet's work. This one aspect can be technical, e.g. use of rhythm, or thematic, e.g. death, love, etc.
- **Engagement with the texts:** You must show that you understand how the poems function and achieve their impact. It is not simply enough to know what the poem is about. A statement such as 'this is a dramatic poem' is useless unless you show *how* the poem is dramatic.

You will lose marks for *Coherency of Delivery* if you:

- Fail to shape your argument. Remember, your essay must have a beginning, a middle and a conclusion.
- Write in disorganised paragraphs that lack focus. Remember, the definition of a paragraph is a group of sentences dealing with one idea.
- Use the wrong register. Your tone of voice and the type of language that you use are important aspects of your essay. While you should try to write in a natural style, the fact that you are writing an essay implies a certain degree of formality.

Efficiency of Language

If you want to obtain the full 15 marks available for *Efficiency of Language*, you must:

- Control your expression. This means that your sentences should flow naturally. Avoid very long sentences. If something can be said clearly in a short sentence, don't try to make it more complicated. You must ensure that the syntax (word order) of your sentences is logical.

- Ensure that your paragraphs are structured correctly. As previously stated, you must write in ordered paragraphs that work together to answer the question. Try to link your paragraphs where possible. Sometimes contrast can work as a link between paragraphs.
- Use lively, interesting language and phrasing. Try to vary your sentence length and avoid repetition of words and phrases. Once again, knowledge of the technical aspects of the poet's work can help make your language more interesting.

You will lose marks for *Efficiency of Language* if you:

- Fail to write clear and logical sentences that make complete sense to the person reading them. The golden rule is, if you are slightly unclear about what your sentence is saying, then the person reading it will be completely lost.
- Use learned-off material that does not logically fit in with the rest of your argument or address the question asked.
- Write an essay that does not contain ordered paragraphs.

Accuracy of Mechanics

There are 5 marks available for grammar and spelling. While the corrector will not punish you for obvious slips of the hand, you will be penalised for poor spelling and grammar. However, if your grammar and spelling are very weak, they will have an impact on other areas of the marking scheme.

Comparing and Contrasting More than One Poem: A Short Exercise

After you have analysed more than one poem by a prescribed poet, you should attempt a comparison of the poems in the table below.

✓ Identify the ideas/images/themes that all three share. You can also comment on any differences there may be.
✓ Include appropriate quotations that support some of the points that you make.

Title of Poem	Similarities	Differences	Supporting Quotations

Paragraph Building

Once you have read several poems by the prescribed poets, it is time to start thinking about how you will approach each poet's work in an essay. As you organise your thoughts, try to do so in focused paragraphs. The following points will help you to achieve this.

1. Generally, the best paragraphs tend to have two or three relevant quotations that fit in with the grammatical logic of the paragraph's sentences.
2. They tend to focus on one aspect of the poet's work.
3. Rather than concentrating on what a poem says, the best paragraphs deal with what the poet has to say on a particular idea or topic.
4. Strong paragraphs also deal with how the poet organises his or her ideas. This usually means that you should discuss the poet's use of language.
5. Finally, you must address the question asked. In recent years, most questions on the Leaving Certificate have tended to be personal responses. This means that

your paragraphs *must* contain a personal reaction. While you do not want to overdo it, the easiest way to achieve this is to include the personal pronoun 'I'.

Using Quotations in Your Paragraphs

Your paragraph is part of *your* argument, so consider the following points when using quotations.

1. Too many quotations can overpower your own argument or voice.
2. Quotations should fit into your argument, not appear out of thin air. Try to avoid simply dropping in the quote out of the blue.
3. Avoid explaining a quote or saying the same thing twice by using a quote.
4. Quotations should be grammatically consistent with the rest of your essay. If punctuation, pronouns and verb tenses don't flow with your own words, paraphrase the necessary material or make minor changes within the quotation, surrounding them with square brackets [ ]. If you want to leave out some words, you should use ellipses […]. All quotations should be unobtrusive. Making them unobtrusive can be very difficult to perfect. However, once you master this skill, you will notice a marked improvement in your ability to argue a point.

You should practise using quotations every time you write about a poet. Take a look at how the examples below incorporate quotations so that they fit in with the grammatical flow of the sentence.

> **Example:** In the extract from 'The Great Hunger', the speaker presents us with a desolate and unforgiving landscape where 'the potato-gatherers [move] like mechanized scare-crows'.

The quotation in this sentence is unobtrusive; it does not take from the point that is being made. Rather, it adds to it. Remember, don't be afraid to alter the flow of the quote to suit the grammar of your sentence. Notice how the small change that was made to the quotation has helped the sentence to flow more smoothly.

Look at the following example.

> **Example**: Eavan Boland points out that they 'speak plainly. [They] hear each other clearly.'

In this sentence, only one word has been changed. However, this simple change from the original 'we' to 'they', indicated by square brackets, allows the sentence to flow more smoothly.

Look at the following example.

> **Example**: In my opinion, Adrienne Rich's poetry is most powerful when it draws on images from the natural world in order to highlight the poet's emotional state. In 'Storm Warnings', she looks outside and detects 'gray unrest [...] moving across the land'. Here, the weather acts as a metaphor for her own feelings of unease.

Some of the words from this quote have been left out. This allows you to make your point in an efficient manner. Notice how the quotation in this short extract supports the personal statement made in the first sentence. It also supports the technical point about Rich's language made in the third sentence. Quotations that help to build on the points you are making are best when it comes to exploiting the marking scheme.

If you want to use a block quotation (usually more than one or two lines of text or to give emphasis to the quote), you drop a line, move to the centre of your page and insert the quotation. Take a look at this extract from an essay on Robert Frost's poetry written by a Leaving Certificate student.

> **Example**: What struck me most about Frost's poetry is the manner in which it gives form to life and shapes experience by reflecting upon it. By inviting his readers to share in these experiences, Frost provides us with a chance to hear one of the most important poetic voices of the 20th century. I suppose my attitude to Frost's poetry can be best summed up by saying that I really never needed to be told what it meant. Few of us can forget such memorable lines as:
>
> > Two roads diverged in a wood, and I—
> > I took the one less traveled by,
> > And that has made all the difference.

Albeit in a much less specific manner than the other quotations above, this block quote still works to support the point being made. Notice how this paragraph is clearly focused on the poetry of Frost in general, rather than on the specific poem quoted. Try to avoid commenting on the poetry in a poem-by-poem manner.

Now that you have read about how to compare and contrast poems and how to use quotations in your paragraphs, look at the following essays, which were written by Leaving Certificate students under examination conditions.

Sample Essay: Robert Frost

'The poetry of Robert Frost is a poetry of deep feeling and sharp observation.' Write a response to this statement, supporting your points with the aid of suitable reference to the poems you have studied.

'I thought of questions that have no reply'.

Robert Frost's poetry is the poetry of philosophy. While his voice was often quiet and languid, he was a passionate individual. He cared deeply about a wide range of issues, from the true nature of man, to the ageing

It can sometimes be a good idea to anchor your essay on a strong quote. If you do this, try to use a quotation that captures the poet's thematic or stylistic concerns.

process, to the arbitrary and random nature of fate. His poetry not only makes the reader think, it allows the reader to view the world through the eyes of the poet. All his poems serve to illustrate the fact that this is a poet with sharp observational skills. The poet uses these skills to create beautiful images, through which he can explore the philosophical issues that interest him.

This is an excellent introduction. It provides a general overview of Frost's poetry while at the same time remaining focused on the question.

A poem that typifies Frost's style is 'The Road Not Taken'. In this poem, Frost reflects on the philosophical puzzles presented by fate. He is interested in the impact a seemingly innocuous decision can have on life.

This is a strong topic sentence. It is straightforward, clear and shows the direction that the paragraph is going to take. Remember that the focus is on Frost's style, not the poem itself. The poem is used as a means to back up the topic sentence.

> Two roads diverged in a yellow wood,
> And sorry I could not travel both
> And be one traveler, long I stood
> And looked down one as far as I could
> To where it bent in the undergrowth.

This stanza shows Frost at his brilliant best. He thinks deeply about the impact a simple decision can have on life, and he couches his thoughts in the simple, instantly recognisable metaphor of the forked road.

The use of technical terms (such as metaphor) adds greatly to any answer.

In the end, he decides to opt for the 'one less traveled by'. The poet is not a complacent man who accepts life without thought. He is a man with a strong desire to examine the impact our decisions have on our lives.

> I took the one less traveled by,
> And that has made all the difference.

'Design' is a poem about nature and God. In 'The Road Not Taken', a simple everyday event is used to explore a great philosophical theme. The poet employs a similar conceit in 'Design'.

The introduction of a second poem helps to avoid the danger of paraphrase. See p. 549 on how to avoid paraphrase.

The poet's sparkling eye for detail and his love of the natural world are immediately apparent.

> I found a dimpled spider, fat and white,
> On a white heal-all, holding up a moth
> Like a white piece of rigid satin cloth—

The detail here is almost forensic. The poet looks at this apparently unimportant scene and finds something profound. The repetition of the word 'white' illustrates his fascination with the scene. It is a scene that, in fact, disturbs him. He is drawn to think about the cruelty of nature – 'Assorted characters of death and blight' – and, being a philosopher, begins to ponder the existence and intent of God. The scene leads to a disturbing conclusion:

> What but design of darkness to appall?—
> If design govern in a thing so small.

The poet's sharp observational eye has led him to a profound conclusion.

The poems 'Mending Wall' and ' "Out, Out—" ' illustrate the importance the poet placed on the understanding of human relationships. In 'Mending Wall', he comments on the divisions all humans build between themselves and their fellow man. Frost uses the metaphor of the stone wall to communicate his message. The building of the wall is described marvellously:

> And some are loaves and some so nearly balls
> We have to use a spell to make them balance:

However, the most powerful image of the poem is the simile used to describe the neighbour, with whom he realises he will never be able to connect, 'like an old-stone savage armed'. The image is evocative and compelling, and allows Frost to communicate a deeply held belief about the nature of man.

Notice how the use of technical terms adds greatly to the depth of the paragraph.

' "Out, Out—" ' is possibly the most impressive of the Robert Frost poems on the course. The poem describes an idyllic New England day that is disturbed by the tragic death of a young boy. Frost uses the death to comment on fate and on our reaction to its intervention. The power of the poem lies in the poet's ability to recreate the atmosphere of the tragic day in order to explore a philosophical issue about which he feels strongly.

> And from there those that lifted eyes could count
> Five mountain ranges one behind the other
> Under the sunset far into Vermont.

The day is beautiful, peaceful, idyllic. However, it is interrupted by the menacing, echoing sound of the buzz saw being used by the young boy. The poet uses the onomatopoeic 'snarled' and 'rattled' to recreate the sound of the saw 'As it ran light, or had to bear a load'. The description of the accident is visceral. The momentous intervention of fate is shown in slow motion to emphasise the poet's sense of powerlessness over cruel, indiscriminate fate. The saw:

> Leaped out at the boy's hand, or seemed to leap—
> He must have given the hand. However it was,
> Neither refused the meeting. [...]

Again in this poem, Frost takes an event from everyday life and uses it to comment on an issue about which he feels deeply. The death is tragic, all the more so given that it happened

It can be a good idea to concentrate on one poem that you found particularly impressive.

to one so young. However, the poet, while sorry, is not devastated. He makes the point that life goes on. Death is a natural part of life:

> [...] And they, since they
> Were not the one dead, turned to their affairs.

The poetry of Robert Frost is the poetry of deep feeling and sharp observation. Any examination of the selection of his work on the Leaving Certificate syllabus proves the truth of this statement. Frost is a man deeply aware of the world around him. He is inspired to think about

Like all good conclusions, this one links to the introduction. It is also focused on the question. Notice how there is no new material here and the key question words are emphasised.

that world by the everyday events of the life. Those events are closely observed and scrutinised in his poetry. These close observations inspire thought, inspire questions, and inspire an emotional response in the reader.

Sample Essay: Patrick Kavanagh

> **Write a personal response to the poetry by Kavanagh that you have studied. Support your essay by reference to the poems by Kavanagh on your course.**

Kavanagh's poetry stands apart from much of the other Leaving Certificate selection that I have studied. His honesty and the 'newness' of his language, together with the manner in which he is inspired by nature, are particularly appealing. I found Kavanagh's poetry to have

This is an excellent introduction. It addresses the thematic and technical appeal of Kavanagh's poetry in a personal manner. In this respect, it is very question focused.

an appeal that often transcends the simplicity of his subject matter. I genuinely feel that Kavanagh is an important Irish poet who will be remembered long into the future.

One of the most remarkable aspects of Kavanagh's poetry is the manner in which he used the material of his life so as to create such unique poems. 'On Raglan Road' is, in my estimation, one of the most haunting love poems ever written. Few can forget having heard this poem for the first time (especially if

sung). The air 'The Dawning of the Day' works to enhance the effect that Kavanagh attempts to create in his poem. Antoinette Quinn described 'On Raglan Road' as one of the 'sweetest songs that tell of the saddest of thoughts'. For me, this is precisely what Kavanagh achieves in this poem. The autumnal setting and the slow, sad, almost funereal pace combined with the intensity of the speaker's emotions all work to create an unforgettable reading experience. The beauty of the woman in the poem symbolised by her 'dark hair' is viewed by the speaker as being a 'snare' that he 'might one day rue'. In my view, there is a startling honesty to what Kavanagh has achieved in this poem. The poet lays his heart bare for all to see and yet manages to evoke something of the importance of poetry:

[…] I had wooed not as I should a creature made of clay –
When the angel woos the clay he'd lose his wings at the dawn of day.

At the poem's close, we are left to realise that the beauty of this song transcends even the earthly, more conventional beauty of the dark-haired woman.

Kavanagh is one of the few poets who speaks openly and honestly about his place as a poet in society. 'Iniskeen Road: July Evening' is rooted firmly in the ordinary, even banal

setting of rural Ireland. The rhythm and cadence of the poem mirror that of the ordinary country people that populate it. We learn that there is to be a 'dance in Billy Brennan's barn tonight' and that the 'bicycles go by in twos and threes'. I particularly admire the manner in which Kavanagh has the honesty and courage to approach such an ordinary subject matter. He transforms the night of this dance into a symbol of poetic isolation. Kavanagh the poet is excluded from the 'wink-and-elbow language of delight'. He may transcend (through the art of his poetry) the here and now, he may even be king of 'banks and stones and every blooming thing', but he will never belong fully to the society about which he writes. This is, of course, very similar to 'On Raglan Road', where the poet 'wooed not as he should a creature made of clay'. Patrick Kavanagh the poet is condemned to a lifetime of isolation. His existence as a poet forces him to look in from the outside and to record but never participate in the beauty he experiences. However, it is not Kavanagh's loneliness, but his honesty that is most attractive to the modern reader.

There is a refreshing, open honesty to the poems on the course by Patrick Kavanagh. The 'canal poems' have a wonderful honesty at their centre that manages to transport the reader beyond the reality of their setting. So successful *Where possible, you should try* is Kavanagh in achieving this that we are taken *to relate to the poems you have* from the Grand Canal in Dublin to a realm of *read on a personal level.* mythology and 'Parnassian' beauty. So much poetry concerns itself with ideas and notions that seem outside the realm of everyday experience. Kavanagh, on the other hand, writes about places and things with which I am familiar. I pass by the Grand Canal in the centre of Dublin every day and I know why Kavanagh describes it as being 'stilly' and 'Greeny'. I also completely understand what he means when he describes the 'tremendous silence' of the Grand Canal. In these poems, the redemptive force of nature is an almost religious experience. However, his message is at all times open, honest and ordinary, he doesn't preach and he is rarely didactic. When I read Kavanagh, I find that I am impressed by the honest conviction of the poet and the ordinariness of his message.

While Kavanagh may not be a didactic *Notice how this paragraph links* poet, it is possible to learn a great deal from *very well with the paragraph* his poems on the course. 'Advent' is a powerful *that went before it. You should* poem that reaches out to the modern reader *try to maintain links between* despite the fact that it celebrates a somewhat *your paragraphs.* forgotten practice. The 'dry black bread and the sugarless tea | Of penance' may be alien to most readers, but the idea that we have 'tasted and tested too much' is something I can certainly appreciate. There is an enduring simplicity to Kavanagh's message. We are made to feel that the ordinary can indeed induce 'prophetic astonishment'. Kavanagh asks us not to analyse or 'reason', but rather accept 'arguments that cannot be proven'.

In a world where cynicism and rational analysis have supplanted faith and acceptance, I find it refreshing to find that we can indeed 'return to Doom | the knowledge that we stole but could not use'.

Kavanagh's message is not, however, always uplifting. For me, the most memorable poem on the course is perhaps his most bleak. The excerpt from 'The Great Hunger' is a dark yet powerful poem. The opening lines present us with an almost stygian landscape. We learn that 'Clay is the word and clay is the flesh' and that this is a place where life is 'broken-backed over the Book | Of Death'. There is a compelling, voyeuristic appeal to this poem that I find mesmerising.

In fact, it is not possible to read Patrick Kavanagh's poetry without being hypnotised by the beauty of his language. I found the uniqueness of his metaphors and the strangeness of his neologisms combined with the inflections of everyday speech to be genuinely impressive. Kavanagh's language has both the variety and the control to underpin the diversity of his themes. Seamus Heaney has pointed out that there is a rough-cast quality in such lines as:

A language-based paragraph will always impress the corrector. Notice how the student does not lose sight of the question.

> Where the potato-gatherers, like mechanized scare-crows move
> Along the side-fall of the hill […]

Similarly, in 'Shancoduff', the bleak desolation of Monaghan is conveyed when the speaker describes the 'sleety winds [fondling] the rushy beards of Shancoduff'. However, this darkness that is often captured in Kavanagh's language is only one aspect of his poetry. Very often, sombre concerns give way to a lyrical, soft yet impassioned quality that I found particularly uplifting. There is an exuberance and childish enthusiasm to the poet's music that allows him to treat nature with, at times, an almost lover's intensity. Kavanagh calls on nature to 'encapture' him and to 'Feed the gaping need of [his] senses'. In a similarly innocent fashion, the 'magical' and wonderful 'Garden that was childhood' is captured in the narrative of 'A Christmas Childhood'.

Patrick Kavanagh's poetry is memorable for its honesty. It charts the spiritual, artistic, intellectual and emotional journey of the poet. It is a journey that takes us from 'Billy Brennan's barn' and the heartbreaking strangeness of the 'dreeping hedges' of Monaghan to unrequited love in 'On Raglan Road', culminating in the inner peace and restoration to be found near the Grand Canal. I suppose my attitude to Kavanagh's poetry can best be summed up by saying that I never really needed to be told what his poetry meant. I would genuinely recommend that everyone should read at least one poem by Patrick Kavanagh.

EXAMINATION TECHNIQUE

Sample Essay: Sylvia Plath

'I do/do not like to read the poetry of Sylvia Plath.' Respond to this statement, with reference to the poetry you have studied on your course.

This is an excellent introduction. It is very question focused in that it combines a personal response with reasons for liking Plath's poetry.

I do like to read the poetry of Sylvia Plath, despite how depressing I sometimes find it. The absolute control which Plath has over her work, her unique use of imagery and the insight her poetry provides into her personality and her state of mind are just a few of the reasons that I was, and still am, drawn to Plath's poetry.

Plath has a masterful poetic style. Her work is intricately sculpted and crafted, which is one of the main reasons why I find it so beautiful and enjoyable to read. The aural quality of Plath's poetry can be both mesmerising and *The topic sentence of this paragraph is clear. Sometimes a short sentence can work well in grabbing the reader's attention.* unsettling. 'Morning Song', one of the most uplifting Plath poems on our course, makes great use of sound in conveying its message. The jaunty rhythm of 'Love set you going like a fat gold watch' gives way to an awestruck, reverential tone when

In this paragraph, the student demonstrates excellent technical knowledge of the poems.

Plath describes her baby as a 'New statue | In a drafty museum'. Here, the assonance of the 'ah' and 'ooh' sounds mimic the baby talk of the new parents. The delicate sound created by the onomatopoeia in lines such as 'your moth-breath | Flickers' provides us with an example of how Plath's technical accomplishment makes her poetry so enjoyable to read.

Often, however, the language in Plath's poetry can be as disturbing as it is beautiful. In 'Child', for example, the poet uses assonance to capture the sound of a child's speech:

> I want to fill it with color and ducks,
> The zoo of the new

The use of enjambment creates a gentle, lilting momentum. However, in the final stanza, Plath uses assonance to create a far darker tone. The repetition of broad vowel sounds ('troublous', 'dark', 'star') creates a brooding, gloomy atmosphere. Furthermore, the sibilance present in the final stanza adds an almost menacing feeling to the poem,

Sometimes only one word, such as 'similarly', is enough to link your paragraphs.

which leaves the reader feeling troubled. A similar effect can be seen in 'Poppies in July'. The first line of the poem is energetic because of the repetitive staccato of the short, disyllabic words 'Little poppies'. However, the broad monosyllabic sounds of the second line's question, 'Do you do no harm', evokes a lethargic atmosphere. The stark contrast in tone between these two lines is an unsettling combination, and a perfect illustration of how Plath expertly sculpts her poems to be both entrancing and disturbing.

Similarly, I found the unusual images in Plath's work captivating and enthralling. Of course I have to admit that I was also unsettled and even alarmed by her imagery. Her description of the hive as 'the coffin of a midget | Or a square baby' in 'Arrival of the Bee Box' is bizarre, disturbing and strangely comical. However, images such as 'African hands' 'Black on black, angrily clambering' are menacing and claustrophobic. Yet it is this dark undercurrent that makes Plath's poetry so distinctive and compelling. In 'Finisterre', Plath depicts a fragile cliff edge that

Notice how the paragraph manages to link two poems together. Such paragraphs can be impressive.

is surrounded by 'trefoils, stars and bells'. However, the darkness is never far from her poetry. The image takes on a sinister tone when Plath goes on to say that the flora looks as if it has been embroidered by 'fingers [...] close to death'. There is an undercurrent of violence

Notice how the student really tries to link the paragraphs.

present in the poet's description of rocks hiding 'their grudges under the water'. This sinister quality is also present in the poem 'Mirror'. There is a disturbing underlying force present in this poem. The mirror feels rewarded by the woman's tears and by the 'agitation of [her] hands'. Old age is portrayed as a menace that 'Rises toward her day after day, like a terrible fish'. I found this image troubling, and yet also intriguing. One of my favourite things about Plath's writing is that it is thought provoking because it shows the world in an entirely new light.

Plath's poetry does not just shed interesting light on the external world, however. The confessional nature of her poetry allows the reader to explore something of her troubled personality through reading her work. 'The Arrival of the Bee Box' provides us with an interesting example of Plath's confessional poetry. The combination of short, one-line sentences and long run-on lines works to make the poem feel almost like a stream of consciousness. In the poem, Plath uses the personal pronoun 'I' a total of 18 times. Plath explores her psyche through the depiction of an external event. I feel that the bees in the box can be taken to refer to Plath's own thoughts and visions. They are maniacal, clambering and dark. She describes them as 'dangerous' and they appal her, yet she is fascinated by them. I think that the poem reveals more about Plath's persona than it ever does about the bees. We get an insight into Plath's obsessive tendencies when she tells us that she 'can't keep away from it'. We glimpse her controlling personality when she proclaims: 'I need feed them nothing, I am the owner.' Her chilling narrative voice is enthralling in its blunt, even cruel honesty, and this honesty is one of the main reasons I enjoy reading Plath's work.

This conclusion is excellent in that it is question focused. It does what all good conclusions should do because it closes down the essay perfectly.

Sylvia Plath has written a vast body of extraordinary poetry. I love her poetry for the beauty of its language and captivating nature of the imagery employed by the poet. I was mesmerised by the latent, brooding violence that underpins so much of her work. Reading Plath provides insight into the often dark mindset of the poet. I sometimes find it uncomfortable to read Sylvia Plath's poetry, but I love it nonetheless.

Sample Essay: Adrienne Rich

Give your personal estimation of the poetry of Adrienne Rich. Support your point of view by reference to the poems of Rich on your course.

I was intrigued by Adrienne Rich's poetry. It is challenging, thought provoking and unique. Many of her poems, such as 'Trying to Talk with a Man', 'Aunt Jennifer's Tigers' and 'The Roofwalker', are figurative and I admired the

This is an excellent question-focused introduction, combining a personal response with clear reasons for admiring Rich's poetry.

poet's ability to use metaphor in an inventive and original way. Rich's use of

A clear topic sentence that provides direction is very important.

language is always very controlled. Her ability to manipulate and control language to create powerful, memorable and at times cinematic imagery means her poetry can be enjoyed on a purely aesthetic level.

Thematically, her work is never less than engaging. Rich is a feminist writer, and, like many of my classmates, hearing this made me approach her work with negative preconceptions. However, those preconceptions were based on ignorance, and I am happy to say that reading her work has educated me. Reading poems like 'Power' and 'The Roofwalker' has allowed me to develop an understanding of the politics of feminism, and this is an aspect of Rich's work I thoroughly enjoyed. Probably the most appealing aspect of this poet's work, however, is her honesty when dealing with difficult personal issues. Poems like 'Living in Sin' are reflective and wry, and 'From a Survivor' and 'Trying to Talk with a Man', written in the aftermath of Alfred Conrad's suicide, are intensely moving and mature. So what is my estimation of Adrienne Rich's work? I think her poetry is fascinating thematically and her use of language is technically brilliant.

Once again, there is a clear topic sentence. This provides the paragraph with a clear direction.

Much of Adrienne Rich's poetry is autobiographical. 'Living in Sin', a brilliantly observant and reflective poem, sees the poet looking back at the young idealistic woman she used to be. She remembers how 'She had thought the studio would keep itself; I no dust upon the furniture of love'. I think the poet is clearly amazed at her youthful naiveté. She remembers living in the cold apartment and thinking it 'Half heresy, to wish the taps less vocal, I the panes relieved of grime'. She captures the universal desire to believe in the power of love, and this helped me to relate to the poem. I believe anybody who has ever experienced the pain of the break-up of a relationship can relate to the poet at the end of the poem when she talks about how 'she woke sometimes to feel the daylight coming I like a relentless milkman up the stairs'. I loved this ending to the poem, and found it refreshing that she was able to look back on a painful memory with humour and insight.

The paragraph makes good use of quotation. Quotation is often most effective when built into the fabric of the sentence.

The maturity obvious in 'Living in Sin' is also apparent in this poet's two most fascinating poems, 'From a Survivor' and 'Trying to Talk with a Man'. These poems deal with the poet's feelings following the suicide of her former husband, Alfred Conrad. Their honesty is compelling. The idealism of youth is again referred to in 'From a Survivor' when the poet says, 'The pact that we made was the ordinary pact | of men & women in those days'. She loved her husband when she married him, but time and reflection have made her realise 'we didn't know | the race had failures of that order | and that we were going to share them'. This is a very moving and plaintive expression of the poet's feelings. In 'Trying to Talk with a Man', I learned that her marriage had been troubled for a long time, and that she felt 'an acute angle of understanding | moving itself like a locus of the sun | into this condemned scenery'. She talks of looking into her husband's eyes and feeling that his 'eyes are stars of a different magnitude | they reflect lights that spell out: EXIT'. I was amazed by the directness and maturity of these lines. The fact that she can look back on the end of a relationship with such a clear eye is an aspect of Rich's poetry that intrigued me. That is particularly true when you read 'From a Survivor' and realise that Conrad is 'wastefully dead', having taken his own life. Rich describes 'the leap | we talked, too late, of making', and how making that leap has meant that her new life is 'a succession of brief, amazing movements'. The brilliance with which the poet deals with such powerful emotions and complex relationships is an aspect of Rich's work that appealed to me.

The final sentence of this paragraph works very well. Notice how it complements the paragraph's topic sentence. The best paragraphs work in this fashion.

That complexity of thought is an aspect of Rich's 'political' poems that I also found intriguing. The poem 'Aunt Jennifer's Tigers' illustrates the fact that Rich had a powerful awareness of her identity as a woman and of the position of women in society from an early age. That poem displays an acute sense of injustice at the role conventional society forced upon women like her aunt. Jennifer is an immensely skilled woman, whose 'fingers fluttering through her wool' draw the poet's eye. In a remarkably effective use of metaphor, something which characterises Rich's poetry, the poet notes how 'The massive weight of Uncle's wedding band | Sits heavily upon Aunt Jennifer's hand'. Clearly, the poet is interested in how women, symbolised by Aunt Jennifer, have been suppressed and unable to express themselves due to their relationships with men. This was an issue that stimulated much thought in the poet, and one of the results was her determination to reassess her identity as a writer.

Notice how both paragraphs are linked. This is one of the hardest essay-writing skills to perfect. The marking scheme rewards students for essays that are coherent and unified.

This concern is dealt with in 'The Roofwalker'. In that brilliantly thoughtful and thought-provoking poem, the poet describes 'Giants, the roofwalkers, | on a listing deck, the wave | of darkness about to break | on their heads'. The giants are symbolic of the patriarchs of literature, the men whose style Rich has learned, and upon whose work she has modelled her writing. There is an awareness in the poem that the time for male dominance has come to an end. The poet must find a new style, a distinctively feminist voice, because she 'lay— | with infinite exertion— | a roof [she] can't live under'. This poem, written in 1962, clearly reflects the poet's growing need to express herself as a woman, free from the influence of men. She knows this will be difficult, and feels 'naked, ignorant'. The sense is that the struggle to find her voice as a feminist writer will be difficult, but she must take the chance.

That awareness of the pain implicit in the struggle for women's liberation, equality and rights is also evident in her most overtly political poem, 'Power'. The poem, written in 1978, reflects back on the struggle radical feminists went through to excavate:

> one bottle   amber   perfect   a hundred-year-old
> cure for fever   or melancholy   a tonic
> for living on this earth   in the winters of this climate

I was fascinated by these lines. I loved the sense that the poet was writing in a stream of consciousness and that the precious bottle that has been excavated represented women's rights, won after a long struggle. Of course, it is easy to take the equality of the sexes for granted in our modern world, where legislation exists to prevent discrimination based on gender. That is why it is interesting, from an historical perspective, to see the poet describe the long, hard struggle women have had to endure to achieve these rights, which she brilliantly describes as 'a tonic | for living on this earth'.

Of course, the central figure in 'Power' is Marie Curie, the great Polish chemist who, for Rich, symbolises the feminist struggle. The decision to employ the image of Curie is typically insightful and clever. Curie had to suffer to achieve greatness, as the visceral description of the 'cracked and suppurating skin of her finger-ends' proves. Rich employs Curie as a symbol for the pain women have had to and will have to endure to achieve equal status with men. This use of symbolism is one of the most memorable characteristics of Rich's work.

Her use of metaphor and figurative imagery really is remarkably effective. In 'Aunt Jennifer's Tigers', the image of 'her terrified hands [...] | Still ringed with ordeals she was mastered by' effectively captures the suppression of women, just as the image of the 'tigers in the panel that she made | [...] prancing, proud and unafraid', captures the resilient spirit of the aunt and of all women. Similarly, in 'Living in Sin', the line 'on the kitchen shelf among the saucers | a pair of beetle-eyes would fix her own' is remarkably effective. There is no escaping the horrified sense of realisation felt by the young woman who has committed herself to a doomed relationship. However, the most effective use of metaphor and symbolism in Rich's poetry lies, for me, in 'Trying to Talk with a Man'. In this extraordinary poem, the poet's relationship with her husband is compared to a desert. She talks about 'an acute angle of understanding | moving itself like a locus of the sun | into this condemned scenery'. She is using metaphor in a memorable and innovative way to communicate her sense that her relationship with her husband has failed. This extraordinary use of figurative language continues in the poem as she describes the emotional distance she feels in her marriage by using a combination of sibilance and metaphor:

> walking at noon in the ghost town
> surrounded by a silence
>
> that sounds like the silence of the place
> except that it came with us
> and is familiar

What is my personal estimation of Adrienne Rich's poetry? I think it is wonderful. I think it is complex and simple, personal and political, moving and challenging. I don't know if Rich *These personal statements are strengthened by use of technical vocabulary.* would agree, but I think her poetry is didactic, because I have learned so much from reading it. I gained an insight into feminist ideology. I have learned that emotional problems and personal crises can be dealt with in a mature fashion. Most of all, I *This strong conclusion rounds off the essay perfectly.* have learned that poetry that is carefully crafted and intensely passionate can be remarkable.

Glossary

This section of the book is aimed at helping you to recognise the various literary terms that apply to poetry. This type of technical vocabulary can appear daunting. However, you should try to approach these terms with an open mind. If you attempt to link these terms to the poems you have read in class, they can add a whole new dimension to your reading of poetry. When writing essays, try to include some technical vocabulary, as it can help you to avoid paraphrasing.

Adjective: A word that is used to describe a noun (the name of a person, place, thing or abstract idea).

Aesthetics: The study of the nature of beauty, especially as it is perceived through art or literature. Much of the poetry on the course can be appreciated from an aesthetic point of view.

Alliteration: Sometimes known as initial rhyme, alliteration is used to create poetic effect through the repetition of the initial sounds of several words in succession. Alliteration usually refers to the repetition of consonant sounds.

Allusion: An indirect reference in one piece of literature to a character, theme or idea found in a historical period or another literary work.

Ambiguity: When a line of poetry contains more than one meaning, it is said to be ambiguous.

Analogy: A likeness or an agreement that is made between things that are otherwise dissimilar. Analogies are regularly found in metaphysical poetry.

Anaphora: The repetition of the same word or phrase at the beginning of consecutive sentences, lines or verses, usually for emphasis or rhetorical effect.

Apostrophe: A figure of speech where something obviously non-human or abstract is spoken to directly.

Assonance: The repetition of vowel sounds. The effect of assonance is generally to create a lonely or haunting quality. By appealing to the ear, it also increases our sense of immediacy, as it makes the experience more accessible.

Asyndetic: An adjective used to describe the act of omitting conjunctions in sentence constructions in which they would usually be used. Gerard Manley Hopkins makes extensive use of asyndeton in many of his poems on the course.

Atmosphere: The overall mood created in a poem.

Aubade: A poem or song that either addresses or announces the dawn. John Donne's 'The Sun Rising' is one of the best-known and, indeed, beautiful aubades.

Ballad: A story in poetic form, often about tragic love and usually sung. Traditionally passed down from generation to generation in oral form, ballads are especially common within the Irish tradition.

Blank verse: A poem written in unrhymed iambic pentameter. Poets tend to favour iambic pentameter, as it is normally the amount of words the average person can get out in a single breath. By using unrhymed iambic pentameter, the poet can create a natural and conversational feel to a poem. This, of course, has the effect of rendering the piece more accessible to the reader. (See also **Iambic pentameter** and **Metre** for more information.)

Cacophony/euphony: Cacophony is an unpleasant combination of sounds. Euphony, the opposite, is a pleasant combination of sounds. These sound effects can be used intentionally to create an effect that works to enhance the meaning of the poem. Cacophonous sounds tend to grate on the ear and often consist of harsh *k* or *c* sounds.

Cadence: This is the rise and fall in rhythm that naturally occurs when we speak. The cadence of a poem can be more powerful than the obvious metre or rhyming.

Caesura: A pause within a line of poetry, which may or may not affect the metrical count. A caesura is usually indicated by the following symbol (//). However, this is not always necessarily so.

Chiasmus: A type of rhetorical construction in which the order of the words in the second of two paired phrases is the reverse of the order in the first. Perhaps the most famous example of this device is to be found in Shakespeare's *Macbeth*, when the witches utter their famous chant, 'Fair is foul foul is fair'.

Cinematic: A poem is said to be cinematic if it presents its subject matter in a manner that recalls the movement of a camera in a movie or if the scene presented is strongly reminiscent of the cinema in general.

Colloquial language/Colloquialism: A form of language used in everyday speech.

Comparison: The act of comparing. Normally in poetry, a comparison falls into two categories: simile and metaphor.

Conceit: A far-fetched simile or metaphor. A literary conceit occurs when the speaker compares two highly dissimilar things.

Concrete poetry: A poem written in the shape of its subject matter.

Confessional style: A poem is said to have a confessional style if it reveals details about the poet's personal life. The term is usually applied to certain poets of the United States from the late 1950s and 1960s.

Consciousness: The perceptive qualities of the speaker in a poem.

Consonance: The repetition of consonant sounds with differing vowel sounds in words near each other in a line or lines of poetry. Consider the following example from Eavan Boland's 'The War Horse': 'the clip, clop, casual I Iron of his shoes'. The repetition of the *c* sound in 'clip', 'clop' and 'casual' creates consonance. The result is that something of the nature of the horse's movement is captured. Consonance is often associated with onomatopoeia.

Continuous present: A form of the present tense used to describe continuous actions, e.g. 'I am singing.'

Contrast: To set in opposition in order to show or emphasise differences between two ideas or two physical objects.

Couplet: A stanza of two lines that usually rhymes. Rhymed couplets are known as **heroic couplets**. In Robert Eager's opinion, such heroic couplets often 'aim at a clear transmission of sense'. For this to succeed, the heroic couplet must be supported by alliteration, assonance and controlled rhythm. (See also **Stanza**.)

Counterpoint: In a piece of music, the sounding together of two or more melodic lines, each of which displays an individual and differentiated melodic contour and rhythmic profile. Gerard Manley Hopkins borrowed this term to describe the reversal of two successive feet in a line.

Courtly love poem: A highly crafted and stylised type of poem. Normally, in the final stanza of such a poem, human love is represented as an ennobling force.

Curtailed or contracted sonnet: Refers to a sonnet of just 11 lines, normally using an *abcabc dcbdc* or *abcabc dbcdc* rhyming scheme. The final line of a curtail sonnet is a half line. The term was coined by Gerard Manley Hopkins to describe the form that he used in the poem 'Pied Beauty'.

Dactyls: Stressed syllables followed by unstressed syllables.

Dirge: A song of mourning for someone's death.

Dramatic monologue: A type of poem developed during the Victorian period in which a fictitious or historical character delivers a speech explaining his or her feelings, actions or motives. This speech or monologue is usually directed toward a silent audience, with the speaker's words influenced by a dramatic or critical situation. Examples of the dramatic monologue can be seen in the poems 'The Love Song of J. Alfred Prufrock' by T.S. Eliot, 'Lady Lazarus' by Sylvia Plath and more recently in 'The Captain of the 1964 Top of the Form Team' by Carol Ann Duffy.

Elegy: A lyric poem lamenting the death of someone or something.

Enjambment: A term describing the continuing of the sense from line to line in a poem, to the extent that it becomes unnatural in speaking the lines to make a pause at the line ending.

Envoi: Sometimes known as a tornada, an envoi is the short stanza at the end of a poem, used for summing up or as a dedication.

Epic: In literature generally, a major work dealing with an important theme that usually incorporates events of universal importance.

Epigraph: A brief quotation which appears at the beginning of a literary work.

Epiphany: A near-spiritual turning point or moment in a poem when the speaker becomes aware of truths that he or she had not previously thought about.

Epithalamium: A poem or song written or performed in celebration of a wedding.

Euphemism: A word or phrase that is substituted for another word or phrase that might be more unpleasant or offensive.

Feminism: This term is used to describe the movement for the advancement and the emancipation of women. This movement became particularly vocal in the 1960s and 1970s. In this anthology, the poet Adrienne Rich can be described as being particularly feminist in her outlook.

Femme fatale: A woman who is considered to be highly attractive and to have a destructive effect on those who succumb to her charms. Keats's 'La Belle Dame sans Merci' provides us with an example of such a dangerously seductive woman.

Figurative language: In literature or poetry, this is a way of saying one thing and meaning something else. In her poem 'Trying to Talk with a Man', Rich compares her relationship to a nuclear test site. Of course, she does not mean that it is literally burned and scorched or even radioactive. The comparison is intended to improve our understanding of how she feels. While figurative language provides a writer with the scope to write imaginatively, it also tests the imagination of the reader, forcing the reader to go below the surface of the poem and explore deeper, hidden meanings.

Figure of speech: An example of figurative language that states something that is not actually true in order to create an effect. Similes, metaphors and personification are figures of speech that are based on comparisons. Metonymy, synecdoche, synesthesia, apostrophe, oxymoron and hyperbole are other commonly used figures of speech.

Foot: The basic unit of measurement in a line of poetry. The metre in a poem is classified according to both its pattern and the number of feet to the line. Below is a list of classifications:

Monometer = one foot to a line
Dimeter = two feet to a line
Trimeter = three feet to a line
Tetrameter = four feet to a line
Pentameter = five feet to a line

If a line of poetry is written in iambic metre with four feet to the line, the line would be referred to as iambic tetrameter. Poets tend to favour iambic pentameter, as it is normally the number of words that an average person can get out in a single breath. This can create a natural and conversational feel to a poem that in turn renders the piece more accessible.

Formalistic: A poem is said to be formalistic if it cultivates artistic technique even at the expense of its subject matter.

Free verse: Unrhymed poetry with lines of varying lengths and containing no specific metrical pattern.

Genre: One of the categories that artistic works of all kinds can be divided into on the basis of form, style or theme. For example, detective novels are a genre of fiction, while Keats's 'La Belle Dame sans Merci' is written in the genre of the literary ballad.

Gustatory imagery: The representation through language of the sensation of taste.

Hendiadys: The substitution of a conjunction for a subordination, where a conjunction is used to link two words to express a single complex idea. Normally, a noun and adjective pairing is transformed into two nouns joined by a conjunction. Perhaps the best-known example of hendiadys can be found in Shakespeare's *Macbeth*, where the protagonist speaks of the 'sound and fury' of life. This provides the reader with a far more striking image than, say, 'furious sound' would have. English names for hendiadys include 'two for one' and 'figure of twinnes'.

Hyperbole: A figure of speech in which an overstatement or exaggeration occurs.

Iamb: A metrical pattern of one unstressed syllable, followed by one stressed syllable.

Iambic pentameter: A line of poetry that is made up of five units of rhythm, e.g. five pairs of stressed and unstressed syllables. Elizabeth Bishop's favourite example of iambic pentameter was 'I hate to see that evenin' sun go down'.

Iambic tetrameter: A line of verse that has four metrical feet.

Imagery: A word or group of words in a poem which appeal to one or more of the senses: sight, taste, touch, hearing and smell. The use of images serves to intensify the impact of the work.

Imagism: Around 1912 in London, some British and American-Irish poets, led by Ezra Pound, started a poetic movement called Imagism. These poets reacted against 19th-century poetry, which they felt was sentimental and emotionally dishonest. Instead, they favoured precision of imagery and clear, sharp language.

Imperative: The order form of the verb. For example, in the sentence 'shut the door', the verb 'shut' is in the imperative.

Impressionism: A style of painting that concentrates on the general tone and effect produced by a subject without elaboration of details. Impressionistic music is characterised by the use of rich harmonies and tones rather than form to express scenes or emotions.

Inference: A judgment based on reasoning rather than on direct or explicit statement or a conclusion based on facts or circumstances.

Internal rhyme: This is the rhyme between a word within a line and another word either at the end of the same line or within another line. The following excerpt from the comic poem 'Bantams in Pine Woods' by Wallace Stevens makes good use of internal rhyme:

> Chieftain Iffucan of Azcan in caftan
> Of tan with henna hackles, halt!

Intransitive verb: A verb that does not normally take a direct object. For example, the verb 'to go' does not normally take a direct object. You cannot say 'to go the car'.

Irish Literary Revival: The Irish Literary Revival, also known as the Celtic Revival, was begun by Lady Gregory, Edward Martyn and William Butler Yeats in Ireland in 1896. This group of writers aimed to stimulate a new appreciation of traditional Irish literature. The movement also encouraged the creation of works written in the spirit of Irish culture, as distinct from British culture. Slowly and perhaps inevitably, the movement became political. Well-known writers such as Yeats, J.M. Synge, George Russell, Æ and Sean O'Casey wrote many plays and poems about the political state of Ireland at the time. Perhaps the greatest symbol of the Irish Literary Revival was the Abbey Theatre. In many respects, the next generation of writers, spearheaded by poets such as Patrick Kavanagh, reacted to the Revival's tendency to romanticise the Irish peasantry.

Irony: Irony takes many forms. Normally, a situation is said to be ironic if there is an incongruity between actual circumstances and those that would seem appropriate.

Kinaesthetic imagery: Imagery associated with the sensation of movement or tension.

Logaoedic rhythm: A poem or line of verse in which different metrical feet are mixed to give an effect like speech or prose. Gerard Manley Hopkins makes extensive use of this type of rhythm in his poetry.

Lyric poem: A short poem wherein the poet expresses an emotion or illuminates some life principle.

Metaphor: A figure of speech wherein a comparison is made between two normally dissimilar quantities, without the use of the words 'like' or 'as', e.g. 'He is lion-hearted.' Most of the poets on your course employ a metaphor in at least one of their poems.

Metaphysical poetry: The term 'metaphysical' is used to designate the work of a group of 17th-century writers who were using similar methods and who turned their backs on many of the romantic conventions of Elizabethan love poetry. In 1692, the English poet John Dryden launched an attack on the poetry of John Donne. In this attack, he claimed that Donne's poetry introduced 'metaphysics' or theoretical assumptions in a manner that was designed to 'Perplexe the minds of the fair sex'. Dryden was, of course, mocking Donne, but the label stuck and was eventually applied to the group of 17th-century poets that included John Donne, George Herbert, Andrew Marvell, Thomas Carew, Henry Vaughan and Richard Crawshaw. Metaphysical poems tend to be short, draw their subject matter from the concerns of their time and appeal to the intellect as much as to the emotions. They tend to use conceits or hidden, extended allusions and contain striking, innovative imagery.

Metonymy: A figure of speech which occurs when some significant aspect or detail of an experience is used to represent the whole experience. For example, in a herd of 50 cows, the herd might be referred to as '50 head of cattle'. The word 'head' is used to represent the herd or, for example, the 'gilded beak' to represent a bird.

Metre: A regular pattern of unstressed and stressed syllables in a line or lines of poetry.

Monologue: An extended speech uttered by one speaker.

Monosyllabic: A word containing only one syllable.

Mood: The atmosphere or feeling created by a literary work, partly by a description of the objects or by the style of the descriptions. A work may contain a mood of loneliness, loss, excitement or childlike wonder, to name a few.

Motif: A situation, idea or image that is repeated in a poem. This is sometimes known as a leitmotif.

Myth/mythology: An unverifiable tale, often based on religious or quasi-religious beliefs. The characters of myths are gods and goddesses, or the children of the pairing of gods or goddesses and humans. Some myths detail the creation of the world, while others may be about love, journeys, deceit or revenge. In all cases, it is the gods and goddesses who control events, while humans may be aided or victimised. Most commentators believe that mythology is the means by which ancient man attempted to account for natural or historical occurrences. Many of the poems in this anthology draw on mythology for their inspiration.

Neologisms: The practice of coining new words or phrases or of extending the meaning of existing words or phrases. Patrick Kavanagh regularly employs neologisms in order to heighten the impact of his poetry. For example, in the poem 'Lines Written on a Seat on the Grand Canal, Dublin', he changes the adjective 'green' into the noun 'greeny'.

Octave: A group of eight lines of verse, especially the first eight lines of a sonnet, or a poem that consists of eight lines.

Ode: An ode is a dignified and elaborately structured lyric poem praising and glorifying an individual, commemorating an event, an intense emotional state or describing nature. Perhaps the greatest odes of the 19th century were written by Keats. After Keats, there have been few major odes in English.

Onomatopoeia: A literary device wherein the sound of a word echoes the sound it represents. The words 'splash', 'wallop' and 'gurgle' are examples.

Parable: A short, simple story or narrative intended to illustrate a moral or religious lesson.

Paradox: A situation or a statement that seems to contradict itself.

Parallelism: The deliberate repetition of particular words or sentence structures for effect.

Pastoral: From *pastor*, Latin for 'shepherd', 'pastoral' refers to a literary work dealing with shepherds and rural life. Poems that present an idealised depiction of the countryside are often described as being pastorals.

Pathetic fallacy: When an author suggests that non-human phenomena act from human feelings, it is described as pathetic fallacy. In this type of literary device, something non-human found in nature – an animal, a plant, a stream, the weather, etc. – performs as though it were acting from human feelings or motivation.

Periphrasis: An expression that states something indirectly or in an overly poetic fashion. A phrase of poetry that is written in this manner is termed as being *periphrastic.*

Persona: An assumed identity or fictional personality taken on by the speaker in a poem.

Personification: A figure of speech in which something non-human is given human characteristics.

Petrarchan: Writing that imitates the Italian poet Francesco Petrarca, or Petrarch (1304–74). Many of Petrarch's poems were addressed to an idealised woman called Laura.

Petrarchan sonnet: The Petrarchan sonnet consists of an octave, or eight-line stanza, and a sestet, or six-line stanza. The octave has two quatrains. These rhyme in the following manner: *abba, abba*. In this type of sonnet, the first quatrain puts forward the theme of the poem and the second develops it. The sestet is usually built on two or three types of rhyming schemes, arranged *cdecde* or *cdcdcd* or *cdedce*; the first three lines illustrate or reflect on the theme, and the last three lines bring the whole poem to a unified close.

Pluperfect: A past tense that denotes an action that happened before another past action.

Prefiguring: This occurs when a poem hints at, or suggests in advance, an idea that is developed later in the poem.

Present participle: The '-ing' part of the verb. For example, 'going', 'doing' and 'seeing' are all in the present participle.

Protagonist: The central figure in a work of literature.

Pun: A play on words wherein a word is used to convey two meanings at the same time.

Quatrain: A four-line stanza, which may be rhymed or unrhymed. A heroic quatrain is a four-line stanza rhymed *abab*.

Renaissance: The term 'renaissance' means revival or rebirth. It is the term given to the cultural revival that occurred in Italy in the 13th century. During this period in European history, there was a rebirth in interest in Greek and Roman arts and culture.

Rhetorical question: A question asked for effect that neither expects nor requires an answer.

Rhyme: In poetry, a pattern of repeated sounds. In **end rhyme**, the rhyme is at the end of the line. When one of the rhyming words occurs in a place in the line other than at the end, it is called **internal rhyme**. **Eye rhyme** is a form of rhyme wherein the look, rather than the sound, is important. 'Cough' and 'tough' do not sound enough alike to constitute a rhyme. However, if these two words appeared at the end of successive lines of poetry, they would be considered eye rhyme. **Half-rhyme** occurs when the final consonants rhyme.

Rhythm: Recurrences of stressed and unstressed syllables at equal intervals, similar to metre. These recurrences lead to a wave-like repetition of motion or sound. Although two lines may be of the same metre, the rhythms of the lines may be different. While the metre of a line is identified by the pattern within each foot, the rhythm is accounted for by larger movements within the poem or individual line.

Romantic: The term used to describe the movement in late 18th- and early 19th-century music, literature and art that departed from the classicism and formality of previous movements. The Romantics emphasised sensibility, the free expression of feelings, nature and the exotic. This freedom of expression was not confined to the arts. Many of the Romantics were committed to revolutionary politics.

Rondel: A poem of 11 lines, employing only two rhymes in its three stanzas.

Run-on line: See **Enjambment**.

Sardonic: Forced or bitter laughter. The term can be applied to the tone of a poem. If the tone is intentionally bitter or mocking, it may be called sardonic.

Satire: A type of poem that ridicules the attitudes of society or individuals.

Second person singular: The second person singular is the 'you' part (archaic thou) of the verb, as in 'you are'.

Sestet: Six lines of poetry that form the second part of a sonnet.

Sibilance: Sibilance is achieved by producing a recurring hissing sound like that of *s* or *sh*.

Simile: A comparison involving the words 'like' or 'as'.

Slant rhyme: Also called near rhyme, oblique rhyme, off rhyme or imperfect rhyme, this type of rhyme occurs when two words that sound approximately the same are placed closely together within a poem. Emily Dickinson makes much use of slant rhyme in her poems.

Sonnet: A sonnet is a lyric poem consisting of 14 lines of roughly equal length. It is usually written in iambic pentameter. There are two basic types of sonnet. The Italian or Petrarchan sonnet is made up of eight lines called an octave, which is broken into two four-line sections called quatrains. A six-line section called a sestet follows this octave. The movement from the octave to the sestet is usually marked by a change in the tone or mood of the poem. This change is often known as a turn or a volta. The second type of sonnet is known as a Shakespearean sonnet. This type of sonnet comprises three quatrains (a grouping of four lines) and a rhyming couplet. Usually, in the Shakespearean sonnet, the change in the tone and mood of the poem occurs in the final couplet.

Sprung rhythm: A flexible metre that resembles patterns of natural speech. By combining stressed and unstressed syllables, the energy, rhythm and cadence of everyday speech are incorporated into lines of poetry. The term was coined by Gerard Manley Hopkins but can be observed in the works of many authors, including Shakespeare. Hopkins never claimed to have invented it, only to have discovered the concept and enfranchised this as a regular and permanent principle of scansion.

Stanza: A group of verse lines that make up a section of a poem. Stanzas usually have the same length and metrical pattern. Sometimes stanzas are referred to as verses. However, strictly speaking, a verse is a single line of poetry.

Symbol: Something that represents something else by association, resemblance or convention. Normally in poetry, material objects are used to represent something invisible or abstract.

Symbolism: Symbolism is a late 19th-century art movement of French and Belgian origin in poetry and other arts. The movement was largely a reaction to other movements, such as Naturalism and Realism, which had attempted to describe nature in realistic terms. Symbolists attempted to represent reality in terms of spirituality, the imagination and dreams. The Symbolist movement in literature has its roots in *Les Fleurs du Mal* by Charles Baudelaire. It was developed and refined by other French writers, such as Stéphane Mallarmé and Paul Verlaine. At the beginning of the 19th century, English-speaking writers such as Ezra Pound, T.E. Hueme and T.S. Eliot were heavily influenced by the French Symbolist movement.

Synaesthesia: The description of a sense impression in terms more appropriate to another sense.

Syncopation: Syncopation, or syncopated rhythm, is any rhythm that puts an emphasis on a beat, or a subdivision of a beat, that is not usually emphasised. One of the most obvious features of Western music, to be heard in most everything from Bach to blues, is a strong, steady beat that can easily be grouped into even measures. T.S. Eliot relies heavily on syncopated rhythms in his poems. In a line from 'A Game of Chess', Eliot borrows from a popular ragtime song by Gene Buck and Herman Ruby. Notice how the rhythm of these lines is syncopated:

> O O O O that Shakespeherian Rag—
> It's so elegant
> So intelligent

Synecdoche: A figure of speech in which the word for part of something is used to mean the whole, e.g. 'I have just bought a new set of wheels [car]' or '10 Downing Street [the British government] has just announced a new financial package'.

Syntax: The order in which words appear on the page.

Tercet: A group of three lines in a poem.

Terza rima: An interlocking rhyming scheme with the pattern *aba bcb cdc,* etc.

Theme: The most important idea that is apparent in a poem.

Tone: Tone expresses the author's attitude toward his or her subject. The concept of tone embraces the idea of emotional colouring or the emotional meaning of a poem.

Transcendentalism: The word used to describe the appearance of radically new ideas in literature, religion, culture and philosophy that emerged in New England in the early to middle 19th century. It is sometimes called *American Transcendentalism* to distinguish it from other uses of the word 'transcendental'.

Transferred epithet: The transferred epithet occurs when the adjective cannot normally be applied to the noun that it is describing, but where its use becomes justified by the added effect it achieves. The following are examples of transferred epithets: a happy one, the angry sea.

Transitive verb: A verb that can take a direct object. For example, in the sentence 'the car hit the wall', 'the car' is the subject and 'the wall' is the object. The verb 'to hit' is a transitive verb because it can take an object. (See also *Intransitive verb.*)

Triplet: Three lines of poetry that share the same rhyme.

Triptych: A work of art or literature that appears in three pieces. Michael Longley's poem 'Wreaths' consists of three poems that are linked in their exploration of violence.

Understatement: A statement that lessens or minimises the importance of what is being said. The opposite is hyperbole. (See also *Hyperbole.*)

Villanelle: A 19-line poem of fixed form, consisting of five tercets and a final quatrain.

Volta: The technical term for the change or turn that occurs in a sonnet.

Copyright Acknowledgements

The Publishers would like to extend their thanks to the following for permission to reproduce poems in this book:

Beacon Press for 'The Sun' by Mary Oliver, from *New and Selected Poems: Volume One*. Copyright © 1992 by Mary Oliver. Reprinted by permission of Beacon Press, Boston.

Bloodaxe Books for 'A Glimpse of Starlings' and 'Eily Kilbride' by Brendan Kennelly, from *Familiar Strangers: New and Selected Poems 1960–2004* (2004). Reprinted by kind permission of Bloodaxe Books.

Carcanet Press Ltd for 'The War Horse', 'Child of Our Time', 'The Famine Road', 'The Black Lace Fan my Mother Gave me', 'The Shadow Doll', 'White Hawthorn in the West of Ireland', 'Outside History', 'This Moment', 'Love' and 'The Pomegrantate' by Eavan Boland, from *New Collected Poems* (2005); 'Thinking of Mr D.', 'Dick King', 'Mirror in February', 'Chrysalides', 'Glenmacnass: VI Littlebody', 'Tear', 'Hen Woman', 'His Father's Hands', 'Settings: Model School, Inchicore', 'The Familiar: VII' and 'Belief and Unbelief: Echo' by Thomas Kinsella, from *Collected Poems* (2001); and 'Eating Poetry' by Mark Strand, from *Selected Poems* (1995). Reprinted by kind permission of Carcanet Press Ltd.

Curtis Brown, Ltd for 'homage to my hips' by Lucille Clifton. First published in *Two-Headed Woman*. Date of original publication 1980, published by the University of Massachusetts Press. Reprinted by kind permission of Curtis Brown, Ltd.

David Higham Associates for 'Meeting Point' by Louis MacNeice, from *Collected Poems* (Faber & Faber); 'Jungian Cows' by Penelope Shuttle, from *Selected Poems 1980–1996* (1998); and 'Do Not Go Gentle into That Good Night' by Dylan Thomas, from *Collected Poems* (Dent). Reprinted by kind permission of David Higham Associates.

Faber & Faber for 'The Forge', 'Bogland', 'The Tollund Man', 'Mossbawn: Sunlight', 'A Constable Calls', 'The Skunk', 'The Harvest Bow', 'The Underground', 'Postscript', 'A Call', 'Tate's Avenue', 'The Pitchfork' and 'Ligetnings viii' by Seamus

renewed 1944 by Carl Sandburg. Reprinted by permission of Houghton Mifflin Harcourt Publishing Company.

Liveright Publishing Corporation for 'Those Winter Sundays'. Copyright © 1966 by Robert Hayden, from *Collected Poems of Robert Hayden* by Robert Hayden, edited by Frederick Glaysher. Used by permission of Liveright Publishing Corporation.

The Marvell Press for 'At Grass', 'Church Going' and 'Wedding-Wind' by Philip Larkin. Reprinted from *The Less Deceived* by permission of The Marvell Press, England and Australia.

New Directions Publishing Corp. for 'What Were They Like?' by Denise Levertov, from *Poems 1960–1967*, copyright © 1966 by Denise Levertov. Reprinted by permission of New Directions Publishing Corp.

PFD for 'Bearhugs' by Roger McGough, from *Defying Gravity* (© Roger McGough 1992). Reproduced by permission of PFD (www.pfd.co.uk) on behalf of Roger McGough.

Rogers, Coleridge & White for 'Going Home to Mayo, Winter, 1949' by Paul Durcan. Copyright © Paul Durcan by kind permission of the author c/o Rogers, Coleridge & White Ltd, 20 Powis Mews, London W11 1JN.

Salmon Poetry for 'All Day Long' by Noel Monahan, from *The Funeral Game* (2004). Reprinted by kind permission of Salmon Poetry.

Virago for 'Phenomenal Woman' from *The Complete Collected Poems of Maya Angelou* by Maya Angelou. Reproduced by kind permission of Virago, an imprint of Little, Brown Book Group.

W.W. Norton for 'The Uncle Speaks in the Drawing Room' and 'Our Whole Life', from *Collected Early Poems: 1950–1970* by Adrienne Rich. Copyright © 1993 by Adrienne Rich. Copyright © 1967, 1963, 1962, 1961, 1960, 1959, 1958, 1957, 1956, 1955, 1954, 1953, 1952, 1951 by Adrienne Rich. Copyright © 1984, 1975, 1971, 1969, 1966 by W.W. Norton & Company, Inc. Used by permission of the author and W.W. Norton & Company, Inc. Excerpts from 'Blood, Bread, and Poetry: The Location of